D0402780

**Popular
Mechanics**

THE COMPLETE BOY MECHANIC

359 FUN & AMAZING THINGS to BUILD

Popular Mechanics

THE COMPLETE BOY MECHANIC

359 FUN & AMAZING THINGS to BUILD

HEARST BOOKS
New York

HEARST BOOKS
New York

An Imprint of Sterling Publishing
387 Park Avenue South
New York, NY 10016

This book was previously published as two paperbacks under the titles *The Boy Mechanic* and *The Boy Mechanic Makes Toys*.

Cover Photo Credit: Lambert/Getty Images

Library of Congress Cataloging-in-Publication Data available upon request.

10 9 8 7 6 5 4 3 2 1

Popular Mechanics is a registered trademark of Hearst Communications, Inc.

www.popularmechanics.com

For information about custom editions, special sales, premium and corporate purchases, please contact Sterling Special Sales Department at 800-805-5489 or specialsales@sterlingpublishing.com.

Distributed in Canada by Sterling Publishing
⁄o Canadian Manda Group, 165 Dufferin Street
Toronto, Ontario, Canada M6K 3H6

Distributed in Australia by Capricorn Link (Australia) Pty. Ltd.
P.O. Box 704, Windsor, NSW 2756 Australia

Manufactured in China

Sterling ISBN 978-1-58816-859-7

Contents

FOREWORD

We've come a long way over the last century or so. From humble beginnings, the car has become the SUV and luxury sedan. Computers, and technological innovations of all stripes, have far exceeded the wildest dreams of visionaries and even science-fiction writers of the early twentieth century. Today's explosion of electronic toys, games, and devices has created a new universe of imagination and given kids the ability to put themselves in incredible make-believe worlds.

But perhaps we've also lost something along the way. The "good old days" of the early 1900s embodied a truly simpler time, but also a time when self-sufficiency was a highly valued skill. It was a period in history when the measure of a man—and a boy—was gauged by his working knowledge of general sciences, his proficiency in outdoor skills, his ability to craft projects in wood and metal, and his old-fashioned ingenuity. The times called for innovation, and the home mechanics of the period rose to that call, using the rawest of materials, a minimum of technology, and a maximum of ingenuity.

This book captures the spirit of that time. It is filled with sparks to fire the young imagination—straight from the pages of *Popular Mechanics* books and magazines spanning the first two decades of the twentieth century. In making this book, we changed very little, allowing the style of writing to evoke the tenor of the times. Some of these topics are quaintly dated. Some, such as passages on setting up camp on an outdoors trip, are still useful and applicable even though the attendant fixtures and technology have changed quite a bit. Others, such as a mission-style candlestick or any of a number of handcrafted toys, are right at home in our modern lives. And, of course, there are those topics which are simply too odd, bizarre, or funny to leave out—the sail for a boy's wagon and a mirror for rowing a boat come to mind.

Given the wide range of projects in these pages, it's a sure bet there's something here for kids of all ages. The young child will no doubt be enchanted by the idea of a toy donkey whose head and tail move as it's pulled along. Older kids will be intrigued by the idea of making their own "parlor cue alley" game, or a ukulele they can really play. And anyone can delight in the idea of a tree swing that moves in great exhilarating circles.

It is, however, important to point out what may already be obvious:

These projects have not been updated. We've left them largely as they first appeared. The modern reader must realize that at the time of first publication, available materials and tools were severely limited by today's standards. So, when tackling any of the projects, feel free to substitute more modern techniques, equipment, and hardware. Children should not undertake any projects in this book without adult supervision. And it should go without saying—but is important enough to reiterate—use all necessary safety precautions called for in today's workshop.

However, you certainly don't have to get your hands dirty to enjoy this book. The topics and text itself make for entertaining reading and say as much about history as they do about skills and crafting.

So enjoy a trip to the not-so-distant past and bygone pastimes, courtesy of *Popular Mechanics*, then and now.

The Editors
Popular Mechanics

CHAPTER 1

WORKSHOP TOOLS
and PROJECTS

—

USEFUL TOOLS *for* HOME MECHANICS

— MAKING T-SQUARES —

The making of a single article of any kind presents a distinct problem in itself, but the production of a large number of the same article must be done in a different way, if efficiency and uniformity in the product are desirable qualities. For instance, making a large number of T-squares means the material is not made up in the same manner as for one. A number of these instruments were required and were made as follows, with no other equipment than bench tools and a band saw. The squares were made of mahogany, having both stock and blade edged with maple. The blades were fastened to the stock with five ⅜-in. button-head screws.

The material for the heads and the blades was glued up and finished to the sizes given in *A* and *B*. The material was cut to gauge lines on the band saw, the blades being a scant ⅛ in. thick, and the stocks, ⅜ in. Two of each were cut from each prepared piece, first from one side and then from the other. They were then faced off on both sides and two more pieces cut. With careful cutting, six blades and six stocks were made from each piece. This left one side of each piece to be planed after sawing. The holes for the screws were drilled with a small hand drill.

For assembling, a jig was made by nailing a piece of stock, ⅜ in. thick,

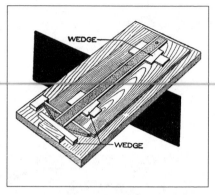

STOCK AND BLADE MATERIAL FOR MAKING THE PARTS, AND THE JIG FOR ASSEMBLING.

to a straight drawing board. One end of the piece was planed straight and true before it was fastened into place. Stops were provided to locate the stock and hold the blade square with it. Wedges were used to keep both stock and blade against the stops while the screws were inserted. The wedges were not driven with a hammer, but pushed in firmly with the fingers.

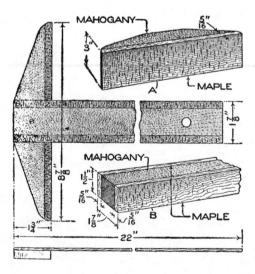

DIMENSIONS FOR A T-SQUARE OF WHICH A NUMBER WERE TO BE MADE IN DUPLICATE.

— A Combination Tool —

Combining a square, plumb, and rule, the tool illustrated is well worth the slight time and trouble required in making it. Wood is used for the T-shaped piece, the long edge of which is graduated in inches and fractions, while the angles at the corners are used as squares. The plumb consists of a weighted pendulum made from a piece of clock spring. Brads or pins are inserted at the proper points on the three ends of the device to indicate the true plumb

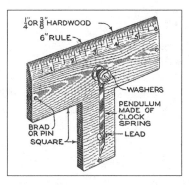

line, when using the tool to test the level of a surface.

— Homemade Carpenter's Vise —

The sketch shows an easily made, quick-working vise composed exclusively of wood that has proven very satisfactory. The usual screw is replaced by an open bar held on one end by a wedge-shaped block, and the excess taken up on the other end by an eccentric lever. The wedge is worked by a string passing through the top of the bench and should be weighted on the other end to facilitate the automatic

downward movement. The capacity of the vise, of course, depends on the size and shape of the wedge-shaped block.

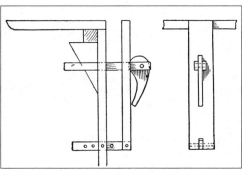

VISE MADE ENTIRELY OF WOOD.

— GROOVE CUTTER FOR WOOD —

Having occasion to cut some grooves in a board and not being properly equipped for such work, I made the tool shown in the sketch. Although rather crude in appearance it will do good work if properly made. It consists of a handle, *A,* shaped to afford a comfortable grip for the hand, and a cutter, *B,* made of a short piece of hacksaw blade, clamped along the left side of the handle by the strip *C,* which is held with screws. A pin, *D,* driven into the handle and allowed to project about 1/16 in., prevents the blade

from sliding back under the clamp. For guiding the blade, the arrangement *F* is employed. An extension, *E,* is nailed on the right side of the handle, and holes made near each end for two screws having round heads, such as may be obtained from discarded dry batteries. These screws are for securing the sliding stop *F,* which is a flat piece of hardwood. The wood has slots cut near the end for screws to pass through to provide for adjustment.

In use, the guide *F* is adjusted until it is the desired distance from

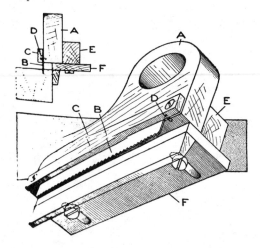

TWO SLOTS ARE MADE WITH THE CUTTER, AND THE STOCK BETWEEN THEM REMOVED WITH A CHISEL.

the cutter and then secured by the screws. The tool is handled like a plane, care being taken not to bear down too hard, because the cutter may bind and cause it to be pulled from the clamp. In cutting a groove, two slots are cut and the stock between them removed with a chisel.

— A Carpenter's Gauge —

The home workshop can be supplied with a carpenter's gauge, without any expense, by the use of a large spool and a round stick of wood. The stick should be dressed to fit the hole in the

ROUND STICK IN A SPOOL.

spool snugly and a small brad driven through one end so that the point will protrude about 1/16 in.

The adjustment of the gauge is secured by driving the stick in the hole in the direction desired. A better way and one that will make the adjusting easy is to file the point end of a screw eye flat and use it as a set screw through a hole in the side of the spool.

— Block Plane Converted for Use on Circular Work —

Few amateur craftsmen can afford to own a circular plane, yet this tool is decidedly necessary for such round work as tabletops, half-round shelves, segments, and the like. Any ordinary block plane will accomplish such work if equipped as illustrated. A piece of half-round hardwood is cut the width of the plane and attached with countersunk machine screws, as indicated. The

block elevates the rear end of the plane, causing it to follow the curve of the work on which it is used.

— HOMEMADE CALIPERS —

A good pair of calipers can be easily and quickly made by anyone in the following manner: Procure a piece of spring wire about 15 in. long and bend it as shown in the sketch, allowing the ends to point inward or outward as the style demands. A loop of heavy wire is fastened around the center so that it can be slid back and forth along the wire. This serves the purpose of an adjuster.

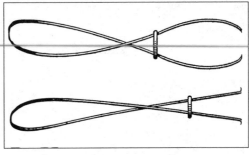

THE SPRING WIRE IS BENT SO THAT THE POINTS TURN IN OR OUT AS DESIRED.

— A HANDY DRILL GAUGE —

The accompanying sketch shows a simple drill gauge that will be found very handy for amateurs. The gauge consists of a piece of hardwood, ¾ in. thick, with a width and length that will be suitable for the size and number of drills you have on hand. Drill a hole through the wood with each drill you have and place a screw eye in one end to be used as a hanger. When you want to drill a hole for a pipe, bolt, screw, etc., you use the gauge to determine what size drill must be used in drilling the hole.

DRILL GAUGE.

The Versatile Querl
and Other Utensils

— A Table Knife Sharpener —

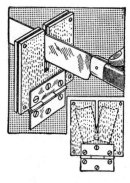

The knife sharpener shown can be easily made of two pieces of thin wood, such as cigar-box covers, about 2 in. wide and 2½ in. long, and two discarded safety-razor blades of the heavier type. Lay the wood pieces together and saw a slot down the center for about 1¾ in. Lay the two razor blades at an angle of about 2 degrees on each side of the slot, as shown, fasten them to one of the boards, and securely attach the other board over them.

To sharpen a knife, run it through the slot two or three times. The sharpener can be fastened with a hinge so that it will swing inside of the drawer or box that the knives are kept in, and it will always be ready for use.

— Clean Pencil Sharpener —

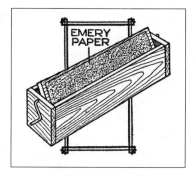

EMERY PAPER

Pencils may be sharpened without spreading the dust from them by the use of the device shown in the illustration. A piece of emery paper is fixed to one side of the cover of the box. By turning over the cover with a handle after a pencil has been sharpened, the dust may be dropped into the box and removed from time to time.

— NAIL CARRIER MADE OF CANS —

Four ordinary tin cans, fastened to a wooden block as shown in the illustration, make a serviceable and practical carrier for nails, staples, or similar materials used in making repairs on the farm or in the shop. The tops of the cans are cut out carefully and the edges smoothed so as not to injure the hand when removing nails from them. The tops are cut to the shape shown and attached to the block. The handle is provided, making it convenient to carry the

contrivance. If cans made with covers that may be pried off are used, the central block should be extended and the handle nailed directly to it.

— KNIFE, FORK, AND SPOON HOLDER —

This holder is made of a piece of sheet copper of sufficient thickness to support the number of pieces of cutlery used. The piece is notched to admit the different pieces, and its back edge is bent at right angles to provide means of fastening it to a support, a wall, or the back of the kitchen cabinet. It will save space as well as time, because it is much easier to grasp one of the articles when

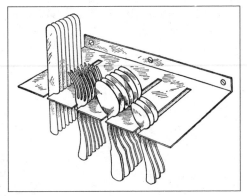

THE HOLDER KEEPS THE CUTLERY IN A POSITION FOR EASY SELECTION AND GRASPING.

wanted than if they are kept in a drawer.

— The Versatile Querl —

"Querl" is the German name for a kitchen utensil that may be used as an eggbeater, potato masher, or lemon squeezer. For beating an egg in a glass, mixing flour and water, or stirring cocoa or chocolate, it is as good as anything on the market.

This utensil is made of hardwood, preferably ash or maple. A circular piece about 2 in. in diameter is cut from ½ in. stock and shaped like a star as shown in *Fig. 1*, and a ⅜-in. hole bored in the center for a handle. The handle should be at least 12 in. in length and fastened in the star as shown in *Fig. 2*.

In use, the star is placed in the dish containing the material to be beaten or mixed, and the handle is rapidly rolled between the palms off the hands.

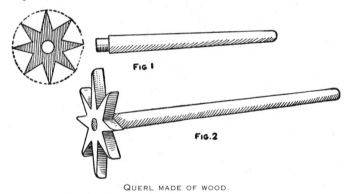

FIG 1

FIG. 2

QUERL MADE OF WOOD.

— Eggshells as Flowerpots —

Here is a novel method of caring for small plants until they are ready to be set out in the garden. Holes were bored in the bottom of the till of an old trunk and eggshells fitted into them. Seeds were planted in the shells and names of the varieties were marked on them. The arrangement is compact, and when the plants are ready for planting, the shells may be broken, and the plants set without disturbing the roots.

IN *the* WORKSHOP

— GUIDE FOR CUTTING MORTISES —

After spending considerable time in cutting one mortise in a piece to make the settee described in *Popular Mechanics* magazine, I devised the plan shown in the sketch, which enabled me to cut all the mortises required in the time that I cut one in the ordinary manner. Two

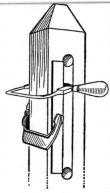

metal plates, one of which is shown in the sketch, having perfectly straight edges, are clamped on the piece with the straight edge on the line of the mortise. A hacksaw is applied through holes bored at the ends and a cut sawed along against the metal edges.

— HOW TO LOCK A TENONED JOINT —

A tenon placed in a blind mortise can be permanently fastened, when putting the joints together, by two wedges driven in the end grain of the wood. In some cases, where the wood to be used is very dry and brittle, it is advisable to dip the tenon in warm water before applying the glue. The glue must be applied immediately after the tenon is removed from the water, and then inserted in the mortise.

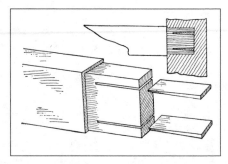

WEDGES IN TENON.

The sketch shows the application of the wedges as the tenon is forced into place.

— Sawhorse with Collapsible Casters —

To save the labor required to carry a sawhorse from one work site to another, a workman equipped it with a set of collapsible casters, as shown in the drawing. The caster axles are inserted through slots in the legs of the sawhorse, and washers and cotter pins are used on the projecting ends to prevent side play. A simple system of wooden toggle levers raises and lowers the casters from the floor. To lower the wheels, when it is desired to move the horse, the handle is pushed inward. To remove them from contact with the floor the handle is given an outward pull.

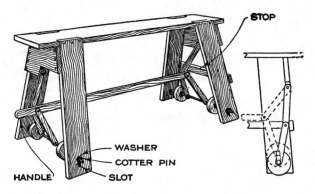

A SAWHORSE EQUIPPED WITH A SET OF CASTERS. BROUGHT TO
BEAR AGAINST THE FLOOR BY PRESSURE ON TOGGLE LEVERS,
THE CASTERS MAKE CHANGES OF LOCATION EASY.

— Sliding Box Cover Fastener —

While traveling through the country as a watchmaker, I found it quite convenient to keep my small drills, taps, small brooches, etc., in boxes with sliding covers. To keep the contents from spilling or getting mixed in my cases, I used a small fastener as shown in the accompanying illustration. The fastener is made of steel or brass and fastened by means of small screws or tacks on the outside of the box. A hole is drilled on the upper part to receive the pin that is driven into the sliding cover. This pin should not stick out beyond the thickness of the spring, which is bent up at the point so the pin will freely pass under it. The pin can be driven through the cover to prevent it from being pulled entirely out of the box.

— HOLDING WOOD IN A SAWBUCK —

Anyone who has used a sawbuck knows how inconvenient it is to have a stick roll or lift up as the saw blade is pulled back for the next cut. With the supplementary device shown in the sketch, which can be easily attached to the sawbuck, these troubles will be eliminated. It consists of two crosspieces hinged to the back uprights of the sawbuck and a foot-pressure stirrup fastened to their front ends as shown. Spikes are driven through the crosspieces so that their protruding ends will gouge into the stick of wood being sawed. The stirrup is easily thrown back for laying a piece of wood in the crotch.

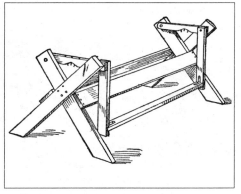

THE HOLDING ATTACHMENT EASILY ADJUSTS ITSELF TO THE STICK OF WOOD PLACED IN THE CROTCH.

— REMOVABLE DRAWER STOP —

When I least expect it, the small-tool drawers of my tool chest have often dropped out after I had left them partly open. The result was a waste of time in picking up the tools, not to mention the possible

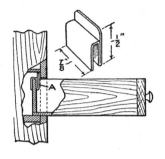

injury to them. I made small clips, like those shown in the sketch, fitted to the back of the drawers as in A. When it is desired to remove the clips, the portion that extends above the drawer may be bent forward. This is necessary only where the space above the drawer is small. The clips may be made large enough to fit drawers of various sizes.

— CUTTING THIN WOODEN DISKS —

Instead of cutting thin wooden disks with a coping saw, making it necessary to smooth off the circumference of the disk, more satisfactory results may be had by the following method: Determine the center from which the circumference of the disk is to be struck. Drive a nail through a strip of wood about 1 in. wide and ¼ in. thick, and into the center of the proposed disk. At a point on the strip, so as to strike the circumference of the disk, drive two sharp brads as shown in the sectional view off the sketch. Arrange

them to act as saw teeth by driving them at an angle, with a slight space between the points. By grasping the end of the strip and drawing it carefully around the center a number of times, the disk may be cut cleanly. By cutting from one side nearly through the board, and then finishing the cut from the other, an especially good job results.

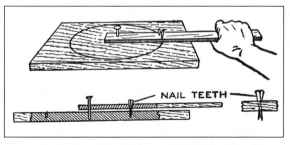

DRAW THE STRIP WITH ITS SAW-TOOTH BRADS AROUND THE CENTER, CUTTING OUT THE DISK.

The first appliance necessary for the boy's workshop is a workbench. The average boy who desires to construct his own apparatus can make the bench as described herein. Four pieces of 2- by 4-in. pine are cut 23 in. long for the legs, and a tenon made on each end of them, ½ in. thick, 3½ in. wide, and 1½ in. long, as shown in *A* and *B*, *Fig. 1*. The crosspieces at the top and bottom of the legs are made from the same material and cut 20 in. long. A mortise is made 1¼ in. from each end of these pieces and in the narrow edge of them, as shown at *C* and *D*, *Fig. 1*. The corners are then cut sloping from the edge of the leg out and to the middle of the piece, as shown. When each pair of legs is fitted to a pair of crosspieces they will form the two supports for the bench. These supports are held together and braced with two braces or reconnecting pieces of 2- by 4-in. pine, 24 in. long. The joints are made between the ends of these pieces and the legs by boring a hole through each leg and into the center of each end of the braces to a depth of 4 in., as shown in *J*, *Fig. 2*. On the backside of the braces bore holes, intersecting the other holes, for a place to insert the

nut of a bolt as shown in *HH*. Four ⅜- by 6-in. bolts are placed in the holes bored, and the joints are drawn together as shown at *J*. The ends of the two braces must be sawn off perfectly square to make the supports stand up straight.

In making this part of the bench be sure to have the joints fit closely and to draw the bolts up tight on the stretchers. There is nothing quite so annoying as to have the bench support sway while work is being done on its top. It would be wise to add a cross brace on the backside to prevent any rocking while planing boards, if the bench is to be used for large work.

The main top board *M*, *Fig. 2*, may be either made from one piece of 2- by 12-in. plank, 3½ ft. long, or made up of 14 strips of maple, ⅞ in. thick by 2 in. wide, and 3½ ft. long, set on edge, each strip glued and screwed to its neighbor. When building up a top like this be careful to put the strips together with the grain running in the same direction so the top may be planed smooth. The back board *N* is the same length as the main top board *M*, 8½ in. wide and only ⅞ in. thick, which

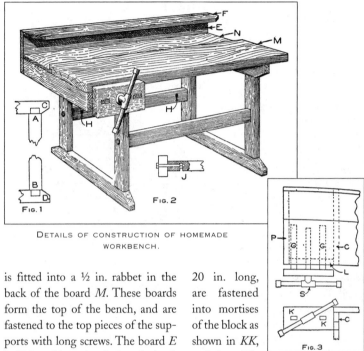

DETAILS OF CONSTRUCTION OF HOMEMADE
WORKBENCH.

is fitted into a ½ in. rabbet in the back of the board *M*. These boards form the top of the bench, and are fastened to the top pieces of the supports with long screws. The board *E* is 10 in. wide and nailed to the back of the bench. On top of this board and at right angles with it is fastened a 2½ in. board, *F*. These two boards are ⅞ in. thick and 3½ ft. long. Holes are bored or notches are cut in the projecting board, *F*, to hold tools.

Details of the vise are shown in *Fig. 3*, which is composed of a 2- by 6-in. block 12 in. long, into which is fastened an iron bench screw, *S*. Two guide rails, *GG*, ⅞ by 1½ in. and 20 in. long, are fastened into mortises of the block as shown in *KK*, and they slide in corresponding mortises in a piece of 2- by 4-in. pine bolted to the underside of the main top board as shown in *L*. The bench screw nut is fastened in the 2- by 4-in. piece, *L*, between the two mortised holes. This piece, *L*, is securely nailed to one of the top crosspieces, *C*, of the supports and to a piece of 2-by 4-in. pine, *P*, that is bolted to the undersides of the top boards at the end of the bench.

— SAFETY CHOPPING BLOCK —

Chopping of pieces of wood, which must be broken into short lengths, is often dangerous. The chopping block shown in the illustration was designed to overcome this element of danger and it may be used for chopping small kindling wood as well as for breaking up heavier pieces. When the blow is struck on the wood to be broken, the pieces are thrown away from the person chopping. The sketch shows the device in use for the chopping of short pieces of wood, and the heavy portion may be used as a seat.

THIS CHOPPING BLOCK MAKES FOR SAFETY IN THAT PIECES CHOPPED ARE THROWN AWAY FROM THE WORKER.

The smaller sketch shows how the block is built up of 2-in. planks, bolted together.

— HOMEMADE PICTURE-FRAME MITER BOX —

Any person wishing to make a picture frame or to cut down an old one requires a miter box for that purpose so that the molding may be properly held while sawing it, and also for nailing the corners together. I made a miter box, as shown, and found it to be just the thing for this purpose. It is built on a base similar to an overturned box, the saw guides being held on the ends of a piece, constructed as shown in *A*. Holes are cut in the top, as shown in *B*, for one of the guides and for the two wedges. Two pieces, *C*, are fastened with their outer edges at perfect right angles on the top.

The frame parts are clamped

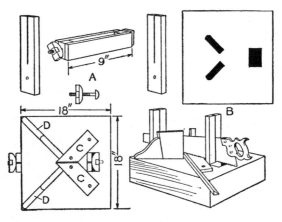

HOMEMADE MITER BOX FOR SAWING FRAME MOLDING AND
TO HOLD THE PARTS FOR FASTENING TOGETHER.

against the pieces on top with the wedges driven in between the frame parts and the brackets *DD*. After cutting the frame parts they are held tightly in place while fastening them, in any manner desired.

— BOX COVER WITHOUT HINGES —

Two ordinary boxes may be fitted together as one without using hinges if nails or screws are inserted at points along the edges so that they will slip into holes bored at corresponding points in the edges of the other box. The nail heads or screw heads should be filed off or cut off after being placed in position.

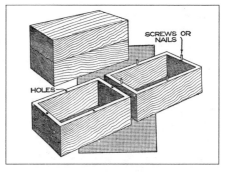

BOX COVER USING PINS INSTEAD OF HINGES TO KEEP IT IN PLACE.

Under Lock *and* Key

— Simple Lock for Drawer or Chest —

A simple lock for a drawer or chest, which will make it impossible for anyone not in on the secret to open the drawer without resorting to force, can be made in a few minutes.

A piece of stiff wire is bent to the shape shown in the drawing and fastened to the inside of the drawer case with screw eyes. A piece of spring wire is wrapped around a rod to make a compression spring, which is slipped over the staple provided for the stem of the lock. This spring locks the drawer automatically when it is closed. A hook, bent on the upper end of the wire, fits into a slot cut in the underside of the chest top.

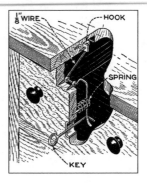

The front of this slot is fitted with a brass wearing plate against which the hook bears. The lock is opened by a bent-wire key, inserted into the keyhole and turned until the bent end comes over the stem end of the lock, which is pulled forward.

— Simple Concealed Locking Device for Cases of Drawers —

A simple method of providing a homemade locking device for a tier of drawers is shown in the sketch. The use of only one keyed lock is necessary, as is common in manufactured cases. This is applicable to new or old cases, where a space of about 1½ in. is available between the back of the drawers and the rear of the case.

The device as detailed consists of a locking bar sliding in guides, screwed or fastened to the back of the case. Attached to the bar are latches one less in number than there are drawers and spaced apart the distance that each drawer top is above the one below. The upper latch is the master feature. The top of this is beveled off, forcing it downward when the top drawer is closed. The locking bar with the other latches also moves down, and the latch fingers engage the backs of the drawers. The connecting bar is operated by a light coil spring set on a shouldered rod at the bottom of the bar, as detailed.

The master latch may be attached at any place on the bar, and should be placed at the bottom drawer for cases too high to be reached handily. To make the device for a small space, a ¼ in. metal rod with metal fingers

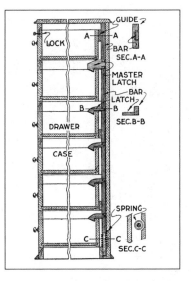

clamped on can be used. Metal striking plates are then put on the back edges of the drawers.

— WOODEN LOCK WITH COMBINATION KEY —

The lock shown in the sketch and detailed drawings is made entirely of wood, and it is nearly impossible to pick or open it without the use of the key. The casing of the lock is 5 by 5 in. and 1 in. thick, of hardwood, oak being suitable for this as well as for the other parts. Three tumblers, a bolt, and a keeper are required. The key is shown inserted, indicating how the tumblers are raised by it. The bolt is slotted and a screw placed through it to prevent it from being moved too far. The lock and keeper are bolted into place on a door with carriage bolts, the heads being placed on the outer side.

The detailed drawing shows the parts, together with the dimensions of each, which must be followed closely. The lock casing is grooved with two grooves extending the length of the

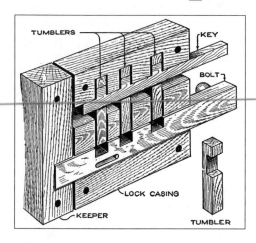

LEFT: THIS LOCK IS MADE ENTIRELY OF WOOD AND CANNOT BE PICKED EASILY.

BELOW: THE DETAILS OF CONSTRUCTION MUST BE OBSERVED CARE-FULLY AND THE PARTS MADE ACCURATELY TO ENSURE SATISFACTORY OPERATION.

grain and connected by open mortises, all ½ in. in depth. The spacing of the mortises and the grooves is shown in the views of the casing. Three tumblers, ½ in. square and 2½ in. long, are required. The bolt is ½ by 1 by 8 in., and the key ¼ by ¾ by 5½ in., and notched as shown. All the parts of the lock must be fitted carefully, sandpapered smooth, and oiled to give a finish that will aid in the operation, as well as protect the wood. Aside from its practical use, this lock is interesting as a piece of mechanical construction.

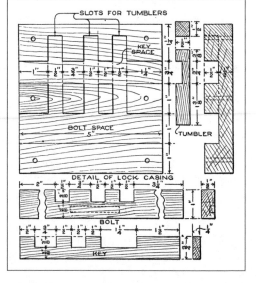

— A Quickly Made Door Latch —

A door latch that is efficient as well as simple may be made by bending a piece of iron rod and pointing one end, as shown in the illustration, then securing it to the door with staples.

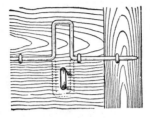

Or small rods may be bent in the shape of a staple and the ends threaded for nuts. The door is locked by turning the handle in the position shown by the dotted lines and securing it with a padlock.

Household Helpers

— A Kitchen Utensil Hanger —

Every cook knows how troublesome it is to have several things hanging on one nail. When one of the articles is wanted it is usually at the back, and the others must be removed to secure it. A revolving rack for hanging a can opener, eggbeater, and cooking spoons, etc., takes up less space than several nails, and places every article within easy reach as well as providing individual hooks for all the pieces.

The rack is easily made of a block of wood 2½ in. in diameter and 1 in. thick, an arm, ¾ in. wide by ¼ in. thick and 6 in. long, and a metal bracket. The arm is fastened to the bracket and the bracket to the wall. A screw is turned through a loose-fitting hole bored in the end of the arm and into the disk. Screw hooks are placed around the edge of the dish as hangers.

— A TROUSER HANGER —

A wood frame, similar to a picture frame, is made up and hinged to the inner side of the closet door with its outer edge hung on two chains. The inside of the frame is fitted with crossbars. After hanging the trousers on the crossbars, the frame is swung up against the door where it is held with a hook. Several pairs of trousers can be hung on the frame, and when flat against the door it takes up very little space. The trousers are kept flat so that they will hold their crease.

TROUSERS CAN BE EASILY HUNG ON THE CROSSBARS TO KEEP THEIR CREASE.

— AN IRONING-BOARD STAND —

An ordinary ironing board is cut square on the large end and a slot cut 1½ in. wide and 4 in. long to admit the angle support. The support is placed against the table and the board is pressed down against the outer notch that jams against the table, thus holding the board rigid and in such a position as to give free access for ironing dresses, etc.

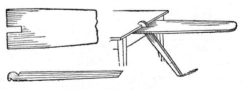

STAND ATTACHED TO TABLE.

— HANDLE FOR A DRINKING GLASS —

Measure the bottom part of the glass and make a band of copper that will neatly fit it. The ends of the copper can be riveted, but if a neat job is desired, flatten or file the copper ends on a slant and braze or solder them together.

Attach to the band an upright copper piece a little longer than the glass is high. To this upright piece rivet or solder a bent piece of copper to form a handle. The glass is set in the band and the upper end of the vertical pieces is bent over the glass edge.

— A HANDY LAUNDRY CABINET —

A cabinet in which all necessary washing materials, such as soap, bluing, soap powder, and the like, may be kept in one place will be appreciated by the laundress. The overall dimensions of the cabinet illustrated are 5 by 12 by 20 in., and the swinging compartment or

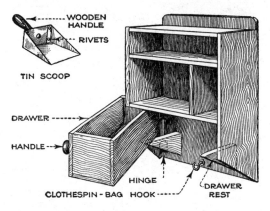

A CABINET FOR THE LAUNDRY, IN WHICH ALL
WASHING MATERIALS ARE KEPT TOGETHER.

drawer, which is used for soap powder or chips, is 4 by 5 by 10 in. If desired, a door can be fitted to cover the upper compartments. A hook is screwed underneath the soap drawer, from which the clothespin bag is hung. A simple scoop for handling the washing powder is easily made from a piece of tin and is kept in the drawer.

— DEVICE FRIGHTENS FLIES AT SCREEN DOOR —

An effective means of frightening flies away from a screen door may be made from a spring curtain rod and cotton duck. Scallops of 8-oz. duck, 6 in. long, are fastened to the pole, on opposite sides, as shown. The ratchet on the end of the pole is arranged so as not to catch. A small cord is wound around the pole and fastened to the screen door. The rod supports are fixed near the top of the door frame.

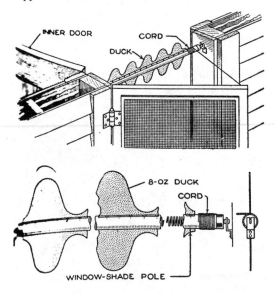

THE SCALLOPED ROLLER REVOLVES RAPIDLY WHEN
THE DOOR IS OPENED, FRIGHTENING FLIES.

— FELT TIRES FOR THE ROCKING CHAIR —

It is aggravating to the housekeeper when the varnished surface of a floor becomes worn by the rockers of a chair. This annoyance can be prevented and longer life given the floor finish by gluing a strip of felt to the underside of each chair rocker. Liquid glue or linoleum cement can be used for holding the felt strip to the wood. In order to bring the felt into contact with the wood at all points, the method of clamping shown in the drawing

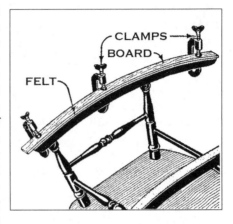

should be used, and the board and clamps allowed to remain overnight.

—SHOE GUARD PREVENTS SOILING AND DAMAGE —

Many good shoes have been ruined by acid, oil, paint, whitewash, and other materials, which, had the shoes been suitably protected, would not have injured them. The shoe cover illustrated is made from a piece of rubber, canvas, or other material, cut to shape and fitted with a cuff of the same material, to which the buckles from a pair of old arctics are fastened. A strap fastened to the projecting ears of the

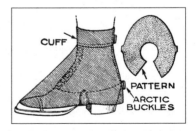

guard passes under the instep like a legging strap. The old buckles are at the back and allow the cover to be slipped on or removed quickly.

— A HINGED WINDOW BOX —

A window box arranged to rest in a hinged bracket on the outside of a window, as shown in the sketch, has advantages over the usual method of fixing the box permanently. The box is separate from the supporting frame and may be removed from it. The frame is attached to the window casing by means of T-hinges and is strongly supported by a bracket. When it is desired to clean the window, the device may be swung around and out of the way. This feature is also desirable when

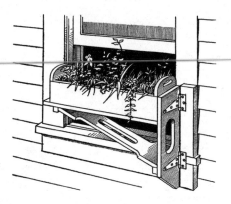

THE FLOWER BOX IS ARRANGED TO SWING AWAY FROM THE WINDOW SO THAT IT WILL NOT BE IN THE WAY.

it is raining, for the flowers in the box may be watered conveniently in this way.

— HAND-OPERATED WHIRLING FAN —

The whirling fan illustrated is more convenient than a fan of the ordinary type, and may be made by a boy of only moderate mechanical skill. The materials necessary for its construction are easily available in the home. The sketch at right illustrates the method of operation. The details of construction are shown in the working drawings on the next page.

The wing of the fan is cut from a sheet of bristol board, and is 6 in. long and 5½ in. wide. It is formed by gluing two pieces together, the upper end of the driving shaft being glued into place at the same time. The small sketch at

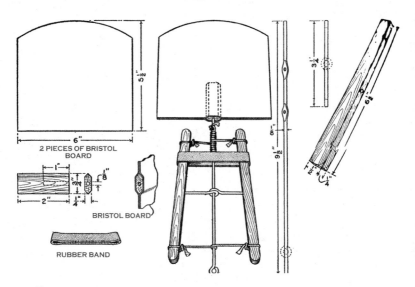

2 PIECES OF BRISTOL BOARD

BRISTOL BOARD

RUBBER BAND

THE WHIRLING FAN IS SUPERIOR TO ONE OF THE ORDINARY VARIETY AND MAY BE MADE AT HOME OF MATERIALS READILY AVAILABLE. THE DETAILS OF CONSTRUCTION ARE SHOWN IN THE SKETCH AND IN THE WORKING DRAWINGS.

the left shows the size and shape of the piece of wood into which the driving shaft is fastened at its upper end.

The driving rod, shown at the right of the larger sketch, is ⅛ in. in diameter and 9½ in. long. The flattened portions near the upper end are drilled to receive the ends of the cords that wind and unwind on the shaft at the top of the handles. A brace of similar wire is fixed near the middle of the handles so that they pivot on its ends when the lower ends of the handles are pressed together, as shown in the sketch at the right. The handles are of wood, ¼ in. thick, ½ in. wide, and 6½ in. long. Their ends are rounded and slight notches are cut into the corners near the ends to provide for the tying of the cords.

A wide rubber band, slipped over the handles near their upper ends, causes them to close at the top. When the fan is in use this will reverse the rotation of the fan. It is necessary only to squeeze the handles inward, and the reverse action is repeated.

Labor Saving Devices

— A Bell-ringing Mailbox —

The annoyance of watching for the arrival of the mailman was overcome by the fitting of an electrical alarm to the mailbox, as shown in the sketch. A strip of metal, A, was pivoted in the box and weighted on one end. A bell, B, was wired to dry cells in the box below the container for the mail. When the mail is dropped

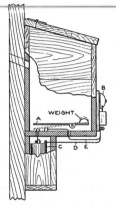

into the box, the end A is forced down, forming an electrical contact and completing the circuit from the cells C through the wire D and back through the wire E. When the mail is removed, the weight raises the metal strip.

— Motor-driven Entertainer for the Baby —

A contrivance that keeps the baby entertained by the hour, at intervals, and is a big help to a busy mother, was made in a short time. I mounted four wooden arms on a small motor as shown. On the ends of two of the arms, I fixed small pinwheels, one blue and the other yellow. The other arms hold curious-shaped pieces of bright cardboard, one red and the other green. The driving motor is run by one two-volt cell. The revolving colored pinwheels amuse baby in his highchair,

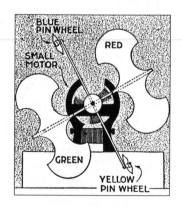

and the device has well repaid the little trouble of making it.

— DEVICE FOR SUSPENDING PARCELS FROM OVERHEAD HOOKS —

To hang small sacks or other articles out of reach overhead, so that they may be easily taken down, I use a double-eye hook that I made of wire. A single piece of wire is used and twisted into two loops, as

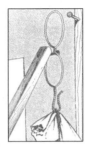

shown, and then formed into a twisted hook. I use a pole with a nail, hooking it into the lower loop to raise the parcel; this leaves the upper loop free to be hooked on the nail above.

— SCRAPER FOR DISHES —

Housekeepers will find the scraper shown to be silent and more rapid than a knife for cleaning dishes. It consists of a handle cut from a piece of straight-grained wood, with a kerf sawn in the wide end to a depth of ¾ in., into which a piece of sheet rubber is inserted. The rubber may be cut from an old bicycle-tire casing

and is fastened with two or three brads driven through the handle. The ends of the brads are bent over or riveted. The edge of the rubber should be made straight.

— A NONROLLING THREAD SPOOL —

A spool of thread may be kept from rolling by gluing squares of cardboard to the ends. The squares should be a little larger than the spool.

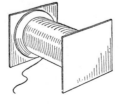

This will save many a step and much bending over to pick up the spool. The spool, when it falls, will stop where it landed.

— EMERGENCY LIFTING DEVICE
OF ROPE AND LEVER —

When block and tackle, chain hoists, or similar equipment are not at hand, the simple arrangement shown in the sketch is useful for lifting heavy loads. Make the lever *A* of a piece of 2- by 4-in. timber and cut notches into it for the ropes, as indicated. From a suitable support, *B*, fix the ropes *C* and *D* to the lever *A* at the proper notches, permitting the ends *C-1* and *D-1* to be drawn down and fastened to the floor or other support as required in raising the load. Fix the rope *E* to the load *W* and suspend it from the lever *A* at the proper notch by means of a loop, *E-1*. To raise the load, bear down on the end of the lever when it is in its original position *A-1*, bringing it to the position *A-2*. This will bring the lower rope to position *E-2*. Draw up the slack in rope *D*, to bring the loop to position *D-2*, and fasten it. Then lift the lever *A* from its position *A-2*, to the position *A-3*, and draw up the slack in rope *C* to bring the loop up to position *C-2*. The lower rope will be brought to position *E-3*. By repeating this process, the load may be raised gradually. The ropes

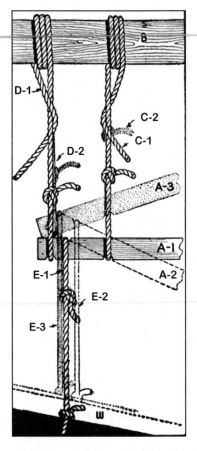

may, of course, be of various lengths within the range of the support and the operators.

SECRET HIDING PLACES

— CONCEALING THE HOUSE KEY —

The time-honored custom of concealing the house key under the doormat or in the letter-box when the family has not enough keys to go around is so well known that an unauthorized person seeking to enter the house would look in these places first of all.

A simple and effective hiding place for the key can be quickly and easily made with the aid of an auger and two pieces of tin. Pick out an obscure section of the porch railing, and in the edge of this bore a ¾-in. hole, about ¼ in. deeper than the length of the key. Make a piece of tin into a cylinder, the same length as the key, so that the latter will slide easily into the hole. At one end of this cylinder solder a 1-in. disk of tin, which will make it appear as in the illustration.

If the key is placed in the cylinder and the latter pushed into the hole until it is flush with the surface, it will scarcely be noticed by anyone not in on the secret. By painting it the same color as the railing it will become still more inconspicuous.

— A SECRET BOX LID —

A simple secret box lid, which cannot be opened by anyone who does not know the secret, is made by pivoting the lid near one end by means of two nails driven through the sides of the box into the edges of the cover. A hole is drilled in the middle of the opposite end of the lid to take a spring and a nail from which the point and head have been cut. When the lid is closed, the nail is pushed into a hole drilled in the end of the box, locking it securely. To open the box, it is necessary to push the bolt out of the hole in the box by inserting a heavy pin through a small hole, which leads from the outside to the nail socket, and by pressing down on the short end of the lid. The lid can be given the appearance of being solidly nailed by using shortened nails and some other side may be made to appear as the cover. A shortened nail can be pushed into a small hole leading to the bolt and, when in position, will conceal this perfectly. Some kind of mark should be made on the head of this nail, to distinguish it from the corresponding one on the opposite end.

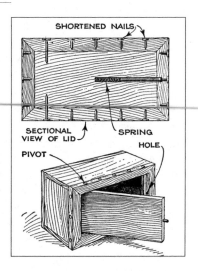

— A SECRET TRINKET CASE FOR THE BOOKSHELF —

Practical use as well as the novelty of its construction makes the trinket case shown in the illustration well worth the time and effort necessary to make it. Various kinds of wood—preferably of the better cabinet varieties—are suited to the design shown, like that used in cigar boxes. The size shown is that of a bound volume of a magazine like *Popular Mechanics,* and may be adapted to special needs. The back and the cover slide in grooves, which are not visible when the "book" is closed. This makes it difficult and interesting for one to discover how the case is opened. The back may be marked and lettered to resemble a bound volume closely. If special secrecy is desired, it may even be covered with leather, in exact duplication of those on a bound set of magazines kept in the bookcase with it.

Make the pieces for the frame of the box first. If possible, make one strip of the proper width—2 in., in this case—and long enough for the two ends and the front. Make another strip 1¾ in. wide and long enough for the partition and false back of the tray.

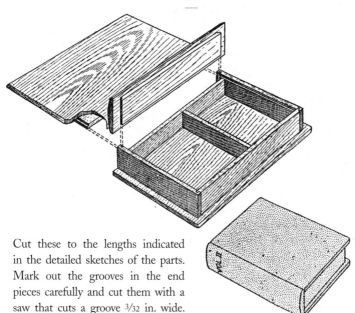

BOX COMPLETED

Cut these to the lengths indicated in the detailed sketches of the parts. Mark out the grooves in the end pieces carefully and cut them with a saw that cuts a groove 3/32 in. wide. The grooves may be cut by clamping a straight strip of wood on the surface of the ends the proper distance from the top and sawing cautiously along the strip to the proper depth. The grooves across the grain may be cut similarly, or in a miter box.

Glue the pieces of the frame together, taking care that the corners are square. If necessary, place blocks inside to ensure that the clamping will not disturb the right angles of the box. Shape the bottom and cover pieces nearly to the final size before gluing them; then, if small nicks are made in the edge, they may be removed

THIS TRINKET CASE IS A PRACTICAL NOVELTY THAT MAY BE USED AS A SECRET CONTAINER TO BE SET ON THE BOOKSHELF WITH SIMILAR BOUND VOLUMES.

by a cut of the plane when the case is complete. Glue the sliding pieces to the cover and to the back. This must be done carefully, and it is convenient to drive small brads part way into the second piece from the inner side to prevent the pieces from slipping while being glued. If proper care is taken, only a small amount of glue will be forced out, and this can be removed with a chisel when dry. The edges may be trimmed off to their exact size and the entire construction given a final light sanding. It is then ready for the stain and shellac or other finish. The parts that slide in grooves should not be shellacked or varnished because this is apt to cause them to stick.

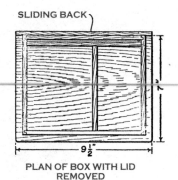

PLAN OF BOX WITH LID
REMOVED

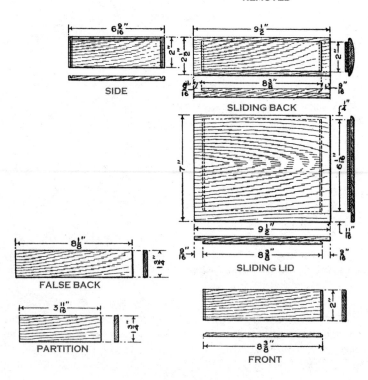

SIDE

SLIDING BACK

SLIDING LID

FALSE BACK

PARTITION

FRONT

ALTERNATIVE LIVING ARRANGEMENTS

— BIRD HOUSE MADE OF AN OLD STRAW HAT —

A birdhouse of an old straw hat is a practical and easily contrived affair. Cut a hole in the crown of the hat. Then nail the hat against a board of proper size. To protect the hat against the rain, put a roof over it, as shown.

A perch is also provided for the birds. A birdhouse such as this one can be hung against the trunk of a tree, or nailed against a wall. Leaving the hat in its natural straw color, and painting the rest a dark brown, produces a satisfactory effect.

— HOUSES MADE OF POLES —

Being forced to take the open-air treatment to regain health, a person adopted the plan of building a pole house in the woods. The scheme was so successful that it was decided to make a resort grounds to attract crowds during holidays, by which income could be realized for living expenses. All the pavilions, stands, furniture, and amusement devices were constructed of straight poles cut from young-growth timber with the bark remaining on them.

Outside of boards for flooring and roofing material, the entire construction of the buildings and fences consisted of poles.

A level spot was selected and a house built having three rooms. The location was in a grove of young timbers, most of them being straight. Thirteen trees were easily found that would make posts 12 ft. long, required of the sides, and two poles 16 ft. long, for the center of the ends, so that they would reach to the ridge.

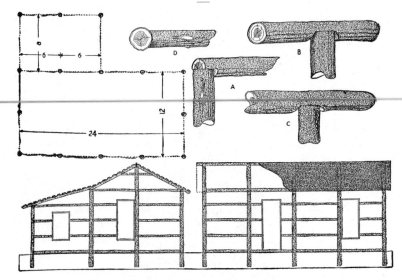

THE FRAME CONSTRUCTION OF THE HOUSE MADE ENTIRELY OF ROUGH POLES,
THE VERTICALS BEING SET IN THE GROUND, PLUMBED, AND SIGHTED
TO MAKE A PERFECT RECTANGLE OF THE DESIRED PROPORTIONS.

The plot was laid out rectangular and marked for the poles, which were set in the ground to a depth of 4 ft., at distances 6 ft. apart. This made the house 8 ft. high at the eaves with a square pitch roof; that is, the ridge was 3 ft. high in the center from the plate surfaces for this width of a house. The rule for finding this height is to take one-quarter of the width of the house for the height in the center from the plate.

The corner poles were carefully located to make the size 12 by 24 ft., with a lean-to 8 by 12 ft., and then plumbed to get them straight vertically. The plates for the sides, consisting of five poles, were selected as straight as possible and their ends and centers hewn down to about one-half their thickness, as shown in *A* and *B*, and nailed to the tops of the vertical poles, the connection for the center poles being as shown in *C*.

The next step was to secure the vertical poles with crosspieces between them, which were used later for supporting the siding. These poles were cut about 6 ft. long, their ends being cut concave to fit the curve of the upright poles, as shown in *D*. These were spaced evenly, about 2 ft. apart from center to center, on the sides and ends, as shown in the sketch, and toe-nailed in place. The door and window openings were cut in the horizontal poles wherever wanted, and casements set in and nailed. The first row of horizontal poles was placed close to the ground and used both as support for the lower ends of the siding and to nail to the ends of the flooring board, which were fastened in the center to poles laid on stones, or better still, placed on top of short blocks, 5 ft. long, set in the ground. These poles for the floor should be placed not over 2 ft. apart to make the flooring solid.

A lean-to was built by setting three poles at a distance of 8 ft. from one side, beginning at the center and extending to the end of the main building. These poles were about 6 ft. long above the ground. The rafter poles for this part were about 9½ ft. long, notched at both ends for the plates, the ends of the house rafters being sawed off even with the outside of the plate along this edge. The rafter poles for the house were 10 in all, 8 ft. long, and were laid off and cut to fit a ridge made of a board. These poles were notched about 15 in. from their lower ends to fit over the rounding edge of the plate pole and were then placed directly over each vertical wall pole. They were nailed both to the plate and to the ridge, also further strengthened by a brace made of a piece of board or a small pole placed under the ridge and nailed to both rafters. On top of the rafters, boards were placed horizontally spaced about 1 ft. apart, but this is optional because other roofing material can be used. In this instance metal roofing was used and it required fastening only at intervals. To prevent rusting, it was well painted on the underside before laying it and coated on the outside when fastened into place. If a more substantial shelter is wanted, it is best to lay the roof solid with boards, then cover it with the regular prepared roofing material.

Some large trees were selected and felled, then cut into 4-ft. lengths and the bark removed. If desired, the bark can be removed in 4-ft. lengths. The bark was nailed on the outside of the poles, beginning at the bottom in the same manner as laying shingles, to form the siding of the house. If a more substantial house is wanted, boards can be nailed on the poles, then the bark fastened to the boards; also, the interior can be finished in wallboard.

The same general construction is used for the porch, with horizontal poles latticed, as shown, to form the railing. It is very easy to make ornamental parts, such as shown, on the eave of the porch by splitting sticks and nailing them on closely together to make a frieze. Floors are laid on the porch and in the house, and doors hung and window sash fitted in the same manner as in an ordinary house.

A bandstand was constructed on sloping ground and, after setting the poles, the floor horizontals were placed about 2 ft. above the ground on

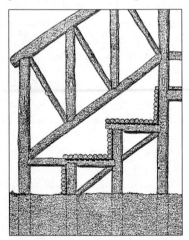

THE STEPS ARE SUPPORTED ON PAIRS OF VERTICAL POLES SET IN THE GROUND TO MAKE DIFFERENT LEVELS.

the upper side, and 4 ft. on the lower side. The poles used were about 18 ft. long. Instead of placing the horizontals 2 ft. apart, the first was placed 1 ft. above the floor, the next at about one-half the distance from the lower one to the plate at the top, and the space between was ornamented with cross poles, as shown. A balcony or bay was constructed at one end, and a fancy roof was made of poles whose ends rested on a curved pole attached to the vertical pieces. Steps were formed of several straight poles, hewn down on their ends to make a level place to rest on horizontal pieces attached to stakes at the ends. A pair of stakes was used at each end of a step, and these were fastened to a slanting piece at the top, their lower ends being set into the ground. The manner of bracing and crossing with horizontals make a rigid form of construction, and if choice poles are selected for the step pieces, they will be comparatively level and of sufficient strength to hold up the entire load put on them. The roof of this building was made for a sunshade only and consisted of boards nailed closely together on the rafters.

An ice-cream parlor was built on the same plan, but without any board floor; the ground, being level, was used instead. There were five vertical poles used for each end with a space left between the two poles at the center, on both sides, for an entrance. This building was covered with prepared roofing so that the items offered for sale could be protected in case of a shower.

A peanut stand was also built without a floor, and to make it with nine sides, nine poles were set in the ground to form a perfect nonagon. The poles were joined at their tops with latticed horizontals. Then a rafter was run from the top of each post to the center, and boards were fitted on each pair of rafters over the V-shaped openings. The boards were then covered with prepared roofing. A railing was formed of horizontals set in notches, cut in the posts, and then ornamented in the same manner as for the other buildings.

Fences were constructed about the grounds, made of pole posts with horizontals on top, hewn down and fitted as the plates for the house. The lower pieces were set in the same as for the house railing. Gates were made of two vertical pieces the height of the posts, and two horizontals.

GATE OPENINGS WERE MADE IN THE FENCE WHERE NECESSARY, AND GATES OF POLES HUNG IN THE ORDINARY MANNER.

They were then braced with a piece running from the lower corner at the hinge side to the upper opposite corner, the other cross brace being joined to the sides of the former, whereupon two short horizontals were fitted in the center. A blacksmith formed some hinges of rods and strap iron, as shown, and these were fastened in holes bored in the post and the gate vertical. A latch was made by boring a hole through the gate vertical and into the end of the short piece. Then a slot was cut in the side to receive a pin inserted in a shaft made to fit the horizontal hole. A keeper was made

TOP OF POST

THE ENTRANCE TO THE GROUNDS WAS GIVEN AN INVITING APPEARANCE WITH LARGE POSTS AND SWINGING GATES.

were considerably higher than the fence poles. The poles were set in a perfect square, having sides about 18 in. long, and a square top put on by mitering the corners, whereupon four small rafters were fitted on top. The gates were swung on hinges made like those for the small gate.

The swings were among the best and most enjoyed amusement devices on the grounds. Several of these were built, with and without tables. Four poles, about 20 ft. long, were set in the ground at an angle, and each pair of side poles was joined with two horizontals, about 12 ft. long. Spreaders were fastened between the two horizontals to keep the tops of the poles evenly spaced. The distance between the poles will depend on the size of the swing and the number of persons to be seated. Each pair of side poles is further strengthened with crossed poles, as shown. If no table is to be used in the swing, the poles may be set closer together so that the top horizontals will be about 8 ft. long. The platform for the swinging part consists of two poles, each 12 ft. long, which are swung on six vertical poles, each about 14 ft. long. These poles are attached to the top

in the post by boring a hole to receive the end of the latch.

Large posts were constructed at the entrance to the grounds. On these, double swing gates made up in the same manner as the small one were attached. These large posts were built up of four slender poles and

horizontals with long bolts, or rods, running through both, the bottom being attached in the same manner. Poles are nailed across the platform horizontals at the bottom for a floor, and a table with seats is formed of poles at the ends. The construction is obvious.

A short space between two trees can be made into a seat by fastening two horizontals, one on each tree, with the ends supported by braces. Poles are nailed on the upper surface for a seat.

Other furniture for the house and grounds was made of poles in the manner illustrated. Tables were built for picnickers by setting four or six poles in the ground and making a top of poles or boards. Horizontals were placed across the legs with extending ends on which seats were made for the tables. Chairs and settees were built in the same manner, poles being used for the entire construction.

Have Trunk, Will Travel

— Making One's Own Steamer and Wardrobe Trunks —

The Steamer Trunk

Only ordinary tools such as a hammer, saw, plane, and an old flatiron are needed to build the steamer trunk described in this article. In addition, a glue pot is needed, and a brush or two, for gluing and painting the finished trunk.

There are several kinds of lumber that can be used and in the order of their desirability they are: three-ply veneer, basswood, spruce, and sugar pine. The veneer costs a trifle more, but is lighter and more durable, and if used in conjunction with fiber, it is possible to make a trunk that

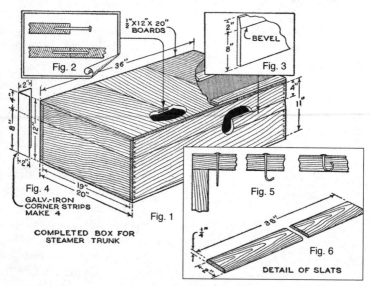

Fig. 2

Fig. 3 BEVEL

Fig. 4
GALV.-IRON
CORNER STRIPS
MAKE 4

COMPLETED BOX FOR STEAMER TRUNK

Fig. 1

Fig. 5

Fig. 6
DETAIL OF SLATS

A PROFITABLE UNDERTAKING DURING THE LONG WINTER MONTHS IS THAT OF MAKING TRUNKS, IN ANTICIPATION OF NEXT SUMMER'S VACATION.

is almost indestructible. If any of these woods is used, secure all ½-in. material, dressed on both sides, and as clear as possible.

In making the steamer trunk, 12-in. material can be used with no waste. A box is made to the dimensions shown in *Fig. 1.* To prevent the top and bottom from warping where the boards are joined, 1½-in. wire nails are driven into the edges of the boards at about 6-in. intervals. Cut off the heads and butt up the next board, as indicated in *Fig. 2;* if desired, these joints can be glued before they are driven together.

After the top and bottom are in place, mark a line on each side 4 in. from the top. Then, starting at a corner, carefully cut through the boards and around the entire box, keeping to the mark, until the box has been sawn into two parts—a lid and a bottom. This method ensures the absolute matching of both parts. The lower part is laid on its side and a line is marked on each side 2 in. below the edge. Another line is marked in the middle of the edge and, using the plane, the outside of the boards is beveled off down to the 2-in. mark, as in *Fig. 3.* Some strips of galvanized iron, as shown

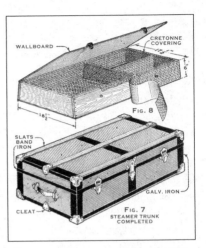

FIG. 8

FIG. 7
STEAMER TRUNK
COMPLETED

THIS STEAMER TRUNK, WHILE NOT COST-ING NEARLY SO MUCH AS A PURCHASED ARTICLE, WLL BE FOUND QUITE AS STRONG AND SERVICEABLE.

in *Fig. 4,* are bent at right angles between two blocks. After bending, they are punched at 1-in. intervals on the edges to take 1-in. clout nails; these nails are easily bent and therefore the punching is necessary. A quarter of an inch from the edge is about the distance to place the holes, which should be punched without raising any burrs.

What is known in the theatrical profession as "scenic linen" is used for covering the trunk, and about 2 yards of this will be needed. This material can usually be obtained from any stage carpenter or scenic artist at little or no expense. Even if bought new, the cost is small. A 14-in. strip, the length of the piece, is cut off. A pot of glue is mixed and the outside of the box is given a light coat; this may be thin, as it is intended only to fill up the pores of the wood. When this has dried, apply a thicker coat as smoothly as possible. While the glue is still hot, lay on the linen and smooth it with a rubbing motion. After the sides have been covered, the top and bottom pieces can be cut and glued on in the same manner; these should be cut ½ in. smaller than the surface they are to cover.

The galvanized iron corners are now nailed in place, the method of clinching the nails being clearly illustrated in *Fig. 5*. The nail is driven through the wood, the point curved with a pair of round-nose pliers, then, holding the old flatiron against the head, the curved point is driven into the wood and clinched by a sharp hammer blow. A strip of galvanized iron about ½ in. wide is nailed on each edge of the box, and strips about 2 in. wide across the center of each side and at the ends of the top and bottom, the nails being clinched as described. The black bands in *Fig. 7* show the location of these strips.

Eighteen running feet of oak, or hickory, cut and formed to the dimensions shown in *Fig. 6*, are needed for the slats, which take up a great deal of the wear a trunk is subjected to. Six 3-ft. slats are cut and fastened with clout nails to the top and bottom of the trunk, 6 in. apart. As the wood is too hard to prevent the entrance of the nails without bending them or splitting the wood, it is necessary to drill a hole wherever a nail is to be inserted. A light strip of band iron is run around the whole trunk at the point where top and bottom join; this iron is applied in the manner described for the sheet-iron corners, the nails being inserted every 6 in. Next place a pair of 6-in. strap hinges on one side; three hinges are better, and even four may be used. The following hardware, which can be obtained from almost any hardware store, is required: Two strong trunk clasps, four slat cleats, eight corner irons, a pair of trunk handles, and a good trunk lock.

The inside of the trunk is lined with a suitable pattern of cretonne, or similar material, which is applied with ordinary flour-and-water paste. Two ¾-in. strips of wood, 1 by 19 in., are screwed to the inside of the trunk, one in each end of the lower part, and 2 in. from the edge, to support the tray.

The tray is made of material as light as can be obtained: ½ in. for the ends, and ¼ in. for the sides. The top and bottom are made of wallboard, about ¼ in. thick. The tray is built to the dimensions shown in *Fig. 8,* and is made narrower at the top so as to give the lid freedom in closing. After the tray is finished and partitions added as desired, the lid is attached with a piece of muslin, which is glued to the tray and acts as a hinge. The tray is then covered with material similar to that with which the trunk is lined. Small straps and buttons are fastened to the lid and tray, respectively, to keep the lid from opening.

The Wardrobe Trunk

For the benefit of those who prefer a wardrobe trunk instead of the steamer trunk, this article describes and illustrates its construction and dimensions.

Covering a trunk with fiber increases the cost of construction but little, while adding immeasurably to its life. However, a little extra work is required to apply it. Either with or without fiber, the box is built in a similar manner to the steamer trunk, the cut in this case being made in the exact center of the box, which is 24 in. deep. The other operations, such as bracing the corners, etc., are the same with the exception that when using fiber, galvanized iron angle pieces are not used on the edges. In their stead, fiber or rawhide, already pressed into shape, is used; 1½ in. angle fiber or rawhide can be obtained from manufacturers of fiber or rawhide and, in many instances, from electrical supply houses. Holes must be drilled in the fiber or rawhide to take the nails, as both are tough. With such a trunk, no wooden slats are necessary, but when the sheet fiber is used, it is riveted down with round-head nails to the wooden base, after lines dividing the surface into 4-in. squares have been drawn on each side of the trunk. The nails are placed along these lines, as shown in *Fig. 9.* In addition to using angle fiber on the corners, all the outside edges are similarly protected. The angle fiber is applied after the sheet fiber has been riveted in place to cover the exposed edges. Metal corners are used on this style of trunk as in the steamer trunk, as an additional protection, the standard practice among baggage handlers being to roll a trunk on its corners. The fiber covering, however, should not be applied until the interior accessories of the trunk have been installed, as it is necessary to fasten some of them through the wood.

Of the interior arrangement of the wardrobe trunk, little need be said, as the taste and needs of individuals will differ. The clothes rack that supports the hangers is made by fastening two tripods—or crowfoots, such as those used in the installation of electric-lighting fixtures—to the inside of the trunk. These fittings can be obtained in various sizes, and should preferably be threaded to take a ⅜-in. pipe or rod. Stove bolts are used to attach them to the trunk before the fiber or canvas covering is applied. The bolt heads are countersunk to prevent a bulge on the outside. The projecting arms, which carry the clothes hangers, are made of ⅜-in. iron rod. Two 8-in. lengths of rod are required

for each arm. One end of the arm is threaded to screw into the fitting and the two sections of rod are joined by a knuckle, as illustrated in *Fig. 10*. The outer end of each arm has a hole drilled through it, and a small ball-head pin, taken from a pair of hinges, is inserted to prevent the hangers from slipping off.

The clothes hangers are best made of three-ply veneer, cut to the form

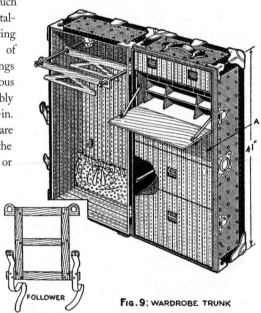

FOLLOWER

FIG. 9: WARDROBE TRUNK

THIS ILLUSTRATION SHOWS A FIBER-COVERED TRUNK, THE INTERIOR ARRANGEMENT OF WHICH MAY BE ALTERED TO SUIT INDIVIDUAL REQUIREMENTS.

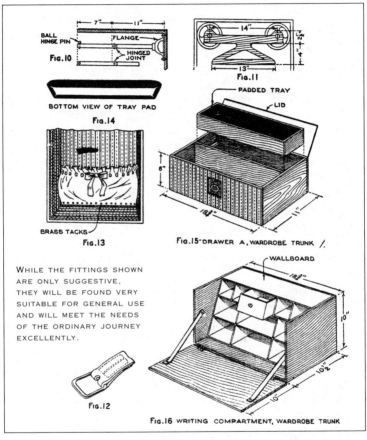

FIG.10

BALL HINGE PIN
FLANGE
HINGED JOINT

FIG.11

BOTTOM VIEW OF TRAY PAD

FIG.14

PADDED TRAY
LID

FIG.13

BRASS TACKS

FIG.15-DRAWER A, WARDROBE TRUNK

WHILE THE FITTINGS SHOWN ARE ONLY SUGGESTIVE, THEY WILL BE FOUND VERY SUITABLE FOR GENERAL USE AND WILL MEET THE NEEDS OF THE ORDINARY JOURNEY EXCELLENTLY.

WALLBOARD

FIG.12

FIG.16 WRITING COMPARTMENT, WARDROBE TRUNK

and dimension shown in *Fig. 11*. The veneer will not crack or warp as readily as straight-grained wood. About nine hangers will be needed, and these can all be sawn out at one time, if a band saw is available.

To hold the clothes securely in place, the follower, shown in *Fig. 9*, is placed on the arms after all the hangers have been put in position. Two straps are riveted to the bottom of this follower, and pass through buckles that are attached to the back of the trunk. The tongues are removed from the buckles, *Fig. 12,* so that the straps can slide through them and be pulled up tight before the trunk is closed.

The drawers are supported by strips of ½-in. angle iron, riveted to the trunk before the covering is applied. The bottom of one section is equipped with a shoe or laundry bag made of the same material as the lining of the trunk. The bag is hemmed all around and, being considerably fuller than the width of the box, it is gathered at the top and provided with a drawstring or an elastic band, as shown in *Fig. 13,* which keeps the shoes or linen in place.

The top drawer may be fitted with a padded compartment for jewelry or other valuables. The padding is best done by cutting snug-fitting pieces of heavy cardboard, corresponding in size to the sides, ends, and bottom of the compartment. Cotton batting is first laid on the cardboard to the required depth, after which it is covered with muslin, which is glued to the underside of the cardboard, as in *Fig. 14.* A piece of dark-colored velvet or similar material is next applied over the muslin and glued in the same manner. The padded compartment is placed at the rear of the drawer, as shown in *Fig. 15,* so as not

to attract attention when the drawer is opened or the trunk left unlocked. Each drawer is fitted with a suitable handle or drawer pull for convenience in opening.

Fig. 16 illustrates the desk compartment, which may be added if desired, although the space it occupies may be devoted to the storage of clothing or other belongings.

When the trunk is packed, the pins in the ends of the horizontal arms supporting the clothes hangers are removed, and the follower is put in place. This is pulled up tightly, the straps buckled, the pins replaced, and the arms turned inward, thus holding all the clothing firmly in place.

The canvas-covered trunk described in Part I is painted before the applications of the slats and metal fittings, with a priming coat of white metal primer. A little lampblack is added to give this coat a grayish tint. The entire outside of the trunk is given a coat of this priming, which is then allowed to dry for at least 24 hours. The body coat, which is usually dark brown or dark olive green, is applied after the priming coat has dried. This paint can be bought ready prepared, but it is best to apply it in the flat and afterward give it a coat of varnish. The flat color is known as color ground in Japan, or gold size; it is thinned down with turpentine to which a few drops of raw linseed oil have been added as a binder. A very neat job can be made by painting the canvas brown or green, and then painting the galvanized iron or fiber fittings black, leaving the brass corners, locks, and clips bright. No paint is placed on the wood slats, which are given two coats of orange shellac. The entire trunk is then given a coat of the best varnish.

If a fiber-coated trunk is to be painted, the priming coat is unnecessary, the color coat being applied directly to the fiber and finished as described above.

— TRUNK BOOKCASE FOR CONVENIENT SHIPMENT —

Mechanics, engineers, and other persons are sometimes engaged in work that keeps them at the same locality only a few months. Those who desire to carry with them a small library will find the trunk bookcase, as shown, convenient. It may be shipped as a trunk and used as a bookcase in one's hotel or dwelling. Articles other than books may be packed in it. The outside dimensions when closed

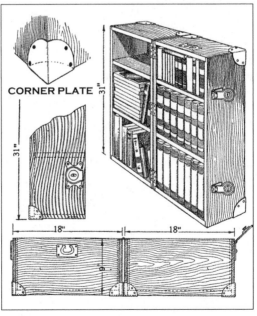

A SMALL LIBRARY MAY BE SHIPPED HANDILY IN THIS BOOKCASE.

are 31 by 18 by 18 in., providing for three shelves. It may be made of ¾-in. pine or whitewood, and stained, or covered with impregnated canvas. The outer corners are reinforced with metal corner plates and suitable hardware is provided.

— THREE-CASTER TRUNK FOR MOVING CRATES AND FURNITURE —

A convenient truck for handling heavy objects, especially in the home where commercial devices for this purpose are not available, is shown in the illustration. It consists of a frame built up of three 1¼- by 2- by 14-in. strips, fixed to a disk, ⅞ by 12 in. in size. Revolving casters are mounted under the ends of the arms, giving great freedom of movement in transporting loads. The three-caster arrangement is better than the use of four casters, because it accommodates itself to irregularities in the floor.

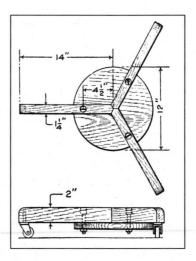

{ CHAPTER 2 }

HANDCRAFTED FURNITURE

BOOK IT

— A BOOK HOLDER —

Books having a flexible back are difficult to hold in an upright position when copying from them. A makeshift combination of paperweights and other books is often used, but with unsatisfactory results.

The book holder shown in the sketch will hold such books securely, allow the pages to be turned easily, and conceal the smallest possible portion of each page.

The holder can be cut out of a box corner and fitted with two screw eyes,

which have the part shown by the dotted lines at *A (Fig. 1)* removed. The length of the backboard determines the slope for the book rest.

— Combination Bookcase and Writing Desk —

In planning a writing desk, much convenience can be added by providing it with a bookcase in which may be stored those reference works most frequently used.

The material required, figuring exact size, is as follows:

- *2 sides, ⅞ by 16½ by 67 in.*
- *1 bottom shelf, ⅞ by 12 by 32¼ in.*
- *1 bottom shelf, ⅞ by 12 by 32¼ in.*
- *1 top shelf, ⅞ by 9¼ by 32¼ in.*
- *1 back, ⅜ by 40 by 31 in., made of pieces of convenient widths*
- *1 desk board, ⅞ by 16⅛ by 30 in.*
- *1 lower bookcase shelf, ⅞ by 9⅛ by 30 in.*
- *1 middle bookcase shelf, ⅞ by 8⅜ by 30 in.*
- *1 desk cover, ⅞ by 15½ by 30 in.*
- *1 upper back rail, ⅞ by 5 by 30 in.*

Bookcase Doors
- 4 stiles, ¾ by 1¼ by 19 in.
- 4 rails, ¾ by 1¼ by 13½ in.
- 2 mullions, ¼ by 1 by 17 ½ in.
- 2 mullions, ¼ by 1 by 13½ in.
- 1 pigeonhole stock, ⅜ by 7 by 72 in.

Main Drawers
- 1 front, ¾ by 4 by 30 in.
- 2 sides, ⅜ by 4 by 15½ in.
- 1 back, ⅜ by 3¼ by 29½ in.
- 1 bottom, ⅜ by 15¼ by 29½ in.
- 2 drawer slides, ⅞ by 1½ by 15 in.
- 1 lower rail, ⅞ by 1½ by 30 in.
- 1 molding strip, ¼ by ⅜ by 120 in.

As the main sides are of considerable width, it would be best to make them of two pieces glued together. In order to obtain a strong and neat joint, have this done by an experienced joiner or in the mill. The back edges should be carefully planed and rabbeted ⅜-in. deep by ½-in. wide for the ⅜-in. thick back. The bottom or foot piece of the sides should be squared up with the back edges, or the completed desk is liable to be winding or warped. The bottom and top shelves or main cross braces should be marked and cut out and, to be in harmony with the shape of the sides, the lower-shelf tenons are made wider than those on the upper shelf. The top shelf should be rabbeted ½ in. deep by ⅜ in. wide, to fit the back boards that are nailed to it. The

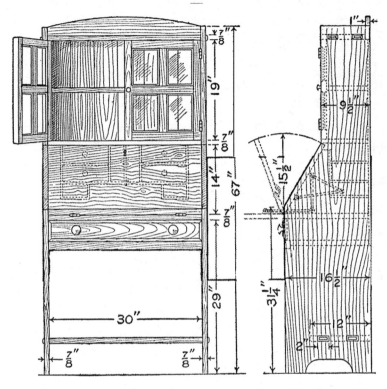

required mortises in the sidepieces are marked from the corresponding tenons of the shelves, and can then be cut out with a chisel. When finished, the four parts constituting the frame should be assembled, and may be held together with blind screws or dowel pins, passed through the tenons.

The desk board and two library shelves should then be fitted and fastened in place with blind screws through the sides, or with cleats from the inside. For a neat, finished appearance, the back boards should be carefully joined, exposing no cracks and fastened with nails driven into the various shelves. The upper rail, resting on the bookcase, and the lower rail, forming part of the drawer support, can then be fitted and secured to the sides with blind screws, either from the outside or diagonally through the

COMBINED BOOKCASE AND WRITING DESK WHICH CAN BE MADE UP IN GOLDEN OAK, MISSION, OR MAHOGANIZED BIRCH AND WILL COMPLEMENT OTHER FURNITURE OF LIKE CONSTRUCTION.

best construction would be to tenon the rails into the stiles about ½ in. The glass panel fits in a notch, ½ in. deep and ¼ in. wide, cut around the inside edge of the door. It is held in position with molding strips. In order to give the door an appearance of being divided into four parts, mullions or cross strips are fitted with the rails and stiles, and fastened to them with brads. The doors are attached with butt hinges.

In making the desk door, a specially selected board should be used because the finished appearance of the desk will greatly depend on this. The ends and sides should be perfectly squared, and the lower or hinge end cut beveled corresponding to the edge of the desk board. Butt hinges are used to secure it in position and hinged brackets or chains are provided to support it when open. When closed, it rests against a strip fastened to the lower side of the bottom bookcase shelf.

In arranging the pigeonholes have the inside boards rest on the desk board so the entire arrangement of the drawers and shelves may be withdrawn easily.

When thoroughly sanded and finished to taste, a serviceable, handy, and attractive piece of furniture is obtained.

rails from the inside. Drawer slides are fitted in place flush with the top edge of the lower rail and fastened to the sides with screws.

In making the drawer, the usual construction should be followed. The front piece should be rabbeted near its lower edge to fit the drawer bottom and notched ½ in. at each end to fit the sides. The bottom and end pieces fit into grooves cut in the sides. Suitable drawer pulls or knobs should be provided.

For the doors of the bookcase, the

— BOOKRACK —

The material necessary for the illustrated bookrack is as follows: 2 end pieces, ⅝ by 5¼ by 6 in.; 1 shelf, ⅝ by 5¼ by 13 in.

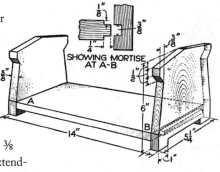

The shelf is cut rectangular, 5¼ in. wide by 14½ in. long. Its two ends should then be provided with tenons ⅜ in. thick by 4¼ in. wide, and extending out ¼ in.

The end pieces, after being cut to the given dimensions, are marked off and cut out for mortises to fit the shelf tenons. In assembling the parts, they are glued in place and clamped with hand screws until the glue has set. Any of the good Mission stains, properly applied, will give a finished appearance to the bookrack.

— A FOLDING BOOKRACK —

Having need of a bookrack that I could pack away in my trunk and still have room for my clothes, I made one as follows: I procured a piece of pine, ⅝ in. thick by 6 in. wide by 18 in. long, and laid out the plan on one side. Holes were drilled in the edges, ¾ in. from the ends, to receive 1½ in. round-head brass screws. The design for the ends was sawn out with a scroll saw and the edges smoothed up with

THE ENDS OF THE RACK TURN DOWN, MAKING A STRAIGHT BOARD.

fine sandpaper, whereupon the surfaces were stained and given a coat of wax. The screws were put in place to make the ends turn on them as on a bearing. In use the ends were turned up.

— A Homemade Book Holder —

A piece of board and four finishing nails furnished me with the necessary materials to construct a book-holding apparatus when in a hurry. Each nail, being driven through the board, could be turned to release and pulled out far enough to accommodate a thicker book. In fact the device was adjustable.

NAILS DRIVEN IN A BOARD AND BENT IN THE SHAPE OF SCREW HOOKS TO HOLD A BOOK.

— Easily Constructed Wall Shelves —

All that is necessary to make and support the simple set of wall shelves, shown in the illustration, is lumber for the shelves, four screw eyes, four screw hooks, sufficient picture-frame wire to form the braces and supports, and wood screws for attaching the wire. On the topside of the upper shelf are fastened the four screw eyes, two near the wall edge and the others near the outer edge. To support the upper shelf four screw hooks are used; two placed in the wall and spaced to match the set of screw eyes nearest

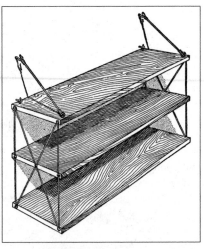

SHELVES FOR BOOKS SUPPORTED WITH PICTURE-FRAME WIRE TO THE WALL.

the wall, the others being placed above the first and connected to the outer set of screw eyes with the wire, thereby forming strong inclined sup-ports. The remaining shelves can be hung to suit by the supporting wires, which can be fastened with screws to the end of each shelf.

Seating *and* Storage

— Hall Seat with Storage Compartment —

The illustration represents a simple design for an easily made and substantial hall seat, provided with a compartment for odds and ends. It is advisable to make it of wood to matching its surroundings. The following material is necessary:

- *2 ends, ⅞ by 14 by 28 in.*
- *2 rails, ⅞ by 6 by 38 in.*
- *1 seat board, ⅞ by 14 by 36¼ in.*
- *1 bottom board, ⅞ by 12¼ by 36¼ in.*
- *2 seat cleats, ⅞ by ⅞ by 12¼ in.*
- *2 bottom cleats, ⅞ by ⅞ by 11½ in.*

The two ends, *A*, are marked to

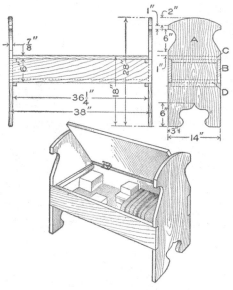

Details showing the construction of a hall seat to be made in mission style.

the same outline and cut with a coping or scroll saw. If a fine-toothed saw is used, the edges of the boards can be easily smoothed with sand-paper. Otherwise a file is necessary to remove the coarse saw traces. The rails *B* are cut to size and squared up at the ends, after which they can be placed at the proper places on the ends *A*, which may then be marked for the notches to receive the rails. In fastening the rails to the end pieces, 2-in. round-head screws can be used. The seat *C* is attached to the back rail by 2-in. butt hinges. To prevent the seat from sagging in the middle, it is supported on each side by cleats screwed to the end pieces *A*. If the seat is liable to warp it can be held straight by two cleats screwed underneath. The bottom board *D* may be held in place by means of screws through the rails, or by resting on cleats screwed to the end pieces. The seat, when assembled and thoroughly sanded, can be finished to suit.

— A Simple Bench —

A bench, substantial enough to hold a machine vise, and of sufficient strength to stand the rough usage incident to this duty, is a necessity around the farm or home workshop. A very simple and cheap bench is shown in the illustration; it consists of a stout barrel, in the center of which is set a heavy post, firmly packed with gravel. A board of the desired dimension is fastened to the post top, and the vise is mounted thereon. A bench of this character does not occupy much space, and is unusually well suited for this purpose.

GRAVEL POST

— Footstool —

The material necessary for the footstool shown in the illustration is as follows:

- *2 end pieces,* 1 by 10 by 15 in.
- *3 cross braces,* 1 by 4 by 12 in.
- *2 end braces,* 7/8 by 4 by 8 in.
- *1 top board,* 1/2 by 10 by 14 in.
- *1 piece of leather,* 11 by 16 in.

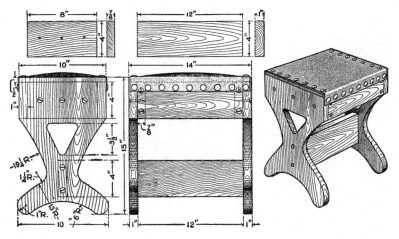

FOOTSTOOL IN MISSION FINISH WITH A LEATHER TOP.

• *Round-head wood screws and nails*

The two end pieces should be marked to a suitable pattern and may be cut out with a scroll or coping saw or, if these are not available, with a keyhole saw. The center opening should first be bored at one end and then cut out with the saw. The three long braces should be accurately squared and finished at the ends; the rigidity of the stool depending on this work. The seat consists of a box form with the open side down. The top is a ½ in. board, 8 in. wide by 12 in. long; the sides are formed by two of the long braces and the ends are the short braces. This box is securely put together with nails and then screwed in position with round-head wood screws so as to be flush with the top edge of the end pieces. The lower brace is secured in place with screws. In putting on the leather top, ½ in. should be turned under at each end and 1½ in. brought down on each side. This will provide sufficient looseness to pad the seat properly. Large round-head brass nails can be used, producing a neat appearance. The stool is then ready for a suitable stain or finish.

— EASILY MADE FOOTREST —

A comfortable and easily made footrest is made from two pieces of ¾-in. board and a pair of metal shelf brackets. The two boards, each 9 by 18 in., are screwed together at right angles to each other, and the shelf brackets are attached underneath to strengthen the construction. All corners of the boards are rounded off smoothly, and the whole is given a coat of paint, varnish, or stain, as desired. The footrest is used as shown in the drawing, and no effort is required to hold it in position.

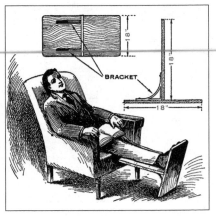

NO EFFORT IS REQUIRED TO HOLD THIS EASILY MADE FOOTREST IN POSITION. TWO BOARDS AND A PAIR OF METAL SHELF BRACKETS ARE THE MATERIALS REQUIRED.

— WOVEN-TOP STOOL —

The material necessary for this stool is as follows:

- *4 legs,* 1¾ by 1¾ by 16 in.
- *4 bottom rails,* ⅞ by 1¾ by 16 in.
- *4 top rails,* ⅞ by 2 by 16½ in.
- *4 diagonal braces,* ⅞ by 1¾ by 6 in.

The legs are mortised so the top rails come level. The upper rails are tenoned on the sides only and beveled at the ends. For the bottom rails, the mortises are made one above the other, the rails being tenoned on all sides. The braces are cut at 45-degree angles on each end and glued into place.

In weaving the top, proceed as follows: Use a wet weaver and wrap one layer over the entire top, the strips being placed close together and tightly wound. Start the second layer at right angles to the first by going under one strip, then over

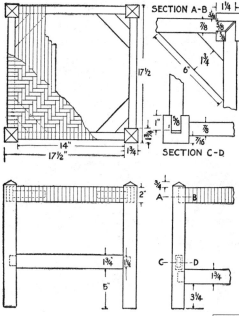

SECTION A-B

17½

6"

14"
17½"

SECTION C-D

as in the preceding; the fifth, start over two, then under and over three, repeatedly. The sixth, and last of the series, begin over three and then continue, by threes, as before. Having finished one series, the remainder of the top should be completed in similar order. Good white shellac makes the best finish for the seat; the stool itself may be finished to suit.

CONSTRUCTION OF THE FRAME AND MANNER OF LAYING THE WEAVERS FOR THE TOP.

three strips, under three, and so on, by threes, until that strip is finished. Start the second by going under two strips, then over three, under three, and so on, as before. The third strip should start by going under three, then over and under three, etc. Start the fourth by going over one, then under three, and over three,

WEAVING THE TOP OF THE STOOL BY USING A WET WEAVER OF REED.

— How to Make a High Stool —

The cast-off handles of four old brooms, three pieces of board cut as shown, and a few screws will make a substantial high stool. The legs should be placed in the holes, as shown at *A*, and secured with screws turned through the edge of the board into the legs in the holes. The seat *B* should be fastened over this and the legs braced by the square piece *C*. Screws are turned through the legs and into the square piece to keep it in position.

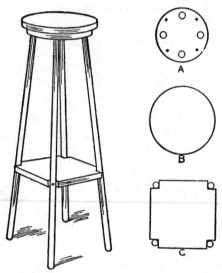

— An Enameled Armchair Made of Wooden Strips —

An armchair suitable for a dressing table was made by a handy women from pine strips. The photograph shows the simple and pleasing lines of the construction. Aside from the board seat, only three sizes of wood are used, 2 by 2 in., 1 by 2 in., and ½ by 2 in.

THE SIMPLE CONSTRUCTION OF
THIS NEAT ARMCHAIR MAKES
IT AN ATTRACTIVE JOB FOR
THE AMATEUR CRAFTSMAN.

at exposed points. The seat is wider from side to side than from front to back. Two coats of white paint and one of white enamel give a good finish.

The dimensions may be varied to suit individual needs. Sizes suggested are: back, 32 in. high and 24 in. wide; side, 26 in. to top of arm and 19 in. wide; seat, 17 in. from floor, 18 in. from front to back, and 20 in. wide between the front supports. The stock is all planed up square to dimensions and sanded smooth. The ends should be cut squarely in a miter box, with a fine-toothed saw, and then sanded smooth, taking care not to round the ends.

The pieces are fastened with screws, round-head brass ones being used

— A Detachable Chair Arm —

The children in the home as well as others can make good use of a chair arm that may be attached quickly to an ordinary chair. The wide arm is clamped to the back of the chair by means of a metal strip fitted with a thumbscrew, and the upright is fixed to the arm by a hinge, making it convenient to store the device. The lower end of the upright is fitted with

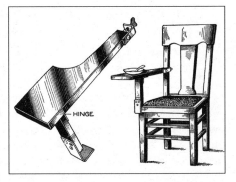

a metal angle that fits on the corner of the chair.

DESKS *and* TABLES

— A PARLOR TABLE —

The material required for the parlor table illustrated is as follows:

- *1 tabletop,*
  1 by 26 by 41 in.
- *1 bottom shelf,*
  1 by 15 by 35 in.
- *2 side rails,*
  ¾ by 4 by 33 in.
- *2 end rails,*
  ¾ by 4 by 21 in.
- *2 top cross braces,*
  1 by 4 by 19½ in.
- *4 feet,*
  1¾ by 4 by 4 in.
- *2 posts, 6 by 6 by 26 in.*
- *2 side corner strips,*
  1 by 1 by 31½ in.
- *2 end corner strips,*
  1 by 1 by 17½ in.

DESIGN OF A TABLE THAT WILL APPEAR WELL IN THE DIFFERENT OAK FINISHES AS WELL AS IN MAHOGANY.

The bottom shelf can be made of two pieces of 1-in. material, 8 in. wide, carefully glued together and reinforced on the underside with two crosspieces glued and screwed to it. The foot pieces are secured to the bottom shelf so as to project 1 in. on the ends and side. In case a center support is deemed advisable, another foot piece can be added. But unless the floor is very level, rocking may result. The uprights, or posts, are made from solid 6- by 6-in. lumber, 26 in. long, carefully squared at the ends and tapered to 4 in. square at the upper end. If desired, the posts can be made of boards cut and fastened together to form a hollow tapered post. In either case, they should be set in about 4 in. from each side of the bottom shelf and fastened to it by means of screws. The rail pieces for the tabletop should be cut and fitted with mitered joints at the corner to form a rectangular frame, 21 by 33 in. This is glued to the top and may be toenailed to it. But to provide a more secure bracing, a 1-in. square strip of material is fastened all around the inside edge of the rails, flush with their upper edge. The top is screwed to this. In order to prevent tipping when the top is resting on the 4- by 4-in. ends of the posts, two cross braces are provided. These should be screwed to the outer end sides of the posts and beveled off on their upper edges to fit the tabletop. They should be of such length as to have a tight fit between the side rails, and are fastened to these by means of finishing nails driven from the outside. Gluing and toenailing can also be used to secure the top more firmly to the braces; care should be taken that no nails cut through the tabletop. After thoroughly sanding and smoothing off the table, it can be finished to suit.

— A FOLDING WALL DESK —

To provide an inexpensive desk in a shop, where space was quite limited, the folding wall desk shown in the sketch was devised. It was cut from a packing box and the hinged lid built up of boards of better quality. To give a good writing surface, a piece of heavy cardboard was fastened to the writing bed with thumb tacks and may be renewed whenever necessary. The inside of the desk was fitted with filing compartments arranged to care for a large variety of shop forms and stationery. An inkwell holder made of a strip of sheet metal was fixed to the end of the desk and the bottle suspended in it, there being space for additional bottles also. The hinged lid is provided with a hasp and padlock.

When not in use, the desk may be tilted upward and locked against the wall with small catches. By using a T-square against the left edge of the writing bed, a convenient drafting table for shop sketching is provided.

The detailed construction for the making of the desk from stock lumber, by boys or amateur workers with tools, may be carried out as follows: Determine upon the size of the proposed desk. Convenient dimensions are 30 in. long, 18 in. wide, 7 in. high at the back, and 4 in. high at the front. Use ⅞-in. softwood; pine and poplar are suitable. Cut and

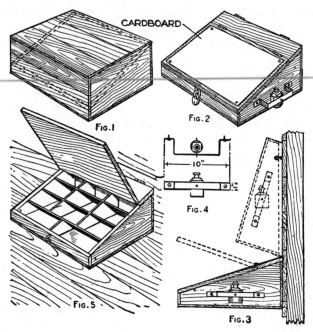

CARDBOARD

Fig. 1

Fig. 2

Fig. 4

10"

Fig. 5

Fig. 3

THE PACKING BOX, FROM WHICH THE DESK WAS MADE, IS SHOWN IN
FIG. 1. THE DOTTED LINES INDICATED WHERE IT WAS CUT TO
GIVE THE SLANTING WRITING SURFACE. THE DEVICE IN ITS
NORMAL POSITION IS SHOWN IN FIG. 2, HOOKED AGAINST
THE WALL IN FIG. 3, AND WITH THE LID RAISED,
SHOWING THE COMPARTMENTS, IN FIG. 5.

shape all the pieces before beginning the assembling of the parts. The wood should be planed smooth and may be sanded lightly when the construction is completed, before applying a finish. A simple arrangement of the pieces so they can be nailed together is that shown in the sketch, which was used in making the box. First shape the pieces for the sides, 5¼ in. wide at the larger end, 2¼ in. wide at the smaller, and 16¼ in. Clamp the boards together or tack them with two wire nails while shaping them so that they will be exactly alike. Make a piece 5 ½ in.

wide and 30 in. long for the back, and one the same length and 2½ in. wide for the front. Nail them to the ends, as shown, permitting the slight excess material to project over the upper edges of the sidepieces. Trim off this extra stock with a plane so that the upper surfaces of the front and back conform to the slant of the sidepieces. Make a strip 4 in. wide for the upper edge of the desk, to which the writing bed is hinged. Cut pieces for the bottom and nail them in place.

Before nailing down the upper hinge strip the interior fittings should be made. Use wood not thicker than ½ in., and fit the pieces into place carefully, nailing them firmly through the outer faces of the desk. A better method is to make the pigeonholes or compartments with a piece off the thin stock on the ends of the partitions so that the compartments are built up as a unit and slid into the desk, no nails being necessary to hold them.

The lid should be made of sound, dry stock and glued up of strips about 3 in. wide to prevent it from warping or twisting easily. If the person making the desk has the necessary skill, it is best to fix a strip 2 in. wide at each end of the writing bed to hold the pieces together and to keep the bed in shape.

The holder for the inkwell is made of a 1-in. strip of metal, bent to the shape shown in *Fig. 4* and drilled to fit small screws. A can is supported in the holder and the bottle rests in it.

The desk may be finished by painting it or giving it a coat of shellac and one of varnish, either after it has been stained to match adjoining woodwork or in the natural color.

— Adjustable and Pivoted Bed Table Attached to a Bedpost —

A table arrangement that can be clamped handily to the bedpost and swung out of the way or removed altogether when not in use is a convenience that has a wide use in the home. A device of this kind, which requires no floor support and can be folded compactly for storage, is shown in the illustration. The table proper consists of a ⅞-in. board, of suitable size, the edges of which are banded with metal or thin wooden strips. The board is supported on a frame of iron rod bent to the form indicated in the dotted lines and clamped with ¹⁄₁₆ in. brass clamps. The end of this frame rod is bent at an angle and pivoted in a metal bracket. A cotter pin guards against accidental loosening of the joint. The clamping device is made of ¼- by 1¼ in band iron, and is bent to fit loosely around the bedpost. A brass plate, *A*, is fitted inside of the main piece *B*, as shown. A thumbscrew is threaded into the piece *B*, its point engaging the brass plate, which acts as a guard. In fastening the piece *B* on the bedpost, the thumbscrew is set and the wing nut also tightened.

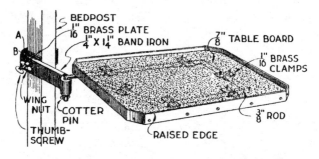

THIS HANDY TABLE CLAMPS ONTO THE BEDPOST AND CAN BE SWUNG ASIDE CONVENIENTLY OR REMOVED ALTOGETHER.

MISSION POSSIBLE

— MISSION CANDLESTICK —

Even though a candlestick is one of the simplest of the smaller household furnishings, it nevertheless can be made a very attractive feature. For the illustrated mission design, a base, 4 by 4 by ⅞ in., should be provided. This is cut, with the grain, for a ½ in.-wide groove, ¼ in. deep, and extending from one side to within ½ in. of the opposite side. In this groove is to fit the handle, which is made from a piece of ½- by 2¼- by 3¾-in. stock. It is provided with a finger-grip hole ¾ by 1¼ in. at one end. Its upper edge should be marked off from the

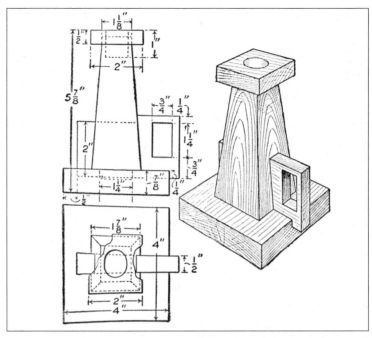

MISSION CANDLESTICK OF PLEASING DESIGN, WHICH WILL
COMPLEMENT OTHER FURNITURE OF THIS CLASS.

center pedestal and fitted to it. The pedestal can be made from stock 1⅞ by 1⅞ by 5 in. A tenon, ¼ in. long by 1¼ in. square, is formed on the lower end. This tenon is to fit a mortise in the center of the base. A slot ½ in. wide is cut centrally in the pedestal and 2 in. above the lower end, to fit the handle. The upper end of the pedestal is cut straight for ¼ in. and squared off to 1⅛ in. This

is to serve as a tenon to fit a corresponding mortise in the ½- by 2-in. square top. The sides of the pedestal are evenly tapered off from the 1⅞-in. square base to the lower end of the 1⅛-in. square tenon, at the top.

The parts, before assembling, should be thoroughly sanded, as considerable difficulty would otherwise be experienced. No nails or screws need be used, because good glue will keep the parts together equally well. When completely assembled, a hole should be drilled through the top and into the pedestal to fit the size of candle to be used. A carefully applied mission stain and varnish will give a proper finish to the candlestick.

— HOW TO MAKE A MISSION LIBRARY TABLE —

The mission library table, the drawings for which are given here, has been found well proportioned and of pleasing appearance. It can be made of any of the several furniture woods in common use, such as selected quarter-sawn white oak, which will be found exceptionally pleasing in the effect produced.

If a planing mill is at hand, the stock can be ordered in such a way as to avoid the hard work of planing and sanding. Of course, if mill-planed stock cannot be had, the following dimensions must be enlarged slightly to allow for "squaring up the rough."

For the top, order 1 piece 1⅛ in. thick by 34 in. wide by 46 in. long. Have it S-4-S (surfaced on four sides) and "squared" to length. Also, specify that it be sanded on the top surface, the edges, and ends.

For the shelf, order 1 piece ⅞ in. thick by 22 in. wide by 42 in. long, with the four sides surfaced, squared, and sanded the same as for the top.

For the side rails, order 2 pieces ⅞ in. thick by 6 in. wide by 37 in.

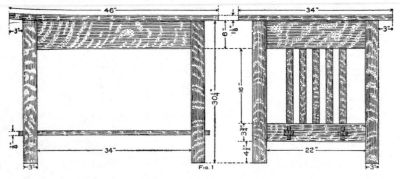

THIS PICTURE IS DRAWN FROM A PHOTOGRAPH
OF THE MISSION TABLE DESCRIBED IN THIS ARTICLE.

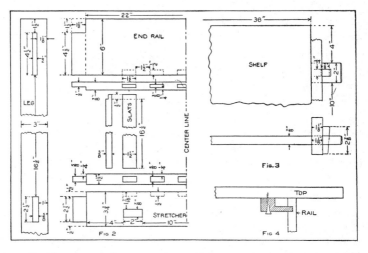

long, S-4-S and sanded on one side. For the end rails, 2 pieces ⅞ in. thick by 6 in. wide by 25 in. long. Other specifications as for the side rails.

For the stretchers, into which the shelf tenons enter, 2 pieces 1⅛ in. thick by 3¾ in. wide by 25 in. long, surfaced and sanded on four sides. For the slats, 10 pieces ⅝ in. thick by 1½ in. wide by 17 in. long, surfaced and sanded on four sides. For the keys, 4 pieces ¾ in. thick by 1¼ in. wide by 2⅞ in. long, S-4-S. This width is a little wide; it will allow the key to be shaped as desired.

The drawings obviate any necessity for going into detail in the description. *Fig. 1* gives an assembly drawing showing the relation of the parts.

Fig. 2 gives the detail of an end. The tenons for the side rails are laid off and the mortises placed in the post, as are those on the end. Care must be taken, however, not to cut any mortises on the post, below, as was done in cutting the stretcher mortises on the ends of the table. A good plan is to set the posts upright in the positions they are to occupy relative to one another and mark with pencil the approximate positions of the mortises. The legs can then be laid flat and the mortises accurately marked out with a fair degree of assurance that they will not be cut where they are not wanted, and that the legs shall "pair" properly when effort is made to assemble the parts of the table.

The table ends should be glued up first and the glue allowed to harden, after which the tenons of the shelf may be inserted and the side rails placed.

There is a reason for the shape, size, and location of each tenon or mortise. For illustration, the shape of the tenon on the top rails permits the surface of the rail to extend almost flush with the surface of the post, at the same time permitting the mortise in the post to be kept away from that surface. Again, the shape of the ends of the slats is such that, though they may vary slightly in length, the fitting of the joints will not be affected. Care must be taken in cutting the mortises to keep their sides clean and sharp and to size.

In making the mortises for the keyed tenons, the length of mortise must be slightly in excess of the width of the tenon—about ⅛ in. of play to each side of each tenon. With a shelf of the width specified for this table, if such allowance is not made so that the tenons may move sideways, the shrinkage would split the shelf.

In cutting across the ends of the shelf between the tenons, leave a hole in the waste so that the turning saw or compass saw can be inserted. Saw within 1/16 of the line, after which this margin may be removed with a chisel and mallet.

Fig. 3 shows two views of the keyed tenon and the key. The mortise for the key is to be placed in the middle of the tenon. It will be noted that this mortise is laid out 11/16 in. from the shoulder of the tenon, while the stretcher is 1⅛ in. thick. This is to ensure the key's pulling the shelf tightly against the side of the stretcher.

Keys may be made in a variety of shapes. The one shown is simple and structurally good. Whatever shape is used, the important thing to keep in mind is that the size of the key and the slat of its forward surface where it passes through the tenon must be kept the same as the mortise made for it in the tenon.

The top is to be fastened to the rails by means either of wooden buttons, *Fig. 4*, or small angle irons.

There are a bewildering number of mission finishes upon the market. A very satisfactory one is obtained by applying a coat of brown Flemish water stain, diluted by the addition of water in the proportion of 2 parts water to 1 part stain. When this has dried, sand with Number 00 paper, being careful to "cut through." Next, apply a coat of dark brown filler; the directions for doing this will be found upon the can in which the filler is bought. One coat usually suffices. However, if an especially smooth surface is desired a second coat may be applied in a similar manner.

After the filler has hardened, a very thin coat of shellac is to be put on. When this has dried it should be sanded lightly and then one or two coats of wax should be properly applied and polished. Directions for waxing are printed upon the cans in which the wax is bought. A beautiful dull gloss so much sought by finishers of modern furniture will be the result of carefully following these directions.

— A MISSION BRACKET SHELF —

The shelf consists of six pieces of wood, *A*, *B*, *C*, *D*, *E* and *F*. The material can be of any wood. I have one made of mahogany finished in natural color, and one made of poplar finished black. The dimensions given in the detail drawings are sufficient for anyone to make this bracket. The amount of material required is very small and can be made from scrap or purchased from a mill, surfaced and sanded. The parts are put together with dowel pins.

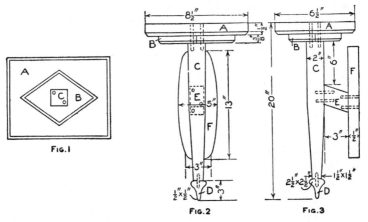

FIG.1   FIG.2   FIG.3

DETAILS OF THE WALL BRACKET

EMBELLISHMENTS

— A COLONIAL MIRROR FRAME —

Black walnut or mahogany is the most effective wood to use in making this simple but artistic frame. It requires a very small amount of stock, and what is used should be of a good quality and carefully worked to the given dimensions with keen tools. The stock required for the frame is as follows:

Black walnut or mahogany
- 2 pieces, 27½ in. long by 1⅜ in. wide by ¾ in. thick
- 1 piece, 22 in. long by 1⅜ in. wide by ¾ in. thick
- 1 piece, 9¼ in. long by 1⅜ in. wide by ¼ in. thick

White holly
- 1 piece 27½ in. long by 1½ in. wide by 1/16 in. thick

Picture board
- 1 piece, 25 in. long by 9 in. wide by ⅛ in. thick.

The dimensions for the walnut and mahogany pieces are rough sizes, oversize to allow for planing to the dimensions given in the sketch. The white holly may be procured smoothly planed on both sides and of the exact thickness required. The

picture backing may be purchased in almost any store that sells frames. It is usually rough pine and inexpensive.

The first operation is to plane the frame pieces on one side and edge, using great care to ensure both being perfectly straight and the edge square with the face. Gauge for, and plane to, the thickness required, although this need not be exactly ⅝ in. as called for, but if the stock will stand 11/16 in. or ¾ in. Do not take the time to cut it down to ⅝ in. The little cross rail must be exactly ⅛ in. thick, because it is to be let ⅛ in. into the rabbet cut for the glass, which makes it come ⅛ in. back from the face of the frame when it is in place. Plane all of these pieces to the width 1⅛ in.

For cutting the rabbet a plow, or a ¾-in grooving, plane is the best tool to use. But if neither is available, a rabbet plane can be used. Be sure to plane the rabbet square and to the lines gauged for the depth and width.

To groove the pieces for the holly strips a special tool is required. This

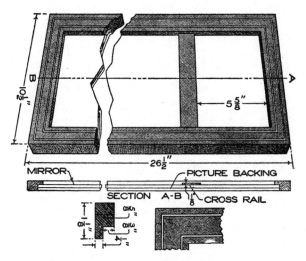

SECTION A-B

MIRROR — PICTURE BACKING — CROSS RAIL

AN INLAY OF HOLLY MAKES AN EXCEEDINGLY PRETTY FRAME
OF COLONIAL DESIGN FOR A MIRROR.

may be made of a piece of soft sheet steel or iron, which must be of a thickness to correspond to that of the holly. A piece 2½ in. long, and of almost any width, will answer the purpose. File one edge of the metal straight, and cut saw teeth in it by filing straight across with a small saw file. Remove the burr raised by the filing by rubbing each side on an oilstone. Drill two holes in it for fastening with screws to a piece of hardwood. The wood serves as a fence, and if properly fastened to the metal, the teeth should cut a groove 1/16 in. deep and 3/16 in. from

the edge. The holly strip should fit the groove tightly so that it can be driven home with light taps of a hammer. It is smart to try the tool on a bit of waste wood first to see if it cuts the groove properly.

The holly is cut into strips ⅛ in. wide with a slitting gauge. An ordinary marking gauge, with the spur filed flat on each side to make a sharp, deep line, will do very well for this work. The gauging is done from both sides of the piece to make the spur cut halfway through from each side. Before the slitting is attempted, one edge of the piece is first straightened. This is readily accomplished with a fore plane, laid on its side and used as a shoot plane. The strip to be planed is laid flat on a piece of ⅞-in. stock with one edge projecting slightly. This raises it above the bench and allows the fore plane to be worked against the projecting edge.

The strips should be applied to the groove to test the fit, and if found to be tight, they must be tapered slightly by filing or scraping the sides. If the fit is good, hot glue may be run into the grooves with a sharp stick, and the strips driven into place. They will project above the surface slightly, but no attempt should be made to plane them off flush until the glue has become thoroughly hardened. Then use a sharp plane and finish with a scraper and No. 00 sandpaper.

The miters are cut in a miter box or planed to the exact 45-degree angle on a miter shoot board. Before gluing the corners, the recesses are cut for the cross rail, but it must not be put in place until the corners of the frame have been fastened and the glue given time to dry.

The frame may be given either a dull or bright finish. The dull finish gives a rich appearance and is very easy to apply. Give the completed frame one coat of white shellac. When it is dry, rub the surface with very fine sandpaper until it has a smooth finish. Finish with any of the prepared waxes, being careful to follow the directions furnished.

Before putting the board back of the mirror, be sure to place two or three sheets of clean paper on the silvered surface. The picture board is fastened with glazier's points or with small bung-head wire nails. The back is finished by gluing a sheet of heavy wrapping paper to the edges of the frame. If the wrapping paper is moistened with a damp cloth before it is applied, it will dry out smooth and tightly drawn over the back.

— A JARDINIÈRE PEDESTAL —

The pedestal may be made of any close-grained wood, such as basswood or maple, if the stain is to be walnut or mahogany, but it can also be constructed of quarter-sawn oak and finished in a waxed mission or varnished surface. The material required is as follows:

- *1 top,* 12 by 12 by ⅞ in, S-2-S
- *2 caps,* 6 by 6 by ⅞ in., S-2-S

85

- *1 upright,* 18 by 4 by 4 in., S-4-S
- *1 base,* 8 by 8 by ⅞ in., S-2-S.

The top is centered and a circle, 11½ in. in diameter, is drawn upon it and sawn out. The caps are also centered, and circles drawn upon them, 5½ in. and 3½ in. in diameter. Saw them out on the larger circles and center them in a wood lathe, and turn out the wood in the smaller circles to a depth of ½ in. The upright is then centered in the lathe and turned to 3½ in. in diameter for its full length.

The base and foot pieces are cut out as shown, fitted together, and fastened with screws from the underside. One of the caps is mounted in the center on the base and the other cap in the center on the underside of the top. The upright is then placed in the turned-out parts of the caps and either glued or fastened with screws.

If lightwood is used, the finish can be walnut or mahogany. A very pretty finish can be worked out in pyrography, if one is familiar with that work.

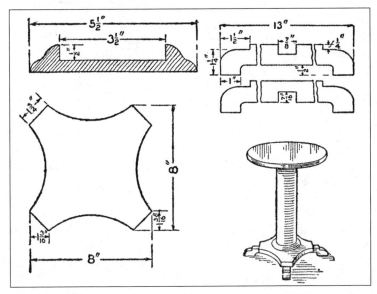

THE PEDESTAL CAN BE MADE OF A WOOD SUITABLE FOR FINISHING TO MATCH OTHER FURNITURE.

— A Turntable Stand
for Potted Flowers —

Potted flowers, if kept in the
house, tend to grow toward
the light. From time to time the pot
should be turned. The turntable stand
shown in the sketch was designed to
do this more readily. It is made up
of a low, four-legged taboret upon
which a 12-in. disk of 1-in. wood is
fixed with a screw. A thin wooden
washer, sanded and shellacked,
ensures easy turning. Rectangular
boxes or circular jars look equally
good upon the stand, the beauty of
which depends much upon its workmanship and finish.

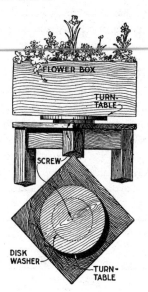

— Stand for a Test-tube
Flower Vase —

A test-tube vase, containing a
single blossom, adds color and
a certain individual touch to the
businessman's desk, or it may be
used with effectiveness in the home.
A simple wooden stand, finished to
harmonize with the surroundings,
may be made easily and affords
a support and protection for the
test tube. The sketch shows a small
stand of this type, made of oak, in the
straight-line mission style. It may be
adapted to other woods and to various
designs in straight or curved lines.

The base is 2½ in. square and
rests on two cross strips, 1 in. wide.
All the material may be about ¼ in.
thick, but it is desirable to have the
base and cap pieces of thicker wood.
The uprights may be of ⅛ to ¼ in.

wood, and are notched together as shown. They are 1 in. wide and 6¼ in. long, a portion being cut to receive the test tube. The cap is 1½ in. square, and its edges are chamfered slightly, as are those on the upper edge of the base. The pieces are fitted together with small brads used as hidden dowels and the joints are glued. Brads may be used to nail the pieces together, and they should be sunk into the wood, the resulting holes filled carefully. The stand should be stained a dark color or left natural and given a coat of shellac or varnish.

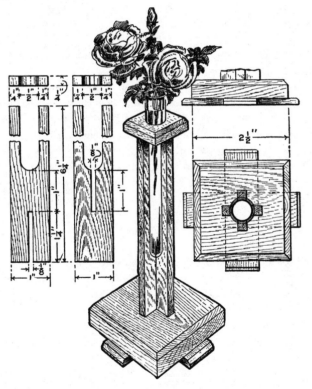

THE STAND PROVIDES A SUPPORT AND PROTECTION FOR THE TEST-TUBE VASE ON THE OFFICE DESK OR IN THE HOME.

— TURN-DOWN SHELF FOR A SMALL SPACE —

The average amateur photographer does not have very much space in which to do his work. The kitchen is the room ordinarily used for finishing the photographs. In many instances there will not be space enough for any extra tables, and so a temporary place is prepared from boxes or a chair on which to place the trays and chemicals. Should there be space enough on one of the walls, a shelf can be made to hang down out of the way when not in use. A shelf constructed on this order may be of any length to suit the space or of such a length for the purpose intended. A heavy piece of wood about 1½ in. thick and 4 to 6 in. wide is first fastened to the wall at the proper height with nails, or much better, large screws.

The shelf is cut and planed

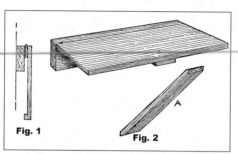

TURN-DOWN SHELF.

smooth from a board 12 in. wide and about 1 in. thick. This board is fastened to the piece on the wall with two hinges, as shown in *Fig. 1*. A small cleat is nailed to the outer and under edges of the board and in the middle, as shown. This is used to place a support under the outer edge of the shelf. The support *A, Fig. 2*, should be long enough to extend diagonally to the floor or top of the baseboard from the inner edge of the cleat when the shelf is up in its proper place.

— ❖ ❖ ❖ —

{ CHAPTER 3 }

IN *the* GARDEN

—

SMALL GARDEN PROJECTS

— DEVICE FOR PACKING EARTH IN TRANSPLANTING —

When tomato or cabbage plants are to be set out in considerable numbers, the simple implement shown here makes stooping over to press the dirt about the plants unnecessary. After a row of plants has been set in dibble holes and watered, the soil can be packed about their roots quickly while one is standing upright. The jaws of the device are activated by means of the hinged lever.

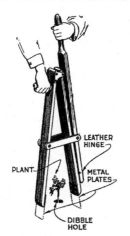

LEATHER HINGE

PLANT

METAL PLATES

DIBBLE HOLE

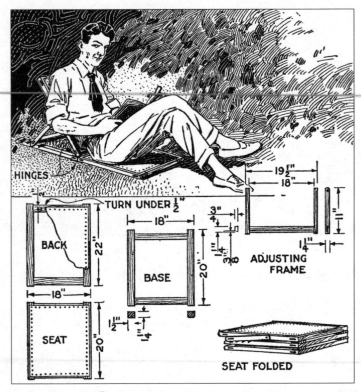

THIS SEAT IS USEFUL OUT OF DOORS
AND ALSO FOR SPECIAL PURPOSES INDOORS.

— A FOLDING GROUND SEAT WITH BACKREST —

Those who enjoy sitting or lying upon the grass while reading will find the device shown in the illustration convenient and comfortable. With this, one may enjoy the coolness of the ground without harm to the person or clothing. The adjustable backrest supports the body in various positions. The device is light, compact, and readily transported. It is useful also in the home and elsewhere. By placing it across the bed, or on a bunk, a good substitute for an extra chair is provided. The seat proper may be folded under and the backrest used as a prop for reading in bed.

Oak is a suitable wood, and other common woods may be used. First construct, according to the dimensions given, three rectangular frames with mortise-and-tenon joints. Cover the seat and back frames with heavy duck, turning it in ½ in. at the edges. The base is an open frame, provided with adjusting notches spaced 2 in. apart. Next make the adjusting frame, as detailed. Hinge the back and the seat to the base, and fasten the adjusting frame to the back with screws, permitting it to fold for convenient storage, as shown.

— PRACTICAL BRACKET FOR GARDEN HOSE —

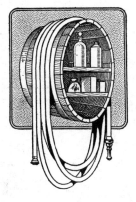

Care in the storage of a garden hose will pay the owner in the longer life of it, and the homemade bracket shown in the sketch suggests a convenient method of caring for the hose. A portion of a barrel was sawn off at one of the hoops and reinforced by nailing the hoops and inserting shelves, after which it was nailed to the wall. The hose may be coiled over it in shape to be easily carried to the lawn or garden for use. The shelves provide space for an oilcan for the lawn mower and other accessories.

— PORTABLE HEAD AND BACK REST —

A convenient and readily portable head and back rest, for use on beach or lawn, is made from several hardwood strips and a length of canvas, combined as in the sketch. The long side strips are mortised at the center and the crosspiece is provided with a corresponding tenon at each end, as in the drawing. The lower ends of the sidepieces are pointed. Near the upper end of each crosspiece, a hole is drilled for a piece of rope, which passes through them and through the hem provided at one edge of the canvas strip. The rope is secured to the outside of the strips with knots.

In use, the rest is placed at an angle, as shown. The pointed sidepieces are forced into the ground, the person sitting on the extended canvas. When not in use, the seat may be taken apart and rolled in a small bundle.

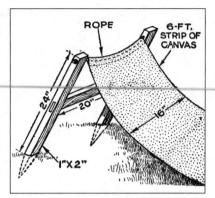

— QUICKLY MADE LAWN TENT —

A very simple way of erecting a lawn tent for the children is to take a large umbrella such as used on delivery wagons and drive the handle into the ground deep enough to hold it solid. Fasten canvas or cotton cloth to the ends of the ribs and let it hang so the bottom edge will touch the ground. Light ropes can be tied to the ends of the ribs and fastened to stakes driven in the ground in a tentlike manner to make the whole more substantial and to stand against a heavy wind.

This makes an exceptionally fine tent, as the umbrella is waterproof. Also, there is more room to stand up in than in a tent that is in the shape of a wigwam.

— A SIMPLE RAIN GAUGE —

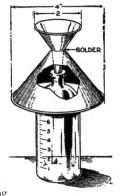

A rain gauge, by which one can ascertain with fair accuracy the precipitation over a certain period, is made from a graduated bottle and two tin funnels. The spout of the larger funnel is removed and that of the smaller one is inserted into the opening and soldered, as indicated. The spout of the smaller funnel is placed in the neck of the bottle. In order to determine the amount of precipitation, the bottle must be graduated in fractions of an inch, and this may be done by marking the bottle with a file, or by making a scale on paper and gluing it to the glass, afterward coating it with varnish. In use, the gauge should be set in the open.

— AN EFFECTIVE CHERRY PICKER —

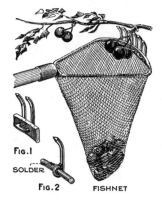

An effective implement can be easily made for picking cherries rapidly with a minimum of climbing. A frame is made of stiff wire or light iron rod, the ends being brought together and forced tightly into a handle of the proper length. On the front of the frame a series of picking fingers or hooks is fastened, about ¼ in. apart, so that the fruit cannot pass between them. *Figs. 1* and *2* illustrate two methods of attaching the hooks. Solder should be used in both cases to make the fingers rigid. The device is completed by attaching a bag of close-woven fish netting to catch the fruit as it is plucked from the tree.

The Birds *and the* Bees

— A Catproof Bird Table —

Our bird table is a source of great enjoyment, particularly since the birds feel secure from cats or other enemies because of the construction of this ornament in our garden. The sketch shows the arrangement of the table braced at the top of a 6-ft. post. Shrubbery surrounds the table and a light evergreen climber clings to the post, yet does not give the cats a good foothold.

Experience has taught us that birds in general prefer breadcrumbs to other varieties of food, and they are also fond of cracked wheat. The linnets like oranges particularly. We cut an orange in two and place the halves on the table. It is amusing to see the birds balance on one side of the orange while they peck at the fruit. Soon the orange peel is almost entirely emptied. We provide a small basin of fresh water on the table, and the birds use it as a drinking cup as well as a bathtub.

— Hollow-log Birdhouses —

Birdhouses that are far more attractive than almost any kind made of boards are easily made by those who delight in watching their feathered friends, using sections of hollow logs.

The type shown in the drawing is made from a length of log mounted on a pole. The piece of log is thoroughly cleaned of all rot and is held in place between the circular bottom platform and the solid top with long bolts, as indicated in the illustration.

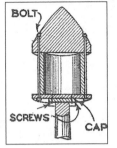

The thickness of the walls will be determined to some extent by the amount of sound wood in the interior of the log, although if this is too thick, it can be cut down by using a carpenter's gouge. Holes are drilled through the sides, and the interior may be divided into several compartments by suitable partitions.

Most pleasing proportions are obtained with a birdhouse of the type shown when the section of log forming the body of the house is about 2 in. longer than its diameter, the height of the cap or top being made a little less than that of the walls. Such a birdhouse can be mounted on the end of a pole. Or it can be mounted by putting a screw eye into the center of the cap and suspending the house from a tree branch.

— CLAY FLOWERPOTS USED FOR BIRDHOUSES —

A novel use of the common garden flowerpot may be made by enlarging the small opening at the bottom with a pair of pliers and carefully breaking the clay away until the opening is large enough to admit a small bird.

Place the pot, bottom side up, on a board 3 in. wider than the diameter of the largest pot used and fasten it to the board with wood cleats and brass screws. Fit the cleats as close as possible to the sides of the pot. One

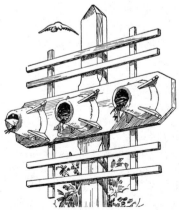

POTS FASTENED TO THE BOARD.

or more pots may be used, as shown on the sketch.

The board on which the pots are fastened is nailed or screwed to a post or pole 10 or 12 ft. in height. The board is braced with lath or similar strips of wood, making a framework suitable for a roost. In designing the roost, the lath can be arranged to make it quite attractive, or the braces may be of twigs and branches of a tree to make a rustic effect.

— BEE FEEDER FOR WINTER USE —

The use of a feeder, like that shown in the sketch, makes the feeding of bees in winter convenient. Syrup is fed to the bees from inverted glass jars, the openings of which are covered with muslin. The jars are encased in a packing of chaff in a wooden covering. The wood box is made to fit over the hive as shown in the sketch, and a 2-in. strip is nailed over the joint.

SYRUP IS FED TO THE BEES IN WINTER AND PROTECTED FROM THE COLD BY THE FEEDING JARS ENCLOSED IN THE BOX.

The device is made as follows: Use wood smoothed on both sides, pine, basswood, or other softwood being satisfactory. Make two pieces, ⅞ in. thick, and the same size as the top of the hive. Into one of these cut two round holes, as shown, to fit the necks of the jars. Make two pieces 6 ¾ in. wide for the sides and two for the ends, the length being suited to the hive, the dimensions given in the sketch being suggestive only. Make four strips 2 in. wide and long enough to fit the four sides of the box. Nail the pieces of the box together, as shown, nailing the sides over the end pieces and the top over the frame of sides and ends. Pack chaff into the box and, after filling the jars with syrup and covering their openings with muslin, pack the jars into the box so that their openings will be level with the bottom through which the holes have been cut. Fasten the board, with holes for the jars, into place with screws so that it may be removed when it is desired to remove the jars for refilling. Nail the 2-in. strips around the lower edge of the box so as to cover the joint between the box and the hive. The feeder is then fitted into place, the bees feeding from the surface of the muslin. The chaff prevents the syrup from congealing in cold weather and so it is always available for the bees. The use of this simple device will prove economical and practical in keeping bees over the winter, assuring them a good food supply, with little effort on the part of the keeper.

LOCKS, GATES *and* FENCES

— DOUBLE-SWING GATE WITH COMMON HINGES —

Ordinary hinges can be easily bent and so placed on posts that a gate can be swung in either direction. As shown in the illustration, hinges can be made to fit either round or square posts. The gate half of the hinge is fastened in the usual way. The post half is bent and so placed that the hinge pin will be approximately on a line between the centers of the posts. The gate and post should be beveled off to permit a full-open gateway.

POST AND GATE ARE CUT AWAY BACK OF THE HINGE TO ALLOW THE GATE TO SWING BACK.

— SELF-CLOSING GATE —

This gate is suspended from a horizontal bar by chains, and swings freely about a 1-in. gas pipe, placed vertically in the center of the gate. The chains are of the same length, being fastened equidistant from the pipe, the upper ends farther out than the lower. The distance depends on the weight of the gate and the desired force with which it should close. Any of the numerous styles of latches can be used, if desired.

THE GATE WILL SWING IN EITHER DIRECTION AND COME TO A REST WHERE IT CLOSES THE OPENING.

— PORCH GATE FOLDS INTO HOLLOW PILLAR —

The porch is a convenient play spot for the children but must be properly safeguarded to prevent not uncommon accidents and injury by falls. The folding gate shown in the sketch provides a substantial barrier to the head of the stairs and may be quickly folded out of the way. It is hardly noticeable when set in the side of the pillar and does not mar the finish or general effect of the latter.

The gate is made of strips of band iron, although wood may be used. The strips are fastened with bolts or rivets, and the forward end is fitted to the section of the pillar, which forms the cover for the recess in which the gate is housed. The cover is hooked to the opposite pillar when the gate is opened. Any suitable height may be chosen for the gate but, for the purpose suggested, 24 to 30 in. is satisfactory. The device may be adapted to a variety of other uses by providing a box or chamber for the collapsed gate, when no hollow recess is otherwise available.

THE GATE IS FOLDED WHEN NOT IN USE AND IS CONCEALED IN THE HOLLOW PORCH PILLAR.

— LOCKING DEVICE FOR LATCH HOOK ON GATE OR DOOR —

The troublesome opening of a latch hook on a gate or door, permitting intruders to enter or possibly injuring the door in the wind, can be easily overcome by fitting a small catch over the hook, as indicated in the sketch.

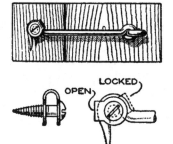

The U-shaped device is cut from a piece of tin and fastened on the screw over which the hook is set. When locked, it is pushed back over the head of the hook, and cannot be easily jarred out of place.

— PORTABLE SECTIONAL POULTRY FENCING —

Sectional poultry fencing has several advantages over stationary fencing: It can be easily moved, the poultry yard being made larger, smaller, or shifted; and an area may be planted to a crop and gradually included in the yard, furnishing greens for the poultry. Also, the tenant who does not care to put down permanent equipment will find sectional fencing desirable.

Sections are practical to about 18 ft. long, and

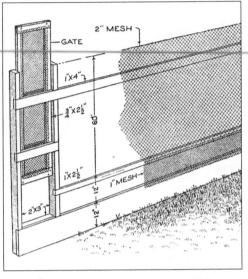

POULTRY FENCING MADE IN PORTABLE SECTIONS HAS SEVERAL ADVANTAGES OVER A STATIONARY BARRIER.

should be 7 ft. high for the lighter breeds of poultry. If the fencing is to be used for grown stock only, the fine-mesh wire below may be omitted and 2-in. mesh used. Some sections should be fitted with gates, and the top batten should be set down about 1 ft. so as not to afford footing for the poultry. The sections are lashed together with wire and supported by an occasional post, or guyed to buildings for supports.

— AN ANIMAL-PROOF GATE LATCH —

One of the farmer's worries is the possibility of his stock opening the gates of their pasture and gaining access to his own or his neighbor's crops. Horses and cattle speedily learn to open gates fitted with an ordinary latch, and when they do this, it usually means retrieving the stock—and paying for the damage.

A simple latch, that is proof against such animal intelligence, consists of a notched wooden bar fitting against a similar notch in one of the rails of the gate. This bar is provided with a handhold and the end slides into a mortise cut into the gatepost. The latch is held in position by guides fastened to each side of the gate.

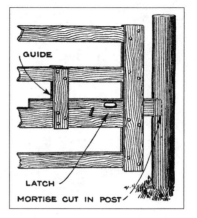

GUIDE

LATCH

MORTISE CUT IN POST

— ❖ ❖ ❖ —

THE GREAT OUTDOORS

—

THE TRICKS *of* CAMPING OUT: PART I

— THE CAMPING OUTFIT —

To enjoy a vacation in the woods thoroughly, it is essential that the camper be provided with the right kind of an outfit. The inexperienced are likely to carry too much rather than too little to the woods—to include many unnecessary luxuries and overlook the more practical necessities. However, camp life does not mean that one must be uncomfortable but rather implies plain and simple living close to nature. An adequate shelter from the sun and rain, a comfortable bed, a good cooking kit, and plenty of wholesome food are the important things to consider. No man or woman requires more, and if unwilling to share the plain fare of the woodsman, the pampered ones should be left at home. The grouchy, complaining individual makes, of all persons, the very worst of camping companions.

The Choice of Tent

There are tents and tents, but for average outings in what may be

THE OLD HAND AT THE CAMPING GAME PREFERS TO CUT POLES ON THE CAMPSITE AND SET THEM UP ON THE OUTSIDE FOR THE CAMPFIRE TENT

considered a permanent camp, the regulation wall, or army, tent is generally used to make a comfortable shelter. It is a splendid utility tent, with generous floor space and plenty of headroom. For the permanent camp, the wall tent is often provided with a fly, which may be set up as an extra covering for the roof or extended over the front to make a kind of porch. An extension may also be purchased to serve the same purpose. The 7-by-9-ft. wall tent will shelter two persons comfortably, but when the camp is seldom moved, the 9-by-12-ft. size, with a 3½-ft. wall, will afford more room. The regulation 8-oz. duck is heavy enough. Or the same tent may be obtained in tan or dark green khaki, if preferred. In any case the tent should have a sod cloth, from 6 to 12 in. wide, extending around the bottom and sewed to the tent. An extra piece of canvas or floor cloth is desirable, but this as well as the fly are extras, and while convenient, are by no means necessary. The wall tent may be erected with the regular poles, or it may be ordered with tapes along the ridge and erected by suspending between it two trees. The old hand at the camping game rarely uses the shop poles supplied with most tents, but prefers to cut them at the camping site and rig them up on the outside, one slender pole fastened with tapes along the ridge and supported at either end in the crotch formed by setting up two poles, tripod or shear fashion.

The "Baker" style is a popular tent with a large sleeping capacity, yet folds compactly. The 7-by-7-ft. size, with a 2-ft. wall, makes a good comfortable home for two and will shelter three or even four, if required. The entire front may be opened to the fire by extending it to form an awning, or it may be thrown back over the ridge to form an open-front lean-to shelter.

THE WALL TENT MAY BE ERECTED WITH THE REGULAR POLES OR, WHEN ORDERED WITH TAPES ALONG THE RIDGE, IT CAN BE SET UP WITH OUTSIDE TRIPOD OR SHEAR POLES.

THE FORESTER'S TENT IS QUICKLY ERECTED BY USING THREE SMALL SAPLINGS, ONE ALONG THE RIDGE AND ONE ON EACH SIDE OF THE OPENING TO FORM A CROTCH FOR THE RIDGEPOLE.

The "Dan Beard," or campfire tent, is a modification of the Baker style, having a slightly steeper pitch with a smaller front opening. The dimensions are practically the same as the Baker, and it may be pitched by suspending it between two trees, by outside poles, or the regular poles may be used.

For traveling light by canoe or pack, a somewhat lighter and less bulky form of tent than the above styles may be chosen, and the woodsman is likely to select the forester's or ranger types. The ranger is a half tent with a 2-ft. wall, and the entire front is open; in fact, this is the same as the Baker tent without the flap. If desired, two half ranger tents with tapes may be purchased and fastened together to form an A, or wedge, tent. This makes a good tent for two on a hike, as each man carries his own half and is assured a good shelter in case one becomes separated from his companion and a tight shelter when the two make camp together.

The forester's tent is another excellent one with good floor space and folding up very compactly. It is a 9-by-9-ft. tent weighing about 5 ½ lb. when made of standard-weight fabric. It may be had with or without hood, and is quickly erected by using three small saplings, one along the ridge, running from peak to ground, and one on each side of the opening, to form a crotch to support the ridgepole, shear fashion. These tents are not provided with sod or floor cloths, although these may be ordered as extras if wanted.

The canoe, or "protean," tents are good styles for the camper who travels light and is often on the move. The canoe tent has a circular front, while the protean style is made with a square front, and the wall is attached to the back and along the two sides. Both tents are quickly set up, either with a single inside pole or with two poles set shear fashion on the outside. A 9-by-9-ft. canoe or protean tent with a 3-ft. wall makes a comfortable home in the open.

Whatever style of tent is chosen, it is smart to pay a fair price and obtain a good quality of material and workmanship. The cheaper tents are made of heavier material to render them waterproof while the better grades are fashioned from lightweight fabric of

THE CANOE OR PROTEAN TENTS ARE GOOD STYLES FOR THE CAMPER WHO TRAVELS LIGHT AND IS OFTEN ON THE MOVE, AND THEY CAN BE QUICKLY SET UP WITH A SINGLE INSIDE POLE.

How to Pitch a Tent

It is, of course, possible to pitch a tent almost anywhere, but for the sake of comfort it is wise to select a site with natural drainage. Many campers dig a shallow trench around the tent to prevent water from running in during a heavy rain. This is a good idea for the permanent camp, but is not often necessary if the soil is sandy or porous or where a sod cloth is used.

THE RANGER'S OR HIKER'S TENT COMES IN HALVES. EACH HALF MAY BE USED INDEPENDENTLY AS A LEAN-TO SHELTER FOR ONE MAN, OR BOTH JOINED TOGETHER TO MAKE ROOM FOR TWO PERSONS.

close weave and treated with a waterproofing process. Many of the cheaper tents will give fair service but the workmanship is often poor, the grommets are apt to pull out, and the seams rip after a little hard use. All tents should be waterproofed, and each provided with a bag in which to pack it.

It is rarely necessary to carry the regular poles to the campground and they may be omitted except when en route to a treeless region. The wall and other large tents may be pitched in several ways. In some places, the woodsman cuts a straight ridgepole about 3 ft. longer than the tent and two crotched uprights, 1 ft. or more longer than the height of the tent. The ridgepole is passed through the opening in the peak of the tent or fastened to the outside of the ridge with tapes sewn to the cloth. The two upright stakes are then firmly planted in the ground, one at the back and the other in front, and the ridgepole is lifted and dropped into these crotched supports. Set up the four corner guys first to get the tent in shape, then peg down the side guys and slide them taut so that all of them will exert an even pull on the tent. Another good method for setting up the side guys is to drive four crotched stakes, each about 4 ft. long, somewhere near 3 ft. from each corner of the tent, and drop a fairly heavy pole in the rest so formed, then fasten the guy ropes to this pole. When a sod cloth is provided it is turned under on the inside, the floor cloth is spread over it, and the camp duffel distributed along the walls of the tent to hold it down and prevent insects and rain from entering.

To overcome the disadvantage of placing the poles in the center of the entrance, the uprights may be formed by lashing two poles together near the top to make a crotch and spreading the bottoms to form a pair of shears. Poles may be dispensed with entirely, providing the tent is ordered with tapes for attaching a rope to suspend the ridge of the tent between two trees. In a wooded country this manner of setting a tent is generally preferred.

Where a wall tent is used in a more permanent camp, it is a good plan to order a fly a couple of sizes larger than the tent. This should be set up by using separate poles and rigged some 6 or 8 in. higher than the ridge of the tent, thus affording an air space to temper the heat of the sun and also serving to keep things dry during long heavy rains.

The Camping Kit

The camping kit, including the few handy articles needed in the woods, as well as the bedding and cooking outfit, may be either elaborate or simple, according to the personal experience and ideas of the camper. In making up a list of things you'll need for your kit, remember that only comparatively few articles are really essential for a comfortable vacation in the wilderness. A comfortable bed must be reckoned one of the chief essentials, and one may choose a deluxe couch—the air mattress or sleeping pocket—use an ordinary sleeping bag, or court slumber on one of the several other styles of camp beds. The fold-over combination bed, the stretcher bed, or a common bag made of ticking 6½ ft. long by 2 ft. wide, which is stuffed with bows or leaves, will suffice for the average person. Folding camp cots, chairs, tables, and other so-called camp furniture have their places in the large, fixed camps, but the woodsman can manage to live comfortably without them. A good pair of warm blankets should be included for each person, providing the sleeping bag is not taken along. The regulation army blankets are a good choice reasonable in price, or the blankets used at home may be pressed into service.

THE BELT AX.

A good ax is the woodsman's everyday companion, and a good-weight tool, weighing 3 or 4 lbs., and a smaller one of 1½ lbs., should be carried. When going light, the belt ax should suffice.

The oil lantern is only suited for the fixed camp, since the fuel is difficult to transport unless it is placed into screw-top cans. The "Stonebridge" and other folding candle lanterns are the most convenient for the woods and give sufficient light for camp life.

The aluminum cooking outfits are light in weight, nest compactly, and will stand many years of hard usage. But like other good things, they are somewhat expensive. A good substitute in tin and steel may be obtained for half the price, having the good feature of nesting within each other but, of course, not being quite so light nor so attractive in appearance as the higher-priced outfits. Both the aluminum and steel outfits are put up in canvas carrying bags, and an outfit for two includes a large and a small cooking pot, coffeepot, frying pan with folding or detachable handle, two plates, cups, knives, forks, and spoons. Outfits may be bought for any number of persons, and almost all sporting-goods stores carry them.

FOLDING CANDLE LANTERN

The Camper's Outfit

The personal outfit should include only the most useful articles, and each member of the party should be provided with a dunnage bag of canvas to hold bedding and clothing, and a smaller, or "ditty," bag for keeping other toilet and personal belongings that most everyone finds necessary for everyday comfort. A mending kit, containing a few yards of silk, linen, and a twist; a length of mending cotton; buttons; a few needles and pins, both safety and the common kinds, should not be overlooked. The veteran usually stows away a bit of wire, a length of strong twine, a few nails and tacks, rivets, etc., for emergency use. It is surprising to the novice how handy these several odds and ends are found while in camp. A compact tin box will form a convenient place to keep them will take up little room in the dunnage bag. A medicine case and a first-aid outfit are well worth packing; the smallest cases containing a few of the common remedies will fully meet the camper's needs.

When carrying food by canoe or pack basket, the canoe duffel and provision bags are a great convenience, enabling the camper to carry different foodstuffs in a compact and sanitary manner. Food bags may be

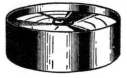

FOOD BAGS WITH FRICTION-TOP
TINS TO FIT THEM.

had in different sizes, and friction-top tins may be purchased to fit them. One or more of these liquidproof containers are desirable for transporting lard, butter, pork, ham, and other greasy necessities. The food bags slip into the larger duffel bags, making a very compact bundle for stowing away in a canoe or pack harness.

Carrying List for Camp Outfit

For permanent camps, take the wall tent with fly, although the Baker or campfire styles are also good. When traveling light by canoe, the canoe or protean tent is recommended. When going very light by pack, use the forester's or ranger's tent. Sod and floor cloths and mosquito netting are optional.

The cooking kit may be of aluminum or steel, all items nesting within the largest pot. Include a folding baker, or reflector, with bread board in a canvas bag, a wood saltbox, and a watertight can for matches.

Furniture for the permanent camp consists of a full-sized ax—double-blade or tomahawk style with straight handle—in a protecting case, whetstone, and file for keeping the ax in shape. A shovel and saw will be needed when a cabin is built. A canteen may be included, but is not required on most trips. A folding candle lantern is the best for the average trip, but an oil, or acetylene, lantern may be used in a fixed camp. Cots, folding chairs, tables, hangers, etc., are useful only in fixed camps.

A pack basket with a waterproof canvas lid and cover, having straps to go over the shoulders, is a general favorite with woodsmen and guides. Canvas packs or dunnage bags may be used if preferred. There are two sizes of food bags, one holding 5 lbs. and another of 10-lb. capacity, with drawstrings at the top. These are the best for carrying provisions.

THE COOKING KIT MAY BE OF ALUMINUM OR STEEL, ALL NESTING WITHIN THE LARGEST POT, AND MAY INCLUDE A FOLDING BAKER, OR REFLECTOR, WITH BREAD BOARD IN CANVAS BAG, A WOOD SALTBOX, AND A WATERTIGHT CAN FOR MATCHES.

A PACK BASKET
WITH A WATERPROOF
CANVAS LID AND COVER.

Pack harness, with a tumpline to go across the forehead, is needed when the outfit must be carried on portages, etc. This may be omitted when pack baskets are used. Packing cases of fiber may be used for shipping the outfit to the camping ground, but ordinary trunks, or wood boxes, will answer as well.

An old ordinary suit that is not worn too thin is sufficient. Corduroy is too heavy for the summer and too cold for winter, and canvas is too stiff and noisy for the woods. Cotton khaki is excellent for the summer and all-wool khaki, or mackinaw coat and trousers are comfortable for winter. Wool is the best material for undergarments in all seasons. Two sets of garments will be sufficient, as the washing is done at night. Be sure the garments are large enough to allow for shrinkage. Lightweight cashmere is the best material for socks during the summer; use a heavier weight for the winter. Three pairs of ordinary-weight and one pair of heavyweight socks will be sufficient. A medium-weight gray flannel overshirt, with breast pockets having button flaps, is the woodsman's choice. On short and light trips one shirt will do. A lightweight, all-wool gray or brown sweater is a good thing to carry along. It is easily wetted through and a famous briar catcher, yet most woodsmen carry one.

The regulation army poncho is more suited to the woods than a rubber coat or oilskins. The larger-size poncho is more bulky to pack, but may be used as a shelter by rigging it up with poles, lean-to fashion. A poncho makes a good ground blanket also.

A medium wide-brimmed hat, in gray or brown, is better than a cap. A gray, or brown, silk handkerchief should be included to wear around the neck to protect it from the sun and cold. Only a few novices will carry one, but not so with the regular woodsman. The moccasin is the only suitable footwear for the woods. The "puckaway," with extra sole, is known to most woodsmen. A pair of larrigans—ankle-high moccasins with single soles—is suitable to wear about the camp.

Each member of the party carries a pair of woolen blankets. Army blankets in tan color are serviceable and inexpensive.

A good, tempered knife should be worn at the belt, preferably one without a hilt and having a blade 5 or 6 in. long.

A small leather pouch containing a few common remedies, such as quinine, laxative, etc.; and a small first-aid kit should be included in each camper's personal pack. Also, a small leather pouch containing an assortment of needles, darning cotton, buttons, and a length of heavy silk twist is a handy companion.

A few sheets of paper and as many envelopes, a notebook, pencil, and a few postcards are usually carried, together with an almanac page of the months covering the intended trip.

The compass is by far the most useful instrument in the woods, but any reliable and inexpensive watch may be carried.

THE COMPASS.

Many woodsmen carry a small hatchet at the belt, and on trips when but the few necessities are carried, the belt ax takes the place of the heavier-weight tool. The tomahawk style gives two cutting edges and is therefore the best tool to carry. A leather or other covering case is needed to protect the blades.

A small tin box containing an assortment of rivets, tacks, a bit of string, brass wire, a few nails, a couple of small files, a tool holder with tools, a sheet of sandpaper, a bit of emery cloth, and any other small articles that the sportsman fancies will come in handy may be carried.

The Tricks *of* Camping Out: Part II

— Cooking in the Woods —

Cooking in the woods requires more of a knack than equipment, and while a camp stove is good enough in a permanent camp, its weight and bulk make this article of camp furniture unsuited for transportation by canoe. Patent cooking grates are less bulky, but the woods-man can learn to do without them very nicely. However, the important item that few woodsmen care to do without is the folding baker, or reflector. The baker is folded flat and carried in a canvas case, including baking pan and kneading board. The largest size, with an 18-in. square pan, weighs about 5 lb., and the smallest, with an 8-by-12-in. pan in aluminum, only 2 lb. In use, the reflector is placed with the open side close to the fire, and cooking is accomplished evenly and well in any

A COOKING RANGE FASHIONED FROM TWO GREEN LOGS LAID IN
A V-SHAPE WITH A FEW STONES BUILT UP AT THE WIDE END
OVER WHICH A FIRE IS MADE OF HARDWOOD STICKS

A GREEN POLE PLACED IN A FORKED STICK PROVIDES
A POT HANGER FOR A NOONDAY MEAL

kind of weather. Bread, fish, game, or meat is easily and perfectly cooked, and the smaller size is large enough for a party of two or three.

The campfire is one of the charms of the outdoors, and if it is built right and of the best kind of wood, cooking may be done over it as well as over a forest range. Many woodsmen prefer to build a second and smaller fire for cooking, and although I have never found this necessary—excepting in large camps where a considerably quantity of food must be prepared— the camper can suit himself, for experimenting is, after all, a large part of the fun of living in and off the woods.

A satisfactory outdoor cooking range may be fashioned by roughly smoothing the top and bottom sides of two green logs and placing them about 6 in. apart at one end, and about 2 ft. apart at the opposite end. At the wide end a few stones are built up, and across these, hickory, ash, and other sticks of hardwood are placed. The reflector is placed close to the coals at this end, and the fire is built between the logs, the broiling and frying being done at the narrow-end opening. Woods that burn slowly when green should be used for back logs and end logs; chestnut, red oak, butternut, red maple, and persimmon being best adapted for this purpose.

The hardwoods are best for cooking and heating because they burn more slowly, give out considerable heat, and burn down to a body of glowing coals. Softwoods are quick to catch fire, burn rapidly, and make a hot fire but burn down to dead ashes. Hickory is by far the best firewood of the north, in that it makes a hot fire, is long-burning, and forms a large body of coals that

6

6

gives an even and intense
heat for a considerable
length of time. Next to
hickory comes chestnut;
the basket oaks, iron-
wood, dogwood, and ash
are the woodsman's favor-
ites. Among the woods
that are easy to split are
the red oak, basket oak,
white oak, ash, and white
birch. A few woods split
more easily when green
than after seasoning, and

A LIMB SUPPORTED AT AN ANGLE OVER THE
FIRE IS ANOTHER MEANS OF HANGING THE POT.

among them are hickory, dogwood,
beech, sugar maple, birch, and elm.
The most stubborn woods to split are
the elder, blue ash, cherry, sour gum,
hemlock, sweet gum, and sycamore.
Of the softer woods, the birches
make the best fuel; black birch in
particular makes a fine campfire and
it is one of the few woods that burn
well when green. The dry bark of the
hemlock makes a quick and hot fire,
and white birch takes fire quickly
even when moist. Driftwood is good
to start a fire with, and dry pine
knots—the limb stubs of a dead pine
tree—are famous kindling. Green
wood will, of course, burn better in
winter when the sap is dormant. And
trees found on high ground make
better fuel than those growing in

moist bottomlands. Hardwoods are
more plentiful on high ground, while
the softer woods are found in abun-
dance along the margins of streams.

For cooking the noonday meal,
a small fire will suffice to boil the
pot and furnish the heat sufficient
to make a fry. Simply drive a forked
stick in the ground and lay a green
stick in the fork with the opposite
end on the ground with a rock laid
on it to keep it down, and hang the
pot on the projecting stub left for this
purpose. A long stick with projecting
stubs, planted in the ground to slant
over the fire at an angle, will serve
as well. Let the pot hang about 2 ft.
from the ground, collect an armful of
dry twigs and plenty of larger kindling
sticks. Now shave three or four of the

larger sticks and leave the shavings on the ends. Stand them up beneath a pot, tripod fashion, and place the smaller sticks around them to build a miniature wigwam. While the pot is boiling, get a couple of bed chunks, or andirons, 4 or 5 in. in diameter, set and level these on each side of the fire, and put the frying pan on them. When the pot has boiled, there will be a nice bed of coals for frying that will not smoke the meal.

When the woodsman makes "one-night stands," he will invariably build the fire and start the kettle boiling while he or a companion stakes the tent. As soon as the meal is prepared, a pot of water is started boiling for dish washing.

For roasting and baking with the reflector, a rather high fire is needed. A few sticks, a yard or more long, resting upright against a back log or rock, will throw the heat forward. When glowing coals are wanted one can take them from the campfire, or split uniform billets of green, or dead, wood about 2 in. thick and pile them in the form of a hollow square, or crib. The fire is built in the center of the crib and more parallel sticks are laid on top until it is a foot or more higher. The crib will act as a chimney, and a roaring fire will result, which upon burning down will give a glowing mass of coals.

Camp cookery implies the preparation of the more simple and nutritious foods, and in making up a list it is wise to include only the more staple foodstuffs, which are known to have these qualities. Personal ideas are certain to differ greatly, but the following list may be depended upon and will serve as a guide.

Provisions List

The items in this list will be sufficient for two persons on an outing of two weeks. Carry in a stout canvas food bag 12 lb. of common wheat flour. The self-raising kind is good but the common flour is better. It is good to bring about 6 lb. of yellow or white cornmeal to be served as a johnnycake, hot, cold, or fried mush. It is fine for rolling a fish in for frying. Rice is very nutritious, easily digested, and easy to cook. It is good when boiled with raisins. When cold, it can be fried in slices. About 3 lb. will be sufficient. Oatmeal is less sustaining than rice but it is good for porridge or sliced when cold and fried. Take along about 3 lb. About 2 lb. of the self-raising buckwheat flour should taken along, as it is the favorite for flapjacks or griddlecakes.

Beans are very nutritious and about 2 lb. of the common baking kind will be required to boil or bake with the salt pork. For soups, take 2 lb. of split peas. They can also be served as a vegetable. Salt pork is a stand-by, and 5 lb. of it is provided and carried in friction-top tins or a greaseproof bag. It should be parboiled before adding to the beans or when fried like bacon. The regulation meat of the wilderness is bacon, and 5 lb. of it is carried in a tin or bag. Carry along 3 lb. of lard in a tin or bag, for bread-making and frying. About 3 lb. of butter are carried in a friction-top tin. For making rice puddings, take along 1 lb. raisins. About 1 lb. of shredded codfish is good for making fish balls. Other small articles, such as ½ lb. of tea, 1 lb. of coffee, 3 lb. of granulated sugar, 1 pt. of molasses, 1 pt. of vinegar, 4 cans of condensed milk, 1 can of milk powder, a good substitute for milk, 1 can egg powder, good for making omelets or can be scrambled, 1 lb. salt, 2 oz. pepper, 1 package each of evaporated potatoes, onions, and fruits, and 3 packages of assorted soup tablets.

This list is by no means complete, but it will suffice for the average person on the average trip, since the occasional addition of a fish or game will help to replenish the stores. When going very light by pack, only the most compact and nutritious foods should be selected. While on short, easy trips the addition of canned goods will supply a greater variety.

— WOODCRAFT —

While shooting, fishing, and camping are chapters in the book of woodcraft, the word is generally defined to mean the knack of using the compass, the map, and in making use of the natural signs of the woods when traveling in the wilderness. If the camper keeps to the beaten paths and does not stray far from the frequently used waterways, he needs no compass, and sufficient knowledge of the ways of the woods may be acquired from the previous articles. But if the camper ventures into an unknown region, the value of more intimate knowledge increases as the distance from civilization lengthens, because it will enable him to keep traveling in the desired direction and prevent the "insane desire to circle," should one discover he has lost the trail.

— The Emergency "Snack" and Kit —

The woodsman well knows that it is an easy matter to stray farther from camp than he intended to when starting out, and that it is a common enough occurrence to lose one's bearings and become temporarily lost. To prepare for this possible emergency and spend a comfortable night away from the camp, he carries in his pocket a little packet of useful articles and stows away a tiny package containing a small amount of nutritious food. When leaving camp for a day's hunting and fishing, the usual lunch is, of course, included. But in addition to this, the woodsman should carry a couple of soup tablets, a piece of summer sausage, and some tea. Wrap this in oiled silk and pack it in a flat tin box. It will take up very little room in the pocket.

The emergency kit is merely a small leather pouch containing a short fishing line, a few fishing hooks, 1 ft. of surgeon's adhesive plaster, needle and thread, a few safety pins, and a small coil of copper or brass wire. These articles, with a gun and few spare cartridges, or rod, a belt knife, match safe, compass, map, a little money, pipe, and tobacco make up the personal outfit without which few woodsmen care to venture far from camp. In addition to the above, I carry a double-edge lightweight ax or tomahawk in a leather sheath at the belt and a tin cup strung to the back of the belt, where it is out of the way and unnoticed until wanted.

— The Compass —

A small pocket compass affixed to a leather thong should be carried in the breast pocket and fastened to a button of the shirt. An instrument costing $1 will be accurate enough for all purposes. Many of the woodsmen do not use a compass, but even the expert woodsman gets lost sometimes, and it may happen that the sun is obscured by clouds, thus making it more difficult to read the natural signs of the wilderness. The compass is of little value if a person does not know how to use it. It will not tell you in what direction to go, but when the needle is allowed to swing freely on its pivot the blue end always points to magnetic north. True north lies a degree or more to either side. In the west, for instance, the needle will be attracted a trifle to the east, while on the Atlantic coast it will swing a trifle to the west of true

north. This magnetic variation need not be taken into account by the woodsman, who may consider it to point to the true north, for absolute accuracy is not required for this purpose. However, I would advise the sportsman to take the precaution of scratching on the back of the case these letters: B=N, meaning blue equals north. If this is done, the novice will be certain to remember and read the compass right no matter how confused he may become on finding that he has lost his way. The watch may be used as a compass on a clear day by pointing the hour hand to the sun. The point halfway between the hour hand and 12 will be due south.

The compass needle is attracted to iron and steel, therefore keep it away from the gun, hatchet, knife, and other metal articles. Hold the compass level and press the stop, if it has one, so that the needle may swing free. Note some landmark as a prominent tree, high cliff, or other conspicuous object lying in the direction of travel, and go directly to this object. Consult the compass frequently when making a detour or when the landmark passes out of sight. When this mark is reached, select another farther on and continue the travel, always picking out new marks along the line indicated by the compass. When making camp, consult a map, study it, and so gain a good general idea of the surrounding country. When leaving camp, take the bearings from the compass. By so doing a person will know in what direction he is traveling, and when the course is changed, keep the general direction in mind. When climbing a hill or making detours, take a mental note of the change in direction and the bearings will not be lost.

— MAPS —

The maps of the U.S. Geological Survey are drawn to a scale of 2 in. to the mile and cost 5 cents each. On the back of each map are printed the symbols showing the character of the land, the contours, roads, and all important rivers and lakes in the district. For convenience, the map should be pasted on a backing of cotton cloth and then cut up into handy sections. Number the sections from left to right and paste a key to the pieces on the back of one of them.

— NATURAL SIGNS —

When traveling through underbrush the woodsman cannot see far ahead, and so plots a true course by noting the position of the sun. For example, here in the northern hemisphere, the sun rises just south of east and sets somewhere south of due west. Therefore, if a person is going north, he should keep the sun on his back and to the right shoulder in the morning hours, full on the back at noon, and on the back and over the left shoulder throughout the afternoon.

If the day is cloudy, set the point of a knife blade on the thumbnail, twist it around until the full shadow is cast on the nail, thus indicating the position of the sun.

The direction of the wind is apt to change, and for this reason is an unreliable guide. The so-called signs of the woods, such as the tips of evergreen trees pointing north, bark being thicker on the north side of trees, or moss growing thicker on the north side of the trees, are by no means to be depended upon. There is absolutely nothing in these signs. However, every woodsman is aware that the foliage of trees grows somewhat thicker on the south side, and that the branches are rather shorter and more knotty on the north side. But these and other signs are scarcely infallible, and if they were, few tenderfeet would recognize them.

When traveling by night, look for the Big Dipper or Great Bear, as the two end stars are known as the pointers, pointing to the north star.

— MARKING THE TRAIL —

roads are crooked and wind about the trees and rocks, while the logging road is fairly straight and broad. Of course, tote roads lead nowhere in particular, but all logging roads are sure to come to a fork and lead to water. When breaking a new trail, blaze it by taking a single clip from a tree from the side it is approached, and on the opposite side make two blazes, indicating the way from the camp. If this is done a person will always know the way back if the trail is crossed from side to

When traveling over old and blind trails look for the old blaze marks, and if doubtful about them, make new ones by breaking down the brushes every 15 or 20 ft., the bent part pointed in the direction of travel. If a road is encountered, it is easy to tell if it is a tote or logging road because tote side. This is the rule of the wilderness, but it is not always observed to the letter, for many woodsmen blaze their trail by clipping the trees as they pass them. Be sure to blaze your own trail correctly, and when you come to a place where two roads or trails fork, set a stick to indicate the right direction.

When a person becomes lost in the woods, as every woodsman is sure to do sometimes, sit down and think it over. Many times a person is nearer camp and companions than it is possible to realize, and if a straight direction is taken, a lumber road or a stream will be found that will give one his bearings. Above all, do not become frightened. If the emergency kit and lunch have not been forgotten, a day and night in the woods alone is not a hardship by any means. Avoid wasting energy by rushing madly about and forgetting to blaze the trail that is being made. Bend the points of the brushes down in the direction of travel. Do not shoot the last cartridge to attract attention, and do not shout until hoarse. Sit down and build a fire of green wood, damp leaves, or moss so that it will smoke. Build a second fire a short distance from the first. This is the recognized signal of the one who is lost. The afternoon may be windy, but the wind is certain to die away at the sundown, and then smoke rising from the fires will visible from a considerable distance. When an experienced woodsman gets lost he merely camps on the spot and awaits the next day for picking up the trail.

TENTS *and* SHELTERS

— CAMPS AND HOW TO BUILD THEM —

There are several ways of building a temporary camp from material that is always to be found in the woods. Whether these improvised shelters are intended to last until a permanent camp is built or only as a camp on a short excursion, a great deal of fun can be had in their construction. An evergreen tree with branches growing well down toward the ground furnishes all the material. By chopping the trunk almost through, so that when the tree falls the upper part will still remain attached to the stump, a serviceable shelter can be quickly provided. The cut should be about 5 ft. from the ground. Then the boughs and branches on the underside of the fallen top are chopped away and piled on top. There is room for several persons under this sort of shelter, which offers fairly good protection against any but the most drenching rains.

The wigwam sheds rain better, and where there are no suitable trees that can be cut, it is the easiest camp to make. Three long poles with the tops tied together and the lower ends spaced 8 to 10 ft. apart make the frame of the wigwam. Branches and brush can easily be piled up and woven in and out on these poles so as to shed a very heavy rain.

The brush camp is shaped like an ordinary "A" tent. The ridgepole should be about 8 ft. long and supported by crotched uprights about 6 ft. from the ground. Often the ridgepole can be laid from one small tree to another. Avoid tall trees on account of lightning. Eight or ten long poles are then laid slanting against the ridgepole on each side. Cedar or hemlock boughs make the best thatch for the brush camp. They should be piled up to a thickness of a foot or more over the slanting poles and woven in and out to keep them from slipping. Then a number of poles should be laid over them to prevent them from blowing away.

In woods where there is plenty of bark available in large slabs, the bark lean-to is a quickly constructed and serviceable camp. The ridgepole is set up like that of the brush camp. Three or four other poles are laid slanting to the ground on one side only. The ends of these poles should be pushed into the earth and fastened with crotched sticks. Long poles are then laid crossways of these slanting poles, and the whole can be covered with brush as in the case of the brush camp or with strips of bark laid overlapping each other like shingles. Where bark is used, nails are necessary to hold it in place. Bark may also be used for a wigwam, and it can be held in place by a cord wrapped tightly around the whole structure, running spiralwise from the ground to the peak. In the early summer, the bark can easily be removed from most trees by making two circular cuts around the trunk and joining them with another vertical cut. The bark is easily pried off with an ax, and if laid on the ground under heavy stones, will dry flat. Sheets of bark, 6 ft. long and 2 or 3 ft. wide, are a convenient size for camp construction.

The small boughs and twigs of hemlock, spruce, and cedar, piled 2 or 3 ft. deep and covered with blankets, make the best kind of a camp bed. For a permanent camp, a bunk can be made by laying small poles close together across two larger poles on a

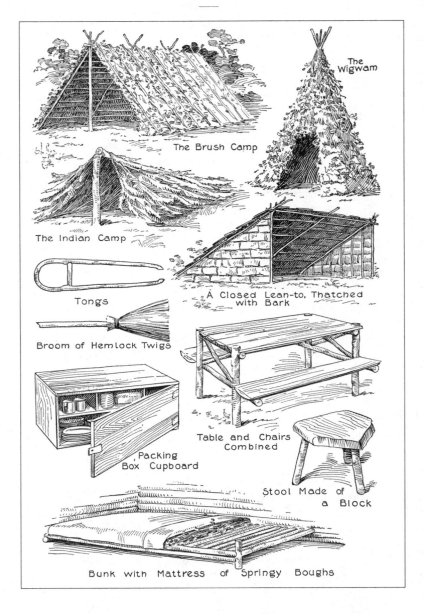

The Wigwam

The Brush Camp

The Indian Camp

Tongs

A Closed Lean-to, Thatched with Bark

Broom of Hemlock Twigs

Packing Box Cupboard

Table and Chairs Combined

Stool Made of a Block

Bunk with Mattress of Springy Boughs

rude framework. Evergreen twigs or dried leaves are piled on this, and a blanket or a piece of canvas stretched across and fastened down to the poles at the sides. A bed like this is soft and springy and will last through an ordinary camping season. A portable cot that does not take up much room in the camp outfit is made of a piece of heavy canvas 40 in. wide and 6 ft. long. Four-inch hems are sewn in each side of the canvas, and when the camp is pitched, a 2-in. pole is run through each hem and the ends of the pole supported on crotch sticks.

Freshwater close at hand and shade for the middle of the day are two points that should always be looked for in a selecting a site for a camp. If the camp is to be occupied for any length of time, useful implements for many purposes can be made out of such material as the woods afford. The simplest way to build a crane for hanging kettles over the campfire is to drive two posts into the ground, each of them a foot or more from one end of the fire space, and split the tops with an ax so that a pole laid from one to the other across the fire will be securely held in the split. Tongs are very useful in camp. A piece of elm or hickory, 4 ft. long and 1½ in. thick, makes a good pair of tongs. For a foot in the middle of the stick, cut half of the thickness away and hold this part over the fire until it can be bent easily to bring the two ends together. Then fasten a crosspiece to hold the ends close together, shape the ends so that anything that drops into the fire can be seized by them, and a serviceable pair of tongs is the result. Any sort of a stick that is easily handled will serve as a poker. Hemlock twigs tied around one end of a stick make an excellent broom. Movable seats for a permanent camp are easily made by splitting a log, boring holes in the rounded side of the slab, and driving pegs into them to serve as legs. A short slab or plank can easily be made into a three-legged stool in the same way.

Campers usually have boxes in which their provisions have been carried. Such a packing box is easily made into a cupboard, and it is not difficult to improvise shelves, hinges, or a lock for the camp larder.

A good way to make a camp table is to set four posts into the ground and nail crosspieces to support slabs cut from chopped wood logs to form a top. Pieces can be nailed onto the legs of the table to hold other slabs to serve as seats, affording accommodation for several persons.

— HOMEMADE SHOULDER-PACK TENT —

After sleeping under various kinds of canvas coverings and not finding any of them entirely to my liking, I made the tent shown in the illustration, which proved quite satisfactory. It is of light weight, easily set up or taken down, and when buttoned closely is practically rain-, wind-, and bug-proof. The cost of materials necessary for making it is slight. I use it not only as a sleeping tent but also as a carryall in packing camping equipment. The canvas is supported by frames made of pliable branches cut in the woods.

The layout for the canvas is shown in the detailed drawings. The sections for the ends are made of three pieces, one for the ground and two, divided vertically, for the end covering. The ground section of the main portion of the tent and the covering are made in one piece,

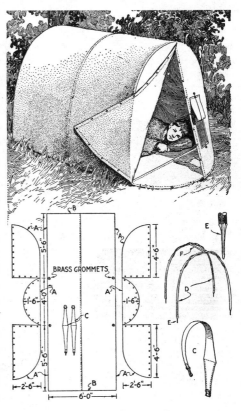

STAKES, ROPE BRACES, AND SUPPORTING POLES ARE NOT REQUIRED FOR THIS SHOULDER-PACK TENT, THE SUPPORTS BEING CUT AT THE CAMP.

6 ft. wide, joined at the middle as shown. The adjoining edges *A*

are sewn together and the edges *B*, which are set at the ridge of the tent, are sewn after the other pieces are joined. Brass grommets are fitted in the canvas, as indicated, and the points of the supporting frames pass through them in driving the supports into the ground. The shoulder straps *C* are placed so that they are in position when the tent is folded and rolled into a pack. Other equipment may be placed inside of it. The tent supports *D* are pointed at the ends *E*

and are twisted together at the top. The ridgepole *F* steadies them and holds the canvas at the middle.

To set up the tent, lay the canvas flat on the ground and place the supports, twisted together, through the grommets. Spring them into the ends of the canvas and insert the ridgepole by springing it between the supports. The canvas is 8-oz. duck, and the fastenings used are snap buttons; buttonholes, buckles, or harness snaps may also be used.

— CARE AND STORAGE OF CAMP EQUIPMENT —

A slovenly sportsman misses much of the joy of the man who takes pride in giving his outfit proper care, not only during its period of use but also during the winter, when occasional overhauling serves to keep one in touch with sports of other seasons. And a real joy it is, each article recalling an experience as one examines it minutely for possible rust spot, scratch, or injury.

Tents usually come in for much abuse, which shortens their life considerably. Cotton duck molds quickly and rots if left rolled up damp. Care should be taken, therefore, to ensure its perfect dryness before storing. Silk and silk-composition tents, being

thoroughly waterproof, are almost as dry after a rain or dew as before, so may be packed for moving at any time. But all tents and tarpaulins should be washed and dried carefully after the season's use.

Blankets absorb much moisture and should be shaken and spread out over bushes to dry in the sun at least once a week. In the cold nights of late summer, the increased warmth of blankets after drying is considerable.

Pack straps and ropes should not be left exposed to the weather. They speedily become hard or brittle. Squirrels like the salt they can obtain by chewing the leather, and if left on the ground in a rabbit country the straps are soon cut into bits. Hang the leather goods in the peak of the tent, keep them away from fire, and oil them occasionally.

A canoe should not be left in the water overnight, or at any time when it is not in use. Simply because use makes it wet, a canoe should not be left so, anymore than a gun should left dirty or an ax dull. If on a cruise with a heavy load, pile the stuff on shore at the night camp and turn the canoe over it. If a canoe is permitted to remain in the water unnecessarily, or its inside exposed to rain, it soon becomes water soaked and heavy for portage, besides drying out when exposed to the sun and developing leaks.

Small punctures in the bottom of a canoe may be mended with spruce, tamarack, or pine gum, melted into place with a glowing firebrand, held close, while blowing at the spot to be repaired. Torn rags of canvas-covered bottoms may be glued with the softer gum of new "blazes," gathered with a knife or a stick.

While traveling on shallow streams, the bottom of a board canoe develops a "fur" of rubbed-up shreds. Every night these should be cut short with a sharp-pointed knife to prevent a shred from pulling out and developing into a large splinter. The paddles, and the setting pole, unless shod with iron, become burred at the ends and require trimming down to solid wood.

The track line, if in use, is wet most of the time. Unless dried frequently it becomes rotten. Every tracker knows the grave danger with a rotten line in a rapids.

During the winter the canoe should be scraped and sandpapered, bulges nailed down, permanent repairs made to the covering, and the canoe painted on the exterior and varnished on the interior.

The average fisherman is an enthusiast who needs no urging in the matter of caring for his outfit, and the user of firearms should profit by this example. Even if not a shot has been fired from a gun all day, moisture from the hands or from the dampness in the woods or marshes may cause rust spots or corrode the bore. Rub an oily rag through the bore and over the outside of the gun every evening before laying it aside.

Cleaning rods are safer and more thorough in cleaning the bore than the common mouse string, which may break when drawing a heavy piece of cloth through, causing much difficulty. A wooden rod, preferably of hickory, is best, although the metal rod is stronger for use in small bores. But care must be taken not wear the muzzle unduly. The hunting weapons should be carefully overhauled before storing them and given a coat of oil to protect the metal parts from rust.

— CAMP SHELTER AFFORDS PROTECTION FROM MOSQUITOES —

When it is undesirable to stay in a camping tent, on warm nights or during the day when a siesta is taken, a mosquito shelter can be made of materials readily available at most camping places. The arrangement, as shown, is made as follows: Procure a number of pliable switches about ¾ in. in diameter and 8 or 10 ft. long—willow or similar growths. Sharpen the butts and force them into the ground in two rows, 3½ ft. apart. Bend the tops together and tie them in arches of the same height, as indicated. Next, tie a ridge binder the entire length. Cover the frame with mosquito netting, providing an entrance at one end. The shelter shown is for one person but may easily be made larger. The fly, supported on a rope between posts or trees, affords shade.

LITHE BRANCHES CUT IN THE WOODS ARE USED FOR FRAMEWORK, WHICH IS COVERED WITH MOSQUITO NETTING.

— A Hammock Sleeping Tent —

Compactness in transportation and general serviceableness are features of the hammock tent shown in the illustration. It is made by sewing a piece of canvas to the sides of an ordinary "dog," or shelter, tent and may be made of a piece of canvas or tarpaulin. The tent is suspended by the ridge from a heavy rope supported on trees or posts. It is kept taut on the sides by tent ropes attached to stakes driven in the ground.

A COMFORTABLE SLEEPING TENT IS PROVIDED BY THE ARRANGEMENT SHOWN IN THE SKETCH.

This form of tent is particularly convenient in providing a good sleeping place in very small space.

It is free from dampness, and the camper is provided with a comfortable rest free from prowling animals, with the use of a cot.

— A Set of Folding Tent Poles —

Motor tourists and others who realize the necessity of traveling light, and with their tent and other equipment stowed away as compactly as possible, will appreciate the merits of the folding tent poles illustrated.

The poles are made of flat bar iron cut into convenient lengths and assembled by means of bolts and wing

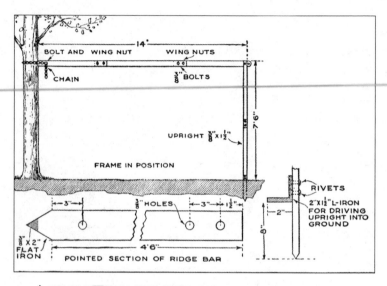

A SET OF SECTIONAL TENT POLES, THE VALUE OF WHICH IS REALIZED
BY MOTOR TOURISTS AND CAMPERS WHO MUST TRAVEL WITH
THEIR EQUIPMENT STOWED IN THE MOST COMPACT MANNER.

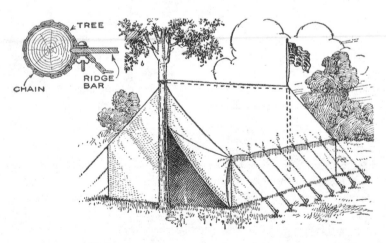

nuts. One section of the horizontal bar is sharpened at one end and provided with a suitable length of chain for securing it to a tree or post. The bottom section of the end pole is pointed and provided with an L-shaped piece, about 8 in. from the end, to serve as a stop and assist in driving it into the ground. After the supports have been assembled and erected, the tent is put up, pegged, and guyed in the usual manner. The bars should be given at least one coat of paint to prevent rust.

The same idea can be applied to the construction of a set of wooden poles if it is found undesirable to make use of the metal sections. However, in this case some form of slip or strap joint should be used so that it will not be necessary to make the ends of the sections overlap each other, which would make an unsightly joint in a wooden pole. The entrance to the tent may be made at either end.

— PORTABLE TENT MADE FROM AN UMBRELLA AND PAPER MUSLIN —

Picnickers desiring to go in bathing are often handicapped by the lack of a convenient place to change clothes. An umbrella and some paper muslin provide a light portable tent that is practical and inexpensive for such uses. Cut the dark paper muslin into as many 9-ft. lengths as there are sections of the umbrella. Sew these strips together. At each seam tie a string about a yard

long and a stout cord 15 ft. long to the handle to hold up the tent. For use, open the umbrella, invert it, and to each rib tie one of the strings. Then tie one end of the cord to the handle of the umbrella and suspend it from a tree or other support, as shown, weighting or tying down the other end.

— Combination Tent and Pack Cover —

For the sportsman or vacation-
ist "roughing it" in the woods or
traveling "light" in a canoe, the
tent shown in the drawing not
only provides a shelter at night
but serves as a cover for his
personal effects.

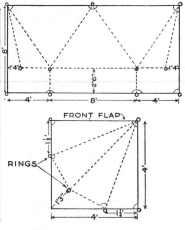

Sportsmen and vacationists "roughing it" and carrying their own beds and boards on their backs, or in a canoe, will appreciate the obvious advantages afforded by a tent that also serves as a cover for the owner's camp effects when not used as a shelter.

There are two methods of making the tent illustrated: One is to use a rectangular tarpaulin, or other suitable material, which is twice as long as the width. Make a strong hem around all edges and sew brass or iron rings, as indicated, at the ends of the dotted lines. The fly, or front flap, is made separately from a square piece of material, the dotted lines showing the folds of the shelter when it is set up. It is unnecessary to do any cutting of material in making a tent of this type.

The alternative method requires more or less cutting of the material, which is cut along the dotted lines as a pattern. The separate pieces are sewn together, with the seam inside. This makes a regulation tent, and by making a few paper models of different sizes it is an easy matter to get the right proportions for a tent of different dimensions from that illustrated. The tent in the drawing is a good average size, and a piece of material 8 ft. wide and 16 ft. long is needed for making it.

It is not necessary for the cloth to be in a single piece, but this is an advantage. In using yard-wide goods, the strips are sewn together with heavy waxed thread, the seams running lengthwise of the 16-ft. piece. To reinforce the tent at the corners, where the greatest strain comes when the tent is pegged and the guys in place, it is a good plan to sew patches of cloth on both sides where the rings are sewn on. The tent is amply large for two occupants. When set up it is 8 ft. wide, 6 ft. deep, 7½ ft. high at the front, sloping to a height of 2½ ft. at the back wall.

For a light summer tent, a heavy grade of unbleached cotton cloth is a good choice, although if heavier material is wanted, regulation canvas duck of several weights can be used.

— A CAVE HOUSE OF BOUGHS AND THATCH —

There is a singular romance attaching to cave dwellers, or troglodytes, which never ceases to fascinate a boy. This is possibly because pirates and other favorite characters of fiction hold forth and store their booty in caves. Cave houses are dangerous because the earth is likely to cave in on the workers, but the house described in this article offers an acceptable substitute.

Two forked sticks are securely set into the ground and a ridgepole laid across the forks, as shown. The sides are formed by placing a number of small poles, or saplings, at an angle to the ridgepole. Additional strength is obtained by burying the bottom ends of the poles in the ground. A number of poles are arranged in a semicircle at the rear of the frame, the poles resting in the crotch of the rear upright and

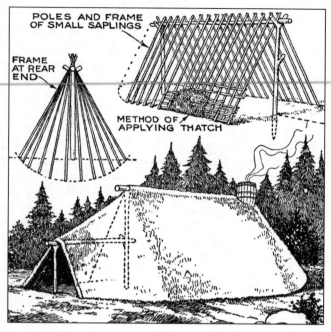

POLES AND FRAME OF SMALL SAPLINGS

FRAME AT REAR END

METHOD OF APPLYING THATCH

LIVING IN CAVES HOLDS A SINGULAR FASCINATION FOR BOYS, BUT IT IS DANGEROUS. THIS CAVE HOUSE CAN BE BUILT ANYWHERE AND IS A PERFECTLY SAFE "ROBBERS'" DEN.

ridgepole. The house is completed by covering it with boughs, thatch, bark, or sod. If thatch is used, it is necessary to nail or tie poles horizontally to the frame, or smaller boughs may be woven between the side poles, basket fashion. Begin applying the thatch at the bottom and work toward the top. When the bottom row of thatch has been applied, another row is put on so that the rows overlap until the top is reached. A hole is left at one end in the roof to permit escape of smoke from the fire, which is built directly underneath. If the front upright has a crotch about the center, a small extension may be added to the house, built in the same manner as the house itself, so that the young "pirates" and "smugglers" will have to crawl into their dwelling after the approved fashion.

— Tent for Permanent Camp —

The interior of an ordinary wall tent may be made more comfortable by setting the tent over a wooden wall, 2 or 3 ft. high, and fastening the guy ropes to a raised railing at the sides, as shown in the drawing. The front end of the wall is provided with a doorframe to which a screen door is attached. A short tent pole is attached over the center of the doorframe to support the front end of the ridgepole; a longer pole will be required at the rear to allow for the height the tent is elevated. Additional ventilation may be obtained by fitting smaller doors in the wall, at each side of the entrance. A window-shade roller to which a strip of canvas is tacked may be fitted at the top of the door to prevent rain from blowing in, and for additional privacy. The tent is attached to the wooden wall by hooking the grommets or eyelets on the bottom edge of the canvas over screw hooks.

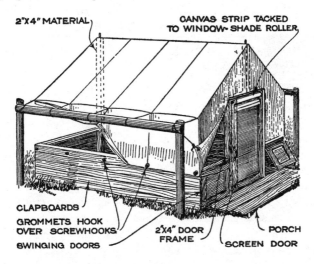

THE INTERIOR OF AN ORDINARY WALL TENT MAY BE GREATLY ENLARGED BY SETTING THE TENT ON TOP OF WOODEN WALLS; A SCREEN DOOR KEEPS OUT INSECTS.

— ERECTING TENTS WITHOUT POLES —

GROMMET IN TENT

KNOTS ON ROPE IN SIDE
OF TENT WILL HOLD TOP STRAIGHT

THE DISADVANTAGES OF TENT POLES ARE ALWAYS APPARENT
TO THE CAMPER, BUT POLES ARE UNNECESSARY
NUISANCES, AS THE DRAWING SHOWS.

Although many a camper has observed and remarked upon the well-known fact that tent poles are a nuisance, it has possibly never occurred to many of them that it is quite possible to erect a tent without poles, using ropes instead. The ridge-pole is eliminated by a rope running through the inside of the tent. The ends of this rope are brought through the grommets provided at each end of the tent for the spikes of the end poles, and a knot is tied under each grommet or eyelet, to prevent the tent from sagging in the center. The outer ends of the rope are attached, at the proper height between two trees, as in the drawing. Should there be only one tree available, one end of the tent rope is tied to the tree; the front end of the tent is supported by a rope running from a branch of the tree to a stake that is firmly driven into the ground somewhat in front of the tent and in line with its center.

— Screen Door for Tent —

While homes are provided with screen doors to prevent entrance of insects, the tent dweller unwillingly entertains a variety of pestiferous insect life, and assumes that an enterprising colony of hornets in his tent is the thing to be expected. By equipping the tent with a screen door, the camper is enabled to show a light in his tent after dark without permitting insects to enter. A light wooden frame is made and covered with wired cloth or mosquito netting, as shown in the drawing. A stake is

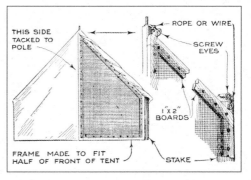

A SCREEN DOOR FOR THE CAMPER'S TENT
IS OPENED BY LIFTING, THE UPPER
EDGE BEING HINGED.

driven at one corner of the tent, to which a corner of the door is attached with screw eyes and a wire link, the upper corner being similarly attached to the end pole.

— How to Make a Bell Tent —

A bell tent is easily made and is nice for lawns, as well as for a boy's camping outfit. The illustrations show a plan of a tent 14 ft. in diameter. To make such a tent, procure unbleached tent duck, which is the very best material for the purpose. Make 22 sections, shaped like *Fig. 3*, each 10 ft. 6 in. long and 2 ft. 2 in. wide at the bottom, tapering in

a straight line to a point at the top. These dimensions allow for the laid or lapped seams, which should be double-stitched on a machine. Sew the last seam only for a distance of 4 ft. from the top, leaving the rest for an opening. At the end of this seam stitch on an extra gusset piece so that it will not rip. Fold back the edges of the opening and the bottom edge of the bell-shaped cover and bind it with wide webbing, 3 in. across and having eyelets at the seams for attaching the stay ropes. Near the apex of the cover cut three triangular holes 8 in. long and 4 in wide at the bottom and hem the edges. These are ventilators. Make the tent wall of the same kind of cloth 2 ft. 2 in. high. Bind it at the upper edge with webbing and at the bottom with canvas. Also stitch on

round galvanized iron, 6 in. diameter. Stitch the canvas at the apex around the hoop and along the sides. Make the apex into a hood and line it with stiff canvas. The tent pole is 3 in. in diameter and should be in two sections, with a socket joint and rounded at the top to fit into the apex.

In raising the tent, fasten down the wall by means of loops of stout line fastened to its lower edge and

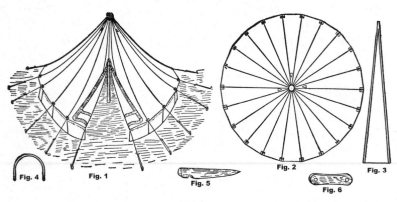

AN INEXPENSIVE HOMEMADE TENT.

coarse canvas 6 in. wide at the bottom, and fill the space between the ground and the wall when the tent is raised with canvas edging. Stitch the upper edge of the wall firmly to the bell cover.

For the top of the tent have the blacksmith make a hoop of ½ in.

small pegs driven through them into the ground, *Fig. 4*. Run the stay ropes from the eyelets in the circular cover to stakes *(Fig. 5)* stuck in the ground. Use blocks, as in *Fig. 6*, on the stay ropes for holding the ends and adjusting the length of the ropes.

PROVISIONS *and* TOOLS

— CAMP WATER BAG —

While out on a camping trip, I devised a way to supply the camp with cool water. A strip of heavy canvas was cut about 2 ft. long and 1 ft. wide, and the edges were sewn up to make a sack 1 ft. square. In one upper corner a large porcelain knob insulator was sewn in for a mouthpiece; the groove around it makes a watertight joint with the cloth. Two metal rings were sewn in the cloth at the top for attaching a strap to carry it. The side and top seams were made as tight as possible.

In use, this sack was filled with as cool water as possible and tightly corked. It was then hung in the shade where a breeze would strike it. The water gradually seeped through the cloth and this, in evaporating, kept the contents cool. This sack also came in handy while fishing or on the road.

— A TABLE BOX FOR CAMPERS —

A very useful combination packing box and camp table may be made from a coffee or other large box. If a box with a three-ply top is available, it makes a neat appearance, but this is not essential. A box 14 in. deep, 20 in. wide, and 29 in. long, outside

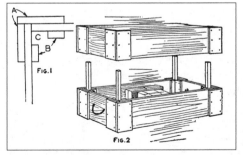

THE STRIPS IN THE CORNERS OF THE BOXES
FORM SOCKETS FOR THE LEGS.

Fig.3

measurements, is convenient. It will slip under the seat of a spring wagon and is of such a size that a person's knees will pass under it when used as a table.

Saw the box in two on the centerline of the narrow way, making two uncovered boxes of the same size and depth. The corners of each box should be well braced on the outside, as shown in *A, Fig. 1*. The strips *B* are fastened to the inside of the box to form sockets, *C*, for the legs. The strips are ½ in. thick, 1¼ in. wide, and as long as the box is deep. Four legs, about 12 in. long and of such size as to fit in the sockets, are used for holding the boxes together in transit. Rope handles are fastened in the ends of each box, and a hook and eye are used to lock them together.

To pack the boxes place one half open side up and insert the legs, as shown in *Fig. 2*. Then fill it and extend the packing to the level of the leg ends; slip the other half of the box on the legs and fasten the two with the hooks. If properly roped, such a box will be taken as baggage. Canvas and other articles that will be removed at once upon arrival in camp, rather than provisions, should be packed in this box so that it can be converted into a table with the least possible work.

To make one table or two of the box, remove the packing legs and insert long legs in the sockets of each section. A set of eight legs, 30 in. long, takes up very little space and can be carried diagonally in the bottom of the box. A piece of oilcloth can be wrapped around them and used later as a cover for the table. The legs should fit loosely in the sockets to provide for swelling in damp weather. Ordinarily they can be wedged to make them rigid. The table is shown in *Fig. 3*.

— A Camper's Salt-and-Pepper Holder —

A camper will find a very clever way to carry salt and pepper by using a piece cut from a joint of bamboo. A piece is selected with the joint in the center, and the ends are stoppered with corks.

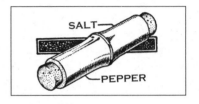

— Kitchen for Hikers —

The kitchen illustrated was constructed with a view to providing all the needs of a commissary department for 36 boys for a period of four days, either on a hike or in a permanent camp. Because it is placed on two wheels, which are removed when the kitchen is in use, it can be moved from one day's camp to another by attaching it to the rear of a horse-drawn wagon by means of a shaft. When the wheels

THE KITCHEN OUTFIT COMPACTED INTO ITS CABINET, MOUNTED ON WHEELS AND UNDER TRANSPORT.

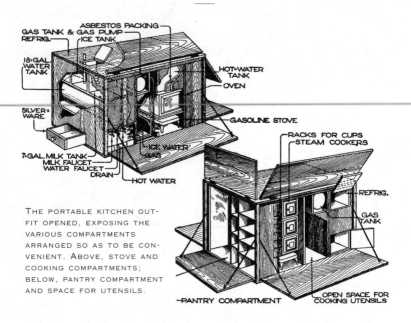

GAS TANK & GAS PUMP
REFRIG.
ASBESTOS PACKING
ICE TANK
18-GAL WATER TANK
HOT-WATER TANK
OVEN
SILVER-WARE
GASOLINE STOVE
7-GAL. MILK TANK
MILK FAUCET
WATER FAUCET
DRAIN
ICE WATER
GAS
HOT WATER
RACKS FOR CUPS
STEAM COOKERS
REFRIG.
GAS TANK
PANTRY COMPARTMENT
OPEN SPACE FOR COOKING UTENSILS

THE PORTABLE KITCHEN OUT-FIT OPENED, EXPOSING THE VARIOUS COMPARTMENTS ARRANGED SO AS TO BE CON-VENIENT. ABOVE, STOVE AND COOKING COMPARTMENTS; BELOW, PANTRY COMPARTMENT AND SPACE FOR UTENSILS.

are removed the entire outfit rests on legs, which are swung down from the bottom. The sides and one end are opened by swinging one half up and resting it on the top, while the other half swings down to a horizontal position where it is used as a work board, making all parts easily accessible.

The outside dimensions of the kitchen, when closed and in the form of a large box on wheels, are 5 ft. 3 in. long, 3 ft. wide, and 2½ ft. high. The main feature of this entire kitchen is its compactness. At

the front, and extending about 1 ft. back, is a kitchen cabinet where the plates, sugar, salt, flour, etc., are kept in separate compartments. Here also are found the necessary cooking utensils such as bread knives, butcher knives, cleaver, cooking spoons, pancake turner, sieves, large forks, lemon squeezer, etc. Small boxes and packages of baking powder, cocoa, etc., are placed on the shelves of galvanized iron. This entire compartment, as well as all others where food is handled and prepared, is lined with No. 28 gauge galvanized iron. Which makes sanitation a feature also.

Upon passing around to one side there can be seen a large three-shelved oven, 21 in. wide, which is heated by a gasoline burner. Between the burner and the bottom of the oven are located coils of pipe for heating water, and these coils are connected to a tank of 7-gal. capacity located just above the oven. An air valve and glass gauge are attached to the tank.

The next compartment to the rear is a large storage space, extending all the way through the kitchen, and a 2½-gal. forged-copper gasoline tank occupies a shelf in the upper portion of this space. At the rear end along this side are located nickel-plated faucets that are connected to the hot-water tank mentioned, a 7-gal., white-enameled milk tank above, an 18-gal. cold-water tank, and an ice-water tank, used when distilled-water ice can be secured. These faucets drain into a small sink, which, in turn, drains off through an ordinary sink drain to a hole dug in the ground beneath it. Practically the entire rear end of the kitchen is occupied by the large water tanks, ice box, and milk tanks, with the exception of a small space at the bottom where the silverware is kept in a drawer.

On the other side, and to the rear, two compartments above and below the large water tank form excellent storage space for ham, bacon, sausage, preserves, butter, etc., which need to kept in a cool place. Next in line is the other end of the large storage space, which extends through from the other side. Pans, pails, canned goods, larger packages, etc., are kept in this space.

Immediately to the rear of the kitchen cabinet, on this side, are located compartment shelves where the tin cups are kept. Adjoining this is found a three-compartment steam cooker. By having the cups and plates near this steam cooker, which is also heated by a gas burner, there is less danger from rust, as they are kept thoroughly dried. Wherever there is a gasoline burner the compartment in which it is located is not only lined with galvanized iron, but sheets of nonflammable material are placed on the inner side so that the heat will not ignite the interior packing or the woodwork. The tanks are accessible from the top of the kitchen for filling and cleaning and are packed with ground cork.

The kitchen has shown its efficiency by giving satisfactory service in camps of many members.

— A Canoe Stove —

Limited space and the rocking motion of salmon-fishing boats in a heavy sea on the Pacific coast brought about the construction of the canoe stove shown in the illustration. It is made of a discarded kerosene can whose form is a square. A draft hole is cut in one side of the

of rocking can cause the vessel to slide from the stovetop, and as the stove is weighted with sand, it cannot be easily moved from the place where it is set in the canoe.

The use of such a stove in a canoe has the advantage that the stove can be cleaned quickly, as the ashes and

can, 4 or 5 in. from the bottom, and a layer of sand placed on the bottom. Two holes are punched through opposite sides, parallel with the draft hole and about 3 in. from the top edge. Rods are run through these holes to provide a support for the cooking utensil. The smoke from the fire passes out at the corners around the vessel.

The main reason for making this stove in this manner is to hold the cooking vessel within the sides extending above the rods. No amount

STOVE MADE OF AN OLD OILCAN WITH EXTENDING SIDES AND WEIGHTED WITH SAND FOR USE ON A FISHING BOAT HOLDS THE COOKING VESSEL SAFELY IN A SEA.

fire can be dumped into the water and the stove used for a storage box. The whole thing may be tossed overboard and a new one made for another trip.

— Utensil Rack for Campfire —

A compact, simple device for holding cooking utensils steady over a campfire is shown in the sketch. It may be collapsed into a small bundle and is of light weight, factors that are important in camping equipment.

The device consists of two sections of pipe, *A*, supported on rods, *B*, having eyes bent at their upper ends. The lower end of the supports is pointed and may be driven into the ground so as to spread the pipes

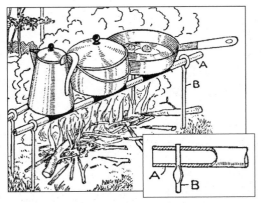

IRON PIPES HELD BY POINTED STEEL RODS PROVIDE A SIMPLE AND SATISFACTORY SUPPORT FOR COOKING UTENSILS IN THE CAMP.

more at one end than at the other, thus providing support for large as well as small utensils.

— Handling Camp Kettles —

Removing a kettle from the campfire demands considerable care and caution if burned fingers are to be avoided and the contents of the kettle prevented from spilling and possibly extinguishing the fire.

Fortunately, there is usually a forked stick of the right size to be found somewhere nearby, and this is converted into a safe handle by cutting three notches in it, as indicated in the drawing. This prevents the handle and edge of the kettle from slipping.

Using this handy little device, it is unnecessary to touch the handle until it is entirely cool, because the kettle can be removed from the fire and the contents poured out in the manner shown.

— HOLDING AX HEADS IN PLACE —

It is not always possible to tell when an ax head is fastened securely enough to prevent the possibility of an accident, especially when using a heavy ax in winter. But by using the simple method shown in the drawing, the ax may be made permanently safe.

A pin is made of 1/16-in. sheet iron to

HOLE FOR SCREW

SCREW

the pattern shown, and after the head has been wedged in place, the pin is driven in until the shoulder bears against the head. A screw is then driven into the handle through the hole in the pin; this will keep the head from flying off, even if the wedges loosen and drop out.

— CAMP STOVE MADE FROM THREE HINGES —

The novel camp stove shown in the drawing is made from three common strap hinges. The hinges are fastened together at the center ends with a small bolt, and the other ends are sunk into the ground. The bolt should be flatheaded and should be screwed up tightly to make the hinge supports as rigid as possible. This stove may be folded up when not in use, and occupies but little space in the camping equipment.

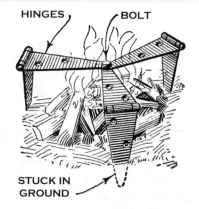

HINGES

BOLT

STUCK IN GROUND

— QUICKLY MADE DIPPER FOR CAMP USE —

When without a dipper or other means for handling water while camping, recourse may be had to an old trick of hunters and trappers, who make serviceable dippers from the bark of trees. A piece of birch bark, stiff paper, or other material is cut about 8 by 10 in., as indicated. The flat piece is bent longitudinally in the center and then slightly along the diagonal lines. To form the dipper, hold the finger at X and push forward on the material inside the triangle until it assumes the shape shown in the drawing. A split stick is forced over the folds

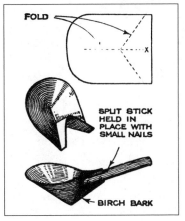

and held in place with small nails or even pins.

— A CAMP PROVISION BOX —

While on a camping and canoeing trip recently, I used a device that added a touch of completeness to our outfit and made camp life really enjoyable. This useful device is none other than a provision, or "grub," box.

From experience, campers know that the first important factor in having a successful trip is compactness of outfit. When undertaking an outing of this kind it is most desirable to have as few bundles to carry as possible, especially if one is going to be on the move part of the time. This device eliminates an unnecessary amount of bundles, thus making the trip easier for the campers, and doubly so if they intend canoeing part of the time. And, apart from its usefulness as a provision container, it affords a general repository for the small articles that mean so much to the camper's welfare.

The box proper may be made in any convenient size, so long as it is

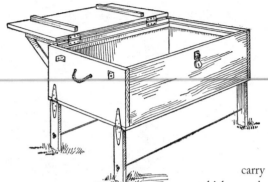

THE PROVISION BOX READY FOR
USE IN CAMP, THE COVER TURNED
BACK ON THE BRACKETS AND
THE LEGS EXTENDED.

not too cumbersome for two people to handle. The dimensions given are for a box I used on a canoe trip of several hundred miles; and from experience I know it to be of a suitable size for canoeists. If the camper is going to have fixed camp and have his luggage hauled, a larger box is much to be preferred. A glance at the figures will show the general proportions of the box. It may be possible, in some cases, to secure a strong packing box near the required dimensions, thus doing away with the trouble of constructing it. The distinguishing features of this box are the hinged cover, the folding legs, and the folding brackets. The brackets, upon which the top rests

when open, fold in against the back of the box when not in use. The same may be said of the legs. They fold up alongside the box and are held there by spring brass clips.

On our trips we carry an alcohol stove on which we do all of our cooking. The inner side of the top is covered with a sheet of flameproof material, this side being uppermost when the hinged top is opened and resting on the folding brackets. The stove rested on this material, thus making everything safe. The cover is large enough to do all the cooking on, and the box is so high that the cooking can be attended to without stooping over, which is much more pleasant than squatting before a campfire getting the eyes full of smoke. The legs are hinged to the box in such a manner that all of the weight of the box rests on the legs rather than on the hinges, and are kept from spreading apart by wire turnbuckles. These, being just bolts and wire, may be tucked inside the box when on the move. The top is fitted with unexposed hinges and with a lock

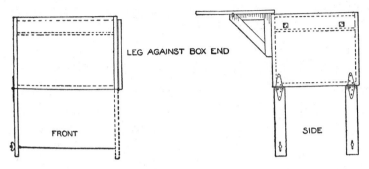

LEG AGAINST BOX END

FRONT

SIDE

THE BRACKETS FOR THE COVER AS WELL AS EACH OF THE FOUR LEGS
FOLD AGAINST THE SIDES OF THE BOX IN SUCH A MANNER
AS TO BE OUT OF THE WAY, MAKING THE BOX EASY TO
CARRY AND STORE AWAY IN A SMALL SPACE.

to make it a safe place for storing valuables.

In constructing the cover it is wise to make it so that it covers the joints of the sides, thus making the box waterproof from the top, if rain should fall on it. A partition can be made in one end to hold odds and ends. A tray could be installed, like the tray in a trunk, to hold knives, forks, spoons, etc., while the perishable supplies are kept underneath the tray. Give the box two coats of paint and shellac the inside.

The wire braces for the legs are made as follows. Procure four machine bolts, about ¼ in. in diameter and 2 in long—any thread will do—with wing nuts and washers to fit. Saw or file off the heads and drill

a small hole in one end of each bolt, large enough to receive a No. 16 galvanized iron wire. Two inches from the bottom of each leg drill a hole to take the bolt loosely. Determine the exact distance between the outside edges of the legs when the box is resting on them. Make the wire braces 1 in. longer than this distance so that the bolts will protrude through the holes in the legs and allow for putting on the nuts and washers. Screwing up on the nuts draws the wire taut, thus holding the legs firm.

The size of the top determines the dimensions of the folding brackets that support it when open. These brackets may be solid blocks of wood, but a lighter and more serviceable bracket is constructed as follows.

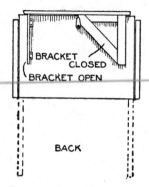

DETAIL OF THE TURNBUCKLE,
BUTTON TO HOLD THE BRACKETS,
AND THE SPRING CLIP FOR HOLDING
THE LEGS ON THE SIDE OF THE BOX.

If the top is 20 in. wide and 30 in. long, make the brackets 10 by 13 in. Constructing the brackets so that their combined length is 4 in. shorter than the total length of the box facilitates their folding against the back of the box when not in use. This point is clearly shown in the drawing. Our brackets were made of ½ in. oak, 1½ in. wide, and the joints halved together. They are hinged to the back of the box as shown, and when folded are held in place by a simple catch. The weight of the lid is sufficient to hold the brackets in place when open, but to make sure they will not creep when in use insert a ¼ in. dowel in the end of each so that it protrudes ¼ in. Drill two holes in the top to

the depth of ¼ in. so that when the top rests on the brackets, these holes engage with the dowels. In hinging the brackets to the back see that they are high enough to support the lid at right angles to the box.

The box here shown is made of ⅞ in. white pine throughout. The legs are ⅞ by 2½ by 18 in. They are fastened to the box with ordinary strap hinges. When folded up against the box they do not come quite to the top, so the box should be at least 19 in. high for 18-in. legs. About 2 in. from the bottom of the legs drive in a brad so it protrudes ⅛ in., as shown. This brad engages in a hole in the spring brass clip when folded up as shown in the illustration.

If in a fixed camp, it is a good idea to stand the legs in tomato cans partly full of water. This prevents ants from crawling up the legs into the box, but it necessitates placing the wire braces higher on the legs.

Our box cost us nothing but the hardware because we knocked some old packing boxes to pieces and planed up enough boards to make the sides. Of course, the builder need not adhere to these dimensions; he can make the size to suit his requirements. The finish is a matter of personal taste.

Camp Furnishings

— A Springy Hammock Support Made of Boughs —

In many camping places, balsam branches, or moss, are available for improvising mattresses. Used in connection with a hammock or a bed made on the spot, such a mattress substitute provides a comfort that adds to the joys of camping. A camp hammock or bed of this kind is shown.

Then cut two poles, 2 in. in diameter and 3½ ft. long, and two smaller poles, 3 ft. long. Also cut two forked poles, 4½ ft. long, for the diagonal braces. Place two of the long poles crossing each other as shown, 1 ft. from the ground. Set up the second pair similarly. Fix the crossbars into place, in the crotches, the ends of the crotch branches being fastened

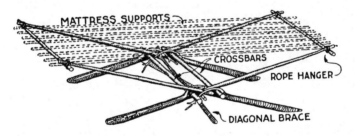

THE CAMP BED CAN BE "KNOCKED DOWN," OR TRANSPORTED CONSIDERABLE DISTANCE AS IT STANDS.

To make it, cut four 6-ft. poles, of nearly the same weight and 1 in. diameter at the small end. These saplings should have a fork about 2½ ft. from the lower ends, as resting places for the crossbars, as shown.

under the opposite crossbar. The end bars are fixed to the crossed poles by means of short rope loops. The mattress is placed on springy poles, 7 ft. long and 2 in. apart, alternating thick and thin ends. The moss is laid over

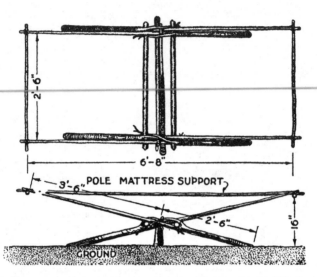

POLE MATTRESS SUPPORT

THE POLES ARE SELECTED CAREFULLY AND SET UP WITH STOUT
CROSS BRACES AT THE MIDDLE AND LIGHTER ONES
FOR THE MATTRESS SUPPORT.

the poles, and the balsam branches used as cover. spread as thickly. Blankets may be

— CAMP LANTERN MADE OF TIN CAN —

Campers and others who have need of an emergency lantern may be interested in the contrivance shown in the sketch, which was used in preference to other lanterns and made quickly when no light was at hand. It consists of an ordinary tin can, in the side of which a candle has been fixed. A ring of holes was punched through the metal around the candle and wires were placed at the opposite side for a support. The glistening interior of the can reflects the light admirably.

— Makeshift Camper's Lantern —

While out camping, our only lantern was accidentally smashed beyond repair and it was necessary for us to devise something that would take its place. We took an empty tomato can and cut out the tin 3 in. wide for a length extending from a point 2 in. below the top and to within ¼ in. of the bottom. Each side of the cutout *A* was bent inward in the shape of a letter S, in which was placed a piece of glass. Four V-shaped notches were cut as shown in *B*, near to the top of the can, and their points turned outward. A slit was cut in the bottom, shaped as shown in *C*, and the pointed ends thus formed were turned up to make a place for holding the base of a candle. A larger can was secured

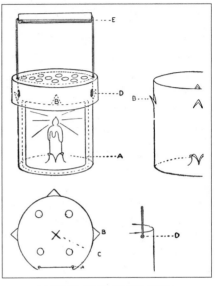

LANTERN MADE OF OLD CANS.

and the bottom perforated. This was turned over the top of the other can. A heavy wire was run through the perforations and a short piece of broom handle used to make a bail.

— How to Make a Camp Stool —

The stool, as shown in *Fig. 1*, is made of beech or any suitable wood with a canvas or carpet top. Provide four lengths for the legs, each 1 in. square and 18½ in. long; two lengths, 1⅛ in. square and 11 in. long for the top, and two lengths ¾ in. square, one 8½ and the other 10½ in. long, for the lower rails.

The legs are shaped at the ends to fit into a ⅝-in. hole bored into the top pieces as shown in *Fig. 2*, the distance between the centers of the holes being 7⅝ in. in one piece and 9⅝ in. in the other. The lower rails are fitted in the same way, using a ½ in. hole bored into each leg 2½ in. up from the lower end.

Each pair of legs has a joint for folding and this joint is made by boring a hole in the middle of each leg, inserting a bolt and riveting it over washers with a washer placed between the legs as shown in *Fig. 3*. The entire length of each part is rounded off for the sake of neatness as well as lightness.

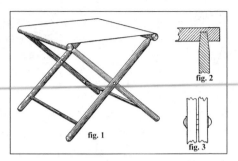

CAMPSTOOL DETAILS

About ½ yd. of 11-in. wide material will be required for the seat, and each end of this is nailed securely on the underside of the top pieces. The woodwork may be stained and varnished or plain varnished, and the cloth may be made to have a pleasing effect by stenciling in some neat pattern.

— A HANGER FOR THE CAMP —

A garment or utensil hanger can be easily made for the camp in the following manner: Procure a long leather strap, about 1¼ in. wide, and attach hooks made of wire to it. Each hook should be about 4 in. long and of about No. 9 gauge wire. Bend a ring on one end of the wire and stick the other end through a hole punched in the center of the strap. The ring will prevent the wire from passing through the leather, and it should be bent in such a manner that the hook end of the wire will hang downward when the width of the strap is vertical. These hooks are placed about 2 in. apart for the length of the strap, allowing sufficient ends for a buckle and holes. The strap can be buckled around a tree or tent pole.

— A Bed for a Camp —

A quickly made bed for a camp is shown in the illustration. The corner posts consist of four forked stakes driven into the earth so that the crotches are on a level and about 1 ft. from the ground. Poles are laid in the crotches, lengthwise of the bed, and canvas covering double-lapped over them. If desired, the

CANVAS BED MADE ON TWO POLES LAID IN THE CROTCHES OF FORKED STAKES.

canvas can be stitched along the inside of the poles.

— A Variety of Camp Furnishings —

When on a camping trip, nothing should be carried but the necessities, and the furnishings should be made up from materials found in the woods. A good spring bed can be made up in the following manner: Cut two stringers from small, straight trees, about 4 in. in diameter, and make them about 6 ft. long. All branches are trimmed off smooth, and a trench is dug in the ground for each piece, the trenches being 24 in. apart. Small saplings, about 1 in. in diameter and as straight as can be found, are cut and trimmed of all branches and nailed across the stringers for the springs. Knots, bulges, etc., should

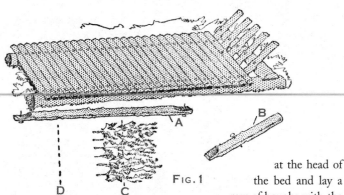

FIG. 1

A CAMP BED MADE OF SAPLINGS WITH
SEVERAL LAYERS OF BOUGHS FOR
THE MATTRESS.

be turned downward as far as possible. The ends of each piece are flattened, as shown in *A, Fig. 1,* to give it a good seat on the stringers.

A larger sapling is cut, flattened, and nailed at the head of the bed across the stringers, and to it a number of head-stay saplings, *B,* are nailed. These head-stay pieces are cut about 12 in. long, sharpened on one end, and driven a little way into the ground, after which they are nailed to the head crosspiece.

In the absence of an empty mattress tick and pillow cover that can be filled with straw, boughs of fir may be used. These boughs should not be larger than a match and crooked stems should be turned down. Begin

at the head of the bed and lay a row of boughs with the stems pointed toward the foot. Over this row, and half-lapping it, place another row so that the tops of the boughs lay on the line *C,* and their stems on the line *D.* The process is continued until the crosspiece springs are entirely covered, and then another layer is laid in the same manner on top of these, and so on, until a depth of 6 or 8 in. is obtained. This will make a good substitute for a mattress. A pillow can be made by filling a meal bag with boughs or leaves.

A good and serviceable table can be constructed from a few fence boards or boards taken from a packing box. The table and chairs are made in one piece, the construction being clearly shown in *Fig. 2.* The height of the ends should be about 29 in., and the seats about

FIG. 2

FIG. 3

A TABLE MADE OF PACKING-BOX MATERIAL AND
A WASH-BASIN STAND OF THREE STAKES.

about 12 in. long and cut from a sapling, into them. The extending ends are supported on legs of the same material. The seat is made of a slab with the rounding side down.

A clothes hanger for the tent ridgepole can be made as shown in *Fig. 5*. The hanger consists of a piece 7 in. long, cut from a 2-in. sapling, nails being driven into its sides for hooks. The upper end is fitted with a rope that is tied over the ridgepole of the tent.

17 in. from the ground. The other dimensions will be governed by the material at hand and the number of campers.

A wash-basin support can be made of three stakes, cut from saplings and driven into the ground, as shown in *Fig. 3*. The basin is hung by its rim between the ends of the stakes.

Wherever a suitable tree is handy, a seat can be constructed as shown in *Fig. 4*. Bore two 1-in. holes 8 in. apart in the trunk, 15 in. above the ground. Drive two pins,

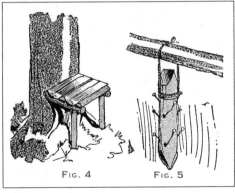

FIG. 4

FIG. 5

A SEAT AGAINST THE TRUNK OF A TREE,
AND A CLOTHES HANGER FOR
THE TENT RIDGEPOLE.

— A SHAVING LAMP AND MIRROR FOR THE CAMP —

To make shaving possible in camp at night or with little daylight, a small mirror was provided with an electric flashlight. The mirror was set to swing free in a wooden support. The light was fastened slightly above and behind the mirror, and swings at its base so that it can be tipped upward or downward, throwing the light correspondingly. A piece of wood 1¼ by 3½ in.,

and as long as the mirror frame is wide, serves as a base. The arms will hold the mirror far enough in front of the lamp to allow room in which to swing. The body of the lamp is set on a block and held between two wooden pieces into which a band of iron was set near the top. The uprights move in an arc, pivoting at their lower fastening on screws.

TWO *for the* PRICE *of* ONE

— COMBINATION CAMP-KITCHEN CABINET AND TABLE —

The combination camp-kitchen cabinet and table is the result of not being able to take the members of my family on an outing unless they could have some home conveniences on the trip. Perhaps the sketch and description may help solve the same problem for others. The table will accommodate four persons comfortably, and extra compartments may be added if desired. The cabinet, when closed, is strong and compact and is well made with a snug-fitting cover. It is bugproof and the contents will not be injured greatly, even if drenched by rain or a mishap in a craft.

For coffee, tea, sugar, salt, etc., I used small screw-top glass jars. They are set in pocket shelves at both ends. When closed, one can sit on the box or even walk on it if necessary when in the boat. If an armful or two of coarse marsh grass is spread over it, the contents will keep quite cool even when out in the hot sun. When open for use, the metal table-top *F* is supported on metal straps, *E*, which also act as braces and supports for the table leaf, *G*, on each side of the box. This affords plenty of table surface, and one can easily get at the contents of the cabinet while cooking or eating. The legs, *D*, are stored inside of the box when closed for traveling. They are held in place under metal straps

THIS OUTFIT PROVIDES ACCOMMODATIONS FOR FOUR PERSONS AND FOLDS COMPACTLY.

when in use and held at their upper ends by the metal plate and blocks, *B* and *C*. The bent metal pieces, *A*, on the ends of the top, spring over the blocks at *B* and *C* and form the handles.

— A Chair Swing —

A comfortable porch or lawn swing can be easily and quickly made with a chair as a seat, as follows. Procure some rope of sufficient strength to bear the weight of the person, and fasten one end securely to one of the front legs of the chair and the other end to the same side of the back, as shown in the illustration, allowing enough slack to form a right angle. Another piece of rope of the same length is then attached to the other side of the chair. The supporting ropes are tied to these ropes

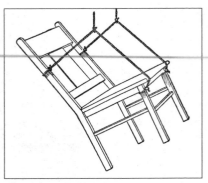

THE ROPES ARE TIED TO THE CHAIR SO THAT IT WILL BE HELD IN RECLINING POSITION.

and to the joist or holding piece overhead.

— How to Attach a Sail to a Bicycle —

This attachment was constructed for use on a bicycle to be ridden on the well-packed sands of a beach, but it could be used on a smooth, level road as well. The illustration shows the main frame to consist of two boards, each about 16 ft. long, bent in the shape of a boat, to give plenty of room for turning the front wheel. On this main frame is built up a triangular mast to carry the mainsail and jib, having a combined area of about 40 sq. ft. The frame is

fastened to the bicycle by numerous pieces of rope.

Sailing on a bicycle is very much different from sailing in a boat, because the bicycle leans up against the wind instead of heeling over with it as the boat does. It takes some time to learn the supporting power of the wind, and the angle at which one must ride makes it appear that a fall is almost sure to result. A turn must be made by turning out of the wind, instead of, as in ordinary

BICYCLE SAILING ON A BEACH.

sailing, into it. The boom supporting the bottom of the mainsail is then swung over to the opposite tack, when one is traveling at a good speed.

— SAIL FOR A BOY'S WAGON —

Every boy who loves a boat and has only a wagon can make a combination affair in which he can sail even though there is no water for miles around. One boy accomplished this as shown in the illustration, and the only assistance he had was in making the sails.

The box of the wagon is removed and the boat deck

THE SAIL WAGON WILL TRAVEL AT A GOOD SPEED IN A STIFF BREEZE.

bolted in its place. The deck is 14 in. wide and 5 ft. long. The mast consists of an old rake handle, 6 ft. long; the boom and gaff are broomsticks, and the tiller is connected with wire to the front axle, which gives perfect control of the steering. The sails are made of drilling.

On brick pavement, the sail wagon can easily pull along two other normal wagons with two boys in each, making in all five boys. Of course a good steady wind must be blowing. With two boys it has made a mile in five minutes on pavement.

— MOTORIST'S FOLDING LUNCHBOX AND TABLE —

For the automobile outing, when lunch is taken along, a compact and substantial combination lunchbox and table can be made along the lines of the one illustrated. In use, the top and bottom hinged covers open horizontally. A pivoted block attached inside one end of the box frame helps to stabilize the outfit. The legs are pivoted on a small iron rod and open downward. They are held rigidly vertical by means of wire braces attached to the underside of

A CLEVERLY DESIGNED COMBINATION TABLE AND LUNCHBOX FOR AUTOMOBILE EXCURSIONS.

the cover, the ends of the wires fitting into a hole on the outside edge of each leg. The legs are provided with buttons on the underside so

that, when folded up in their slots, the buttons can be turned, locking the legs and forming a continuous cover.

OUTDOOR HELPERS

— A WOODSMAN'S LOG RAFT —

Making a raft for crossing a stream or other small body of water is often a diversion for campers who have the usual supply of camp tools and materials. The woodsman is sometimes confronted with a different situation: He has only a hand ax as his tool equipment, and to construct a fairly safe raft of crude materials becomes necessary in order to pursue his course. Logs are readily available, and he may be fortunate enough to find willow withes, various stringy kinds of bark, or even coarse seaweed. If they are not available, the practical woodsman, particularly of the northern regions, builds a raft of logs pinned together firmly with poles and pointed wooden spikes cut on the spot. The method, as shown in the illustration, is simple and interesting. It may be of service in the woods even when other methods of binding the logs into a raft

are possible, and as a practical test of woodcraft for the amateur or boy camper it is of interest. The sketch shows the completed raft, bound together by wooden pins notched into the poles, and the inset details show the manner in which the poles are clamped by the crossed pins.

This method of construction may be applied to a variety of rafts for carrying small or large loads. In selecting the material for the raft, several points must be considered. Dry logs are preferable to wet or green ones, and if the latter are used, a relatively larger raft will be needed to carry a certain load. For one passenger, three logs 9 to 12 in. in diameter, 12 to 16 ft. long, and spaced to a width of 5 ft. will provide a stable raft. Poles may be laid across the raft to give sufficient footing. For heavier loads, the logs should be about the same length and diameter

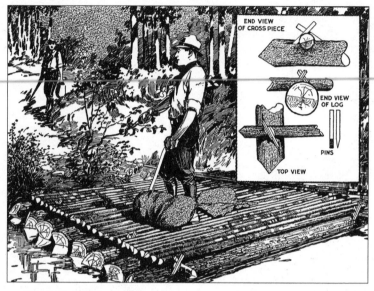

THE INVENTIVE WOODSMAN BUILDS HIS LOG RAFT OF SIMPLE MATERIALS
GATHERED AT THE RIVERBANK; THE LOGS AND POLES ARE NOTCHED
TOGETHER FIRMLY AND HELD WITH WOODEN PINS.

but spaced closer together and laid to form a raft of considerably greater width and buoyancy.

Select a shore sloping gently into the water, if possible, and cut the logs and poles as near this place as is convenient. Cut the logs and roll them to the bank, alternating the butts, if there is any considerable difference in the diameter of the ends. Cut a supply of poles of about 3 in. diameter and of the length necessary to reach across the proposed raft. Then

cut a number of pins of hardwood 1 ft. long and sharpened on one end as shown in the detailed sketch.

Roll the first log—one of the largest—into the water until it is nearly floating. If it is bowed or crooked, place the "humped" side toward the outer edge of the raft. Chop notches 2 in. deep in the top of the log about 1½ ft. from the ends, and squarely across. Place a pole in the notch with its end projecting slightly beyond the log, and cut a double notch in the upper edge of the pole, as shown in the detail sketches, so that when the pins are driven into the log they will rest diagonally in the notches cut into the poles. Make rifts in the log with the ax, cutting as though to split off a slab of bark and wood, rather than toward the center of the log, and drive two of the pins into place. Properly done, this will make a remarkably strong joint. Fasten a second pole at the other end of the log and prop up both poles so as to permit the next log to be rolled into the water under the poles.

Notch the second log before slipping it finally into place. Alternate ends only of the inner logs need to be fastened. If time is important, some of the logs may be left unfastened provided they are held tightly between the logs that are pinned. Shove the raft out into the water as each log is added. If there is a strong current it is desirable to guy the raft with a pole to the bank, downstream. The last log, which should also be a large one, is then floated down and pinned at both ends.

The raft may then be floated and is ready to be covered with light poles or brush to provide dry footing and place for the dunnage. The dunnage is placed near the forward end of the raft, and the person controlling it sculls with a pole at the rear.

— BIRCH-BARK LEGGINGS MADE IN THE WOODS —

An excellent pair of leggings for use in brush and forest land can be made in a few minutes from birch bark cut in the woods. Select a suitable tree, about 6 or 8 in. in diameter, and cut into the heavy bark to obtain two rolls around the circumference of the tree,

taking care not to cut deep enough to injure it. Fit these sections around the legs leaving 6-in. portions overlapping. Trim the bark to the proper shape and soak it in water to soften the grain. Place the bark close to the fire until it curls. The leggings are then ready to use.

— ATTACHMENT FOR GLASSES AIDS MARKSMAN —

The elderly marksman, on account of changing eyesight, often finds himself handicapped by the limitations of focus. If he uses glasses to overcome a tendency to far-sightedness, the target and front sight are clear but the rear sight is more or less indistinct. If "nearsighted" glasses are used, the target and front sight are blurred while the rear sight is clear and sharp. The little device shown in the drawing, which one sharpshooter has found eliminates these troubles, is made from a narrow piece of card-

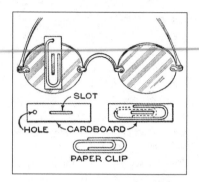

board having a narrow slot cut in the center; it is held to the lens of the "sighting" eye by a wire paper clip.

— A MIRROR AN AID IN ROWING A BOAT —

The young oarsman is apt to experience difficulty in keeping a straight course until he has had some practice. Rowing a boat in a narrow chan-

nel calls for considerable skill to hold a course in midstream. A variation of force in pulling the oars almost instantly results in the rowboat mak-ing a

THE MIRROR ATTACHED TO THE BOAT.

landfall on one of the other of the banks.

The skilled oarsman does not need an appliance that the beginner might welcome. With the aid of a mirror conveniently supported at a suitable angle and height before the oarsman's face, the water, the shores, and approaching boats may be seen with distinctness. The mirror may be set directly in front or a little distance to one side, as shown in the sketch.

— WEBFOOT ATTACHMENTS FOR SWIMMERS —

In order to make the feet more effective in swimming, webfoot devices are frequently used. A simple arrangement for this purpose is shown in the illustration. It consists of three thin sections of metal or wood fastened together on the back side with spring hinges, which tend to remain open thereby keeping all the sections spread out in one straight surface. The center section should be cut to conform closely to the shape of the foot or

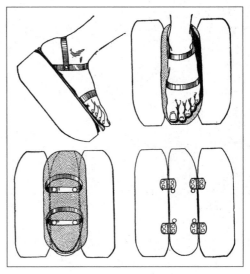

DEVICE FOR ATTACHING TO THE FEET
TO WORK LIKE WEBFEET.

it will produce considerable resistance during the inward stroke of the foot and tend to stop the forward movement of the swimmer. Straps should be provided for attaching the device to the foot; one to fit across the toes and the other adjusted around the ankle by a buckle.

When using the device, the upward or forward stroke of the legs will cause the wings to brush against the water, creating sufficient resistance to overcome the slight force of the springs, thereby pushing the wings parallel with the direction of the stroke. During the opposite, or pushing, stroke, the resistance of the water combined with the opening tendency of the hinges will quickly spread the wings out flat, greatly increasing the effectiveness of the feet.

— DUCK DECOYS MOUNTED ON A FOLDED FRAME —

The duck hunter who wishes to economize by making some of his equipment will be interested in the folding frame for duck decoys, shown in the illustration. It is made of two strips, ¾ in. by 2 in. by 3 ft. 6 in., of softwood, and fitted with a bolt at the middle so that it may be folded for convenience in carrying. The decoys are cut from a sheet of tinned metal and are painted to resemble the game.

DUCK DECOYS MOUNTED ON A FOLDING FRAME MAY BE MADE BY THE HUNTER.

— ❖ ❖ ❖ —

{CHAPTER 5}

TOYS, GAMES, *and* OTHER AMUSEMENTS

—

THE ONE TOY *that* GUARANTEES *a* HAPPY CHILDHOOD

— HOMEMADE ELECTRIC-LOCOMOTIVE MODEL
AND TRACK SYSTEM: THE MOTOR —

The electric locomotive des-cribed may be constructed by boys having average mechanical ability and the necessary tools. However, in any piece of mechanical construction care must be taken to follow the instructions. The material required is inexpensive and the pleasure derived

from such a toy is well worth the time used in its construction.

The making of the outfit may be divided into three parts, the first of which is the motor; second, the truck that is to carry the motor and the body of the car; and third, the track

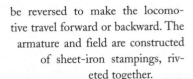

be reversed to make the locomotive travel forward or backward. The armature and field are constructed of sheet-iron stampings, riveted together.

The detailed construction of the armature and its dimensions are shown in *Fig. 2*. The shaft upon which the armature core and commutator are to be rigidly mounted is made of a piece of steel rod, $7/32$ in. in diameter. A portion of this rod, $2\frac{1}{4}$ in. long, is threaded with a fine thread, and two small brass or iron nuts are provided to fit it. The ends of the rod are turned down to a diameter of $\frac{1}{8}$ in. for a distance of $\frac{1}{8}$ in. These are to fit in the bearings that are to be made later.

system upon which the engine is to operate. A side view of the locomotive is shown in *Fig. 1*.

The motor is of the series type, having its field and armature terminals connected to the source of electrical energy through a special reversing switch. By this means, the rotation of the armature may

Fig. 1

SIDE VIEW OF A LOCOMOTIVE DESIGNED TO BE OPERATED WITH EITHER END FORWARD.

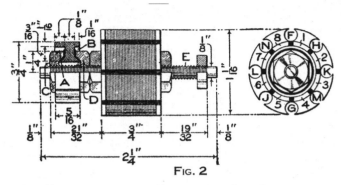

FIG. 2

HOW THE ARMATURE CORE IS MADE OF SOFT-IRON
DISKS FOR THE LAMINATION.

Cut from thin sheet iron a sufficient number of disks 1⅛ in. in
diameter, to make a pile exactly ⅝ in.
thick when they are securely clamped
together. Drill a hole in the center
of each of these disks of such a size
that they will slip on the shaft snugly.
Remove the rough edges from the
disks and see that they are flat. Cut
two disks of the same size from a
piece of 1/16-in. spring brass, and drill
a hole in the center of each so that
they will slip onto the shaft. Place
all these disks on the shaft, with the
brass ones on the outside, and draw
them up tightly with the nuts provided. Be sure to get the laminated
core in the proper position on the
shaft by observing the dimensions
given in the illustration, *Fig. 2.*

After the disks have been fastened, clamp the shaft in the chuck

of a lathe and turn down the edges
of all the disks so that they form a
smooth cylinder, 1 1/16 in. in diameter. Draw a circle on the side of one
of the brass disks, 3/32 in. from the
edge, while the shaft is held in the
chuck. Divide this circle into eight
equal parts and make a center-punch
mark at each division. Drill eight
holes through the core lengthwise
with a 3/16-in. drill. If the centers of
the holes have been properly located,
all the metal on the outside will be
cut away, as shown in the end view
at the right in *Fig. 2.* The width of
the gaps *F, G, H,* etc., thus formed,
should be about 1/16 in. Smooth off
all the edges with a fine file after the
holes are drilled.

A cross-sectional view of the
commutator is shown at the extreme
left, *Fig. 2.* It is constructed as follows:

Clamp one end of a rod of copper or brass, ⅞ in. in diameter and 1¼ in. long, in the chuck of a lathe. Turn the other end down to a diameter of ¾ in., and drill a ½-in. hole through it at the center. Cut away the metal from the end to form a disklike recess.

Cut off a disk, 5/16 in. thick measuring from the finished end, from the piece of stock. Place this disk in a chuck, with the unfinished end exposed, and cut away the metal in a dish form, as shown at *B*. Cut small slots, into which the ends of the wires used in the winding are to be soldered, as shown in 1, 2, 3, etc., in the right-hand view of *Fig. 2*. Obtain two brass nuts, about ¼ in. in thickness, and turn their edges down so that they correspond in form to those shown in *C* and *D*. Divide the disk ring, just made, into eight equal parts by lines drawn across it through the center. Cut eight slots at these points, in the rim of the disk. These cuts should be through the rim. Fill each of the slots with a piece of mica insulation.

Place one of the nuts on the shaft, and then a washer of mica insulation, shown by the heavy lines, near *A* and *B*; then the ring, a second piece of mica, and last the nut, *C*. The latter

should be drawn up tightly so that the insulation in the slots in the disk is opposite the drilled slots in the armature core, as shown in the right-hand view of *Fig. 2*. After the disk has been fastened securely, test it to learn whether it is insulated from the shaft. This is done by means of a battery and bell connected in series, one terminal of the circuit being connected to the disk and the other to the shaft. If the bell rings when these connections are made, the ring and shaft are not insulated. The disk must then be remounted, using new washers of mica insulation. Mica is used because of its ability to withstand a higher degree of heat than most other forms of insulation.

Each of the eight segments of the dished disk should be insulated from the others. Make a test to see if the adjacent commutator segments are insulated from each other, and also from the shaft. If the test indicates that any segment is electrically connected to another, or to the shaft, the commutator must be dismantled and the trouble corrected.

The armature is now ready to be wound. Procure ⅛ lb. of No. 26 gauge insulated copper wire. Insulate the shaft, at *E*, with several turns of thin cloth insulation. Also insulate similarly the nuts holding the armature core and the inside nut holding the commutator. Cut several pieces from the cloth insulation wide enough to cover the walls of the slots in the core, and long enough to extend at least 1/16 in. beyond the core at the ends. Insulate slots *F* and *G* thus, and wind 15 turns of the wire around the core lengthwise, passing the wire back through the slot *F*, across the back end of the core, then forward the front end through slot *G*, and back through *F*, and so on. About 2 in. of free wire should be provided at each end off the coils.

In passing across the ends of the armature, all the turns are placed on one side of the shaft, and so as to pass on the left side, the armature being viewed from the commutator

end. The second coil, which is wound in the same grooves, is then passed on the right side, the third on the left, and so on. After this coil is completed, test it to see if it is connected to the armature core. If such a condition is found, the coil must be rewound. If the insulation is good, wind the second coil, which is wound in the same slots, *F* and *G*, and composed of the same number of turns. Insulate the slots *H* and *J*, and wind two coils of 15 turns each in them, observing the same precautions as with the first two coils. The fifth and sixth coils are placed in slots *K* and *L*, and the seventh and eighth in slots *M* and *N*.

The arrangement of the half coils, slots, and commutator segments is given in detail in *Fig. 3*. Each coil is reduced to one turn in the illustration, in order to simplify it. From an inspection of this diagram it may be seen that the outside end of the second coil in the upper row of figures, at the left end, is connected to the inside end of the fourth coil at segment 1, in the lower row of figures, representing the segments of the

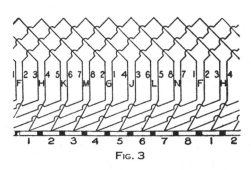

FIG. 3

DIAGRAM FOR THE WINDING OF THE ARMATURE COILS AND THEIR CONNECTION TO THE COMMUTATOR.

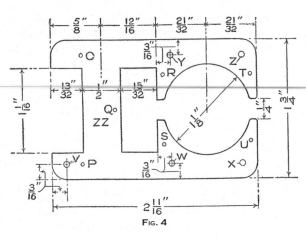

Fig. 4

PATTERN FOR THE FIELD STAMPINGS, SEVERAL PIECES
BEING USED TO MAKE THE DESIRED THICKNESS.

commutator. The outside end of the fourth coil is connected with the inside end of the sixth coil, at segment 2; the outside end of the sixth coil is connected with the inside end of the eighth coil at segment 3; the outside end of the eighth coil is connected to the inside end of the coil 1 at segment 4; the outside end of the coil 1 is connected to the inside end of the coil 3 at segment 5; the outside end of the third coil is connected to the inside end of the fifth coil at segment 6; the outside end of the fifth coil is connected to the inside end of the seventh coil at segment 7; the outside end of the seventh coil is connected to the inside end of the second coil at segment 8, and the outside end of the second coil is connected to segment 1, completing the circuit.

In winding the coils on the core, their ends should be terminated close to the commutator segments to which they are to be connected, in order to simplify the end connections. After all the coils are wound and properly tested, their ends may be connected as indicated. They are then soldered into the slots in the ends of the commutator segments. The completed winding is given a coating of shellac.

The dimensions and form of the field stampings are given in *Fig. 4.*

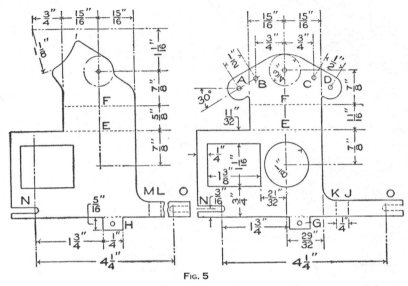

Fig. 5

DETAIL OF THE FIELD-STRUCTURE SUPPORTS, ONE BEING
FOR THE LEFT SIDE AND THE OTHER FOR THE RIGHT.
THE SUPPORTS ARE SHOWN IN PLACE BELOW.

A number of these are cut from thin sheet iron to make a pile ⅝ in. thick when clamped together. The dimensions of the opening to carry the armature should be a little less than that indicated in the sketch, as it will be necessary to true it up after the stampings are fastened together. Use one of the stampings as a pattern and drill seven small holes in each, as indicated by the letters O,

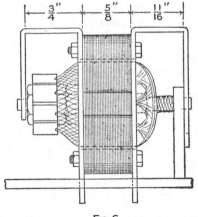

Fig. 6

P, Q, R, S, T, and U. Fasten them together with small rivets, and true up the opening for the armature to a diameter of 1⅛ in. Drill five ⅛-in. holes, as indicated by the letters V, W, X, Y, and Z, to be used in mounting the pieces, which are to form the armature bearings, brush supports, and base of the motor.

Cut two rectangular washers from a piece of thin fiber insulation with outside dimensions of 1⅛ in. and 1¼ in., and inside opening, ½ in. by ⅝ in. Cut open these washers and slip them in position on the portion of the field marked ZZ. Wrap two turns of the cloth insulation about this part, which is to form the field core, and wind the space full of No. 18 gauge enamel-insulated copper wire. Give the completed winding a coat of shellac. The terminals of this winding should be brought out through two holes drilled in one of the fiber washers, one near the core and the other near the outer edge. It is better to have the field terminals at the lower end of the part ZZ than at the upper end.

Now cut two pieces from 1/16 in. sheet brass, similar to those shown in Fig. 5. Place them on opposite sides of the laminated field structure, shown in Fig. 4, and carefully mark the position of the holes, V, W, X, Y, and Z, as indicated in Fig. 4, and drill ⅛-in. holes where the marks were made. Lay out and drill ⅛ in. holes, A, B, C, and D, Fig. 5. Bend the upper portion of the pieces at right angles to the lower portion, along the dotted lines E, and then bend the end of the horizontal portions down along the dotted lines F, until they are parallel with the main vertical parts of the pieces. The latter should be bent so that one forms the left support and the other the right, as shown in Fig. 6.

Bend the projections G and H at right angles to the vertical main parts. The parts at the bottom are bent, one back along the dotted line J and forward on the line K; the other forward on the line L and back on the line M. The pieces are then mounted on the side of the field structure, as shown in Fig. 6; the supports are fastened in place with five small bolts. The grooves N and O, in Fig. 5, are used in mounting the motor on the axles of the truck. They will not be cut until after the truck is constructed.

The brush holders are made of two pieces of hexagonal brass, each 1 in. in length, having a ⅛-in. hole drilled in one end to a depth of

⅞ in., and a threaded hole in the other end, for a small machine screw, as shown in *Fig. 7.* Two holes are drilled and threaded in one side of each of these pieces. These holders are to be mounted by means of screws, through the holes *A, B, C,* and *D, Fig. 5.* Each holder must be insulated from its support. The distance of the holder from its support should be such that the opening in its end is in the center of the commutator. The brushes are made of very fine copper gauze, rolled to form a rod. They are made long enough to extend about ½ in. into the holder when they are resting on the commutator. A small

 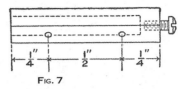

Fig. 7

DETAIL OF THE BRUSH HOLDERS, ONE INCH LONG, WITH HOLES AS SHOWN.

spiral spring is placed on the holder, in back of the end of the brush, and will serve to keep the latter in contact with the commutator.

Temporary connections are made, and the motor is tested with a six-volt battery. The construction of the motor may be modified as to the length of shaft, and other minor details, and may be used for other purposes by fitting it with pulleys, a countershaft, or other transmission devices.

— THE LOCOMOTIVE TRUCK AND CAB —

Successful operation and construction that is feasible, yet of a reasonable standard of workmanship, are the essentials of the locomotive truck and cab described as the second feature of the locomotive and track system under consideration. The materials suggested are those found to be satisfactory, but substitutes may be used if caution is observed. The completed locomotive

is shown in *Figs. 1* and *2.* The outward aspect only is presented and, for the sake of clarity, the portions of the motor and driving rigging attached to it that project below the cab are omitted. These parts are shown assembled in *Fig. 12,* and in detail in the succeeding sketches.

The locomotive, apart from the motor, consists of two main portions: the truck and the cab. Consideration

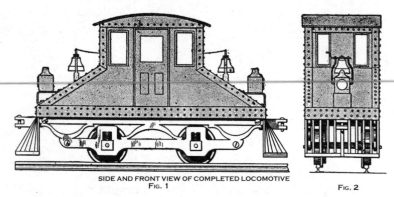

SIDE AND FRONT VIEW OF COMPLETED LOCOMOTIVE
Fig. 1

Fig. 2

THE CONSTRUCTION OF THE CAB IS SUGGESTIVE ONLY, AND THE INVENTIVE
BUILDER MAY DESIGN ONE IN CONFORMITY WITH THE MATERIALS
AVAILABLE OR WITH THE INDIVIDUAL BUILDER'S TASTE.

will be given first to the building of the truck and the fitting of the motor into it. The mechanical and operative features are to be completed before beginning work on the cab, which is merely a hood fixed into place with screws, set onto the wooden cab base.

Begin the construction with the wheels shown in *Fig. 3*. Make the axles of ⅛ in. round steel rod, cut 3³⁄₁₆ in. long.

Turn four wheels of ⅜-in. brass. Drill a ⅛-in. hole in two of them so that they may be forced on the slightly tapered ends of the axle. Drill a ¼-in. hole in each of the other wheels and solder a collar, *A, Fig. 3,* on the inside surfaces of them. Two

fiber bushings, *B*, should be provided to fit in the ¼-in. openings in the wheels and to fit tightly on the ends of the axles. This insulates the wheels on one side of the truck from those on the other. If the rails forming the track are insulated from each other, the current supplied to the motor may pass in on one rail to the two insulated wheels, then to a brush, which bears on the brass collar *A*, through the windings of the motor, through the reversing switch to the other set of wheels, and back to the source of energy over the other rail, as shown in *Fig. 15*.

The wheels of the truck should fit on the axles tightly, because no means other than the friction will

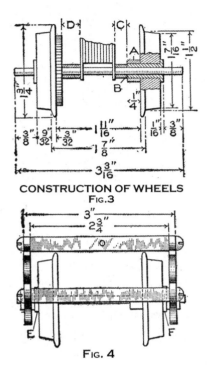

CONSTRUCTION OF WHEELS
Fɪɢ.3

Fɪɢ. 4

be employed in holding them in position. If the ends of the axles are tapered slightly, the wheels may be forced into place and will stay firmly. Do not force them on until the truck is finally assembled.

The truck frame should be constructed next, and its details are shown in *Figs. 4* and *5*. Make two sidepieces of 1/16 in. brass, 9¾ in. long by 1⅝ in. wide, cutting out portions as shown, in order to reduce the weight. This also gives the appearance of leaf springs.

SUCCESSFUL OPERATION, BASED ON FEASIBLE CONSTRUCTION AND A REASONABLE STANDARD OF WORKMANSHIP, IS THE FIRST CONSIDERATION IN THE LOCOMOTIVE. THE DIMENSIONS SHOULD BE OBSERVED CLOSELY IN ORDER THAT THE PARTS MAY BE ASSEMBLED SATISFACTORILY.

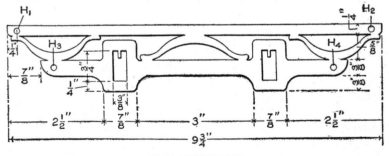

SIDE OF TRUCK
Fɪɢ. 5

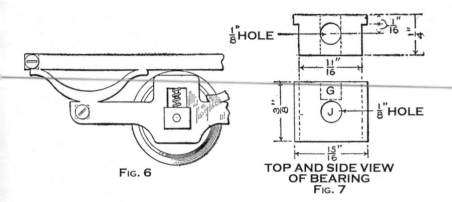

FIG. 6

$\frac{1}{8}$" HOLE

$\frac{11}{16}$"

$\frac{3}{8}$" $\frac{15}{16}$"

$\frac{1}{16}$"

$\frac{1}{4}$"

$\frac{1}{8}$" HOLE

TOP AND SIDE VIEW
OF BEARING
FIG. 7

The two rectangular openings are to accommodate the axle bearings. They should be cut to precise dimensions and their edges should be squared off. Extensions, $\frac{1}{16}$ in. wide, are provided at the middle of the upper edges of each of these openings. They are to hold the upper end of the coil springs, which are set to rest in the holes cut into the bearings, as shown at *G, Fig. 7,* and also in assembled form, *Fig. 6.*

Next, drill four $\frac{1}{8}$ in. holes in each of the sidepieces, as indicated at the letters *H1* to *H4, Fig. 5.* For the cross supports use four pieces of brass rod, $\frac{1}{4}$ in. square, and square off the ends to a length of $2\frac{3}{4}$ in. Drill holes in the center of the ends and tap them for $\frac{1}{8}$ in. machine screws. Join the side and crosspieces as shown in

Fig. 4. Two fiber washers about $\frac{1}{16}$ in. thick should be placed on each axle at *E* and *F*, to hold the wheels from contact with the sidepieces.

Details of a bearing for the axles are shown in *Fig. 7.* The hole *G* carries the lower end of the coil spring and the hole *J* is the bearing socket for the axle. Four spiral springs, having an outside diameter of $\frac{1}{8}$ in. and a length of $\frac{1}{2}$ in. when extended, should be provided. The extensions on the sides of the bearings fit against the inner faces of the sides of the truck. They hold the bearings in position and prevent them from falling out.

The base of the cab is made of wood, dimensioned as in *Fig. 10.* The center of the piece is cut away so as to provide a space for the motor, which extends above the upper edge

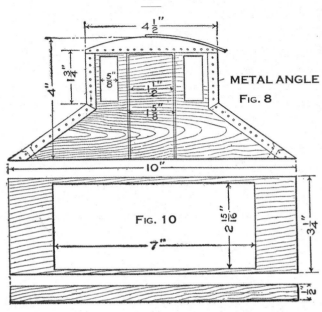

METAL ANGLE
FIG. 8

FIG. 10

BOTTOM OF LOCOMOTIVE CAB

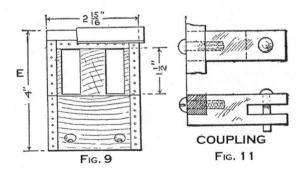

E

FIG. 9

COUPLING
FIG. 11

of the truck as shown in *Fig. 12.*
This block is fastened in place by four
screws through the upper crosspieces

at the ends of the truck. The base
should be made and fitted into place
temporarily so as to be available in

observing how the motor and its fittings are placed in relation to it. For convenience in assembling the parts of the truck and setting the motor, it may be removed readily.

Assembling the truck, including the motor, probably requires the most painstaking effort of any part of the construction of the locomotive. Too great care cannot be taken with it, as the dimensions are carefully worked out and failure to observe them may cause errors sufficient to make the locomotive unserviceable. Before undertaking this work it would be wise to examine carefully the arrangement of the parts as shown in *Fig. 12*. The upper view shows the relation of the driving gears in mesh and the lower view shows the machinery of the truck as seen from above.

The power from the motor is transmitted to one set of wheels by

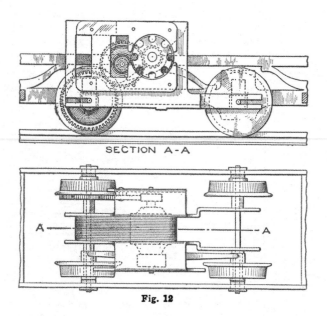

SECTION A-A

Fig. 12

INSTALLATION OF THE MOTOR, SHOWING GEARS
AND SWITCH CONTACT SPRING.

means of a small gear on the armature shaft engaging an intermediate gear, which in turn engages a large gear attached to the inside of one of the truck wheels. The center of the armature shaft is $1^5/16$ in. from the center of the power axle, when both axles are in the slots provided in the motor frame, *Fig. 12*. The gears for the transmission may now be selected. The gear on the armature shaft should be as small, and that on the axle as large, as practicable. The intermediate gear should be of such a size that it will close the space between the small gear on the armature shaft and the large one on the axle. Gears suitable for the transmission may be purchased at a clock store for a small sum. If gears of exactly the proper size cannot be obtained readily, the position of the intermediate gear may be adjusted to produce a proper meshing of the gears.

Mount the small gear on the end of the armature shaft away from the commutator so that there will be about $1/16$ in. clearance between the outside surface and the shoulder at the end of the shaft. Fit it on tightly so that no other means of fastening will be necessary. Mount the large gear on the inside surface of one of the truck wheels as shown in *Figs. 3* and *12*. Place the axle of the truck into the proper grooves in the motor frame, and mark the position of the center of the intermediate gear, when it engages the other gear. Drill a hole in the extension on the motor frame, provided as a support, to fit a small bolt with which the intermediate gear is fastened.

Place a washer between the gear and the piece upon which it is mounted and a locknut on the threaded end of the bolt, drawing it up so that the gear has only sufficient play.

The slots in the motor frame to fit the free axle may now be cut, as shown in *Fig. 12*. Place the motor in position on the axle so that the gears all mesh properly. Fit tubes of insulating material with an outside diameter of $3/8$ in. at *C* and *D, Fig. 3,* and as also shown in *Fig. 12*. Insulation tubes should be provided for the second axle so as to hold the motor in position and to keep the wheels in line. In mounting the various parts sufficient play should be allowed to prevent excessive friction.

The reversing switch, which is to be mounted on the underside of the motor frame, is shown in *Figs. 13* and *14*. It is provided with a control

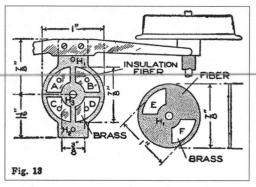

Fig. 13

DETAILS OF THE SWITCH, SHADED PORTIONS
BEING OF FIBER INSULATION.

lever that projects out from under the truck frame. A small movement of the lever will produce the necessary changes in the connections. The operation of the switch may be understood readily from the diagram shown in *Fig. 15*. The moving element of the switch carries two pieces of copper, *E* and *F*, which connect the four stationary pieces of copper, *A, B, C,* and *D,* when the lever attached to *E* and *F* is moved to either side of its central position. The pieces of copper that are moved—*E* and *F*—are shown outside of the stationary pieces in *Fig. 15* for purposes of a diagram only, and are actually directly over the ring formed by the stationary pieces.

The operation of the switch is as follows: Assuming that the current enters at a terminal marked 1 and leaves at the terminal marked 2, then the direction of the current in the armature and series field will be as indicated in the diagrams. The direction of the current in the series-field winding is different in the two cases, which will result in opposite rotation of the armature.

The base of the switch is made of 1/16 in. fiber insulation; its dimensions are shown in *Fig. 13*. It is to be mounted on the two pieces projecting outward on the underside of the motor frame, as shown in *Fig. 14*. Drill a small hole in each of these projections, as indicated by the letters *H1* and *H2,* and tap them to take a small machine screw. Next drill two holes, *H1* and *H2, Fig. 13,* in the piece of insulation, with centers the same distance apart as those drilled in the projections. One end of this piece of insulation is extended to form a mounting for a thin brass spring, the ends of which

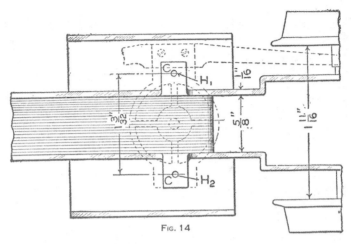

FIG. 14

VIEW OF THE UNDERSIDE OF THE MOTOR, SHOWING
HOW SWITCH IS FIXED INTO PLACE.

bear on the brass collars insulated from the axles, as shown in *Figs. 12* and *13*. The form of this spring and the method of mounting it are also shown in *Fig. 13*.

The sections that come into contact in the switch are made as follows: Mount four pieces of thin copper or brass on the fiber base with rivets having their heads countersunk. Cut a disk, 1 in. in diameter, from a piece of sheet insulation and drill a hole *H1*, in the center of it. Also drill a similar hole, *H3*, in the center of the switch base. Mount two pieces of copper or brass, *E* and *F*, on the underside of this disk. The

edges and ends of all six pieces of metal should be rounded off so that the pieces *E* and *F* will move freely over those on the base. The disk, or upper part of the switch, may be attached to the base by means of a small bolt placed through the holes at the center. A small spiral spring should be placed between the disk and the lower end of this bolt so as to keep the pieces of metal on the disk in contact with those on the base. Attach a small handle to the disk so that it will extend out on one side of the truck. Fix the switch into place by bolts through the holes *H1* and *H2*, *Fig. 14*, on the bottom of

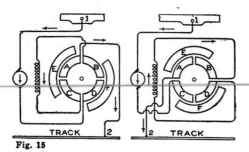

Fig. 15

DIAGRAMS OF THE REVERSING OF MOTOR
BY SHIFTING SWITCH TO FORM CONTACT
BETWEEN PAIRS OF BRASS SECTORS
SET IN THE FIBER SWITCH BASE.

the motor frame. The electrical connections should be made as shown in *Fig. 15*.

The detail of the couplers is shown in *Fig. 11*. They are made of brass fitted to the upper crosspieces and fixed to them by machine screws. "Cowcatchers" may be made for the ends of the locomotive. Sheet metal, corrugated appropriately and bent to the proper shape, will afford the easiest method of making them. Those shown in *Figs. 1* (page 180) are made of strips soldered together, and also the upper crosspieces; they are strengthened by a cross-strip at the bottom, opposite the point.

The cab is to be made apart from the truck and is to fit upon the base, as shown in *Figs. 1* and *2*. It is fixed

into place by four screws and can be removed easily for examination of the locomotive mechanism. The dimensions for the cab are shown in *Figs. 8* and *9*, and may be varied by the builder.

Sheet metal or wood may be used in the construction, and the joints soldered on the inside or riveted, as shown in the illustration. The window and door openings may be cut out or painted on. Small bells may be mounted on the ends of the cab, adding to its appearance. The headlights shown in *Figs. 1* and *2* may be cut from wood or made of sheet metal. Lightbulbs may be installed, and their voltage should correspond to that of the motive energy. The terminals for the sockets of the headlight lamps should be connected to the frame of the truck and to the spring, which bears upon the brass collars on the wheels, which are insulated from the axles, as shown in *A, Fig. 3*.

This completes the locomotive in all essential details and it is ready to be placed upon the track to be tested.

— THE TRACK SYSTEM —

Operation of the electric-loco-motive model described in the previous article is feasible only on a properly constructed track system. This equipment, including curves and switches, is to be described in this article. Two functions are to be performed by the track system: It must serve as a support and guide for the locomotive and provide a path over which the current from the source of energy is supplied to the motor within the locomotive and returned to the source. On this basis, then, the construction may be divided into two parts: the mechanical and the electrical features. If the mechanical construction is not practical and accurate, the locomotive will not operate satisfactorily. The electrical connections must be given due care also.

The track should be of uniform gauge; the joints should be solid and free from irregularities, which cause "bumping" in passing over them. The material used should be stiff, so that it will retain its form, and preferably nonrusting. The rails must be insulated from each other, and proper means must be provided for making suitable electrical connections between the various sections.

The construction of a straight and a curved section of track, together with a switch and signal adaptable to various places on the system, will be considered in detail.

The straight sections may be made any suitable length. Sections 16 in. long will be found convenient, because the metal pieces forming the rails may be bent into shape easily when they are short rather than long. The possibility of various combinations of straight and curved sections in a given area is increased by having the sections shorter. The rails may be made from tinned sheet-metal strips by taking pieces 16 in. long by 1½ in. wide and bending them into the form shown in *Fig. 1*. The rails should be mounted on small wooden sleepers, ½ by ½ by 4 in., by means of small nails or preferably small screws. The distance between the centers of the rails should be 2 in. The sections of track may be fastened together at the ends by means of a special connector, shown in *Fig. 2*, made from thin metal, preferably spring brass. The type of connector shown in *Fig. 2* will not prevent the sections from pulling apart. To prevent this, a second connector similar to

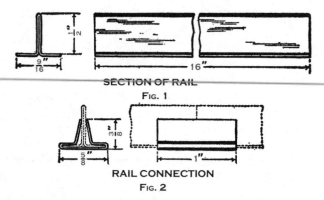

SECTION OF RAIL

FIG. 1

RAIL CONNECTION

FIG. 2

SHAPE THE RAILS FROM SHEET-METAL STRIPS, 1 1/2 INCHES WIDE
BY 16 INCHES LONG, TO THE FORM SHOWN IN FIG. 1.
THE RAIL CONNECTIONS ARE FORMED
AS SHOWN IN FIG. 2.

that shown in *Fig. 3* should be made. The sleepers at the ends of each section should have one side beveled as shown, and these edges should be exactly 1 in. from the end of the rails. A spring clip should be made, similar to that shown, which will slip down on the inside of the end sleepers and hold the sections together.

A better form of rail is shown in *Figs. 3* and *4,* but it is somewhat more difficult to construct. In this case, instead of bending the piece of metal forming the rail over on itself and closing the space entirely, the metal is bent over a round form, such as a piece of wire. The form may be removed, leaving an opening through the upper part of the rail from end to end. This gives a better form to the tread of the rail and at the same time provides an easy means of connecting the ends of the rails, as shown in *Fig. 5*. Small metal pins, about 1 in. long and of such a diameter that they will just fit the circular opening in the top of the rail, are provided. One of these pins should be fastened in one rail at each end of a section, making sure that no rail has more than one pin in it, and that the arrangement of pins and rails corresponds in all sections. With proper care the various sections should fit together equally well, and they may be held together as shown in *Fig. 3.*

The curved sections may be made from rails similar to those described above, but some difficulty will be experienced in bending them into a curve because of the necessity of bending the lower flange on edge. The difficulty may be overcome by crimping in the inner edge of the lower flange and expanding the outer edge by hammering it on a smooth surface. The radius of the curve to which the inner rail should be bent in order to give a section of convenient length, and not too abrupt a curve, is 21 in. The circumference of such a circle is approximately 132 in., which, divided into eight sections, gives 16½ in. as the length of the inner rail of each section. Because the tread of the track is 2 in., the radius of the curve of the outer rail will be 23 in. The circumference of the circle formed by the outer rail is 145 in., which divided into eight sections gives 18⅛ in. as the length of the outer rail of each section. These curved rails may be mounted on sleepers, their ends being held in place, and the various sections fastened together, just as in the case of the straight sections.

Some trouble may be experienced

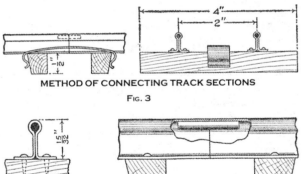

METHOD OF CONNECTING TRACK SECTIONS

Fig. 3

SECTION OF RAIL
Fig. 4

END CONNECTION OF RAILS
Fig. 5

A spring clamp for the joints in the sections is shown in Fig. 3. An improved form of rail is shown in Fig. 4, and in Fig. 5 is indicated the method of joining its sections.

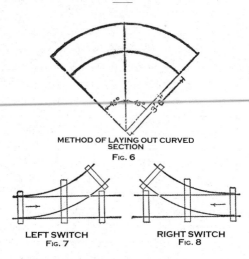

METHOD OF LAYING OUT CURVED SECTION
Fig. 6

LEFT SWITCH
Fig. 7

RIGHT SWITCH
Fig. 8

LAY OUT THE SWITCHES AND CURVES, FULL SIZE, AND FIT THE RAILS TO THE CURVES ACCURATELY.

in getting the curved rails properly shaped, and it would be a good plan to lay them out full size. Draw two circles on a smooth surface having diameters of 42 and 46 in., respectively, and divide each of the latter into eight equal parts. The form of the curve between these division lines and the lengths of the curves will correspond to the shape and lengths of the rails forming the curved sections of the track. The pieces should be cut slightly longer than required, and after they are bent into shape their length can be determined precisely and extra portions cut off. Each curved section will cor-respond to ⅛ of the complete circle, or 45 degrees, as shown in *Fig. 6.*

The switches for the track may be of two kinds: left or right. They are named according to whether the car is carried to the left or right of the main track with reference to the direction in which the car moves in entering the switch. A left switch is shown in *Fig. 7,* and a right switch in *Fig. 8,* the direction of movement being indicated by arrows.

A detailed drawing of a right switch is shown in *Fig. 9.* Rail *A* corresponds in form and length to the outer rail of one of the curved sections previously described. Rail *B* corresponds to the inner rail of one of the curved sections, except that 2 ½ in. of straight rail is added at the left end. Rail *C* is a straight portion of rail, 18 in. in length, with a part of the base cut away at the switch. Rail *D* is a section of straight rail, 15½ in. in length, with the base cut away where it crosses rail *A*. The ends of rails *D* and *A* are hinged at the points *E* and *F*, 3¾ in. from the left end, with pins driven into the ties. The outside edges of the pieces *G* and *H* are filed off so they will fit up against the rails *C* and *B* respectively. Both the pieces *G* and *H* are attached to a strip of fiber insulating material, *I*, at their left-hand ends, in such a way

that when the piece *H* is against the rail *B*, the piece *G* is away from the rail *C* about 3/16 in. When the end of the piece *G* is drawn over against the rail *C*, the end of the piece *H* is drawn away from the rail *B* about 3/16 in. With these two combinations the car may be made to move along the main track or to the right on a curved track. The two long sleepers *J* and *K* are to provide a mounting for the switch-control lever and signal.

The rail *A* is not continuous where the rail *D* crosses it, but is broken as shown in the figure. A small notch should be cut in the surface off the rail *D* where it crosses the rail *A*, for the flange of the car wheels to roll

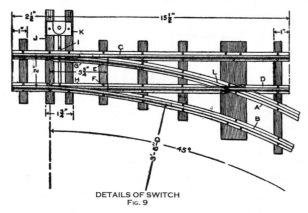

DETAILS OF SWITCH
Fig. 9

THE CROSSINGS OF THE RAILS MUST BE FITTED CAREFULLY AND THE MOVABLE SECTIONS G AND H ARRANGED TO MAKE THE PROPER CONTACTS.

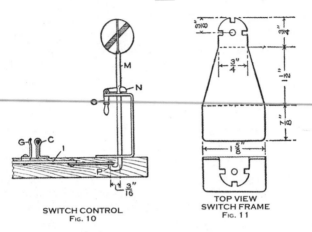

SWITCH CONTROL
FIG. 10

TOP VIEW
SWITCH FRAME
FIG. 11

THE SIGNALS INDICATE THE OPEN OR CLOSED CONDITION
OF THE SWITCH BY THE SMALL DISK, WHICH IS
REGULATED BY THE LEVER SWITCH CONTROL.

through when the car is moving onto or off the switch. The sections of the rails *A* and *D* must be connected electrically. Rail *A* must be connected to rail *C*, and rail *B* to rail *D*.

It is obvious from an inspection of *Fig. 9*, at *L*, that rail *D* will be connected to rail *A* when the car is on the switch, the car wheels passing over the point *L*, and a short circuit will result. This may be prevented by insulating the short section of the rail *D* at this point from the remainder of the rail, but the length of the insulated section must not be greater than the distance between the wheels on one side of the car. Otherwise the circuit through the motor would be broken. If this is the case, and the car stops on the main track with both wheels on the insulated section, it would be impossible to start the locomotive until one wheel was moved to a live part of the rail.

The switch control is shown in *Fig. 10*, and the letters *C*, *G*, and *I* correspond to those given in *Fig. 9*. A ⅛ in. rod, about 4 in. in length, is bent into the form shown at *M*. It is mounted in a frame, the details of which are shown in *Fig. 11*. A small arm, *N*, with a hinged handle, *O*, is soldered to the rod, after the rod is placed in position in the switch frame. The arm *N* and the lever *P* should be parallel with each other.

If properly constructed, the handle O will drop into the notches in the top of the switch frame, and prevent the rod M from turning. A connection should be made from the lever P to the end of the piece I, which will result in the switch being operated when the rod M is rotated one-fourth of a turn. After this connection is made, the frame of the switch should be fastened to the ends of the long sleepers, which were provided when the track part of the switch was constructed. Two small disks, mounted at right angles to each other, will serve as signals when properly painted, or as an indication of the open or closed position of the switch. The speed of the car on the track may be controlled by inserting resistance in series with the battery or source of electrical energy, or by altering the value of the voltage between the rails, by changing the connections of the cells forming the battery. The direction of movement of the locomotive cannot be changed unless the car is turned end for end, or the connections of the armature or field winding—not both—are reversed. The switch on the bottom of the locomotive reverses these connections.

A small rheostat, which will give the desired resistance, may be constructed as follows: obtain a piece of

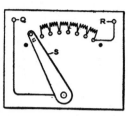

Fig. 12

hardwood 4 by 5 in., and ⅜ in. in thickness. Lay out a curve on this piece, as shown in *Fig. 12* by the row of small circles. Procure eight round-head brass machine screws, about ⅛ in. in diameter and ¾ in. in length, and 16 nuts to fit them. Drill eight ⅛ in. holes along the curve, spacing them ⅜ in. apart. File the heads of the screws in these holes. Make a metal arm, S, and mount it on a small bolt passing through a hole drilled at the center from which the curve was drawn, along which the screws were mounted. This arm should be of such a length that its outer end will move over the heads of the screws. Mount two binding posts, Q and R, to the bolt holding the arm S in place. Connect small resistance coils between the screws, starting with screw No. 2; screw No. 1 corresponds to an open circuit shown in contact with the arm S. Two stops, indicated by the black spots, should be provided to prevent the arm from moving back of screw No. 1 or beyond screw No. 8. The board may now be mounted on a suitable hollow base, and the rheostat is complete.

Two binding posts should be mounted on the ties of one section of the track, and one of them electrically connected to each of the two rails, which will give an easy means of making the necessary electrical connections to the source of energy. After careful examination to make certain that the locomotive is in running order, a test run may be made. If the locomotive operates properly and difficulty is experienced when it is placed upon the track, check up thoroughly on all rail connections, insulations, and other elements in the electrical equipment. Cars of a proper gauge may be coupled to the locomotive, and "runs" made as extensively as the track system will permit.

TOPS, PUZZLES *and* GAMES

— AN AUSTRIAN TOP —

All parts of the top are wood and they are simple to make. The handle is a piece of pine 5¼ in. long, 1¼ in. wide, and ¾ in. thick. A handle, ¾ in. in diameter, is formed on one end allowing only 1¼ in. of the other end to remain rectangular in shape. Bore a ¾-in. hole in this end for the top. A 1/16-in. hole is bored in the edge to enter the large hole as shown. The top can be cut from a broom handle or a round stick of hardwood.

To spring the top, pass one end of a stout cord about 2 ft. long through the 1/16-in. hole and wind

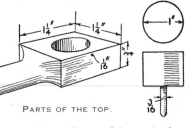

PARTS OF THE TOP.

it on the small part of the top in the usual way, starting at the bottom and winding upward. When the shank is covered, set the top in the ¾-in. hole. Take hold of the handle with the left hand and the end of the cord with the right hand, give a quick pull on the cord, and the top will jump clear of the handle and spin vigorously.

— WILD TOP —

The amateur wood turner can easily make a wooden top that will hop across the floor and howl. The top consists of a hollow two-piece wooden ball, which is turned to form a piece of soft dowel. A hole is drilled through the shell of the ball at one of the center marks and fitted with a hardwood peg having a slightly rounded end, as shown. A ¾-in.

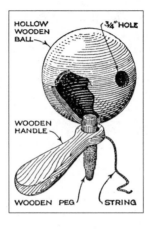

hole is drilled at right angles to the peg. To spin this top, a wooden handle, such as the one shown, is required. The top string is wound around the peg and the end is brought through the hole in the handle, as indicated. A quick jerk on the string sets the top in motion and pulls it free of the handle.

— A RING-AND-PEG PUZZLE —

A short piece of board is provided with ten short wooden pegs. Eight wooden disks are drilled through the center to fit over the pegs easily; four of the disks are white and the others are either made of dark wood or painted black. When the block and disks have been made, the disks are placed on the first eight pegs, white disks alternately

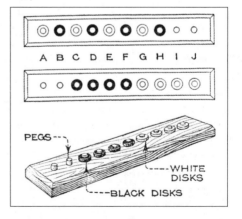

with black. The last two pegs are left vacant. The object of the puzzle is to get the four white and four black disks grouped together without leaving any pegs vacant, except two at either end. The disks must be moved two at a time and the rearrangement made in four moves, two disks at a time.

The upper drawing shows the arrangement of the disks at the commencement of the puzzle and the center one shows how the disks should appear at the conclusion. The secret of the puzzle is as follows: Move the disks *B* and *C* to the vacant pegs *I* and *J*; *E* and *F* to *B* and *C*; *H* and *I* to *E* and *F*; and *A* and *B* to *H* and *I*. This gives the necessary transposition, and the disks can be returned to their original positions by reversing the movements.

— BEWITCHED-CUBE PUZZLE —

This simple puzzle, which requires six numbered cubes, will require considerable concentration to "make it come out right." Six wooden cubes are provided and numbered on each of their six faces from 1 to 6, the order of numbering being different for each cube, as shown in *Figs. 1* and *2*.

The object is to arrange the six cubes in any shape—preferably in a straight line—as in *Fig. 3*, so that the figures 1, 2, 3, 4, 5, and 6 will appear at once on the top, bottom, front, back, right-, and left-hand faces. They will not be in consecutive order, but the six numbers must each show from every side. Separating the cubes slightly will show the right- and left-hand faces. When

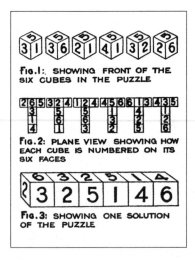

FIG.1: SHOWING FRONT OF THE SIX CUBES IN THE PUZZLE

FIG.2: PLANE VIEW SHOWING HOW EACH CUBE IS NUMBERED ON ITS SIX FACES

FIG.3: SHOWING ONE SOLUTION OF THE PUZZLE

properly arranged, the blocks may be transposed hundreds of different ways in a straight line, fulfilling the conditions each time.

— Mothball Puzzle as Window-advertising Novelty —

A druggist recently puzzled thousands with a novel window display. A small white ball displayed in a show window in a 1-in. glass tube about 10 in. long would sink to the bottom then slowly ascend, only to sink as before. A sign reading "What Makes It Move?" kept the crowd guessing. The tube was apparently filled with water. The construction is simple.

The tube is about three-quarters full of carbonated soda water. The white ball is an ordinary mothball. The ball sinks, and when it becomes soaked gradually as it lowers, bubbles of gas cling to it carrying it to the top of the solution. There, the gas escapes, destroying the ball's buoyancy and causing it to sink again. This process is repeated over and over again.

— Wooden Key-and-Ring Puzzle —

A puzzle that will baffle the ingenuity of many a skilled mechanic is illustrated by the drawing. The mystery of course is as to how the two blocks are put together. The small block, or key, may be made to slide very tightly into the hole in the larger one; it is thus apparent that it could not have been fitted in by any cutting process. The frame, or ring, should be made

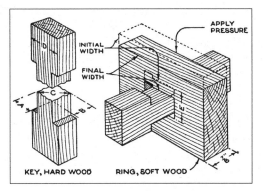

NOT ONLY THE AMATEUR BUT EVEN THE SKILLED MECHANIC MAY BE MYSTIFIED BY A PUZZLE THAT ANY BOY CAN MAKE OUT OF TWO WOODEN BLOCKS.

of good straight-grained softwood, and the key of hardwood, both of

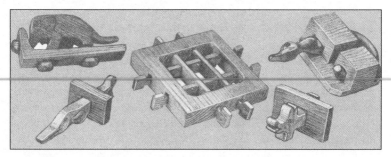

VARIOUS WOODEN ANIMALS ARE SHOWN HELD IN WOODEN FRAMES, OR "TRAPS," ALL MADE ON THE SAME PRINCIPLE AS THE SIMPLE PUZZLE. IN THE CENTER IS A RATHER MORE COMPLICATED SPECIMEN, BUT ALSO MADE WITHOUT JOINTS OF ANY KIND.

about the same thickness. The surface of both blocks may be planed smooth so that the blocks can be inspected all over for glued joints; there are no joints in either block.

The method of making the puzzle is as follows: Cut the two blocks to shape outside, and cut notches in the sides of the key so that dimension A in the drawing will be just slightly less than dimension B. Now caliper the diagonal of this smaller section, thus giving the dimension C. Cut a rectangular hole in the center of the large block of a width E, just slightly greater than this diagonal, and a length greater than the width D of the smaller block. Some notches can be made in the sides of the rectangular hole, as illustrated; these have nothing to do with the puzzle except

that they are quite likely to lead the victim astray in guessing at its solution. If the hole is made according to these directions, the small block can be thrust through it and turned upon its side so as to occupy the position it will have in the completed puzzle.

The ring block is now thoroughly steamed or boiled in water for one hour. It is then gripped in a good bench vise, with the key fitted into it, and screwed up as tightly as possible. When the wood has yielded a little the vise is screwed up again, and so on until the ring is compressed to grip the key tightly between its two sides. Then let the puzzle stand in the vise until the next day, when it will be dry and can be removed. Two stout, hard clamps can be used instead of a vise.

After one's friends have been sufficiently mystified by the question of how the two blocks were ever put together in this fashion, it is a simple matter to place the puzzle in boiling water again for about 20 minutes, when the ring block will swell to its original dimensions and the key can be taken out quite easily.

The photograph shows a number of modifications of the puzzle. All of them involve the same principle as the simple key-and-ring puzzle. Such a collection will form a curious ornament to the craftsman's shop or home.

— A PERPETUAL-MOTION PUZZLE —

The fallacy of perpetual motion is now so generally understood that the description of a new scheme for attaining it is justified only in so far as it may be instructive. The sketch illustrates such a device, apparently successful, and the discovery of the error in it is both instructive and interesting.

Mount a horseshoe magnet on a wooden base, and into the base cut a continuous groove along the three sides of a triangle opposite the poles of the magnet, *N* and *S*. Suspend a long, narrow bar magnet on a universal joint from a standard. A pin projects into the groove from the lower end, which is its north pole, and can move only along the triangular course.

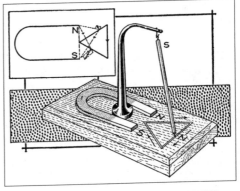

THE INTERACTION BETWEEN POLES OF THE MAGNETS CAUSES THE TRAVELER TO MOVE AROUND THE TRIANGLE.

Start the device with the suspended magnet in the position shown. The lower end will tend to move in the direction of the arrows, because in so doing it is getting farther away from the repelling north pole of the horseshoe magnet and nearer to the attracting south pole, which will bring it to the corner of the triangle in the foreground. It will next move down the side as indicated by the arrow, because along that line it is nearer to the attracting south than the repelling north pole. When it reaches the end of its trip, at the angle between the poles of the magnet, the attraction and repulsion will be balanced, but a slight jar will carry the traveler beyond the angle.

The third leg of the triangle will be covered similarly, the north pole repelling the traveler. On this basis the motion should continue indefinitely, but a test will show that it will not do so.

The corners of the triangle should be rounded slightly, and it would be better to use several hanging magnets, flexibly connected, so that when one is at the dead center the others will carry the traveler on.

— How to Make an Inlaid Checkerboard —

In the checkerboard design illustrated, each square is a miniature checkerboard in itself, composed of 64 light and dark squares.

For the dark squares, 16 strips each of ebony and mahogany, $3/16$ by $\frac{1}{2}$ by 17 in., are needed. As many strips of maple and oak of the same size will be needed for the white squares, a total of 64 strips. Using alternate strips of light and dark-colored wood, eight strips are glued together to make a laminated piece $1\frac{1}{2}$ in. wide. From this piece, after it has been glued and both faces sanded, $3/16$-in. sections are cut transversely, and eight such sections glued together to form a square of the board, using the gluing jig

illustrated for the purpose. The sections are cut $3/16$ in. wide in a miter box. The strips are glued together so that light squares will come next to dark ones, the mahogany and ebony being used for the "black" squares, and oak and maple for the "white" ones.

All of the gluing operations should be done in a warm room and the stock should also be warmed. The wooden gluing jig should be made long enough to accommodate about eight squares at a time, each being separated from the other by a strip of paper. By rubbing the edges of the jig with paraffin, the glue will be prevented from sticking, and the blocks can easily be removed.

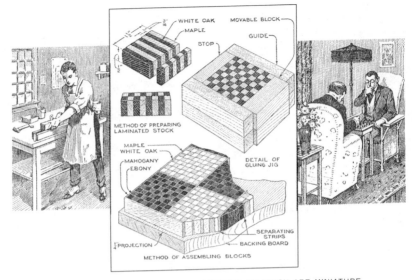

AN INLAID CHECKERBOARD, THE SQUARES OF WHICH ARE MINIATURE
CHECKERBOARDS THEMSELVES, BEING BUILT UP OF
LIGHT- AND DARK-COLORED WOODS.

For a backing board use a ½-in. pine board, 14½ in. square. Nail and glue two ¹⁄₁₆ by ½ in. red-oak strips near two edges, to form a right angle, and also prepare seven strips of red oak, ¹⁄₁₆ by ½ by 12½ in., and 56 similar strips, 1½ in. long. Paint the face of the board with glue and place in the angle formed by the strips at the edge, which should be at the lower left corner, one of the dark squares, with an ebony square in the corner, and the grain running parallel with the left edge of the board.

Glue one of the short separator strips to the upper edge, and then place a light block in position, with the grain at right angles to that of the dark, and with the light maple square in the lower left corner. When the row of eight squares has been placed against the pine strip at the left, glue one of the long separator strips to the inner edge of the row and start building up the next row. When all the blocks are assembled, enclose the two open sides with strips, and clamp them tightly until the glue sets.

When the glue has dried thoroughly, trim the ends of the separator strips flush, and glue 1/16-in. strips around the remaining two sides. Cut off the edges of the backing board to leave a 1/4-in. projection, and scrape and sand the surface smooth. Wax it or, if a higher gloss is desired, fill with a light paste filler and give three coats of varnish.

— A WIRE-WALKING TOY —

Boys can easily make a toy featuring a daring, wire-walking performer who, unmindful of the fact that a misstep may mean destruction, keeps on going, back and forth—so long as the motor runs or the crank is turned. The wire is stretched, not across Broadway, but between two 1- by 1-in. standards held upright by guy cords or fixed to a baseboard. They are fitted with forked tops, in A and B, and pulley wheels, C and D. A wire, F, is fastened to two of the prongs, in E, and a black thread, G, runs over the pulley wheels. A carriage, I, is formed from a 12-in. length of stiff wire, and weighted, in L, to balance upon the tight wire. The figure K is cut from stiff paper and made to turn upon the carriage upright J, and braced with thread, in H. Thus the figure is always drawn forward, revolving on the support J at the end of each trip. Power to turn the thread is transmitted from a hand crank or motor, M, by means of the double pulley wheel in D.

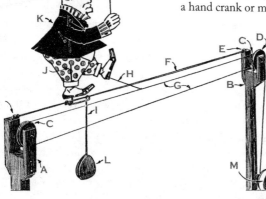

ADAPTED TO WINDOW DISPLAYS, THIS AMUSING TOY HAS AN ADVERTISING VALUE.

— AUTO HORN FOR CHILD'S PLAY VEHICLE —

A baking-powder or other tin can may be used to make the small automobile horn, shown in the illustration, for use on a child's coaster wagon. The device consists of a toothed wheel operating against several metal pawls within the can, and the warning sound is produced by turn-

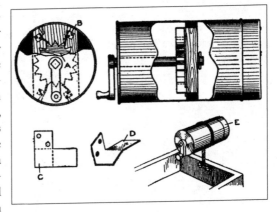

THIS SMALL AUTO HORN WAS MADE OF A TINNED CAN FITTED WITH A NOTCHED WHEEL AND PAWLS.

ing a small crank at the end of the can. The can is fixed to the side of the vehicle by means of a wire or strap-iron bracket, as shown in the sketch in E.

A piece of wood is fitted into the can to support the ratchet wheel. It is bored to carry a shaft, which bears in the end of the can, and at the exposed end of which is fixed a crank. A disk of wood, about ½ in. thick, is cut to have a notched edge as shown in A. The notched wheel is placed upon the shaft and fastened securely to it so that the ratchet

wheel revolves with the shaft when the crank on the shaft is turned. Four small pawls of sheet metal are fixed on the inner support, as shown in B. They are made by cutting pieces of metal to the shape shown in C, and folding them, as shown in D. They are fastened to the support with small screws or nails. The cover is placed on the end of the can when the device is used. The action of the ratchet wheel against the pawls produces a loud grating sound, resembling that of a horn of the siren type.

— "Moving-picture" Toy for Children —

A very interesting "moving-picture" toy for the small child can be made of cigar boxes, some wire, babbitt or lead, and a few pieces of pipe cane.

A rectangular opening is cut in the bottom of a cigar box of the size made to contain 100 cigars. A piece of window glass, cut to fit, is placed behind the opening and held in place by tacks. A frame made of cigar-box wood, shown at the upper right, fits neatly into the box. This holds the picture ribbon against the glass and carries the spools on which the ribbon is wound. A piece of pipe can is mounted at each corner of the frame to serve as a roller.

The spindles, one of which has a crank formed on one end, are made of No. 9 galvanized wire, and are provided with babbitt or lead "keys" to turn the wooden spools on which the ribbon is wound. To make these keys, a portion of the wire should be flattened as shown. A cork stopper with a groove cut in the top and a hole drilled through the center is pushed on the wire directly underneath the flattened portion. A cup is formed by wrapping heavy paper around this cork, into which the bab-

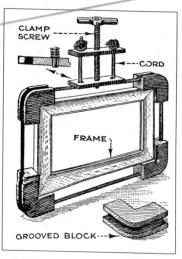

A "MOVING-PICTURE" TOY THAT IS INSTRUCTIVE AS WELL AS AMUSING CAN BE VERY EASILY MADE FROM SCRAP MATERIALS.

bitt can be poured. The wooden spools upon which the ribbon is wound can be made from old film spools, cut at one end to fit the babbitt key.

Children can be amused for hours with this little toy, which can be made instructive as well as amusing. Pictures cut from the comic or rotogravure sections of newspapers and pasted to the ribbon in order make very interesting moving pictures of this kind, although, of course, any suitable pictures may be used.

— A MINIATURE FIGHTING TANK THAT HURDLES TRENCHES —

Among the engines of war in action on land, probably none has created greater interest than the now famous "fighting tank." According to reports, this machine pours out missiles of destruction on the enemy from armored turrets, and crawls over trenches, shell craters, and similar obstructions like a fabled giant creature of prehistoric ages. The tank described in this article, while not as deadly as those on the battlefields of Europe, performs remarkable feats of hurdling trenches and crawling over obstructions large in proportion to its size. The model, as shown in the heading sketches, is fully armored, and has a striking resemblance to these war monsters. The turret is mounted with a magazine gun that fires 20 projectiles automatically as the tank makes it way over the rough ground. The motive power for the tractor bands is furnished by linked rubber bands, stretched by a winding drum and ratchet device on the rear axle, as shown in *Fig. 1*. When the ratchet is released the rear axle drives the fluted wheels on it, and they in turn drive the tractor bands as shown in the side elevation,

Fig. 6. The wire-wrapped flywheel conserves the initial power of the rubber-band motor and makes its action more nearly uniform.

The tank will run upward of 10 ft. on the rubber-motor power, depending on the size and number of the bands used. The gun is fired by a spring hammer, activated by a rubber band. The trigger device is shown in *Fig. 1*. The pulley *A* is belted, with cord, to the front axle. Four pins on its inner side successively engage the wire trigger, drawing it out of the gun breech *B*, and permitting another shell to drop into place. As the pulley revolves, the trigger is released, firing the projectile. This process goes on until the motor runs down or the supply of shells is exhausted.

The tank is guided by the pilot wheel, shown in *Fig. 1*. The sheet-metal armor, with its turret, is fitted over the mechanism and can be removed quickly. It bears on angles bent up, as detailed in *Fig. 2*, to fit on the ends of the wooden center crosspiece of the main frame, and is held by removable pins at the ends of this frame. Though the rubber motor is easy to make and install, the

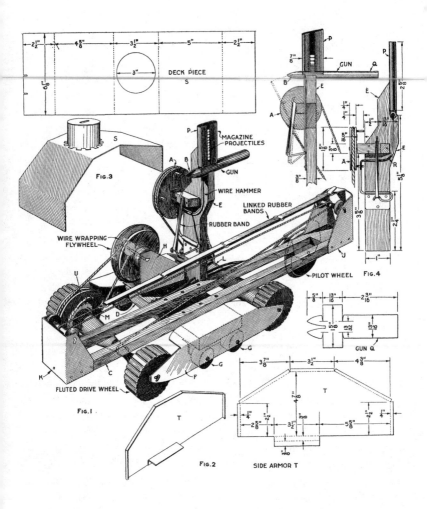

Fig.3

DECK PIECE
S

MAGAZINE
PROJECTILES

GUN

WIRE HAMMER

LINKED RUBBER
BANDS

RUBBER BAND

WIRE WRAPPING
FLYWHEEL

PILOT WHEEL

Fig.4

GUN

Fig.1

Fig.2

FLUTED DRIVE WHEEL

SIDE ARMOR T

GUN Q

PERSPECTIVE SKETCH, SHOWING THE ARRANGEMENT OF THE PARTS
WITH THE ARMOR AND THE TRACTOR BANDS REMOVED, AND
DETAILS OF THE GUN MECHANISM AND THE ARMOR.

range of the tank can be increased by using a strong spring motor, the construction otherwise being similar.

The construction is best begun by making the wooden frame that supports the armor. The perspective sketch, *Fig. 1,* used in connection with the working and detailed drawings, will aid in making the latter clear. Make the frame *C,* as detailed in *Figs. 5* and *6,* ⅜ by 1¾ by 11 in. long, with an opening cut in the center, 1 in. wide, 1 in. from the rear, and 1¼ in. from the front end. Make the crosspiece *D* ⅜ by 1¾ by 5⅞ in. long; the gun support *E,* as detailed in *Fig. 4,* ⅜ by 1⁵⁄₁₆ by 6¼ in. long. Shape the support *E* as shown. Fasten the frame *C* and the crosspiece *D* with screws, setting the piece *D* 5¾ in. from the front, and its left end 3 in. from the side of the frame, as shown in *Fig. 5.* This is important, as the fitting of the other parts depends on the position of these wooden supports.

The drive-wheel axles are carried in sheet-metal hangers, *F,* shown in *Figs. 1* and *5,* and detailed in *Fig. 6.* These hangers also carry bearing wheels, *G, Fig. 1,* which are held between the hanger *F* and a metal angle, as detailed in *G, Fig. 6.* These wheels are cut from a broomstick and mounted on nail axles. The metal for the hangers *F* is drilled as shown and bent double at the ends to make a strong bearing for the drive-wheel axles. The upper portion is bent at a right angle and fits over the top surface at the end of the crosspiece *D,* and is fastened to it with small screws or nails. Cut the stock for the hangers 2 by 6⅜ in. long.

Next make the sheet-metal support *H, Fig. 1,* for the flywheel. The rim of this is wrapped with wire to give it added weight. Cut the stock as detailed in *Fig. 6,* 1¾ by 4³⁄₁₆ in. long, and notch it to form the spring arrangement that holds the flywheel so that the belt will be tight. The other sheet-metal support may then be made. Cut the stock for the front support *J,* for the rubber motor, 4⅛ by 3¾ in. long, and shape it as shown in the detail, *Fig. 6.* Make the support *K* from a piece of sheet metal, in general shape similar to that used for support *H,* the dimensions being made as required and no spring arrangement being provided. Drill these metal fittings as indicated for the points of fastening, and mark the places for the holes in which shafts or axles run very carefully.

The driving mechanism can then be made, as shown in *Fig. 1,* and detailed in *Figs. 5* and *6*. The driving shafts and their parts, as well as the pulleys, can be turned in a lathe. Or they can be made from spools, round rods, etc. Make the front axle *L* and wheels, joined solidly, 5¾ in. overall. The grooved wheels are ¾ in. thick by 1 7/16 in. in diameter. Wires are used as bearings for shafts for the driving axles. If the rear axle is turned in a lathe, it is cut down to the shape indicated, thinner at the middle, to provide a place for the cord connected to the rubber motor. The grooved pulley and the fluted drive wheel at the winding-key end, shown in *Fig. 5,* are then cut loose. The drive wheel on the other end is cut loose, forming three sections mounted on the wire axle, one end of which is the winding key. Ratchet wheels, *M*, are fitted between the ends of the center section and adjoining pieces. The ratchet wheels are nailed to the center section and soldered to the wire axle. Pawls, *U*, are fitted to the inside of the two end sections as indicated in *Figs. 1* and *5*. When the rubber motor is wound up on the drum, the tractor bands are gripped until it is desired to start the tank on its trip. Then the power is communicated from the drum, or center section of the axle, to the

drive wheels by means of the ratchet wheels acting on the pawls.

Mount the hangers *F* on the center crosspiece *D*, fitting the axles of the drive wheels into place. Make the weighted flywheel and mount it on its shaft, as shown, lining it up with the pulley on the rear drive shaft. Fit the supports *J* and *K* into place, setting spools for the rubber-motor cord in place on wire axles. Arrange the belt from the flywheel to the driveshaft, and connect the rubber bands for the rubber motor as shown. Fasten one end in the hook of support *J*, and pass the winding cord through the spools. Fix it to the driveshaft. The device can then be operated with the fluted drive wheels bearing on strips of wood for tracks.

The tractor bands *N* are fitted over the drive wheels, as shown in *Fig. 6*. They are built up of canvas strips on which wooden shoes are glued and sewn, as detailed in *Fig. 5*. The stitches that reinforce the gluing are taken in the order indicated by the numerals. The pilot wheel is 2 in. in diameter, and sharpened at its circumference. Make a metal shell, *O*, for it as detailed in *Fig. 6*. Solder the shell to the double wire, which supports the wheel and gives it a spring tension to take obstructions nicely.

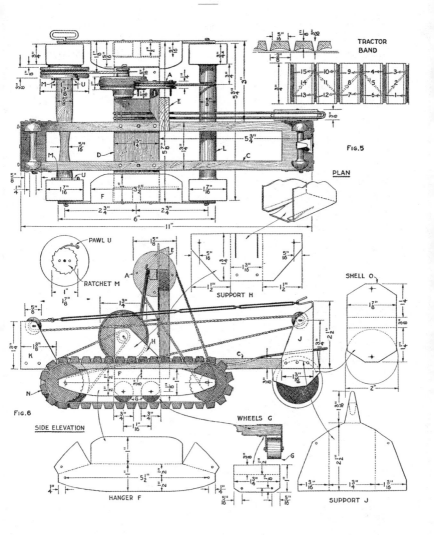

TRACTOR BAND

FIG.5

PLAN

PAWL U

RATCHET M

SUPPORT H

SHELL O

FIG.6

SIDE ELEVATION

WHEELS G

HANGER F

SUPPORT J

PLAN AND SIDE ELEVATION OF THE INTERIOR MECHANISM, WITH
THE ARMOR REMOVED AND DETAILS OF THE METAL FITTINGS,
THREE RATCHETS, AND THE TRACTOR BANDS.

The wire is fastened to the crosspiece *D*, as shown in *Fig. 5*.

The gun and its mechanism can be made handily before the support *E* is fixed into place at the front of the crosspiece *D*. Shape the magazine *P* from sheet metal, making it 2⅝ in. high, as detailed in *Fig. 4*. Make the gun *Q* from a piece of sheet metal, as detailed, cutting the metal to the exact dimensions indicated. Mount the magazine and the gun, and arrange the wire hammer *R*, and the rubber band that holds it. Fix the pulley *A* into place on its axle, supported by a small block of wood. Belt it to the front drive-wheel axle, as shown in *Fig. 5*, after the gun support is fastened into place with screws. Make the projectiles of wood, as shown, and the fighting tank is ready to be tested before putting on the armor.

The armor is made of one deck piece, *S*, *Fig. 3*, into which the covered turret is set with two sidepieces *T*, as detailed in *Fig. 2*. Make one left- and one right-sidepiece, allowing the flanges all around to be bent over and used for riveting or soldering the armor together. The bottom extension on the sidepieces is bent double to form an angle on which the armor is supported, where it rests on the top of the hangers *F*. The turret is fitted to the deck by cutting notches along its lower edge, the resulting strips being alternately turned in and out along the point of joining, as shown in *Fig. 3*. When the armor is completed, it is fitted over the main frame, the gun projecting from the turret. Small pins hold the ends of the armor solid against the ends of the main frame *C*, so that the armor can be lifted off readily. The various parts of the fighting tank can be painted as desired, care being taken not to injure the points of bearing on the axles and pulleys, which should be oiled. Silver bronze is a good finish for the exterior of the armor, which may be decorated with a coat of arms.

— TOY PAPER WARSHIPS —

With a pair of scissors, pins, and a newspaper or two, a fleet of warships can be made to sail the seven seas of polished floors. Strips of paper, through which holes at opposite points have been cut and pinned together at one end as shown in *Fig. 1*, are used for the sides of the boat. Rolls of paper are slipped through the opposite holes, as shown in *Fig. 2,* and provide support for the deck. The deck is a flat piece of paper pointed at the end to fit between the sides of the craft. A second deck fitted with funnels and masts, as shown in *Fig. 3,* is made of a folded piece of paper with holes cut through it for

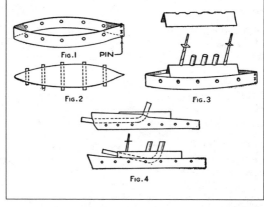

FLEETS OF BATTLESHIPS MAY BE MADE OF PAPER.

the masts and funnels, which are rolls of paper. If plain paper is used, the warships may be made in several colors, which adds to the effect of rivalry between the fleets. Other types of craft may easily be devised, two of which are shown in *Fig. 4.* Not

only the youngsters in the household, but their elders as well, may find not a little amusement and diversion in the making of a fleet of such warships, modeled after battleships, destroyers, battle cruisers, and other vessels.

— A COME-BACK ROLLING CAN —

An interesting toy may be made by fitting a rubber band into a tin can and weighting it as shown. When the can is rolled on the floor it will return to its original place by reason of the weight that is supported on a string at the middle

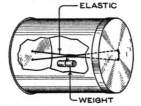

of the rubber band. The latter is passed through two holes at each end of the can, and when the can is rolled along the floor the elastic is wound at the middle. The weight reverses the direction of rolling.

— MECHANICAL TOY PIGEON MADE OF WOOD —

When the head of the mechanical pigeon is lowered the tail rises, and vice versa. It is constructed as follows: Make paper patterns for the parts, which consist of two body pieces, a head, a tail, and the foot piece. The shape of the parts is shown in the sketch, the front body piece being removed to show the connections of the rubber and wire controlling the movements. The view above shows the fastening of the parts, which are made of ⅛ to ¼ in. softwood: head, 1¾ by 3½ in.; body, 2 by 5¼ in.; tail 1¼ by 3¼ in.; foot piece, 1⅜ by 1½ in. Mark the shapes on the wood, cut them out and mount them, with a rubber band connecting the head

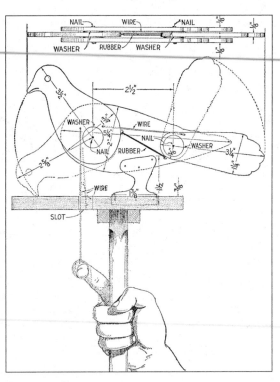

DRAW ON THE WIRE AND THE HEAD
AND TAIL BOB UP AND DOWN.

and tail as shown. Nail the foot piece between the body pieces and pivot the head and tail on nails. Connect the head with a wire with a loop on one end. Make the holder, and cut a slot into it for the draw wire, operated with the finger.

SLEIGHT *of* HAND

— TOSSING A CARD AT A MARK ACCURATELY —

There is an interesting old game that can be played instead of solitaire. It consists of trying to toss the greatest number of cards into a small basket or an upturned stiff hat, set at a distance. If the cards are held as shown in *A*, and tossed as in *B*, the card may be thrown with surprising accuracy after a little practice.

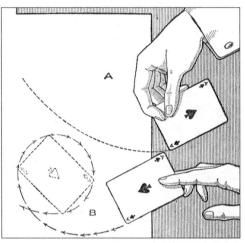

TOSSING CARDS ACCURATELY SO THAT THEY WILL FALL INTO A RECEPTACLE SET AT A DISTANCE.

— A SIMPLE CARD DECEPTION —

The effect of this trick is not new, but the method is. A card is selected by a spectator and noted, then returned to the pack, which is shuffled by the one drawing the card. Despite the thorough mixing, the correct card is located by cutting the pack. The secret is this: When the card is chosen, the chooser is allowed to remove it from the pack. The performer then takes it and holds it up and asks the audience to fix it in their minds. While doing this, allow the thumbnail of the index finger to slightly graze the edge of the card. This will not show, nor can it be detected by the holder, and he suspects nothing of the kind. When returned to the deck and shuffled, the pack is evened up for cutting. A glance at the edges will show a small white spot distinctly, as the scraped edge will contrast with the other soiled cards. It is simple to cut the pack from this key.

— A DIMINISHING CARD TRICK —

A clever diminishing card trick may be played with a piece of paper made up as shown in the illustration. Show the audience the whole card, *Fig. 1,* then fold it halfway and show again, *Fig. 2,* then again, *Fig. 3.* If this is done quickly it will not be noticed. A piece of paper is used the size of a regular playing card, and an ace is made on one side. When it is folded over, one side of the reduced size is made to show the same ace, then another fold is made and the smaller ace is made.

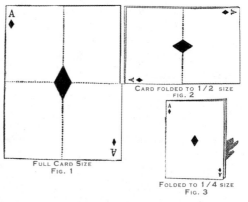

REDUCING THE SIZE OF A PLAYING CARD WHILE HOLDING IT IN ONE HAND.

— DISAPPEARING-COIN TRICK —

To make a quarter disappear from a glass of water after hearing it drop is a very puzzling trick. The articles necessary to perform this trick are a glass of water, a handkerchief, a quarter, and a piece of clear glass the exact size of a quarter. The glass can be cut and ground round on an emery wheel, and the edge polished.

To perform the trick, advance with the piece of glass hidden between the second and third fingers of the left hand and holding the quarter in plain sight between the thumb and first finger of the same hand, with the handkerchief in the right hand. Throw the handkerchief over the left hand and gather up the glass piece in the fold of the cloth, allowing the coin to drop into the palm of the left hand while covered. Remove the left hand and hold out the piece of glass with the handkerchief drawn tightly around it.

Anyone can touch the cloth-covered glass, but it cannot be distinguished from the quarter. While this is being shown, slip the quarter into a pocket. Spread the handkerchief over the glass of water and allow the glass disk to drop. A distinct click will be heard when it strikes the bottom. Raise the handkerchief and nothing will be seen, as the glass will be invisible in the water.

— Tricks with Knives and Glasses —

An interesting trick may be performed with three tumblers and three table knives. Place the tumblers in an equilateral triangle on a table so that the knife ends, when the knives are laid between the glasses as shown in the plan sketch, are about 1 in. away from the tumblers. The trick is to arrange the knives so that they are supported by the tops of the three tumblers and nothing else. Most observers will say that it is impossible; some will try it and in most cases fail. It can be done, and the illustration shows how simply it may be accomplished.

KNIVES PLACED IN SUCH A MANNER AS TO BE SUPPORTED BY THE THREE GLASSES.

— A SIMPLE GEOMETRICAL TRICK —

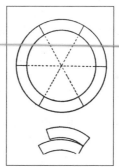

A simple geometrical trick that can be made from a piece of cardboard will provide plenty of entertainment at the efforts of others to prove that two identical circular-ring sections are of different sizes.

Two concentric circles are drawn on the cardboard with a compass, and these are carefully divided into six equal parts. Two ring sectors are cut out. Place the sectors one above the other as below, and ask someone how much longer one piece is than the other. Unless the person has seen the experiment before, he will invariably say that one is considerably longer than the other. Now reverse the pieces and repeat the question. The fact that the two pieces are the same size can be established to the satisfaction of anyone by placing one on top of the other.

— THE MAGIC PILLBOX —

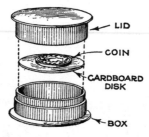

The magic pillbox makes coins disappear and return at will. The trick is very simple, and any pillbox can be fixed for performing it in a few minutes.

Cut a cardboard disk just large enough to fit into the bottom of a regulation round pillbox. Drop a coin in the box and put the lid on. Then turn it upside down and shake it, calling attention to the fact that the coin is still there by the rattling inside. Now, pull the box apart, holding the lid in the left hand so that the cardboard disk covers the coin, which has vanished. Then, still holding the lid upside down, put the box together again and reverse the operation, holding the bottom in the right hand. Upon opening the box the coin will reappear.

So That's How They Do It!

— The Magic Cabinet —

The performer calls the attention of his audience to a cabinet mounted on short legs and having doors in the front, back, and top. The back door is opened, then the top and front, and an arm is thrust through to show that the cabinet is empty and without double doors or double walls. The performer also puts his "magic" wand beneath the box to show that there is no deception there. The doors are then closed, except the top, and reaching down he takes out any number of articles, from handkerchiefs to rabbits, and then the front door is opened to show the box is empty. But upon closing the front door again, he is still able to produce articles until the supply is exhausted. Wonderful though this trick may appear, it is very simple. If a person is handy with tools, it can be made from lumber taken from a packing box.

To make the cabinet, nail together, in the shape of a rectangle, two pieces 16 in. long, 14 in. wide, and ½ in. thick, and two pieces 14 in. square by ½ in. thick. To one of the latter pieces fasten four legs, one at each corner. In the opposite piece, or the top, make an opening in the

TILTING BOX IN BACK DOOR

OPEN THE FRONT DOOR AND TOP OF THE CABINET AND IT WILL APPEAR EMPTY.

center 8 in. square. This opening is covered with a door 8½ in. square, supplied with a knob to open it easily. A piece 16 in. long by 14 in. wide, with an attached knob, is hinged to the front for a door; and another is made for the back, hinged in the same manner and with a knob. In the back there is a cutout, 9 in. long and 7 in. wide, made in the center. In this opening a swinging box is hung to hold the articles taken from the cabinet. The swinging box is made of two pieces, 9 in. long and 7 in. wide, and two pieces about ½ in. larger each way, nailed together on ends, cut triangular. This box is hinged in the opening so that it will swing in or out as desired and show a panel on either side of the door. The front door should have a panel nailed on each side of equal size to make both doors appear alike.

After loading all the things desired to be shown in the triangular box, start the trick by pushing this box into the cabinet and showing the outside. Then open the back, and in doing so, push the triangular box out as the door swings back and away from the audience. This shows that there is nothing to be seen but the panel. Open the front door and top, and the cabinet will appear empty. Close both front and back doors, and in making this change, push the triangular box in and begin to take things out through the top door.

By careful construction, the cabinet can be made so that the doors will open freely and the triangular box swing easily so that it will not be seen in operating it. With a clever performer this trick is without equal, as many variations can be made in the performance.

Go Fly a Kite

— How to Make Combined Kites: A Dragon Kite —

Dragon kites are made as hideous as the maker can possibly imagine them. Although the one to be considered is no beauty, it is more droll than fierce-looking. In general appearance the dragon and centipede kites are like huge caterpillars floating about in the air.

The kite sometimes twists and the balancer sticks appear to be large, hairy spines. Usually the tail end swings higher than the head. It is like so many single kites, pulling hard and requiring a strong cord for the line. The individual circular sections may number 20 and if placed 30 in. apart would make a kite about 50 ft. in length, or the number of sections may be more or less to make the kite longer or shorter. The kite will fold up into a very small space, for carrying about or for storage. But care should

IN GENERAL APPEARANCE THE DRAGON KITE IS LIKE A HUGE CATERPILLAR FLOATING ABOUT IN THE AIR.

be taken in folding not to entangle the harness.

The Head

The head requires much more work than any of the other sections. There are two principle rings to this section, as shown in *Fig. 1*. The inner ring is the more important, the outer one being added for the protection of the points when alighting. The construction of the framework is shown in *Fig. 2*. It is made entirely of bamboo. The bamboo is split into strips, about 3/16 in. wide, for the ring *A*. As the bamboo strips will be much too thick, they must be pared down to less than 1/16 in. The diameter of the ring *A* is 12 in., and a strip of bamboo to make this ring should be about 38 in. long, so that there will be some end for making a lap joint. The ends of the strip are held securely together by winding them with linen thread. Some boys use strips of rice paper that are about ½ in. wide and torn lengthwise. The rice-paper strips are made wet with

FIG. I

THE KITE-HEAD SECTION, HAVING HORNS, EARS,
AND REVOLVING EYES, IS VERY HIDEOUS.

paste before winding them on the joint. When they dry out, the shrinkage will bind the ends securely.

Two crosspieces, of the same weight as the ring stick, are placed 3½ in. apart, at equal distances from the center and parallel, as shown in *B* and *C*. The ends of these pieces are turned at a sharp angle and lashed to the inside surface of the ring *A*. To make these bends, heat the bamboo over a candle flame until it will give under pressure, and then bend it. The bamboo will stay in shape after it becomes cold. This method of bending should be remembered, because

it is useful in making all kinds of kites. Two small rings, each 3½ in. in diameter, are put in between the two parallel pieces, as shown in *D* and *E*. These are for the eyes of the dragon. The rings are lashed to the two crosspieces *B* and *C*. Because the eyes revolve in the rings, they should be made perfectly true. This can be done by shaping the bamboo about a perfectly round cylinder, 3½ in. in diameter. To stiffen the whole framework, two pieces of bamboo, 1/16 in. thick, ⅛ in. wide, and 20 in. long, are lashed to the back as shown by *F* and *G*. There is a space of 3 in. between the inner ring *A* and the outer ring *H*, giving the latter a diameter of 18 in. It is made of a bamboo strip, ⅛ in. wide, and should be less than 1/16 in. thick. It may be necessary to make this large ring from two pieces of bamboo to get the length. In such a case be careful to make a perfect ring with the ends well lashed together. Two short pieces are lashed together to the two rings, as shown in *J* and *K*.

The supports for the horns consist of two pieces, ⅛ in. wide and less than 1/16 in. thick, and they are lashed to the upper crosspiece and to both rings, so that the parts L and M are exactly halfway between the ends of the pieces F and G, and radiate out from the center of the ring A. The other parts, N and O, point to the center of the eye rings, respectively. The ears are unimportant and may be put on if desired. The rings on the horns and the stick ends may be from ½ to 2 in. in diameter, cut from stiff paper, but if larger, made of bamboo.

Chinese rice paper is the best material for covering, and it should be stretched tightly so that there will be no buckling or bagging places. The only part covered is that inside of the inner ring *A*, the horns and the ears, leaving the eye rings open. The shades are put on with a brush and watercolors, leaving the face white, or it can be tinted in brilliant colors. Leave the horns white and color the tongue red.

The Eyes

The frame for each eye is made of bamboo, pared down to 1/32 in. in thickness and formed into a perfect ring, 3¼ in. in diameter. Each ring revolves on an axle made of wire passed through the bamboo exactly on the diameter, as shown in *P, Fig. 3.* The wire should be long enough to pass through the socket ring *D* or *E, Fig. 2,* also, and after the eye ring is in place in the socket ring and the axle adjusted, the latter is fastened to the eye ring with a strip of paper wrapped tightly around the wire and

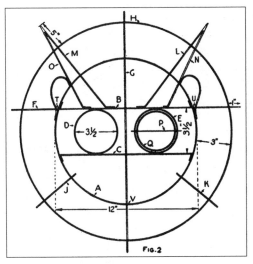

THE FRAMEWORK FOR THE HEAD SECTION IS MADE ENTIRELY OF BAMBOO STRIPS LASHED AT THE JOINTS.

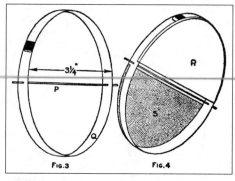

of it will show on both front and back of the eyepiece. When the eyepiece is given a half turn in its socket, the backside will come to the front and will appear just the same as the other side. Some kite builders add pieces of mirror glass to the eyes, to reflect the light and cause flashes as the eyes revolve in their sockets.

pasted to the bamboo of the ring. A glass bead, placed on the wire axle between the socket rings D or E and the eye ring Q on each side, keeps them apart and the revolving one from striking the other.

Each side of the eye ring is covered halfway with rice paper, as shown in *Fig. 4*. The part R is on the upper front half, and that shown by S is on the back lower half. Placing the two halves in this manner causes an unequal pressure of the wind on the whole eyepiece, and thus causes it to revolve on the axle. The front upper half of the eyepiece is made black, and the smaller dark portion extending below the darkened half is a round piece of paper placed just between the two halves so that half

A Section Kite

The ring for the section kite is made the same size as the inner ring of the head kite, or in this case 12 in. in diameter. The bamboo for making this ring should be ⅛ in. wide and ¹⁄₁₆ in. thick. The balancer stick, 36 in. long, is located about the same place as the cross stick F, as shown in *Fig. 2*, and must be made small, light, and well balanced. Small tufts of tissue paper or feathers are attached to the tip ends of the balancer sticks, as shown in *Fig. 5*. The cover for the section kite is put on tightly, the same as for the head; the builder can color them as desired. The balancer on the last section should have streamers, as shown in *Fig. 6*, for a finish. The streamers are made of light cloth.

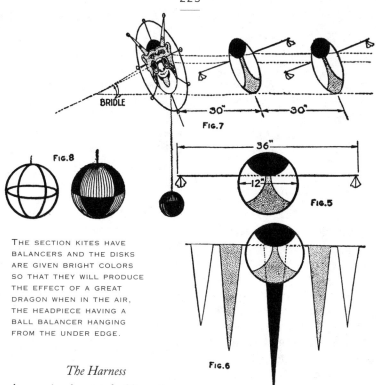

BRIDLE

FIG.7

30"   30"

36"

12"

FIG.5

FIG.8

THE SECTION KITES HAVE
BALANCERS AND THE DISKS
ARE GIVEN BRIGHT COLORS
SO THAT THEY WILL PRODUCE
THE EFFECT OF A GREAT
DRAGON WHEN IN THE AIR,
THE HEADPIECE HAVING A
BALL BALANCER HANGING
FROM THE UNDER EDGE.

FIG.6

The Harness

As previously stated, 20 sections more or less can be used, and the number means so many separate kites which are joined together with three long cords, spacing the sections 30 in. apart. The cords should be as long as the kite from the head to the tail, allowing sufficient extra length for the knots. As such a kite will make a hard pull, the cord used should be six-ply, hard-twisted seine twine. Start by tying the three long cords to the head kite at the points *T*, *U*, and *V*, *Fig. 2*. Tie the next section at corresponding places just 30 in. from the head kite. The construction will be much easier if the head kite is fastened to a wall so that each cord may be drawn out to its proper length. Continue the tying until all sections are attached just 30 in. apart. Other spacing can be used, but the distance selected must be uniform throughout the length of the kite. The individual kites, or sections, may vary in size, or they can all be 9 in. in diameter instead of 12 in., and the balancer sticks 30 in. long instead of 36 in., but a kite of uniform sections is much better and is easier to make. The positions of the sections as they will appear in the kite are shown in *Fig. 7.*

The Bridle

The Chinese bridle is usually made of three strings, which are attached to the same points on the head kite as the harness cords, or at *T, U,* and *V.* The lower string is longer than the two upper ones so that the proper inclination will be presented to the breeze. As the head is inclined, all the section kites will also be inclined. Some makers prefer a balancer on the head kite, and in one instance such a balancer was made in the shape of a ball. A ball made of bamboo strips is shown in *Fig. 8,* and is attached as shown in *Fig. 7.*

Flying the Kite

It will be necessary to have a helper, and perhaps two, in starting the kite up because the harness might become entangled. Quite a little run will be necessary, but when up the kite will make a steady flier and will pull very hard. If the first attempt is unsuccessful, try readjustment of the bridle or a little different position in the breeze, and see that the balancers are not tangled. Quite a number of changes may be worked out on these plans, but it is necessary to bear in mind that the distances between sections must be equal and that the general construction must be maintained.

— HOW TO MAKE COMBINED KITES: A FESTOONED KITE —

More than one kite on the same framework is known as a compound kite. The one illustrated consists of three tailless kites on one long stick, called the spine. The upper one is 3 ft., the center one, 2 ft., and the lower one, 1 ft. in width. A stick of light wood will be needed for the construction of this kite—spruce is best, but it may be pine or bass—7 ft. long by ¼ by ½ in. If the wood breaks easily it will be better to increase the width from ½ in. to ¾ in., or the stick might be made ⅜ in. thick without increasing the width, but with a good spruce stick the dimensions first given will be sufficient. The stick should be straight grained and without a twist. If the spine is twisted, the kites will not lie flat or in a plane with each other. If one is out of true, it will cause the kite to be unsteady in the air. The bow sticks are three, the upper one being 4 ft. long by ¼ by ½ in., the center one, 2 ft. long by ¼ by ⅜ in., and the lower one, 1 ft. long by ¼ by ¼ in. About five sheets

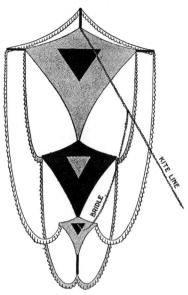

THE KITE AS IT APPEARS WITH THE FESTOONS HUNG TO THE ENDS OF THE STICKS.

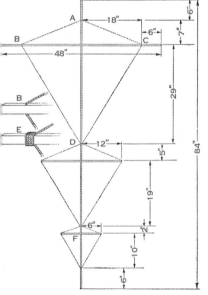

THE SPINE WITH THE BOW STICKS PROPERLY SPACED AS SHOWN BY THE DIMENSIONS.

of tissue paper will be required, but more may be needed for color combinations. The so-called French tissue paper is much better, as it comes in fine colors and is much stronger than the ordinary tissue. It costs a trifle more, but it pays in making a beautiful kite. The Chinese rice paper is the strongest, but comes only in natural colors.

It will be seen that the kites do not extend to the top and bottom of the spine stick. The first bow stick is placed 13 in. from the top end of the spine, and each of its ends extends 6 in. beyond the kite for fastening the festoons. The bow sticks should be lashed to the spine, not nailed. Wind diagonally around the two sticks, both left and right, then wind between the two, around the other windings. This draws all windings up tightly to prevent slipping.

To string up the upper kite, drill a small hole through the spine 6 in. from the top, at *A*. Also drill 6 in. from each end of the bow stick, at *B* and *C*. If a small drill is not available, notch the stick with a knife or saw to hold the string. Another hole is made in the spine 29 in. from the upper bow stick, or at *D*. Tie the outline string at *A*, then pass through the hole at *C*, then through *D*, up through *B* and back to the starting point at *A*. In tying the last point, draw up the string tightly, but not enough to spring the spine or bow. Measure carefully to see if the distance *AC* is the same as *AB* and if *CD* is equal to *BD*. If they are not, shift the string until they are equal and wind at all points, as shown in *E*, to prevent further slipping. Proceed in the same way with the center and lower kite, and it will be ready for the cover.

The cover tissue should be cut about 1 in. larger all around than the surface to be covered, but turn over about half of this allowance. This will give plenty of looseness to the cover. For the fringe festoons, cut strips of tissue paper 2½ in. wide, past ½ in. of one long edge over a string, and cut slits with scissors at intervals of 1 in. along the loose edge. After the fringe has been made, attach it as shown in the illustration. Do not stretch it tightly but give sufficient looseness to make each length form a graceful curve and keep the sides well balanced.

To bend the bows of the upper and center kites, attach a string from end to end of each bow on the back side of the kite and spring in short brace sticks.

Attach the upper end of the bridle at A. The length of the bridle string is 87 in. and the kite line is attached to it 30 in. from *A*, leaving the lower part from this point to *F*, where it is tied to the spine, 57 in. long.

The kite should fly without a tail, but if it dodges too much attach extra streamers to the ends of the bow sticks of the lower kite and to the bottom of the spine.

If good combinations of colors are used a very beautiful kite will be the result and one that will fly well.

— An Eight-pointed Star Kite —

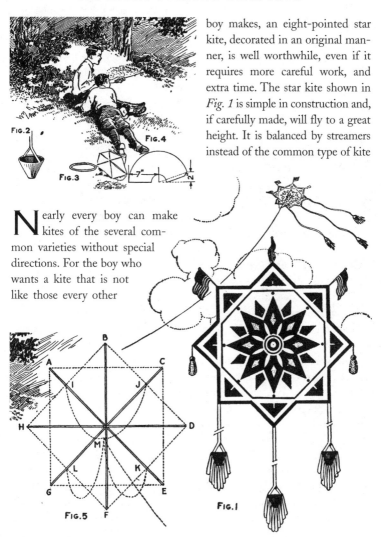

boy makes, an eight-pointed star kite, decorated in an original manner, is well worthwhile, even if it requires more careful work, and extra time. The star kite shown in *Fig. 1* is simple in construction and, if carefully made, will fly to a great height. It is balanced by streamers instead of the common type of kite

Nearly every boy can make kites of the several common varieties without special directions. For the boy who wants a kite that is not like those every other

FIG.2

FIG.3

FIG.4

FIG.5

FIG.1

tail. Any regular-shaped kite should be laid out accurately, as otherwise the error appears very prominent, and unbalances the poise of the kite.

The frame for this star kite is made of four sticks joined, as indicated in *Fig. 5*, with strings running from one corner to the second corner beyond, as from *A* to *C*, from *C* to *E*, etc. A little notching of each pair of sticks lessens the thickness of the sticks at the center crossing and strengthens the frame. The sticks are ¼ by ½ in. by 4 ft. long. They are set at right angles to each other in pairs and lashed together with cord. They are also held by a ¾-in. brad at the center. The strings that form the sides of the squares, *A* to *G*, and *B* to *H*, must be equal in length when tied. The points where the strings forming the squares cross each other and the sticks are also tied.

The first cover, which is put on with paste laying it out on a smooth floor or table as usual in kite making, is plain, light-colored paper. The darker decorations are pasted onto this. The outside edges of the cover are turned over the string outline and pasted down. The colors may be in many combinations, such as red and white, purple and gold, green, and white, etc. Brilliant and contrasting colors are best. The decoration may proceed from the center out, or the reverse. The outside edge in the design shown has a 1½ in. black stripe. The figures are black. The next octagonal black line binds the design together. The points of the star are dark blue with a gilt stripe on each. The center design is done in black, dark blue, and gilt.

The flags are tied on, and the tassels are easily made of cord. The outside streamers are at least 6 ft. long and balanced carefully. Ribbons or dark-colored lining cambric are used for them. The funnel-shaped ends balance the kite. They are shown in detail in *Figs. 2, 3,* and *4,* and have 1-in. openings at the bottom, through which the air passes, causing a pull that steadies the kite. They are of dark blue, and the cloth fringe is of light blue. A thin reed or fine wire is used for the hoop that stiffens the top. Heavy wrapping or cover paper is used to cover the hoop. It is cut as shown in *Fig. 4* and rolled into shape.

A four-string bridle is fastened to the frame at *I, J, K,* and *L,* as shown. The upper strings are each 18 in., and the lower ones 32 in. long, to the point where they come together, and must be adjusted after the kite line is fastened at *M*.

— How to Make and Fly a Chinese Kite —

A serious kite-flying boy is not satisfied with simply holding the end of a kite string and running up and down the block or field trying to raise a heavy paper kite with a half pound of rags for a tail. He makes a kite as light as possible without any tail, which has the peculiar property of being able to move in every direction. Sometimes an expert can make one of these kites travel across the wind for several hundred feet. In fact, I have seen boys a full block apart bring their kites together

and engage in a combat until one of their kites floated away with a broken string, or was punctured by the swift dives of the other and sent to earth, a wreck.

The boy makes his kite as follows: From a sheet of thin but tough tissue paper about 20 in. square, which he folds and cuts along the dotted line as shown in *Fig. 1,* he gets a perfectly square kite having all the properties of a good flyer, light and strong. He shapes two pieces of bamboo, one for the backbone

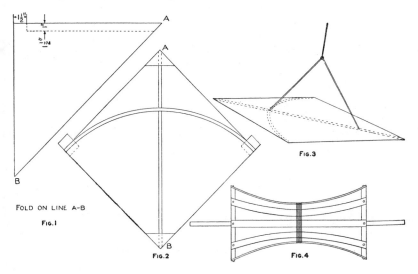

PARTS OF A CHINESE KITE.

and one for the bow. The backbone is flat, ¼ by 3/32 in. and 18 in long. This he smears along one side with common boiled rice. Boiled rice is one of the best adhesives for use on paper that can be obtained, and the Chinese have used it for centuries, while we are just waking up to the fact that it makes fine photo paste. Having placed the backbone in position, paste two triangular pieces of paper over the ends of the stick to prevent tearing. The bow is now bent and the lugs extending from the sides of the square paper are bent over the ends of the bow and pasted down. If the rice is quite dry or mealy it can be smeared on and will dry almost immediately; therefore no strings are needed to hold the bow bent while the paste dries.

After the sticks are in position, the kite will appear as shown in *Fig. 2*. The dotted lines show the lugs bent over the ends of the bow and pasted down. *Fig. 3* shows how the band is put on and how the kite is balanced. This is the most important part and cannot be explained very well. This must be done by experimenting, and it is enough to say that the kite must balance perfectly. The string is fastened by a slipknot to the band, moved back and forth until the kite

flies properly, and then it is securely fastened.

A reel is made next. Two ends—the bottoms of two small peach baskets will do—are fastened to a dowel stick or broom handle if nothing better is at hand. These ends are placed about 14 in. apart and strips nailed between them, as shown in *Fig. 4*, and the center drawn in and bound with a string. The kite string used is generally a heavy packing thread. This is run through a thin flour or rice paste until it is thoroughly coated, then it is run through a quantity of crushed glass. The glass should be beaten up fine and run through a fine sieve to make it about the same as No. 2 emery. The particles should be extremely sharp and full of splinters. These particles adhere to the pasted string and when dry are so sharp that it cannot be handled without scratching the fingers. Therefore the kite is flown entirely from the reel. To wind the string upon the reel, all that is necessary is to lay one end of the reel stick in the bend of the left arm and twirl the other end between the fingers of the right hand.

In China, a boy will be flying a gaily colored little kite from the roof of a house (if it is in one of the large cities that have flat-roofed houses) and a second boy will appear on the roof of another house perhaps 200 ft. away. Both have large reels full of string, often several hundred yards of it. The first hundred feet or so is glass-covered string, the balance common packing thread or glass-covered string. As soon as the second boy has his kite aloft, he begins maneuvering to drive it across the wind and over to the first kite. First, he pays out a large amount of string. Then, as the kite wobbles to one side with its nose pointing toward the first kite, he tightens his line and commences a steady quick pull. If properly done, his kite crosses over to the other and above it. The string is now paid out until the second kite is hanging over the first one's line. The wind now tends to take the second kite back to its parallel and in so doing makes a turn about the first kite's string. If the second kite is close enough, the first tries to spear him by swift dives. The second boy in the meantime is see-sawing his string and presently the first kite's string is cut and it drifts away.

It is not considered sport to haul the other fellow's kite down as might be done, and therefore a very interesting battle is often witnessed when the experts clash their kites.

— HOW TO MAKE A WAR KITE —

The material required is three pine sticks, each 60 in. long, one stick 54 in. long, one stick 18 in. long, all ½ in. square; 4 yards of cambric; a box of tacks; some linen thread, and 16 ft. of stout twine.

Place two 60-in. sticks parallel with each other and 18 in. apart. Then lay the 54-in. piece across at right angles to them 18 in. from the upper ends, as shown in *Fig. 1,* and fasten the joints with brads. At a point 21 in. below this crosspiece, attach the 18-in. crosspiece.

The extending ends of all three long pieces are notched, *Fig. 2,* and the line is stretched taut around them as shown by the dotted lines. If the cambric is not of sufficient size to cover the frame, two pieces must be sewn together. Then a piece is cut out to the shape of the string, allowing 1 in. to project all around for a lap. The cambric is sewn fast to the string with the linen thread. Fasten the cloth to the frame part with the tacks, spacing them 1 in. apart. The space in the center, between the sticks, is cut out. Make two pieces of the remaining goods, one 36 in. by 18 in., and the other 36 in. by 21 in. The remaining 60-in. stick is fastened to these pieces of cambric, as shown in *Fig. 3*, and the whole is fastened to the main frame so as to make a V-shaped projection. The bridle strings, for giving the proper distribution of pull on the line to the kite, are fastened one to the upper end of the long stick in the V-shaped piece attached to the kite. The other is fastened to the lower end, as shown in *Fig. 4*. The inclination can be varied to suit the builder by changing the point of attachment of the kite line to the bridle. If it is desired to fly the kite directly overhead, attach the line above the regular point. For low

THE LINE SHOULD BE A VERY STRONG ONE, THEN BANNERS CAN BE FLOWN ON IT.

flying make the connection below this point. The regular point is found by trial flights with the line fastened temporarily to the bridle, after which the fastening is made permanent.

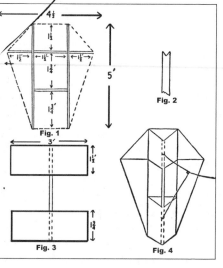

$4\frac{1}{2}$

$1\frac{1}{2}$

$1\frac{1}{2}'$ $1\frac{1}{4}'$ $1\frac{1}{2}'$

$1\frac{3}{4}'$

$1\frac{3}{4}'$

5'

Fig. 1

Fig. 2

3'

$1\frac{1}{4}'$

$1\frac{3}{4}'$

Fig. 3

Fig. 4

— AN AEROPLANE KITE —

After building a number of kites from recent description in *Amateur Mechanics* I branched out and constructed the aeroplane kite shown in the illustration, which has excited considerable comment in the neighborhood on account of its appearance and behavior in the air.

THE KITE BEING TAILLESS RIDES THE AIRWAVES LIKE AN AEROPLANE IN A STEADY BREEZE.

The main frame consists of a 31-in.-long center stick, *A*, and two cross sticks, of which one, *B*, is 31 in. long and the other, *C*, 15½ in. long.

The location of the cross-pieces on the centerpiece *A* is shown in the sketch, the front piece *B* being 1¾ in. from the end, and the rear piece *C*, 2¼ in. from the other end. The ends of the sticks have small notches cut to receive a string, *D*, which is run around the outside to make the outline of the frame and to brace the parts. Two cross strings are placed at *E* and *F*, 7 in. from either end of the centerpiece *A*. Other brace strings are crossed, as shown in *G*, and then tied to the cross string *F* on both sides, as in *H*.

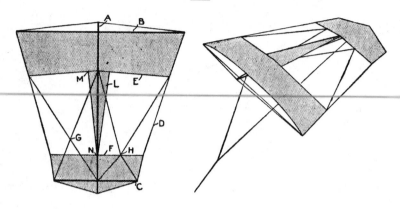

The long crosspiece B is curved upward to form a bow, the center of which should be 3¼ in. above the string by which its ends are tied together. The shorter crosspiece is bent and tied in the same manner to make the curve 2½ in, and the centerpiece to curve 1¾ in., both upward. The front and rear parts, between the end and the cross strings E and F, are covered with yellow tissue paper. This is pasted to the crosspieces and strings. The small wings L are purple tissue paper, 4 in. wide at M and tapering to a point at N.

The bridle string is attached on the centerpiece A, at the junction of the crosspieces B and C, and must be adjusted for the size and weight of the kite. The kite is tailless and requires a steady breeze to make it float in the air currents like an aeroplane.

The bridle string and the bending of the sticks must be adjusted until the desired results are obtained. The bridle string should be tied so that it will about center under the cross stick B for the best results. But a slight change from this location may be necessary to make the kite ride the air currents properly. The center of gravity will not be the same in the construction of each kite, and the string can be located only by trial, after which it is permanently fastened.

— CAMERA FOR TAKING PICTURES FROM A KITE —

When watching a kite flying at a considerable height, one frequently wonders how the landscape appears from such a viewpoint as would be possible from a kite. Few of us can have the experience of a ride in an airplane, but it is quite possible to obtain a view from the kite, by proxy as it were, through the use of a kite camera. A kite of large dimensions would be necessary to carry an ordinary camera taking pictures of fair size; hence it is necessary to devise a camera of lighter construction so that a kite of moderate size may carry it to a height of several hundred feet. Such a camera is shown in the illustration, attached to a box kite. Details of construction are shown in the smaller sketches.

A camera consists, briefly, of a lightproof box with a lens at one end and a sensitive plate of film at the other. For a kite camera, a single achromatic lens will suit the purpose. Such a lens is not expensive and may be taken from a small camera. It must be obtained before the camera is begun, because the size of the camera is dependent upon the focal length of the lens and the size of the picture to be made. A camera taking pictures 2 in. square is satisfactory for kite photography. If it is desired to enlarge the pictures, this may be done in the usual manner.

The box of the camera is made cone shaped in order to reduce the weight and air resistance. Its sides are of lightweight, stiff cardboard, reinforced at the corners to ensure that no light will enter. The back of the camera is a tight-fitting cover of cardboard having the same measurements as the picture to be taken. The lens is fitted to an intermediate partition, as shown in the sketch. It is necessary to determine the focal length of the lens and to set it at a distance from the inner side of the cardboard back of the camera—the film surface—so that it will focus properly for photographing distant objects.

The front is provided with a circular opening of a size large enough not to obstruct the view of the lens. A shutter made of thin pressboard is fitted over the opening, as shown in the sketch on the next page. A slit is cut in the shutter through which light is admitted in making the exposure as the shutter is drawn back. The size and width of the slit

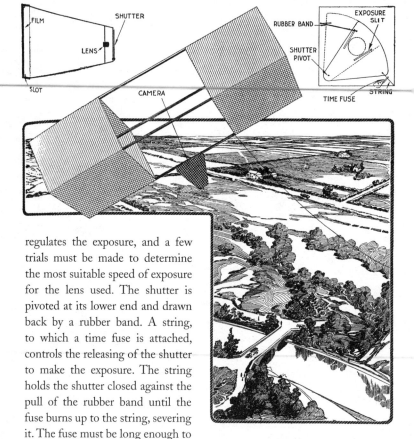

FILM

SHUTTER

LENS

SLOT

CAMERA

RUBBER BAND

EXPOSURE SLIT

SHUTTER PIVOT

STRING

TIME FUSE

regulates the exposure, and a few trials must be made to determine the most suitable speed of exposure for the lens used. The shutter is pivoted at its lower end and drawn back by a rubber band. A string, to which a time fuse is attached, controls the releasing of the shutter to make the exposure. The string holds the shutter closed against the pull of the rubber band until the fuse burns up to the string, severing it. The fuse must be long enough to enable the kite to attain a suitable height before the string is burned. When the shutter has been set and the fuse attached ready for lighting, the camera may be taken into the darkroom for loading. A piece of film, cut to the proper size, is placed

THE KITE CAMERA OFFERS A DIVERSION IN PHOTOGRAPHY AND HAS PRACTICAL AND COMMERCIAL USES. THE CAMERA SHOWN IS OF LIGHTWEIGHT, SIMPLE CONSTRUCTION, AND PRODUCES FILM EXPOSURES 2 IN. SQUARE. A SECTIONAL VIEW IS GIVEN AT THE LEFT, AND THE DETAILS OF THE SHUTTER DEVICE AT THE RIGHT.

carefully into the lightproof sliding cover, as with a film pack. The sensitive side is, of course, placed nearest the lens.

The camera is attached to the kite securely at the middle, as shown, so that when the kite is in flight a view nearly straight down will be obtained. When all is in readiness, the fuse is lighted and the kite started on its flight. By timing experimental flights, the required length of fuse may be determined in order to permit the kite to attain the desired height at the time of exposure.

The kite used for taking pictures from the air should be large enough to carry the camera easily. One of the box type illustrated is satisfactory, although other types may be used. A kite camera for the amateur has great possibilities for experimentation, but requires care in construction and a reasonable knowledge of photography. To the person willing to master the details, kite photography offers a pleasurable diversion as well as practical uses in photographing plots of ground, groups of buildings, manufacturing plants, and other subjects that cannot be photographed by other methods.

FLYBOYS

— A MODEL PAPER MONOPLANE THAT CAN BE STEERED —

An interesting bit of paper construction is a small monoplane made from a 7-in. square of paper, folded as indicated in the diagram, and provided with a paper tail. This little monoplane can be steered by adjusting the tail and can even be made to loop the loop in varying air currents. For the boy who enjoys experimenting with such a model, this little construction offers much instruction and entertainment. And the grown-up who still has an interest in such things will also find it a worthwhile job.

To make this model, fold a square of medium-weight paper on the dotted lines as indicated in *Fig. 1* in the diagram. Then unfold the sheet and refold it as in *Fig. 2*. Then bring the folded corners *A* and *B* into position as shown in *A* and *B* in *Fig. 3*. Fold

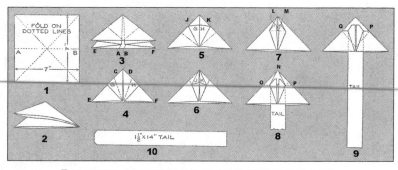

the corners *C* and *D* upward to the position *C* and *D* in *Fig. 4*. Fold corners *G* and *H* to the corresponding letters in *Fig. 5*. Fold points *J* and *K* to the corresponding letters in *Fig. 6*. Raise the points *J* and *K*, *Fig. 6*, and fold them in so that the corners that were below them in *Fig. 6* now come above them, as in *L*

and *M* in *Fig. 7*. Fold the corner *N* back along the line *OP*, *Fig. 8*, so that the shape of the main portion of the model is as shown in *Fig. 9*, in *OP*. Make the tail 1½ by 14 in. long, as shown in *Fig. 10*, and paste it into position. This completes the model, which can be steered by bending or twisting the tail.

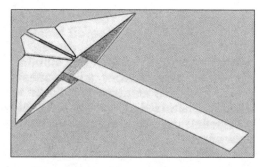

THIS MODEL MONOPLANE IS MADE OF A SHEET OF PAPER, SEVEN INCHES
SQUARE, AND CAN BE STEERED BY BENDING OR TWISTING THE TAIL.

— TOY PAPER GLIDER CAREFULLY DESIGNED —

A paper glider is an interesting and useful toy that can be made quickly. It may be used out of doors, but occasions when weather conditions make it necessary to remain indoors are especially good a pin, as shown in the upper sketch. The inventive boy may devise many play uses for the glider, in tournaments, competitions, and for "military" flights, in which the "drivers" of the devices may "annihilate armies."

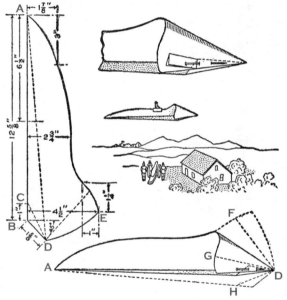

THE GLIDER WILL TRAVEL 30 FT.
CARRYING A MESSAGE IF CAREFULLY MADE.

for this form of pastime. The glider shown in the sketch was worked out after considerable testing. With a toss, it travels 20 to 30 ft. on a level keel, with a message slipped behind Practical use of the toy was made in a series of air-current tests.

The glider is made as follows: Fold a piece of 10- by 15-in. paper lengthwise, and mark the outline shown at the left upon it. The dimensions should be followed carefully. Measure first from the end A to the point B, and then draw the slanting line to D, at an angle of 45 degrees. Mark the width to E, and measure the other distances from A and at the middle, to determine the curve of the edge. Mark the dotted lines extending from D, which are guides for the folding of the paper to form the glider, as shown in the lower sketch. Curl the points under the side so that the line FD comes to the position DG, and pin them to the corners H, as shown in the lower sketch. The glider is tossed by holding it between the thumb and forefinger at the middle of the fold underneath it.

— MAKING A TOY CATAPULT —

A 10-cent rat trap of the type shown in the drawing can easily be made into a marble-throwing catapult, the range of the missile being regulated by an adjustable stop. The trap is fastened to the edges of the ammunition box and the bait hook is removed. The stop is then bent from a strip of sheet metal and fastened to opposite edges of the trap as indicated. Two side arms that serve as braces for the stop are adjusted by means of a wire pin passing through holes in the stop and arms. The throwing arm should be made of ½- by ½ in. hardwood, about 10 in. long, although the length is best determined by trial. A small metal cup at the end of the arm provides a pocket for the ammunition. If desired, a trigger

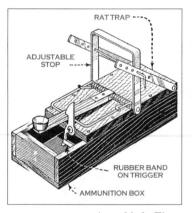

arrangement can be added. Flour tied in tissue paper may be used to make a realistic bomb because it gives off a smokelike puff when it strikes and is harmless. The longest throw the device is capable of will usually be attained when the stop is set at an angle of about 45 degrees.

— PAPER GLIDER THAT LOOPS THE LOOP —

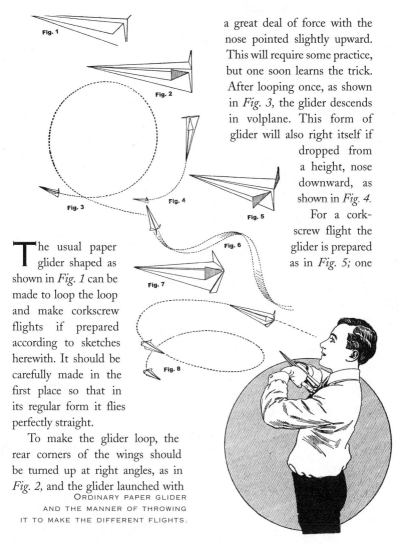

a great deal of force with the nose pointed slightly upward. This will require some practice, but one soon learns the trick. After looping once, as shown in *Fig. 3,* the glider descends in volplane. This form of glider will also right itself if dropped from a height, nose downward, as shown in *Fig. 4.*

For a corkscrew flight the glider is prepared as in *Fig. 5;* one

The usual paper glider shaped as shown in *Fig. 1* can be made to loop the loop and make corkscrew flights if prepared according to sketches herewith. It should be carefully made in the first place so that in its regular form it flies perfectly straight.

To make the glider loop, the rear corners of the wings should be turned up at right angles, as in *Fig. 2,* and the glider launched with

ORDINARY PAPER GLIDER AND THE MANNER OF THROWING IT TO MAKE THE DIFFERENT FLIGHTS.

rear corner being bent up and the other down. In this form it flies horizontally, or downward, while rapidly rotating around its longitudinal axis, as shown in *Fig. 6.*

To make a spiral descent, the rear corners of the wings are bent up as in *Fig. 2,* and the rear corner of the keel is bent at right angles, *Fig. 7,* whereupon it is thrown in the ordinary manner. It then takes the course shown in *Fig. 8.*

— BOOMERANGS AND HOW TO MAKE THEM —

A boomerang is a weapon invented and used by native Australians. The boomerang is a curved stick of hardwood, *Fig. 1,* about $5/16$ in. thick by 2 ½ in. wide by 2 ft. long, flat on one side with the ends and the other side rounding. One end of the stick is grasped in one hand with the convex edge forward and the flat side up, and thrown upward. After going some distance and ascending slowly to a great height in the air with a quick rotary motion, it suddenly returns in an elliptical orbit to a spot near the starting point. If thrown down on the ground the boomerang rebounds in a straight line, pursuing a ricochet motion until the object is struck at which it was thrown.

Two other types of boomerangs are illustrated herewith and they can be made as described. The materials necessary for the T-shaped boomerang are: one piece of hard maple $5/16$ in. thick by 2½ in. wide by 3 ft. long; five ½ in. flathead screws. Cut the piece of hard maple into two pieces, one 11½ in. and the other 18 in. long. The corners are cut from these pieces, as shown in *Fig. 2,* taking care to cut exactly the same amount from each corner. Bevel both sides of the pieces, making the edges very thin so they will cut the air better. Find the exact center of the long piece and make a line 1¼ in. on each side of the center, and fasten the short length between the lines with the screws, as shown in *Fig. 3.* The short piece should be fastened perfectly square and at right angles to the long one.

The materials necessary for the cross-shaped boomerang are one piece hard maple $5/16$ in. thick by 2 in. wide by 30 in. long, and five ½-in. flathead screws. Cut the maple into two 14-in. pieces and plane the edges of these pieces so

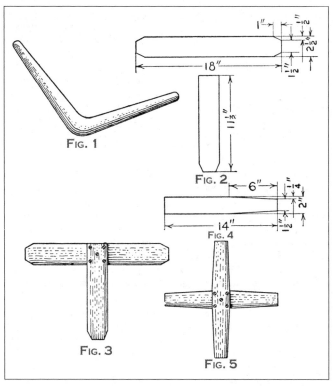

that the ends will be 1½ in. wide, as shown in *Fig. 4*. Bevel these pieces the same as the ones for the T-shaped boomerang. The two pieces are fastened together as shown in *Fig. 5*. All of the boomerangs when completed should be given several coats of linseed oil and thoroughly dried. This will keep the wood from absorbing water and becoming heavy. The last two boomerangs are thrown in a similar way to the first one, except that one of the pieces is grasped in the hand and the throw given with a quick underhand motion. A little practice is all that is necessary for one to become skillful in throwing them.

Water (*and* Frozen Water) Toys

— How to Make a Water Telescope —

Before you decide on a place to cast your hook it is best to look into the water to see whether any fish are there. Yes, certainly, you can look into the water and see the fish that are swimming about, if you have the proper equipment. What

use the water telescope regularly in searching for herring shoals or cod.

All that is necessary to make a wooden water telescope is a long wooden box, a piece of glass for one end and some paint and putty for making the seams watertight. Fix the

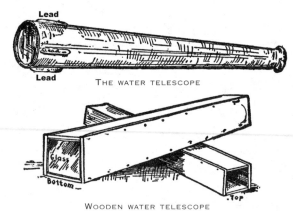

THE WATER TELESCOPE

WOODEN WATER TELESCOPE

you need is a water telescope. This is a device made of wood or metal with one end of glass. When the glass end is submerged, by looking in at the open end, objects in the water are made plainly visible to a considerable depth. In Norway, the fishermen

glass in one end of the box and leave the other open to look through.

A tin water telescope is more convenient than the wooden one, but more difficult to make. The principal essential for this is a circular piece of glass for the large end. A funnel-shaped tin horn will do for the rest. Solder in the glass at the large end, and the telescope is made. Sinkers consisting of strips of lead should be soldered on or near the bottom to counteract the buoyancy of the air contained in the watertight funnel and also to help submerge the big end. The inside of the funnel should be painted black to prevent the light from being reflected on the bright surface of the tin. If difficulty is found in obtaining a circular piece of glass, the bottom may be made square and square glass used. Use plain, clear glass, not magnifying class. To picnic parties the water telescope is of great amusement, revealing numerous odd sights in the water which may never have been seen before.

— A SIMPLE DIVING RAFT —

Campers on the shores of a lake or river frequently discover to their dismay that the water near the shore is too shallow to permit diving. The answer to this is a floating springboard, such as shown in the drawing. Two logs, about 20 ft. long and 18 in. in diameter, are fastened, about 5 ft. apart, with heavy planks that form the platform. The springboard rests on a heavy wooden crosspiece, and the end underneath is attached to a similar crosspiece. To prevent the springboard from shifting its position, a wooden pin is driven into the front crosspiece on each side of the board. Instead of using one heavy plank for the diving board, two comparatively thin planks may be arranged like the leaves of an elliptic spring, the longer board being on top. A stone anchor prevents the raft from drifting too far from shore.

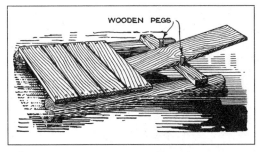

SPRINGBOARD MOUNTED ON A HEAVY RAFT MAKES DIVING POSSIBLE WHEN THE WATER OFF SHORE IS SHALLOW.

— A Homemade Punt —

A flat-bottom boat is easy to make and is one of the safest boats, as it is not readily overturned. It has the advantage of being rowed from either end, and has plenty of good seating capacity.

This punt, as shown in *Fig. 1,* is built 15 ft. long, about 20 in. deep, and 4 ft. wide. The ends are cut sloping for about 20 in. back and under. The sides are each made up from boards held together with battens on the inside of the boat near the ends and in the middle. One wide board should be used for the bottom piece. Two pins are driven in the top board of each side to serve as oarlocks.

The bottom is covered with matched boards not more than 5 in. wide. These pieces are placed together as closely as possible, using caulk between the joints and nailing them to the edges of the sideboards and to a keel strip that runs the length of the punt, as shown in *Fig. 2.* Before nailing the boards place lamp wicking between them and the edges of the sideboards. Only galvanized nails should be used. In order to make the punt perfectly watertight, it is best to use the driest lumber obtainable. At one end of the punt a skeg and a rudder can be attached as shown in *Fig. 3.*

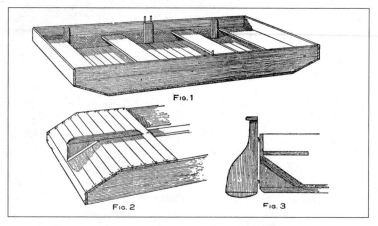

FIG. 1

FIG. 2

FIG. 3

FLAT-BOTTOM BOATS ARE EASY TO BUILD AND SAFE TO USE.

— How to build a "Pushboat" —

Much fun can be had during the swimming season with a "pushboat" of the type illustrated, which operates on the same principle as a variety of popular small-wheeled vehicles.

The hull—for lack of a better name—is made from a single thick plank, the bow end of which is pointed. After smoothing off the surface of the board, it is given at least two coats of good paint. A piece of 10-in. plank, 3 ft. long, is spiked to the deck and in the center of the hull as shown. Then a seat, made from a 10- by 18-in. board, is nailed to the stern end of the upright. Round off the edges so that they won't cut

A HAND-PROPELLED PADDLE-WHEEL WATERCRAFT OF THE CATAMARAN TYPE;
THE BACK-AND-FORTH MOVEMENT OF THE HAND LEVERS DRIVES THE
PADDLES THROUGH CONNECTING RODS AND A CRANKSHAFT.
A CURVED OUTRIGGER SUPPORTS WOODEN AND
PNEUMATIC FLOATS ON EITHER SIDE.

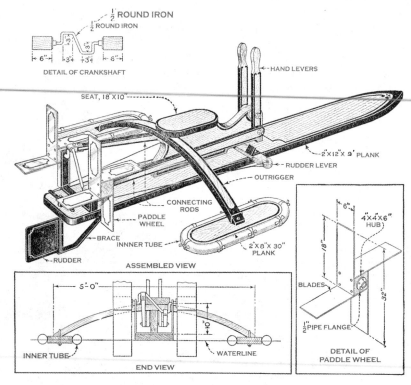

½" ROUND IRON

½" ROUND IRON

← 6" → |←3"→| |←3"→| ← 6" →

DETAIL OF CRANKSHAFT

HAND LEVERS

SEAT, 18"X10"

2"X12"X 9' PLANK

RUDDER LEVER

OUTRIGGER

CONNECTING RODS

PADDLE WHEEL

INNNER TUBE

2"X8"X 30" PLANK

BRACE

RUDDER

ASSEMBLED VIEW

4"X4"X6" HUB

BLADES

½" PIPE FLANGE

DETAIL OF PADDLE WHEEL

← 5'-0" →

INNER TUBE

WATERLINE

END VIEW

DETAIL DRAWINGS OF THE "PUSHBOAT" THAT CLEARLY SHOW HOW THE CRAFT
IS ASSEMBLED. SUCH A BOAT IS INEXPENSIVE TO BUILD AND CAN BE
MADE EASILY WITH FEW TOOLS. THE OUTRIGGER FLOATS MAKE
CAPSIZING OR SINKING DIFFICULT IF NOT IMPOSSIBLE, AND
IT CAN BE DRIVEN AT GOOD SPEED IN QUIET WATERS.

the legs. A mortise is cut into the upper edge of the upright under the stern end of the seat, to receive the outrigger, and a recess under the forward end, to clear the rudder lever. A curved piece of timber 5 ft. long is used for the outrigger, and two round-end planks are fastened to its ends, as in the drawing. These outboard planks should be slightly lower than the hull. The outrigger is then spiked to its mortise in the upright so that the planks will be at the same distance away from the hull and parallel to it. The planks are given buoyancy by tying an inflated inner tube around the edge of each; they can be protected with a wrapping of canvas or burlap.

Movement—forward or backward—of the craft is made by paddle wheels, operated by a pair of levers mounted in front of the seat. The paddle wheels are made by screwing four sheet-metal blades to the sides of an oak hub, as indicated in the detail drawing. Two such paddle wheels are required, and they are attached to the ends of a crankshaft, as detailed. Each end of the shaft is threaded to screw into the pipe flanges fastened to the paddle wheels. The crankshaft is supported on a U-shaped piece of heavy iron, the bearing holes being drilled 10 in. above the deck. In screwing the paddle wheels onto the crankshaft, the flange threads should be coated with white lead and screwed as tightly as possible to prevent them from turning loose by the action of the wheels in motion.

Then bolt a pair of levers, about 30 in. long, one on each side of the bow end of the upright in front of the seat. The pivot bolt goes through the top corner of the upright and should be provided with washers. Form smooth handles at the top of

the levers and drill holes about 6 in. below the pivot bolt, for the connecting-rod bolts. The levers must work back and forth freely. Motion from the levers is communicated to the paddle wheels by means of connecting rods, which are made of oak or ash. These rods are loosely bolted to the levers in front, while the rear ends are round-notched and fitted with flat-iron bearing straps that fit around the crankshaft. By moving the levers back and forth, the paddle wheels are revolved.

Any sort of rudder can be hung from the stern and fitted with a tiller as in the drawing, so that the hands are not required to guide the craft. After completion, the whole craft is given several coats of paint to protect it from the water.

With the operator aboard, the hull will be nearly submerged, but the two inner-tube floats at the ends of the outrigger will keep it afloat and steady so that there will be no possibility of its capsizing or sinking in smooth water.

Sit facing the bow, grasping a lever in each hand and the feet on the steering lever, and then commence to pump the hand levers back and forth at the same time steadying the rudder.

— A Portable Folding Boat —

A boat that is inexpensive, easily made, and readily transported is shown in the illustration. Because the bow section folds inside of the stern portion, it is important that the dimensions be followed closely. The material used is ⅞-in. throughout.

Make a full-size diagram of the plan to determine the exact sizes of the pieces. Brass screws are best for fastening this type of work, but copperplated nails may be used. Tongue-and-groove stock is best for the bottom. The joints should not be driven together too firmly, to allow for expansion, and all joints in the boat should be packed with pitch.

The adjoining ends of the sections should be made at the same

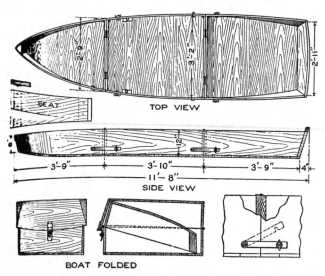

THE CONSTRUCTION OF THE PORTABLE BOAT IS SIMPLE. WHEN FOLDED IT MAY BE TRANSPORTED READILY AND MAY EVEN BE CARRIED IN THREE PARTS. IT IS INEXPENSIVE AND SHOULD PROVE A VALUABLE ADDITION TO THE CAMPING OUTFIT.

time to ensure a satisfactory fit when joined. Braces are fixed into corners.

Metal straps hold the sections together at the bottom of the hinged joints. These should be fitted so that there is little possibility of their becoming loosened accidentally. The front end of each strip is pivoted in a hole and the other end is slotted vertically on the lower edge. Their bolts are set firmly into the side of the boat, being held with nuts on both sides of the wood. A wing nut, prevented from coming off by riveting the end of the bolt, holds the slotted end. Sockets for the oars may be cut into hardwood pieces fastened to the gunwales. The construction of the seats is shown in the small sketch at the left.

— A SNOWBALL MAKER —

Snowball making is slow when carried on by hand. Where a thrower is employed in a snow fort it becomes necessary to have a number of assistants in making the snowballs. The time of making these balls can be greatly reduced by the use of the snowball maker shown in the illustration.

The base consists of a board, 24 in. long by 6½ in. wide by 1 in. thick. A block of wood, A, is hollowed out in the center to make a depression in the shape of a hemisphere, 2 1/12 in. in diameter by 1¼ in. deep. This block is nailed to the base about 1 in. from one end. To make the dimensions come out right, fasten a block, B, 6 in. high—made of one or more pieces—at the other end of the base with its back edge 14½ in. from the center of the hemispherical depression. On top of this block a 20-in.-long lever, C, is hinged. Another block, D, is

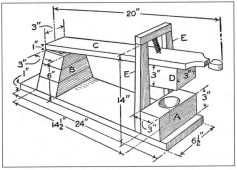

A DEVICE FOR MAKING SNOWBALLS QUICKLY AND PERFECTLY SPHERICAL IN SHAPE.

made with a hemispherical depression like the block *A*, and fastened to the underside of the lever so that the depressions in both blocks will coincide. The lever end is shaped into a handle.

Two uprights, *E*, are fastened to the backside of the block *A* as guides for the lever *C*. A piece is fastened across their tops and a spring is attached between it and the lever. A curtain-roller spring will be suitable.

In making the balls a bunch of snow is thrown into the lower depression and the lever brought down with considerable force.

— AN INEXPENSIVE BOBSLED —

Any boy who can drive a nail and bore a hole can make a bobsled on short notice. The materials necessary are four good, solid barrel staves; four blocks of wood 4 in. long, 4 in. wide, and 2 in. thick; two pieces 12 in. long, 4 in. wide, and 1 in. thick; one piece 12 in. long, 2 in. wide, and 1¾ in. thick; and a good board, 4 ft. long, 12 in. wide, and 1 in. thick.

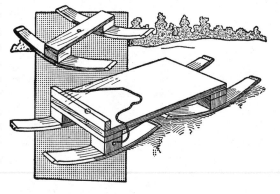

A BOBSLED OF SIMPLE CONSTRUCTION USING ORDINARY BARREL STAVES FOR THE RUNNERS.

The crosspieces and knees are made with the blocks and the 1-in. pieces, 12 in. long, as shown, to which the staves are nailed for runners. One of these pieces with the runners is fastened to one end of the board, the other is attached with a bolt in the center. The 1¾-by 2-in. piece, 12 in. long, is fastened across the top of the board at the front end. A rope fastened to the knees of the front runners provides a means of steering the sled.

The sled can be quickly made, and it will serve the purpose well when an expensive one cannot be had.

— A HOMEMADE YANKEE BOBSLED —

A good coasting sled, which I call a Yankee bob, can be made from two hardwood barrel staves, two pieces of 2- by 6-in. pine, a piece of hardwood for the rudder, and few pieces of boards. The 2- by 6-in. pieces should be a little longer than one-third the length of the staves, and each piece cut tapering from the widest part, 6 in., down to 2 in., and then fastened to the staves with large wood screws as shown in *Fig. 1*. Boards 1 in. thick are nailed on top of the pieces for a seat and to hold the runner together. The boards should be of such a length as to make the runners about 18 in. apart.

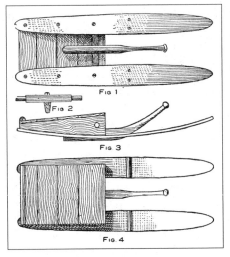

RUNNERS MADE OF BARREL STAVES.

A 2-in. shaft of wood, *Fig. 2,* is turned down to 1 in. on the ends and put through holes that must be bored in the front ends of the 2- by 6-in. pieces. A small pin is put through each end of the shaft to keep it in place. The rudder is a 1½ in. hardwood piece that should be tapered to ½ in. at the bottom and shod with a thin piece of iron. A ½ in. hole is bored through the center of the shaft and a lag screw put through and turned in the rudder piece, making it so the rudder will turn right and left and up and down. Two cleats are nailed to the upper sides of the runner and in the middle lengthways for the person's heels to rest against.

Any child can guide this bob. All he has to do is to guide the rudder right and left to go in the direction named. If he wants to stop, he pulls up on the handle and the heel of the rudder will dig into the snow, causing too much friction for the sled to go any farther.

— Making a Coasting Toboggan —

Essentials of good toboggan, whether for coasting or use in transportation, are strength and lightness. And when it is to be made in the home shop, the construction must be simple. That shown in the illustration and detailed in the working sketches was designed to meet these requirements. The materials for the toboggan proper and the forms over which it is bent may be obtained at small expense.

Smoothness of finished surface, freedom from tendency to splinter, and ability to stand up under abuse being requisite qualities in the wood used to make a toboggan, three varieties may be mentioned in their order of merit: hickory, birch, and oak. Birch is softer than hickory and easily splintered but acquires an excellent polish on the bottom. Oak stands bending well but does not become as smooth on the running surface as close-grained woods. Do not use quarter-sawn oak because of the cross-grain flakes in its structure.

THIS TOBOGGAN WILL AFFORD THE MAKER MUCH PLEASURE. IT MAY BE MADE AS AN INDIVIDUAL PROJECT OR AS A JOINT UNDERTAKING BY SEVERAL BOYS.

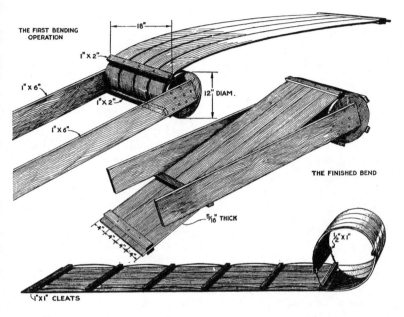

THE BOARDS FOR THE BOTTOM ARE STEAMED OR BOILED AT THE BOW
ENDS AND BENT OVER THE FORM. AS THE BENDING OPERATION
PROGRESSES, THE BOARDS ARE NAILED TO THE FORM WITH
CLEATS AND PERMITTED TO DRY IN THIS POSITION.

Though the best toboggan is made of a single board, both the securing of material and its construction are rather difficult. Narrow strips are easily bent to shape but do not make a durable article. A toboggan made of four boards is practical. The mill bill for one 7 ½ ft. long by 16 in. wide and for the bending frame is as follows: 4 pieces, 5/16 by 4 in. by 10 ft., hardwood; 7 pieces, 1 by 1 in.

by 16 in., hardwood; 2 pieces, ½ by 1 in. by 16 in., hardwood; 2 pieces 1 by 6 in. by 6 ft., common boards; 6 pieces 1 by 2 in. by 18 in., common boards; 1 cylindrical block, 12 in. diameter by 18 in. long.

The form for the bending of the pieces is made of the common boards and the block. A block sawn from the end of a dry log is excellent. Heat it, if convenient, just before bending the strips. The boards for the bottom should be selected for straightness or grain and freedom from knots and burls. Carefully plane the side intended for the wearing surface, and bevel the edges so that, when placed together, they form a wide "V" joint half the depth of the boards. The 1- by 1-in. pieces are for cross cleats and should be notched on one side, 1 in. from each end, to receive the side ropes. The two ½- by 1-in. pieces are to be placed one at each side of the extreme end of the bent portion, to reinforce it.

Bore a gimlet hole through the centers of the 1- by 2- by 18-in. pieces, and 4¼ in. each side of this hole, bore two others. Nail the end of one of the 6-ft. boards to each end of the block so that their extended ends are parallel. With 3-in. nails, fasten one of the bored pieces to the block between the boards, temporarily inserting a ½-in. piece to hold it out that distance from the block.

Steam about 3-ft. of the ends of the boards, or boil them in a tank. Clamp or nail the boards together at the dry ends, edge to edge, between two of the 1- by 2-in. pieces. Leave about ¼-in. opening between boards. Thrust the steamed ends under the cleat nailed on the block, the nails

that hold it slipping up between the boards. Bear down on the toboggan carefully, nailing on another of the bored cleats when the toboggan boards have been curved around the block as far as he floor will permit. The nails, of course, go between the boards.

Now turn the construction over and bend up the toboggan, following the boards around the block with more of the nailed cleats, until the clamped end is down between the two 6-ft. boards where it can be held by a piece nailed across. More of the cleats may be nailed on if desired. In fact, the closer together the cleats are the less danger there is of splintering the boards, and the more perfect the conformity of the boards to the mold.

Allow at least four days for drying before removing the boards from the form. Clamp the ½- by 1-in. pieces on each side of the extreme ends of the bent bows, drill holes through, and rivet them. A 1- by 1-in. crossbar is riveted to the inside of the bow at the extreme front and another directly under the extremity of the curved end. These cleats are wired together to hold the bend of the bow. The tail-end crossbar should be placed not nearer than

2½ in. from the end of the boards, while the remainder of the crossbars are evenly spaced between the front and back pieces, taking care that the notched side is always placed down. Trim off uneven ends, scrape and sand the bottom well, and finish the toboggan with oil. Run a ⅜-in. rope through the notches under the ends of the crosspieces and the toboggan is completed.

Screws are satisfactory substitutes for rivets in fastening together the parts; and wire nails, of a length to allow for about ¼ in. clinch, give a fair job.

In *the* Playground

— A Ferris Wheel —

The whole wheel is carried on two uprights, each 3 by 4 in., by 10 ft. long. In the upper ends of these pieces, *A*, a half circle is cut out to receive the main shaft *B*. The end of the uprights are sunk 3 ft. into the earth and about 4 ft. apart, then braced as shown. They are further braced by wires attached to rings that are secured with staples near the top. The bearings should each have a cap to keep the shaft in place. These

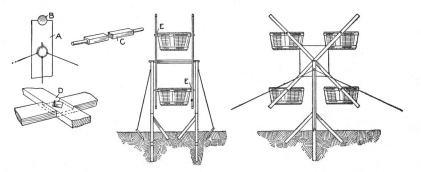

DETAIL OF THE UPRIGHTS, AXLE, AND SPOKES, AND THE END
AND SIDE ELEVATIONS OF THE COMPLETED WHEEL,
SHOWING BRACES AND CARS ATTACHED.

can be made of blocks of wood with a semicircle cut out, the blocks being nailed over the shaft, while it is in place, the nails entering the ends of the uprights.

The main shaft *C* is made of a 2½ in. square piece of good material, 4 ft. long. The ends are made round to serve as bearings, and the square part is fitted with the spokes or car carriers. These consist of 4 pieces, each 1 in. thick by 4 in. wide by 13 ft. long. In the center of each piece cut a notch one-half the thickness, so that when each pair of pieces is crossed they will fit together with the surfaces smooth, as shown in *D*. A square hole is cut through the pieces as shown to fit on the square part of the main axle. Though it is not shown in the illustration, it is best to strengthen this joint with another piece of wood, cut to fit on the axle and securely attached to the spokes.

The cars or carriers are made of two sugar barrels cut in half. The hoops are then securely nailed inside and outside. A block of wood, *E*, is securely attached to the half barrels on the outside, and another block on the inside opposite the outside block. Holes are bored 2½ ft. from the ends of the spokes and a bolt run through them and through the blocks on the edges of the half barrels. The extending ends of the spokes are used to propel the wheel. Four children can ride in the wheel at one time.

— A TWISTY THRILLER MERRY-GO-ROUND —

"Step right up! Three twisting thrillers for a penny—a tenth of a dime!" was the familiar invitation that attracted customers to the delights of a homemade merry-go-round of novel design. The patrons were not disappointed but came back for more. The power for the whirling thriller is produced by the heavy, twisted rope suspended from the limb of a tree or other suitable support. The rope is cranked up by means off a notched disk, *A*, grasped at the handle *B*, the car being lifted off. The thriller is stopped when the brake plate *I*, rests on the weighted box *L*.

Manila rope, ¾ in. or more in diameter, is used for the support. It is rigged with a spreader about 2 ft. long, at the top, as shown. The disk is built up of wood as detailed, and notches, *C*, provided for the ropes. The rope is wound up and the car is suspended from it by the hook, which should be strong and deep enough so that the rope cannot slip out, as indicated at *H*.

The car is made of a section of 2- by 4-in. lumber, *D*. The lumber should be 10 ft. long, to which braces, *E*, of 1-by 4-in. lumber are fastened with nails or screws. The upper ends of the pieces *E* are blocked up with the centerpiece *F*, nailed securely, and the wire link *G* is fastened

through the joint.

The seats, *J*, are suspended at the ends of the 2- by 3-in. bar, with their inner ends lower, as shown. This provides better seating when the thriller is in action. The seats are supported by rope or strap-iron brackets, *K*, set 15 in. apart. The box should be high enough so that the seats do not strike the ground.

THE SUPPORTING ROPES ARE WOUND UP AT THE DISK A.
THE CAR IS HOOKED INTO PLACE AND THE PASSENGERS TAKE THEIR SEATS
FOR A THRILLING RIDE, UNTIL THE BRAKE PLATE I RESTS ON THE BOX.

— Child's Swing Built of Pipes in a Narrow Space —

A narrow space between two city houses was used to erect a swing as detailed in the illustration. A piece of 2-in. iron pipe, *A*, was cut 1 ft. longer than the space between the walls. Two pieces of 2½ in. pipe and a 2½- by 2½- by 1¼-in. tee, as shown in the detail, was slipped over the 2-in. pipe, which was built into the walls. A 1¼-in. pipe, *B*, 20 ft. long, bent as shown, was joined to the tee. And a seat, *C*, was attached. The construction of the seat is shown in detail, being fixed to the wooden part with washers, nuts, and a threaded nipple,

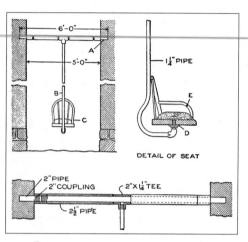

THIS SUBSTANTIAL SWING GUARDS THE YOUNGSTERS FROM INJURY BRUSHING AGAINST THE BRICK WALLS.

D. A cushion and a removable safety bar, *E*, were also features. This swing is safer than one of rope, and will stand much greater wear.

— Adjustable Stilts —

The beginner with stilts always selects short sticks so that he will not be very far from the ground. But as he becomes more experienced, the longer the sticks the better. Then, too, the small boy and the large boy require different lengths of sticks.

The device shown makes a pair of sticks universal for the use of beginners or a boy of any age or height.

To make the stilts, procure two long hardwood sticks of even length, and smooth up the edges; then begin at a point 1 ft. from one end and bore

12 holes, ⅜ in. in diameter and 2 in. apart from center to center. If there is no diestock at hand, have a blacksmith or mechanic make a thread on both ends of a ⅜-in. rod, 12 in. long. Bend the rod in the shape shown, so that the two threaded ends will be just 2 in. apart from center to center. The thread on the straight horizontal end should be so long that a nut can be placed on both sides of the stick. A piece of garden hose or small rubber hose, slipped on the rod, will keep the shoe sole from slipping. The steps can be set in any two adjacent holes to give the desired height.

STILTS HAVING STIRRUPS THAT CAN BE SET AT ANY DESIRED HEIGHT.

— BEGINNER'S HELPER FOR ROLLER SKATING —

One of the most amusing as well as useful devices for a beginner on roller skates is shown in the sketch. The device is made of ¾-in. pipe and pipe fittings, with a strip of sheet metal 1 in. wide fastened about halfway down on the legs. On the bottom of each leg is fastened one ordinary furniture caster that allows the machine to roll easily on the floor. The rear is left open to allow the beginner to enter, then by grasping the top rail he is able to move about the floor at ease, without fear of falling.

BEGINNER CANNOT FALL.

— A MERRY-GO-ROUND POLE —

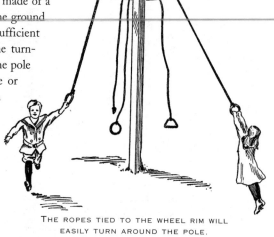

THE ROPES TIED TO THE WHEEL RIM WILL EASILY TURN AROUND THE POLE.

An inexpensive merry-go-round can be made of a single pole set in the ground where there is sufficient vacant space for the turning of the ropes. The pole may be of gas pipe or wood, long enough to extend about 12 ft. above the ground. An iron wheel is attached on the upper end so that it will revolve easily on an axle, which may be an iron pin driven into the post. A few iron washers placed on the pin under the wheel will reduce the friction.

Ropes of varying lengths are tied to the rim of the wheel. The rider takes hold of a rope and runs around the pole to start the wheel in motion. He then swings clear of the ground. Streamers of different colors, and flowers for special occasions, may be attached to make a pretty display.

— SEESAW BUILT FOR ONE —

A single child, seeking means of entertaining herself, has a hard time in getting any pleasure out of the ordinary seesaw.

The drawing shows a combination of seesaw and rocking horse that can be used by one child. The construction is quite simple, the dimensions and weight of the counterweight being varied to meet different requirements. The seat is supported on an iron axle by a pair of strap hinges, one end of each hinge being bent to fit around the axle. The counterweight, which may be an iron casting or a block of cement, is attached to a curved iron bined weight of child and board, and a little experimenting will be necessary to strike the correct balance. The exact mass of weight can be found by first attaching a bucket

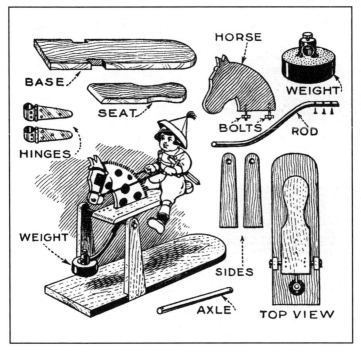

A COMBINATION OF ROCKING HORSE AND SEESAW THAT MAKES IT POSSIBLE FOR A LONE YOUNGSTER TO ENTERTAIN HERSELF. A COUNTERWEIGHT IS PROVIDED FOR BALANCING THE WEIGHT OF THE CHILD AND SEAT.

rod fastened under the front end of the seat. The counterweight should be a trifle heavier than the com- or bag of sand to the end of the rod, and adding or removing sand until the proper weight has been found.

MAKING MAGIC

—

SLICK TRICKS

— A FINGER-TRAP TRICK —

You can fool your friends with the little joker made to trap a finger. It consists of a piece of paper, about 6 in. wide and 12 in. or longer. To prepare the paper, cut two slots in the one end as shown and then roll it up in tube form, beginning at the end with the cuts, then fasten the end with glue. The inside diameter should be ½ in.

When the glue is dry, ask someone to push a finger into either end. This will be easy enough to do, but to remove the finger is a different matter. The end coils tend to pull out and hold the finger. If the tube is made of tough paper, it will stand considerable pull.

IT IS EASY TO INSERT A FINGER IN THE TUBE, BUT TO GET IT OUT IS ALMOST IMPOSSIBLE.

— A Ring-and-Egg Trick —

This trick consists in borrowing a ring and wrapping it in a handkerchief from which it is made to disappear, only to be found in an egg, taken from a number on a plate.

Obtain a wedding ring and sew it into one corner of a handkerchief. After borrowing a ring from a member of the audience, pretend to wrap it in the center of the handkerchief, but instead wrap up the one concealed in the corner, retaining the borrowed one in the hand. Before beginning the performance, place in the bottom of an egg cup a small quantity of soft wax. When getting the cup, slip the borrowed ring into the wax in an upright position. An egg is then chosen by anyone in the audience. This is placed in the egg cup, the ring in the bottom being pressed into the shell. With a buttonhook break the top of the shell and fish out the ring. The handkerchief is then shaken out to show that the ring has vanished.

— A Matchbox Trick —

All that is required to perform this trick is a box of safety matches. Four matches are removed and three of them arranged as shown in the sketch. The performer then tells his friends that he will light the fourth match and set the cross match on fire in the center, then asks which match of the standing ones will light first. Most people will not stop to think and will guess either one or the other. As a matter of fact, after the cross match is set on fire, it soon burns the wood away, and the pressure of the two side matches will

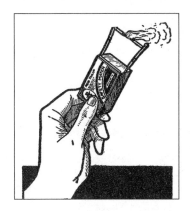

cause it to spring out so that neither catches fire.

— VANISHING HANDKERCHIEF TRICK —

The necessary articles used in performing this trick are the handkerchief, vanishing wand, a long piece of glass tubing about ½ in. shorter than the wand, and a paper tube closed at one end and covered with a cap at the other. The handkerchief rod, shown at *C,* is concealed in the paper tube *A* before the performance. The glass tube *B,* after being shown empty, is put into the paper tube *A* so that, unknown to the spectators, the handkerchief rod now is within it. The handkerchief is then placed over the opening of

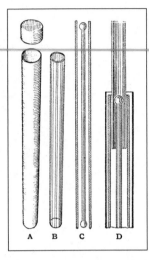

the tube and pushed in by means of the wand. In doing this, the handkerchief and the rod are pushed into the wand, as shown in *D.* After the wand is removed, the cap is placed over the paper tube, and this is given to someone to hold. The command for the handkerchief to vanish is given, and it is found to be gone when the glass tube is taken out of the paper cover. This is a novel way of making a handkerchief vanish. It can be used in a great number of tricks and can be varied to suit the performer.

— DEVICE FOR A FINGER TUG-OF-WAR GAME—

Considerable pleasure is afforded by this tug-of-war game. Two contestants, one at each end, take hold of the rollers with their forefingers and thumbs and endeavor to move the pointer to their respective ends. The game is fun for people of all ages, and they will all want to try it.

The device should be made strong enough to stand up to wear and tear. The top and bottom are boards, ½ by 8 by 24 in. Four blocks, 3 in. high and 2½ in. square, are fastened between them at the corners with screws. The rollers are set in the blocks and held by small nails passing through them and against the inner faces of the blocks. The pointer is made of a strip of brass, bent to a rectangle around the top board, in line with numbers from 9 to zero and back to 9 (scores for each contestant). Cords extend from the pointer inside the box and are tied to the rollers.

— THE DIE-AND-BOX TRICK —

The die-and-box trick, often performed on the stage, is a very interesting and mystifying one. The apparatus, however, is simple. It consists of a box, die, a piece of tin in the form of three adjacent sides of the die, and a hat. The die and box are constructed entirely of wood, ⅛ in. thick; the piece of tin can

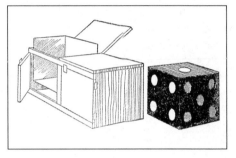

WITH THE FALSE DIE IN PLACE
THE BOX APPEARS TO BE EMPTY.

be cut from any large coffee can. The box is closed by four doors, as shown in *Fig. 1,* two of which are 2¾ in. square, and the others, 3⅛ by 3¼ in. The first two are the front doors and are preferably hinged with cloth to the two uprights *A* and *B.* Small pieces of tin are fastened on the doors at *C* and *D,* to provide a means to open them. The other doors are placed on top and are hinged to the back, as shown.

The die is 3 in. square on all sides, and is constructed of two pieces, 3 in. square; two pieces, 2¾ by 3 in., and two pieces, 2¾ in. square. These are fastened together with ½-in. brads. The tin, forming the false die, is cut out as shown in *Fig. 2,* and is then bent on the dotted lines and soldered together on the joint formed by the two edges *E* and *F.* All parts should be painted a dull black with white spots on the die and false die.

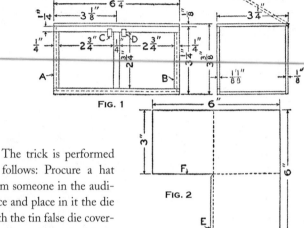

FIG. 1

FIG. 2

THE BOX WITH DOORS ON ONE SIDE AND
THE TOP, AND THE FALSE-DIE PATTERN.

The trick is performed as follows: Procure a hat from someone in the audience and place in it the die with the tin false die covering three sides of a block, at the same time telling the audience that the block will be caused to pass from the hat into the box, the latter being placed some distance away. Inform the audience that it would be more difficult for the die to pass from the box into the hat. Remove the tin piece from the hat and leave the die, holding the surfaces of the false die toward the audience. This will give the impression that the die has been removed. Set the hat on the table above the level of the eyes of the audience. With the back of the box toward the audience, open one top door and insert the tin piece in the right-hand compartment so that one side touches the back, another the side, and the other the bottom of the box. Close the door and open the two doors of the opposite compartment, which, when shown, will appear to be empty. Tilt the box to this side and open the doors of the side opposite to the one just opened, which, of course, will be empty. This should be done several times until someone asks that all doors be opened at the same time. After a few more reversals and openings, open all doors and show it empty, then take the die from the hat.

— Wireless Lighted Lamp Deception —

Window displays of a puzzling nature usually draw crowds. A lighted globe lying in full view, yet apparently not connected to any source of electricity, could easily be arranged as a window display, deceiving the closest observer. A mirror, or window glass, backed with some opaque material, should be used for the foundation of the device. For the display lamp, it is best to use a 25- or 40-watt tungsten, as these will lie

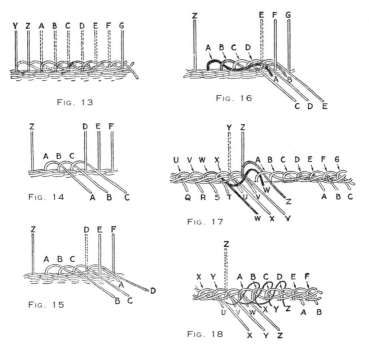

FIG. 13

FIG. 16

FIG. 14

FIG. 17

FIG. 15

FIG. 18

A SIMPLE BREAKDOWN ROLE FOR THE TOP.
ALSO A METHOD OF FORMING A ROLL BETWEEN
THE FIRST AND SECOND SPOKES, WHERE ONLY THREE
SPOKES ARE TURNED DOWN BEFORE THE
THROWING-ACROSS PROCESS BEGINS.

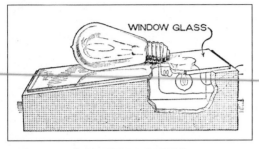

AN ELECTRIC LIGHTBULB
LIGHTED ON A PIECE OF GLASS
MAKES A GOOD WINDOW ATTRACTION.

to pass through. One of the wires should be looped, passed through the hole in the cap, and hooked onto the bare wire connecting with the plug on top of the lamp. The other wire should be fastened to the brass cap near the drilled hole, after which the lamp may be placed in position and the two wires connected to a source of electricity. If proper care has been taken and no crosses occur, the lamp will light. And if the display is placed in the proper surroundings, it will prove very deceiving. To protect against a fuse blow-out from a short circuit, it is advisable to run another lamp in series with the display lamp as shown.

flatter on the glass than the larger sizes, and the deception will not be as easily discovered. The place where the brass cap of the lamp touches the glass should be marked and a small hole drilled through to the wire connecting the tungsten filament to the plug on the top of the lamp. At any suitable place, a hole should be drilled in the glass plate, no larger than is necessary, to permit two small cotton-covered magnet wires

— THE MAGIC CLOCK HAND —

The hand, or pointer, is the only working part needed to perform this trick. A clock face can be drawn on any piece of white paper and a pin stuck in its center on which the hand revolves. The hand *A* is cut from a piece of sheet brass and may be in any form or design desired. It must, however, balance perfectly on the axle, which passes through a ¼-in. hole in the center, or else the magic part will fail. The illustration shows a good design with dimensions that will cause it to balance well; however, this can be adjusted by removing some metal from the end that is heavier with a file or tinner's snips, or a bit of solder may be stuck to the lighter end.

A disk, *B*, is cut from a piece of sheet brass, 1⅛ in. in diameter. Twelve ³/₃₂-in. holes are drilled at equal distance apart near the edge, and a ¼-in. hole is drilled in its center. This disk is soldered to the hand where both ¼-in. holes will coincide. It is necessary to procure two washers, *C* and *D*, which are embossed—raised—in the center, and about 1¼ in. in diameter. These can be purchased from a dealer in curtain rods, and are the washers

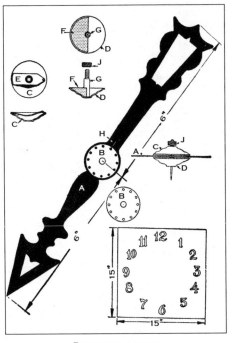

used on the ends of the rods. A careful mechanic can raise the center portion of a brass disk by beating it over a hole with a ball-peen hammer.

One of the washers, *C*, has a spring, *E*, soldered at one end, and the other carries a small projection that will engage the holes in the disk, *B*. The projection can be made by

driving the metal out with a center punch, set on the opposite side.

The washer, *D*, is provided with a lead weight, *F*, and a ¼-in. stud, *G*, is soldered in the center. The stud has a ¹/₁₆-in. hole drilled through its center for the pin axle. The weight is made by filling the washer with melted metal, which when cold is removed and sawn in two. One piece is then stuck in the washer with shellac. The stud is ⅞ in. long with the upper part, about ¼ in. in length, filed, or turned down, smaller, and threaded. Just below the thread, or on the shoulder, the body is filed square to fit a square hole filed in the face of washer *C* carrying the spring. This square hole and stud end are necessary for both washers to turn together.

The dial can be made of a piece of thick cardboard, or thin wood, with the numbers 1 to 12 painted on, like a clock face. A pin, 1/16 in. in diameter, or an ordinary large pin, is run through the center so that it will project on the face side on which the hand is to revolve.

The washer *D* with the weight is placed on the rear side of the hand with the fixed stud running through the hole in the center of the hand; then the washer *C* is placed on the square part of the stud, and the nut, *J*, which should have a round, knurled edge, is turned on the threads. This will cause the projection on the spring *E* to engage one

A NUMBER IS MENTIONED AND THE PERFORMER GIVES THE WASHERS A TWIST TO SET THE CONCEALED WEIGHT SO THAT THE HAND WHEN HUNG ON THE DIAL WILL BE DRAWN TO POINT OUT THE NUMBER SELECTED.

of the small holes on the disk *B*. In turning the two washers, *C* and *D*, with the thumb and first finger of the right hand, the projection snapping into the holes of the disk *B* can be felt. The hand is placed on the pin of the clock face, and the washers are turned so that the weight will make it point to 12. Scratch a mark on the hand at *H*. Also mark a line on the front washer at this point. These lines are necessary, as they enable the performer to know how many holes to snap the spring over to have the hand point at any desired number.

By reversing the hand it will point to a different number; for instance, if set for 8 and put on the pin backward, it will point to 4, and so on with other settings. The dial can be held in the hand, hung on a stand, or fastened to a wall, and can be used to the day of the week, time of day, cards selected, etc. The audience can call for any number on the clock face, and the setting of the disks is an easy matter while holding the hand, or pointer, in the hands, so that it cannot be detected.

— THE MYSTIC CLIMBING RING —

The performer hands out a wand for examination and borrows a finger ring. He holds the wand in his hand, point upward, and drops the ring on it. Then he makes hypnotizing passes over the wand with the other hand, and causes the ring to climb toward the top, stop at any place desired, pass backward, and at last fall from the wand. The wand and ring are examined again by the audience.

To produce this little trick, the performer must first provide himself with a round, black stick, about 14 in. long, a piece of No. 60 black cotton thread, about 18 in. long, and a small bit of beeswax. Tie one end of the thread to the top button on the coat and to the free end stick the beeswax, which is stuck to the lower button until ready for the trick.

After the wand is returned, secretly stick the waxed end to the top of the wand, and then drop the ring on it. Moving the wand slightly from oneself will cause the ring to move upward, and relaxing it causes the ring to fall. In the final stage remove the thread and hand out the wand for examination.

CRAZY CARDS

— THE "X-RAY" PACK OF CARDS —

This trick is a "mind-reading" stunt that is worked on a new principle and is very puzzling. A full pack of cards is shown and half of them are handed out, the other half being kept by the performer. A spectator is asked to select any card from those he holds, and insert it in the pack held by the performer, while the latter's eyes are closed or his head is turned. Without manipulating the pack in any way, the performer places it against his forehead and instantly names the card chosen by the spectator.

The cards held by the performer are prepared for the trick by cutting a slot ⅛ in. wide and 1 in. long in one corner of 25 cards, with the sharp point of a penknife, in such a manner that all the slots coincide. In presenting the trick the performer keeps all the prepared cards, and also one card that has no slot, the latter being kept on top of the pack so that the slots cannot be seen by the spectators. The performer's thumb is held over the slots when the bottom of the pack is shown. A spectator is asked to insert a card face down into the cards the performer holds in his hand. When this is done, the thumb is lifted from the slot as the cards are raised to the forehead, when the performer can look through the pack and see the index on the card the spectator has selected. After the forehead "stall," the performer announces the card selected. The trick is repeated by "fanning" out the cards and extracting the card named.

— The Enchanted Card Frame —

A mystifying card trick, in which the performer makes use of the enchanted card frame shown in detail in the illustration, is performed as follows: A pack of playing cards is given to one of the spectators, who selects a card, noting the number and suit. The card is then placed in an envelope and burned by the spectator. The performer takes the ashes and loads them into a pistol, which he aims at a small frame, shown as empty, and set upon a table a few feet distant. The frame is covered with a handkerchief, and the pistol is fired at a frame. On removing the handkerchief the selected and destroyed card appears in the frame, from which it is taken at the back.

The trick is performed as follows: A forced deck is prepared having 24 like cards, and the backs of the cards are held to the spectators when a card is selected. The frame is made of molding 2 in. wide, mitered at the corners, and of the size indicated, the opening being 6⅜ by 7½ in. The general views of the frame in normal position and inverted are shown in *Figs. 1* and *5*. A pocket is cut in the lower edge of the frame at

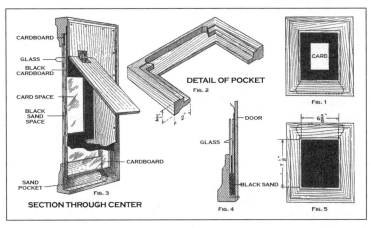

A POCKET IS CUT INTO THE FRAME AND FILLED WITH BLACK SAND, OBSCURING THE CARD WHEN THE FRAME IS INVERTED.

the back, as shown in detail in *Fig. 2*. A pane of glass is fitted into the frame, and on the three edges other than the one having a pocket, ⅛ in. thick strips of cardboard are glued as a bearing for the second piece of glass, as shown in *Fig. 4*. The back of the frame is fitted with a cover of thin wood, and a hinged door is arranged in the center of the back, as shown in *Fig. 3*.

A mat of black cardboard is fitted into the frame to form a background behind the card, *Fig. 1*. The pocket at the bottom is filled with black sand—that used by sign painters is satisfactory—and the frame is ready to receive the card for the performance of the trick. One of the cards from the forced deck is placed in the frame. By inverting the latter the sand is caused to run between the glass partitions, concealing the card on the black mat behind it. In this condition it is exhibited to the spectators and then placed upon the table. A handkerchief is thrown over it. The pistol is one of the toy variety and a cap is fired in it. In picking up the frame the performer turns it over, while removing the handkerchief, so that the black sand runs back into the pocket in the frame.

— A Magic Change Card —

Procure two cards, the 5 of diamonds and the 5 of spades, for example. Bend each exactly in the center, with the face of the cards in, and then paste any card on the back, with its face against the two ends of the bent cards. The two opposite ends will then have their backs together, and these are also pasted. The illustration clearly shows this arrangement.

A CARD HAVING TWO FACES, EITHER OF WHICH CAN BE SHOWN TO THE AUDIENCE INSTANTLY.

To perform the trick pick up this card, which is placed in the pack beforehand, and show to the audience both the front and back of the card, being sure to keep the center part flat against one end or the other, then pass the hand over the card, and in doing so catch the center part and turn it over. The card can be changed back again in the same manner.

— Two Effective Card Tricks —

The first trick involves the use of four cards, which are "fanned" out to show a corresponding number of kings. The performer repeats the magical "abracadabra," and, presto! The same hand has changed to four aces when it is again displayed—a third pass, and only blank cards are shown. Six cards are required for this trick, three of which are unprepared, the other three being "prepared." The three unprepared cards are the king, ace, and blank card shown in *Fig. 1*. The three other cards are prepared by pasting a part of the remaining three kings over a corner of the aces of their corresponding suits as shown in *Fig. 2*. In the presentation of this trick, the four kings are first displayed to the audience. The real king being on the top, the cards are fanned as in *Fig. 3*, so as to show only the kings on the corners of the other three cards. Then, the performer picks up the ace of spades, which has been left face up on the table, and announces that he will place it directly behind the king of spades, which he does. He then lays the king of spades on the table. The cards are then closed up and turned over so that the cards are held at

what is the top of the cards in the first presentation of the four kings. Then, the cards are fanned out to show the four aces, as in *Fig. 4*. The index numbers in the corners of the aces should be erased or covered up, otherwise it will be impossible to show the blank cards.

The manipulator now states that by placing a blank card, which he picks up from the table where the aces of spades are, the spots will disappear from all of the cards. The ace of spades is placed on the table, the blank card taking its place. The cards are then closed and fanned out, the hand showing four blank cards, as in *Fig. 5*.

In the second trick, an ace of diamonds is held in one hand and ace of spades in the other, but while held in full view of the audience, the cards change places. The prepared cards are made from two aces of diamonds, from which the corner index pips and letters have been erased. An ace of spades is also required, the center of which is cut from the rest of the card as indicated in *Fig. 6*, which shows the appearance of the three prepared cards. In presenting this particular trick, an ace of diamonds

281

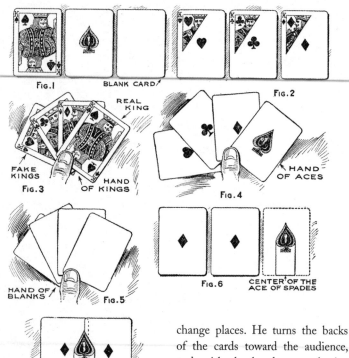

FIG.1   BLANK CARD

FIG.2

FAKE KINGS   FIG.3   HAND OF KINGS

HAND OF ACES   FIG.4

HAND OF BLANKS   FIG.5

FIG.6   CENTER OF THE ACE OF SPADES

THE FAKE SPADE IS SLIPPED FROM ONE CARD TO ANOTHER
FIG.7

is held in each hand, but only one of them is visible to the audience, the other being concealed underneath the ace that has been cut from the card. The performer then announces his intention of making the cards

change places. He turns the backs of the cards toward the audience, and, with the hands apart, begins moving the cards back and forth, bringing them a little closer to each other at each pass. Finally, when the edges touch, as in *Fig. 7*, the false center from the card is slipped over and onto the other card; this done, the cards are moved back and forth, gradually separating them, and their faces are again turned to the audience, when, to all appearances, the cards have changed positions.

— Mind-reading Effect with Cards —

Five cards are shown, and one person is asked to think of two cards in the lot, after which the performer places the cards behind his back and removes any two cards, then shows the remaining three and asks if the two cards in mind have been removed. The answer is always yes, as it cannot be otherwise.

To prepare the cards, take any 10 cards from the pack and paste the back of one card to another, making five double cards. Removing any two cards behind the performer's back reduces the number of cards to three, and when these are turned over they will not have the same faces so that the ones first seen cannot be shown the second time even though all five cards were turned over and shown.

— Mechanical Trick with Cards —

The following mechanical card trick is easy to prepare and simple to perform: First, procure a new deck and divide it into two piles, one containing the red cards and the other the black ones, all cards facing the same way. Take the red cards, square them up, and place in a vise. Then, with a plane, plane off the upper right-hand corner and lower left-hand corner, as in *Fig. 1*, about 1/16 in.

Then take the black cards, square them up, and plane off about 1/16 in. on the upper left-hand corner and lower right-hand corner, as in *Fig. 2*.

Next, restore all the cards to one pack, taking care to have the first card red, the next black, and so on, every

Card trick

alternate card being the same color. Bend the pack so as to give some spring to the cards, and by holding one thumb on the upper left-hand corner all the cards will appear red to the audience; place your thumb in the center at top of pack and they will appear mixed, red and black; with thumb on upper right-hand corner all cards appear black. You can display either color called for.

MONEY MAGIC

— TRICK OF TAKING A DOLLAR BILL FROM AN APPLE —

A rather pleasing, yet puzzling, deception is to pass a dollar bill into the interior of an examined lemon or apple. This can be accomplished in several ways, either mechanically or purely by sleight of hand. The mechanical method, of course, is the easier and just as effective. In performing, a plate with three apples is first exhibited, and the audience is given choice of any one for use in the experiment. The selected one is tossed out for examination and then returned to the performer, who places it in full view of the spectators while he makes the dollar bill vanish. Taking the knife he cuts the apple into two pieces, requesting the audience to select one of them. Squeezing this piece he extracts the dollar bill. The entire secret is in the unsuspected article—the table knife.

The knife is prepared by boring out the wooden handle to make it hollow. Enough space must be made to hold a dollar bill. The knife lies on the table with the fruit, the open end facing the performer. After the bill has

THE DOLLAR BILL IS HIDDEN IN THE KNIFE HANDLE THAT CUTS THE APPLE.

been made to vanish and the examined apple returned to the entertainer, he takes it and cuts in half. One of the halves is chosen, the performer impaling it on the end of the knife blade and holding it out to view. While still holding the knife he turns the blade downward and grasps the half apple and crushes it with a slight pass toward the knife handle end where the bill is grasped along with the apple, which makes a perfect illusion of taking the bill out of the apple.

As to the disappearance of the dollar bill, there are many ways in which this may be accomplished. Perhaps the method requiring the least practice is to place the bill in the trousers pocket, and then show the audience that the pocket is empty. This can be done by rolling the bill into a small compass, and pushing it into the extreme upper corner of the pocket where it will remain undetected while the pocket is pulled out for inspection. Other combinations can be arranged with the use of the knife, which is simple to make and very inexpensive.

— DROPPING COINS IN A GLASS FULL OF WATER —

Take a glass and fill it to the brim with water, taking care that the surface of the water is raised a little above the edge of the glass but not running over. Place a number of nickels or dimes on the table near the glass and ask your spectators how many coins can be put into the water without making it overflow. No doubt the reply will be that the water will run over before two coins are dropped in. But it is possible to put in ten or twelve of them. With a great deal of care the coins may be made to fall without disturbing the water, the surface of which will become more and more convex before the water overflows.

— A MYSTERY COIN BOX —

The effect of this trick is as follows: A small metal box, just large enough to hold a half dollar and about ½ in. high with a cover that fits snugly over the top, is passed out to be examined. When handed back to the performer he places it on the finger ends of his left hand and a half dollar is dropped into it and the cover put on. The box is then shaken to prove that the coin is still there. The performer then taps the box with his fingers and picks it up with the other hand and the coin will appear to have fallen through the bottom. Both the coin and box are then handed out for examination.

This seemingly impossible effect is made when the performer places the cover on the box. The box is resting on the fingers of the left hand and the cover is held between the thumb and forefinger of the right hand, but just before placing the cover on, the box is turned over with the right thumb, and the cover is placed on the bottom instead of the top.

The trick can be done within a foot of the spectators without their seeing the deception. It is a good plan to hide the box with the right hand when placing the cover, although this is not necessary.

— OLD-TIME MAGIC: CHANGING A BUTTON INTO A COIN —

Place a button in the palm of the left hand, then place a coin between the second and third fingers of the right hand. Keep the right hand faced down and the left hand faced up, so as to conceal the coin and expose the button. With a quick motion bring the left hand under the right, stop quick and the button will go up the right-hand coat sleeve. Press the hands together, allowing the coin to

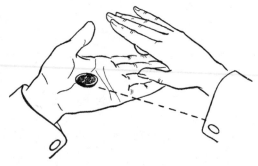

MAKING THE CHANGE

drop into the left hand, then expose again, or rub the hands a little before doing so, saying that you are rubbing a button into a coin.

— Coin and Tumbler Trick —

The accompanying sketch shows how a good trick may be easily performed by anyone. Lay a piece of heavy paper that is free from creases on a board or table. Secure three tumblers that are alike and stick a piece of the same heavy paper over the openings in two of them, neatly trimming it all around the edges so as to leave nothing of the paper for anyone to see. Make three covers of paper as shown in *Fig. 1* to put over the tumblers. Place three coins on the sheet of paper, then the tumblers with covers on top of the coins, the unprepared tumbler being in the middle. Now lift the covers off the end tumblers, and you will see that the paper on the openings covers the coins. Replace the covers, lift the middle one, and a coin will be seen under the tumbler, as the opening of this tumbler is not covered. Drop the cover back again and lift the other tumblers and covers bodily, so that the spectators can see the coins, remarking at the same time that you can make them vanish from one to the other. The openings of the tumblers must never be exposed so that anyone can see them, and a safe way to do this is to keep them level with the table.

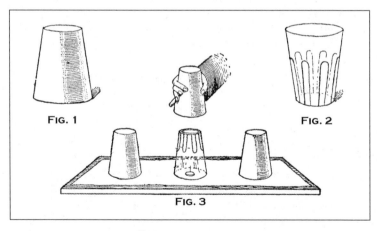

FIG. 1 FIG. 2 FIG. 3

THIS IS A GOOD TRICK.

SLEIGHT *of* HAND

— STRING-AND-BALL TRICK—

Stopping of a ball on a string at a desired point is a technique understood by almost every person, but to make one that can be worked only when the operator so desires is a mysterious trick. Procure a wooden ball, about 2 in. in diameter, and cut it into two equal parts.

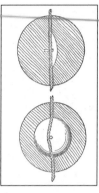

Insert a small peg in the flat surface of one half, a little to one side of the center, as shown, and allow the end to project about 3/16 in. The flat surface of the other half is cut out concave, as shown, to make it ½ in. deep. The two halves are then glued together, and a hole is drilled centrally on the division line for a string to pass through.

To do the trick, hold an end of the string in each hand tightly and draw it taut with the ball at the top, then slacken the string enough to allow the ball to slide down the string. To stop the ball at any point, pull the string taut.

Before handing the ball out and string for inspection, push the string from each side of the ball and turn it slightly to throw it off the peg. This will allow the string to pass freely through the ball, and it cannot be stopped at will. To replace the string, reverse the operation.

— MAGIC SPIRIT HAND —

This magic hand is made of wax and given to the audience for examination, along with a board that is suspended by four pieces of common picture-frame wire. The hand is placed upon the board and answers, by rapping, any question asked by members of the audience. The hand and the board may be examined at any time and yet the rapping can be continued, though surrounded by the audience.

The secret of this spirit hand is as follows: The hand is prepared by concealing in the wrist a few soft iron plates, the wrist being afterward bound with black velvet as shown in *Fig. 1*. The board is hollow, the top being made of thin veneer (*Fig. 2*). A small magnet, *A*, is connected to a small flat pocket-lamp battery, *B*. The board is suspended by four lengths of picture-frame wire, one of which, *E*, is connected to the battery and another, *D*, to the magnet. The other wires, *F* and *G*, are only holding wires. All the wires are fastened to a small ornamental switch, *H*, which is fitted with a connecting plug at the top. The plug can be taken out or put in as desired.

The top of the board must be made to open or slide off so that when the battery is exhausted a new one can be installed. Everything must be firmly fixed to the board and the hollow space filled in with wax, which will make the board sound solid when tapped.

In presenting the trick, the performer gives the hand and board with wires and switch for examina-

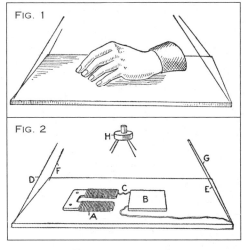

WAX HAND ON BOARD
AND ELECTRICAL CONNECTIONS

tion, keeping the plug concealed in his right hand. When receiving the board back, the plug is secretly pushed into the switch, which is held in the right hand. The hand is then placed on the board over the magnet. When the performer wishes the hand to move he pushes the plug in, which turns on the current and causes the magnet to attract the iron in the wrist, and will, therefore, make the hand rap. The switch can be made similar to an ordinary push button so the rapping may be easily controlled without detection by the audience.

— THE MAGIC THUMB TIE —

The prestidigitator crosses his thumbs and requests some-one from the audience to tie them together with a piece of tape, as shown in the drawing. A hoop is then thrown at the performer and, to the surprise of the audience, it is seen hanging upon one of his arms, although his thumbs are still securely tied.

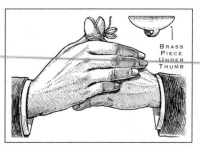

"THERE ARE TRICKS IN ALL TRADES:" CATCHING A HOOP ON THE ARM WITH THE THUMBS TIED TOGETHER IS ONE OF THE MAGICIAN'S TRICKS.

The explanation of this, like most other tricks of legerdemain, is simple. A piece of sheet brass or heavy tin is made into the ring shown in the small drawing, to fit over the right thumb. The broad portion is next to the ball of the thumb; when the thumbs are crossed, the ring is on the underside of the thumb and quite invisible to the person tying the knot. To minimize the possibility of detection, the ring is painted a flesh color. When the hoop is thrown, the performer quickly removes his thumb from the ring, catches the hoop on his arm and slips his thumbs back into the ring too rapidly to be detected.

POWERFUL ILLUSIONS

— CORKS-IN-A-BOX TRICK —

Procure a pillbox and a clean cork. Cut two disks from the cork to fit in the box and fasten one of the pieces centrally to the inside bottom of the pillbox with glue.

To perform the trick, put the loose disk in with the one that is fast and then open the box to show both corks. Close the box and in doing so turn it over, then open and only one cork will be seen. Be careful not to show the inside of the other part of the box with the cork that is fastened.

— MYSTERY SOUNDING GLASS —

Procure a thin, tapering drinking glass, a piece of thin, black thread about 2 ft. long, and a long lead pencil. Cut a small groove around the pencil near one end. Make a slip noose in each end of the thread and slip one into the notch and place the thin glass in the other with the thread near the top. When the pencil is revolved slowly the thread will be wound on it slightly and it will slip back with a jerk that produces a ring in the glass. This may be kept up indefinitely. The movement necessary is so small that it is imperceptible. The glass can be made to answer questions by two rings for "yes" and one ring for "no."

— A ONE-PIECE BRACELET CUT FROM A CALLING CARD —

A trick that will amuse and interest both old and young can be performed with a calling card, cigarette paper, or other similar material, cut with a scissor or knife, as indicated in the diagram. The card is shown, and the performer announces that he will pass his hand through the card, making a bracelet of it. He will, of course, be challenged, and proceeds as follows: He folds the card lengthwise and cuts through two thicknesses from 1 to 2, 3 to 4, etc.; then opens the card, and cuts from 1 to 13. By stretching

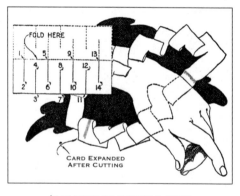

CARD EXPANDED
AFTER CUTTING

IT IS HARD TO IMITATE A QUICK
AND SKILLFUL PERFORMANCE
OF THIS SIMPLE TRICK.

the paper, as shown in the sketch, the hand may be passed through the card readily. The spectators are soon trying to duplicate the trick.

— AN ELECTRIC ILLUSION BOX —

The accompanying engravings show a most interesting form of electrically operated illusion consisting of a box divided diagonally and each division alternately lighted with an electric lamp. By means of an automatic thermostat arranged in the lamp circuit causing the lamps to light successively, an aquarium apparently without fish one moment is in the next instant swarming with live goldfish; an empty vase viewed through the opening in the box suddenly is filled with flowers, or an empty cigar box is seen and immediately is filled with cigars.

The electric magic boxes are shown and made of metal and finished with oxidized copper. But for ordinary use they can be made of wood in the same shape and size. The upper magic boxes as are shown in the engraving are about 12 in. square and 8½ in. high for parlor use and the lower boxes are 18 in. square and 10½ in. high for use in window displays. There is a partition arranged diagonally in the box as shown in the plan view, which completely divides the box into two parts. One-half the partition is fitted with a plain, clear glass as shown.

The partition and interior of the box are rendered nonreflecting by painting them matte black. When made of wood, a door must be provided on the side or rear to make changes of exhibits. If the box is made large enough, or in the larger size mentioned, openings may be made in the bottom for this purpose. The openings can also be used to perform the magic trick of allowing two people to place their heads in the box and change from one to the other.

The electric globes are inserted as shown at *LL* through the top of the box, one in each division. When the rear part is illuminated, any article arranged within that part will be visible to the spectator looking into the box through the front opening, but when the front part is illuminated, and the back left dark, any article placed therein will be reflected in the glass, which takes the same position to the observer as the one in the rear. Thus a plain aquarium is set in the rear part and one with swimming fish placed in the front, and with the proper illumination one is changed, as it appears, into the other. When using as a window display, place the goods in one part and the price in

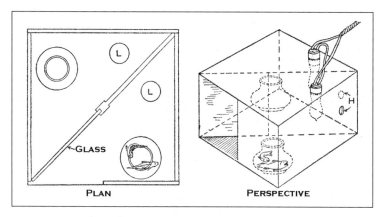

CONSTRUCTION OF MAGIC BOXES

the other. Many other changes can be made at the will of the operator.

Electric lamps may be controlled by various means to produce different effects. Lamps may be connected in parallel and each turned on or off by means of a hand-operated switch or the button on the lamp socket. Or, if desired, a hand-operated adjustable resistance may be included in the circuit of each lamp for gradually causing the object to fade away or reappear slowly.

Instead of changing the current operated by hand, this may be done automatically by connecting the lamps in parallel on the lighting circuit and each connected in series with a thermostatic switch plug provided with a heating coil that operates to automatically open and close the circuit through the respective lamp.

When there is no electric current available, matches or candles may be used and inserted through the holes *H,* as shown in the sketch.

— A Trunk Mystery —

Doubtless every person has seen the trunk mystery, the effect of which is as follows: A trunk, mounted upon four legs, is brought out on the stage and proven to be empty by turning it all the way around to show that there is nothing on the back. Then pieces of plate

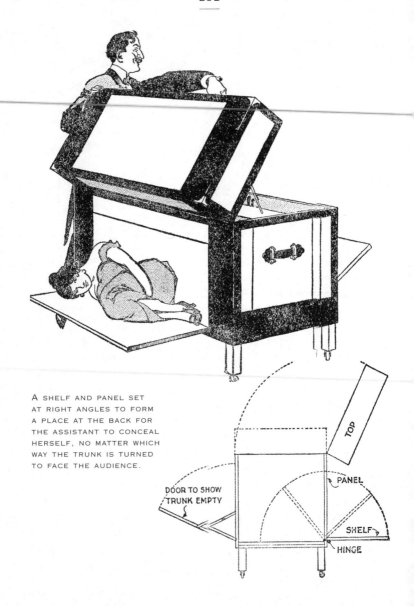

A SHELF AND PANEL SET AT RIGHT ANGLES TO FORM A PLACE AT THE BACK FOR THE ASSISTANT TO CONCEAL HERSELF, NO MATTER WHICH WAY THE TRUNK IS TURNED TO FACE THE AUDIENCE.

TOP

PANEL

DOOR TO SHOW TRUNK EMPTY

SHELF

HINGE

glass are placed along the back, sides, and front, the trunk is closed and given a swift turn and then opened. To the amazement of all, a lady steps out appearing to come from nowhere. The secret of this trick is very simple, and the trunk can be made up very cheaply.

In the back of the trunk there is a movable panel with a shelf exactly the same size as the panel attached to its bottom, forming a right angle. The corner of the right angle is hinged to the bottom of the trunk. The back panel can be turned in until it rests on the bottom of the trunk and, when this is done, the shelf part rises and takes its place, making the back of the trunk appear solid.

When the trunk is brought out upon the stage, the assistant is crouching on the shelf. The trunk can then be shown empty. This is all very simple until the trunk is turned around, when it takes skill not to give the trick away. As soon as the performer starts to turn the trunk around, the assistant shifts her weight on the panel, thus causing it to fall inward and bring the shelf up to make the back appear solid. The assistant is now in the trunk, and the back can be shown clear of any

apparatus. When the trunk is turned to the front, again, the lady repeats the previous operation in the opposite direction, thus bringing her body to the back of the trunk again.

To make the trick appear more difficult, glass plates are made to insert in the ends, front and back of the trunk. In making the trunk, the back should be the same size as the bottom. Fit the piece of glass for the back into a light frame, similar to a window frame. This frame is hinged to the bottom of the trunk and is ½ in. smaller all around than the back of the trunk. This is so that the two pieces of glass can be put in the ends and also allow the back frame and glass to fall flush in the bottom of the trunk. A few rubber bumpers are fastened in the bottom of the trunk to ensure the glass falls without noise. The best way to work this is for the performer to let the frame down with his right hand while he is closing up the front with his left.

As soon as the trunk is closed, the assistant again shifts her weight to cause the panel to fall in. The trunk can be turned to show the back or whirled around and turned to the front again, then opened up, whereupon the assistant steps out, bows to the audience, and leaves the stage.

— A MYSTIC FORTUNE-TELLER —

Fortune-telling by means of weights striking glasses or bottles is quite mysterious if controlled in a manner that cannot be seen by the audience. The performer can propose two strikes for "no," and three for "yes" to answer questions. Any kind of bottles, glass, or cups may be used. In the bottles the pendulum can be suspended from the cork, and in the glasses from small tripods set on the table.

BULB

BULB

THE ROCKING OF THE TABLE IS CAUSED BY THE PRESSURE OF AIR IN THE BULB UNDER THE FOOT, THE MOVEMENT CAUSING THE PENDULUM TO SWING AND STRIKE THE GLASS.

The secret of the trick is as follows: A rubber tube with a bulb attached to each end is placed under a rug, one bulb being located under one table leg and the other near the chair of the performer set at some distance from the table where it can be pressed with the foot. Someone selects a pendulum. The performer gazes intently at it, and presses the bulb under his foot lightly at first. Then, by watching the swaying of the pendulum selected, he will know when to give the second impulse, and continue until the weight strikes the glass. As the pendulums are of different lengths they must necessarily swing at different rates per second. The impulses must be given at the proper time or else the pendulum will be retarded instead of increased in amplitude. A table with four legs is best, and the leg diagonally opposite that with the bulb beneath it must not touch the carpet or floor. This can be arranged by placing pieces of cardboard under the other two legs.

— RUBBER-BAND-CHANGE TRICK —

The trick of changing a rubber band from the first and second fingers to the third and fourth, if done quickly, can be performed without detection by the audience. The band on the first two fingers is shown to the spectator as in *Fig. 1*, with the back of the hand up. The hand is then turned over and the band drawn out quickly, as shown in *Fig. 2*, in a manner as to give the impression that the band is whole and on the two fingers. While doing this, quickly fold all the fingers so that their ends enter the band, and turn the hand over and let go the band, then show the back with the fingers doubled up. In reality the fingers will be in the

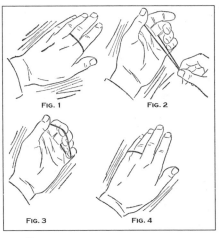

TRANSFERRING RUBBER BAND FROM THE FIRST TWO FINGERS TO THE LAST PAIR, LIKE MAGIC.

band, as in *Fig. 3*, and the back will still show the band on the first two fingers. Quickly straighten out all the fingers, and the band will snap over the last two fingers.

— OLD-TIME MAGIC: THE GROWING FLOWER —

This trick is performed with a widemouthed jar that is about 10 in. high. If an earthen jar of this kind is not at hand, use a glass fruit jar and cover it with black cloth or paper so that the contents cannot be seen. Two pieces of wire are bent as shown in *Fig. 1* and put together as in *Fig. 2*. These wires are put in the jar, about one-third the way down from the top, with the circle centrally located. The wires can be held in place by carefully bending the ends, or using small wedges of wood.

Cut a wire shorter in length than the height of the jar and tie a rose or several flowers on one end. Put a cork in the bottom of the jar and stick the opposite end of the wire from where the flowers are tied through the circle of the two wires and into the cork. The dotted lines in *Fig. 3* show the position of the wires and flowers.

To make the flowers grow in an instant, pour water into the jar at one side of the wide mouth. The cork will float and carry the wire with the flowers attached upward, causing the flowers to grow, apparently, in a few second's time. Do not pour in too much water or you will raise the flowers so far that the wire will be seen.

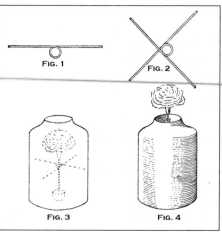

FIG. 1

FIG. 2

FIG. 3

FIG. 4

FLOWER GROWS INSTANTLY.

— OLD-TIME MAGIC: BALANCING FORKS ON A PIN HEAD —

Two, three, or four common table forks can be made to balance on a pinhead as follows: Procure an empty bottle and insert a cork in the neck. Stick a pin in the center of this cork so that the end will be about 1½ in. above the top. Procure another cork about 1 in. in diameter by 1¾ in. long. The forks are now stuck into the latter cork at equal distances apart, each having the same angle from the cork. A long needle with a good sharp point is run through the cork with the forks and

½ in. of the needle end allowed to project through the lower end.

The point of the needle now may be placed on the pinhead. The forks will balance, and if given a slight push they will appear to dance. Different angles of the forks will produce various feats of balancing.

— COMIC CHEST EXPANDER FOR PLAY OR STAGE USE —

A device used in an amateur vaudeville sketch with good effect, and that is interesting for play purposes and magic tricks of various kinds, is made of a 1/32-by-9-by-14-in. piece of sheet spring brass, rigged as shown. In the center, near the upper edge, a small pulley is soldered. At the center of the bottom edge a small hole is drilled. In it is fastened one end of a 4-ft. string that runs up through the pulley. The other end is fastened to a strap to fit around the leg just above the knee. At the two upper corners of the brass sheet two slots are cut to accommodate similar straps, as fastenings. When the wearer stands in a normal position the chest is as usual, but by straightening the body and slightly moving the strapped leg back, the brass sheet is bowed outward, giving the appearance indicated.

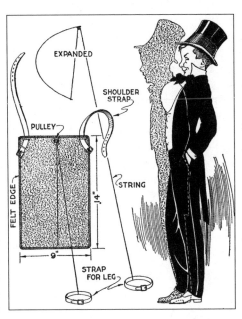

THE PERFORMER'S CHEST "SWELLS WITH PRIDE" WHEN HE DRAWS ON THE STRING BY SHIFTING HIS POSITIONS.

— A Trick "Letter" —

Endless amusement can be obtained from the simple device illustrated, which is attached to an ordinary sheet of letter paper, folded up and placed in an envelope. On opening the supposed "letter," the recipient gets something of a surprise when the ring revolves rapidly.

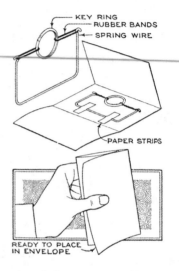

A U-shaped piece of spring wire is fastened to the paper by paper strips. An iron washer, or ring of the type shown, is held across the open part of the "U" by rubber bands. In use, the rubber bands are twisted so that as soon as the letter is opened they begin to untwist and the ring to revolve, causing it to whiz and whir as though there were something very much alive in the letter.

— ❖ ❖ ❖ —

CHAPTER 7

THE SCIENCE
of FUN

—

AMAZING MOTORS

— A SIMPLE MOTOR CONTROLLER —

The controller described here is very similar in operation to the types of controllers used on electric automobiles, and its operation may be easily followed in the diagrammatic representation of its circuits, and those of a two-pole series motor to which it is connected, as shown in *Fig. 1*. The controller consists of six flat springs, represented as small circles and lettered *A, B, C, D, E,* and *F.* These make contact with pieces of narrow sheet brass mounted on a small wood cylinder, arranged so that it may be turned by means of a small handle located on top of the controller case. The handle can be turned in either direction from a point called neutral, which is marked *N.* When the cylinder of the controller is in the neutral position, all six contact springs are free from contact with any metal on the cylinder. The contacts around the cylinder in the six different horizontal positions are lettered *G, H, J, K,*

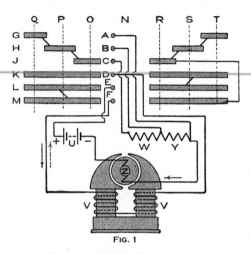

FIG. 1

DIAGRAM OF THE ELECTRICAL CONNECTIONS
OF A CONTROLLER TO A TWO-POLE
SERIES MOTOR.

If the cylinder was rotated to the position marked *O*, the circuit could be traced from the positive terminal of the battery *U*, as follows: To contact spring *E*, to strip of brass *L*, to strip of brass *M*, to contact spring *F*, through the field windings *V V*, to contact spring *D*, to strip of brass *K*, to strip of brass *J*, to contact spring *C*, through resistance *W* and *Y*, to armature *Z*, through armature to the negative terminal of the battery. Moving the cylinder to the position *P* merely cuts out the resistance *W*, and to the position *Q*, cuts out the remaining resistance *Y*. The direction of the current through the armature and series field, for all positions of the cylinder to the left, is indicated by the full-line arrows. Moving the controller to the positions marked *R*, *S*, and *T* will result in the same changes in circuit connections as in the previous case, except the direction of the current in the series field windings will be reversed.

L, and *M*. There are three different positions of the controller in either direction from the neutral point. Moving the cylinder in one direction will cause the armature of the motor to rotate in a certain direction at three different speeds, while moving the cylinder in a reverse will cause the armature to rotate in the opposite direction at three different speeds, depending upon the exact position of the cylinder. These positions are designated by the letters *O*, *P*, and *Q*, for one way, and *R*, *S*, and *T*, for the other.

The construction of the controller may be carried out as follows: Obtain a cylinder of wood, 1¾ in. in diameter and 3⅛ in. long, preferably hardwood. Turn one end of this cylinder down to a diameter of ½ in., and drill a ¼-in. hole through its center from end to end. Divide the circumference of the small-diameter portion into eight equal parts and drive a small nail into the cylinder at each division point, the nail being placed in the center of the surface lengthwise and perpendicular to the axis of the cylinder. Cut off all the nail heads so that the outer ends of the nails extend even with the surface off the outer, or larger size, end.

Divide the large end into eight equal parts so that the division points will be midway between the ends of the nails, and draw lines the full length of the cylinder on these points. Divide the cylinder lengthwise into seven equal parts and draw a line around it at each division point. Cut some ⅛-in. strips from thin sheet brass and mount them on the cylinder to correspond to those shown in *Fig. 1*. Any one of the vertical division lines drawn on the cylinder may be taken as the neutral point. The pieces may be mounted by bending the ends over and sharpening them so that they can be driven into the wood. The various strips of brass should be connected electrically, as shown by the heavy lines in *Fig. 1*, but these connections must all be made so that they will not extend beyond the outer surface of the strips or brass.

A small rectangular frame is made, and the cylinder is mounted in a vertical position in it by means of a rod passing down through a hole in the top of the rectangle, through the hole in the

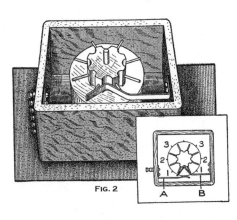

UPPER-END VIEW OF THE CONTROLLER SHOWING THE MANNER OF ATTACHING THE SPRINGS.

cylinder, and partly through the bottom of the rectangle. The upper part of the rod may be bent so as to form a handle. The rod must be fastened to the cylinder in some convenient way.

Make six flat springs similar to the one shown at *A, Fig. 2,* and mount them on the inside of the rectangle so that they will correspond in their vertical positions to the strips of brass on the cylinder. Six small binding posts mounted on the outside of the box and connected to these springs serve to make the external connections, and they should be marked so that they may be easily identified.

A flat spring, ¼ in. wide, is made similar to the one shown in *B, Fig. 2.* Mount this spring on the inside of the rectangle so that it will mesh with the ends of the nails in the small part of the cylinder. The action of this spring is to make the cylinder stop at definite positions. The top of the case should be marked so that the position of the handle will indicate the position of the cylinder. Stops should also be provided so that the cylinder case cannot be turned all the way around.

— MOTOR MADE OF CANDLES —

A tube of tin or cardboard, with an inside diameter that allows it to accommodate a candle snugly, is hung on an axle in the center that turns in bearings made of wood. The construction of the bearings is simple, and they can be made from three pieces of wood as shown. The tube should be well balanced. Pieces of candle are then inserted in the ends, also well balanced. If one is heavier than the other, light it and allow the tallow to run off until it rises; then light the other end. The alternate dripping from the candles will cause the tube to tip back and forth like a walking beam. It will keep going automatically until the candles are entirely consumed.

TALLOW DRIPPING FROM THE ENDS ALTERNATELY LESSENS THE WEIGHT OF THE ARMS AND CAUSES THE TUBE TO TIP.

— How to Wind Wire on Electrical Apparatus —

Beginners are bound to find it difficult to reproduce in a homemade apparatus the mathematical regularity and perfection of the winding on the electrical instrument coils found in the supply stores. But they can achieve a professional and workmanlike finish with the help of a simple contrivance and a little care and attention to details before beginning. Experimental work suddenly takes on a new interest.

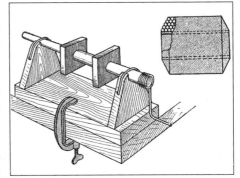

WINDING A COIL OF WIRE SO THAT THE LAYERS WILL BE EVEN AND SMOOTH.

At the outset let it be stated that wire should never be wound directly on the iron core, not only because it cannot be done satisfactorily in that manner, but because the home mechanic often desires to remove a coil from a piece of apparatus after it has served its purpose. It is therefore advisable to make a bobbin, which consists of a thin, hard tube with two ends. The tube may be easily formed by wrapping a suitable length of medium-weight paper on the core, having first coated it with ordinary fish glue, excepting, of course, the first 2 or 3 in. in direct contact with the core. Wind tightly until the thickness is from 1/32 in. to 1/16 in., depending upon the diameter of the core, and then wrap with string until the glue hardens, after which the tube may be sandpapered and trimmed up as desired.

Where the wire is not of too small a gauge and is not to be wound to too great a depth, no ends will be necessary. This is true if each layer of wire is stopped one-half turn before the preceding one, as indicated in the accompanying sketch, and is also thoroughly shellacked. With ordinary care magnet wire may be wound in this manner to a depth of over one-half inch.

The tube having been made ready—with or without ends as may be necessary—the small winding jig illustrated is made. All that is essential is to provide a suitable means for rotating by hand a slightly tapering wood spindle, upon which the tube is pushed. The bearings can be just notches made in the upper ends of two standards, through each of which a hole is drilled at right angles to the length of the spindle, so that some string or wire may be laced through to hold the spindle down.

A crank may be formed by winding a piece of heavy wire around the larger end of the spindle. A loop of wire or string should be attached at some convenient point, so that the crank may be held from unwinding while adjusting matters at the end of each layer, or while making a connection. There should also be provided a suitable support for the spool of wire, which is generally placed below the table to good advantage. Much depends, in this sort of work, upon attention to these small details. After which it will be found that the actual winding will require very little time.

— HOW TO MAKE A TOY STEAM ENGINE —

A toy engine can be easily made from old implements that can be found in nearly every house.

The cylinder *A, Fig. 1*, is an old bicycle pump cut in half. The steam chest *D* is part of the piston tube of the same pump, the other parts being used for the bearing *B*, and the crank bearing *C*. The flywheel *Q* can be any small-sized iron wheel—either an old sewing-machine wheel, pulley wheel, or anything available. We used a wheel from an old high chair for our engine. If the bore in

the wheel is too large for the shaft, it may be bushed with a piece of hardwood. The shaft is made of heavy steel wire, the size of the hole in the bearing *B*.

The base is made of wood, and has two wood blocks, *H* and *K*, ⅜ in. thick, to support bearing *B* and valve crank *S*, which is made of tin. The hose *E* connects to the boiler, which will be described later. The clips *F* are soldered to the cylinder and nailed to the base, and the bearing *B* is fastened by staples.

The valve motion is shown in *Figs. 2* and *3.* In *Fig. 2* the steam is entering the cylinder, and in *Fig. 3* the valve *B* has closed the steam inlet and opened the exhaust, thus allowing the steam in the cylinder to escape.

The piston is made of a stove bolt, *E, Fig. 2,* with two washers, *F,* and a cylindrical piece of hardwood, *G.* This is wound with soft string, as shown in *Fig. 3,* and saturated with thick oil. A slot is cut in the end of the bolt *E* to receive the connecting rod *H.* The valve *B* is made of an old bicycle spoke *C,* with the nut cut in half and filed down as shown, the space between the two halves being filled with string and oiled.

The valve crank *S, Fig. 1,* is cut out of tin, or galvanized iron, and is moved by a small crank on the shaft. This crank should be at right angles to the main crank.

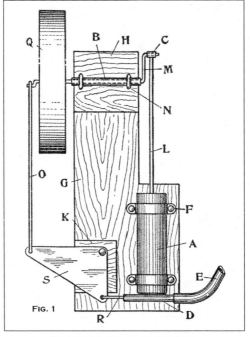

FIG. 1

THE STEAM ENGINE ASSEMBLED.

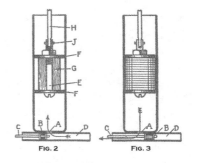

FIG. 2   FIG. 3

VALVE MOTION AND
CONSTRUCTION OF PISTON.

The boiler, *Fig. 4,* can be an old oil can, powder can, or a syrup can with a tube soldered to it, and is connected to the engine by a piece of rubber tubing. The heat from a small gas stove will furnish steam fast enough to run the engine at high speed.

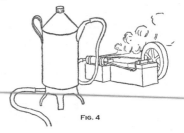

Fig. 4

ENGINE IN OPERATION.

— WORM GEARS FOR TOY MACHINERY —

Every youngster who owns a small battery motor delights in rigging up hoists, mills, and all manner of "machinery" for the motor to drive. Because these motors necessarily run at high speed and have only a very small torque, or turning force, it is always necessary to have some sort of speed-reduction gear. This is usually a system of large and small pulleys using strings as belts. A better arrangement is to use worm gearing, and the fine thing about this is the fact that a speed reduction of 100 to 1 is just as easy to obtain, or perhaps easier, than a 10-to-1 reduction. And because the speed is much reduced, the turning force is greatly increased. This means that a very small motor will, when provided with a worm-gear drive, operate mechanism it could not even turn by means of the strings running over small V-pulleys.

In worm gearing, the driving member, or "worm," is nothing but a screw; a special kind of thread is used on large screws made for this purpose, but this is not at all necessary for small worms to drive toys. Any bolt or machine screw that has a good, full thread will do for the driving worm, provided that the proper gear, or worm wheel, can be obtained to serve as the driven member. The worm wheel must have a number of teeth equal to the desired speed ratio, one with 50 teeth giving a reduction of 50 to 1, when used with an ordinary single-thread screw.

The only special tool needed for cutting worm wheels is an ordinary machinists' tap. It should be of some common size, such as ¼-20, and the worm or screw must, of course, be of the same pitch, in this case, 20 threads to the inch.

Two methods of cutting the worm wheel are illustrated. *Fig. 1* shows a fixture that can be made of three wooden blocks nailed together. A screw for holding the gear blank, a wire nail, and a large wire staple are the only other materials needed. *Fig. 2* shows how the work is done in a lathe; any lathe having a cross feed can be used. It may be remarked that although the shank of the wooden block may be held quite rigidly in the tool post, some kind of bracing

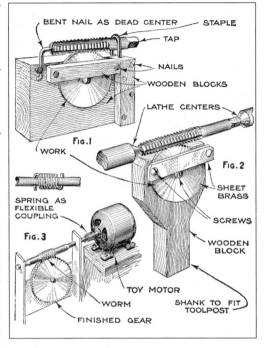

TWO FIXTURES ARE SHOWN FOR CUTTING SMALL WORM WHEELS; THE FIRST IS FOR USE BY HAND AND THE SECOND WITH A LATHE. THE LAST PICTURE SHOWS HOW THE WORM DRIVE IS CONNECTED.

block will have to be wedged under the forward end of the block to prevent chattering.

The blank for the worm wheel is merely a disk of sheet brass or soft iron, with a hole in the center. It can be turned out of the sheet, or filed if no lathe is handy. The diameter need

not be determined accurately, unless the speed reduction must be exact. The rule for determining the diameter of the worm wheel is to multiply the pitch (distance between teeth) by the number of teeth wanted, and take $7/22$ of the result. Thus, for a 100-tooth wheel to fit a ¼-20 worm, the diameter would be 100 x $\frac{1}{20}$ x $\frac{7}{22}$, or $1\frac{13}{22}$ in. In practice, the diameter should be somewhere near $1\frac{5}{8}$ in., the main thing being to get the disk as nearly round as possible. In the hand fixture, shown in *Fig. 1*, the feed is obtained by striking light blows on the heavy staple. The staple should at first be driven in just so far that the teeth of the tap scratch the edge of the blank. The tap is then revolved with a bit brace or wrench; when it has made 100 revolutions the blank will be scratched clear around. As the turning is continued, notice whether the tap teeth have worked into the scratches previously made or are cutting new ones. If the latter is the case, apply a little backward or forward pressure with the hand on the blank. As the turning is continued and the tap is fed in with an occasional blow on the staple, so that the teeth will revolve in the grooves previously cut, and not cut double-pitch.

Fig. 3 gives an idea as to how the motor is connected to drive the slow-speed shaft by means of the worm and wheel. There must be plenty of play between the worm and gear, as the simple teeth of this type will not work well if pressed tightly together. The worm in *Fig. 3* is made by turning or filing down a screw or bolt having the proper thread, so that journals are formed on the ends. The thread is also filed off for the sake of appearance, except at the center, where it meshes with the gear.

— Toy Sand Engine —

A toy sand engine that will provide the amateur mechanic with some interesting applications of mechanical movements and give endless entertainment to the children can be made from a few easily obtained parts. The machine is operated by the weight of sand, which runs from the bin at the top into the hods. As only one of the hods is filled at a time, one of the crossheads and connecting rods is forced down alternately, the small flywheel preventing the device from stopping on dead center. As the hod reaches the lowest point of its travel, one end of it comes into contact with the tripper, which overbalances the load and dumps the sand.

The hods are alternately filled with sand from the overhead bin by a slide valve that, when the engine

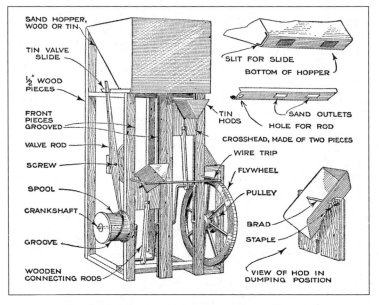

A TOY ENGINE, IN WHICH SOME WELL-KNOWN
MECHANICAL MOVEMENTS ARE APPLIED. THE SAND HODS
ARE AUTOMATICALLY FILLED FROM THE BIN BY A SLIDE-VALVE
ARRANGEMENT, SIMILAR TO THAT USED ON STEAM ENGINES.

is started, is automatic in action. The valve consists of a strip of tin with two openings that correspond to similar openings in the bottom of the bin. These openings are so spaced that when one hod is receiving sand, the opening on the opposite side is closed and the hod on that side is descending. The valve slides horizontally and is operated by a valve rod pivoted to a bracket on the frame. The valve is timed to open and close the sand openings by a grooved cam firmly secured to the end of the crankshafts. An old spool forms the basis for the cam, and an elliptical groove is cut into it large enough to take the end of the valve rod. The cutting and proportioning of this cam so as to have the slide valve open and close at the proper time will probably require more or less experimenting before the valve is properly "timed." The nearer the cam groove comes to the ends of the spool, the greater the travel of the valve rod. The upper end of the valve rod fits into a hole provided for it in the end of the slide valve. The valve should be "timed" so that it will remain open until the hod that is being filled with sand is halfway down. Also, the valve should be adjusted so that just before one hod is being tripped at the end of its travel, the other hod begins to receive sand.

— MAKING A STATIONARY ENGINE PROPEL ITSELF —

Different jobs for the stationary engine—first at the well, in the pasture, and then at the barn a half-mile away—prompted the farmer to rig the engine so as to eliminate the necessity of loading and unloading it into a wagon for each trip.

LOADING EVEN A SMALL STATIONARY ENGINE FOR TRANSPORT TO DIFFERENT JOBS WAS TOO BOTHERSOME FOR THIS FARMER, SO HE MADE THE ENGINE HAUL ITSELF.

The photograph shows at a glance the details of this arrangement. The power of the engine is conveyed to the old mower wheel at the rear, which provides traction. A clutch pulley is keyed to the shaft of the rear wheel. The inner periphery of this is provided with studs that serve as gear teeth and engage with the link chain, to which power is delivered through a horizontal jackshaft connected to the engine pulley by a short belt. The engine is steered by manipulating the long lever shown, which is connected to the front axle by iron rods.

— A Quickly Made Toy Electric Motor —

The illustration shows a small electric motor of such simple construction that it can be easily made from odds and ends found in any amateur workshop. Cut six strips, ½ in. wide and 3½ in. long, from an old tin can, and bend them together in a U-shape. This forms the magnet *A*. The outside piece should be a trifle longer than the others so that its ends can be turned over the other ends to keep them all in place. Screw this down on a small wood base. At one side of the wood base, fix an upright, *B*, and on top, a light wood bracket, *C*, to take the upper bearing of the motor. The shaft *D* is simply a wire nail with the head filed off and filed to a point. Drive it through a 1½-in. length of the same kind of material as used for the magnet. This forms the rotating armature *E*.

Make a slight indentation with a center punch or strong nail, exactly in the center of the base portion of the magnet to take the lower end of the shaft. For the upper bearing,

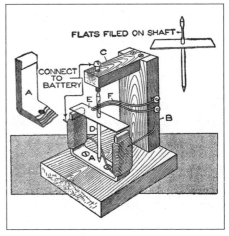

THE MOTOR IS CONSTRUCTED OF PIECES OF TIN, A NAIL, AND SOME WOOD BLOCKS.

file the end of a brass screw off flat and make a similar indentation with a center punch, or by a few turns of a small drill. This screw should be adjusted in the bracket until the shaft rotates freely with the armature just clearing the tips of the magnet. Wind about 40 turns of fairly thin cotton-covered copper wire—No. 24 or 26 gauge is suitable—around each limb of the magnet, first covering the latter with paper, to prevent the possibility of short-circuiting. The windings should be in opposite directions so that the connecting piece of the wire from one coil to the other passes across diagonally as shown in the illustration.

The brush *F* is formed by doubling up one of the free ends of the windings after removing the cotton covering and fixing it firmly with two screws to the side of the upright. After attaching, it should be bent until the outer end bears lightly on the shaft. Remove the shaft and at the point where the brush touched, file two flat surfaces on opposite sides of the nail in a direction at right angles to the longitudinal centerline of the armature. On replacing the shaft the brush should be adjusted so that it makes contact twice in a revolution and remains clear at the flat portions. Connect to a battery, one wire to the screw at the top of the motor and the other end to the open end of the windings. Give the armature a start and it will run at a terrific speed.

GIZMOS *and* GADGETS

— HOW TO MAKE AN EXPERIMENTAL LEAD SCREW —

Often in experimental work a long narrow, parallel screw is desired for regulating, or moving, some part of the apparatus in a straight line. A simple way of making such a screw is to tin thoroughly a small straight rod of the required length and diameter. After wiping off all the surplus solder while it is still hot, wrap the rod with a sufficient length of bright copper wire and fasten the ends. This wire is then securely soldered in place by running the solder on while

A COPPER WIRE WRAPPED AROUND AND SOLDERED TO A STRAIGHT ROD FOR A LEAD SCREW.

holding the screw over a blue gas flame. To make the solder run freely, brush frequently during the heating with a small mucilage brush dipped into the soldering acid. An even pitch can be secured by winding on two wires side by side at the same time, the second one being unwound before soldering.

— BUILDING A SIMPLE RADIO RECEIVER —

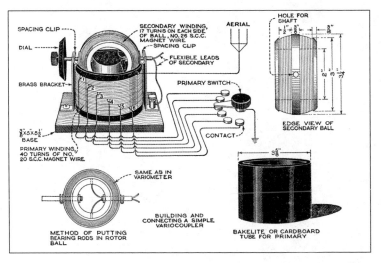

SPACING CLIP

DIAL

BRASS BRACKET

3"/8X5X5 1/2"
BASE

PRIMARY WINDING,
40 TURNS OF NO.
20 S.C.C. MAGNET WIRE.

SECONDARY WINDING,
17 TURNS ON EACH SIDE
OF BALL, NO. 26 S.C.C.
MAGNET WIRE.
SPACING CLIP

AERIAL

FLEXIBLE LEADS
OF SECONDARY

PRIMARY SWITCH

CONTACT

HOLE FOR
SHAFT

EDGE VIEW OF
SECONDARY BALL

SAME AS IN
VARIOMETER

BUILDING AND
CONNECTING A SIMPLE
VARIOCOUPLER

METHOD OF PUTTING
BEARING RODS IN ROTOR
BALL

BAKELITE OR CARDBOARD
TUBE FOR PRIMARY

This receiver is a popular one for reception from broadcasting stations; it gives excellent results for distances up to 250 miles and can be built at small cost. Under average conditions, telegraphic signals can be received within a radius of 1,500 miles, on wavelengths from 150 to 400 meters. The instruments are mounted on a 3/16-in. Bakelite panel, fastened to a wooden base by two angle irons. The variable condenser used is of .001-mf. capacity and is of the panel-mounting, 43-plate type. The variocoupler may either be bought ready-wound, or the knockdown parts are wound and assembled. The stationary Bakelite or cardboard tube is wound with 40 turns of No. 20 single cotton-covered magnet wire and six taps are taken off at approximately equal steps; these taps are led off to the contact points of the primary switch, as shown. The secondary, or rotor, of the variocoupler is wound with 34 turns of No. 26 single cotton-covered wire, 17 turns on each half, and the leads are brought out through the hollow shaft to a pair of binding posts. The tube socket is mounted on the base, at the left of the variocoupler; in front of the

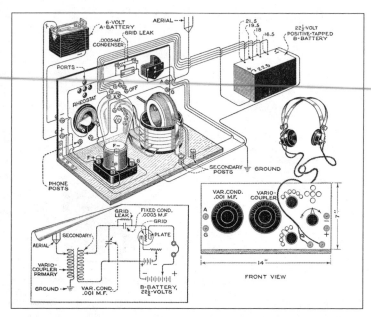

A SIMPLE AND EASILY MADE RECEIVER FOR BROADCASTING-STATION WORK.
IT HAS A WAVELENGTH RANGE OF 150 TO 400 METERS, AND A
WORKING RADIUS FOR TELEPHONE WORK OF 250 MILES. TELEGRAPH
STATIONS CAN BE HEARD AT A DISTANCE OF 1,500 MILES.
STANDARD INSTRUMENTS ARE USED THROUGHOUT.

socket, the 6-ohm battery-type rheostat is placed, and above it several holes are drilled through the Bakelite for observing the brilliancy of the tube filament when in operation. The binding posts for the earphones are located in the panel directly in front of the socket. The switch for the primary of the variocoupler is mounted on the panel, at the right

of the socket, looking at it from the rear. The switch lever is connected to the ground post. Above the primary switch is located the B-battery switch, which has the "off" point at the right; this switch is for the purpose of varying the B-battery voltage on the plate of the detector tube. The grid condenser is placed on the panel above the variocoupler; this condenser is of standard type with a capacity of .0005 mf. The grid leak has a resistance of 2 megohms, and is of the ordinary type, obtainable from any dealer in radio supplies. Six binding posts are placed on the panel, one for the aerial, one for the ground, two for the A battery, which is a 6-volt, 40- or 60-ampere-hour type, and the other two are for the earphones. The B battery is a positive-tapped 22 ½-volt unit of standard make. The taps are connected to the B-battery switch taps on the panel; the various voltages are plainly marked on the battery unit and should be connected to the switch in the order shown.

Use No. 18 insulated fixture wire for the circuit and carefully solder every connection. Bare, tinned copper wire, with varnished cambric tubing, or "spaghetti," slipped over it, can be used, but the fixture wire is cheaper and serves just as well. The detector tube used is a UV-200. The dials for the variable condenser and variocoupler are of standard make.

The proper aerial to use with this type of receiver is one wire, 125 to 150 ft. long, placed from 30 to 50 ft. above the ground. The phones should be wound for at least 2,000 ohms resistance. If desired,

the instruments can be placed in a cabinet, to make a neat and compact set, at the same time protecting the various parts from dust. Many operators prefer the variable condenser in series with the aerial with a receiver of this type, instead of across the secondary, as shown in the diagram, as closer tuning may be had for the radiophone broadcasting stations. Try both ways to find out which best suits the aerial used, as under varying conditions the results will differ.

List of Materials

1 variable condenser, .001-mf. capacity

1 grid condenser, .0005-mf. capacity

1 UV-200 detector tube

1 tube socket

6 binding posts

2 angle irons

1 battery rheostat

1 Bakelite panel, 3/16 by 7 by 14 in.

1 wood base, ½ by 6 by 14 in.

1 variocoupler

2 switch levers

12 contact points

1 22 ½-volt B-battery unit

1 storage battery; 6 volt, 40 or 60 ampere-hour

1 pair 2,000-ohm phones

— An Electrical Dancer —

The modification of the well-known mechanical dancer shown in the illustration is based on the principle of the electric bell. While the amusing antics of the mechanical dancer are controlled by the hand, the manikin shown is actuated by the electromagnet.

The mechanism is contained in a box. It consists of an electromagnet with a soft-iron armature carried by a spring. A wire from the battery goes to the magnet. The other terminal of the magnet connects with the armature spring at L1. The spring is bent at a right angle at its other end, L2, and carries a platform, L3, strengthened by a smaller disk underneath. The dancer performs upon this platform.

A contact spring, S, is carried by the armature spring. A. Contact screw, C, is adjustable in its contact with the spring S. A wire runs from the contact screw to the binding post B, to which the other battery wire is connected.

The current keeps the platform in constant vibration, causing the dancer to "dance." By means of the screw C, the action of the current may be varied, and the "dancing" will vary correspondingly.

The figure is made of wood with very loose joints and is suspended so that feet barely touch the platform.

WHEN THE CONTACT IS MADE THE FIGURE DANCES.

— How to Make a Heliograph —

THE HELIOGRAPH AS IT IS USED BY NEIGHBORING BOYS TO SEND MESSAGES ON A CLEAR DAY BY FLASHING THE SUN'S RAYS FROM ONE TO THE OTHER. THE MESSAGES CAN BE READ AS FAR AS THE EYE CAN SEE THE LIGHT.

The heliograph used in the army provides a good method of sending messages using the reflection of the sun's rays. There are stations in the mountains from which messages are sent by the heliograph for great distances, and guides carry them for use in case of trouble or accident. The wireless telegraph delivers messages by electricity through the air, but the heliograph sends them by flashes of light.

The main part of the instrument is the mirror, which should be about 4 in. square, set in a wood frame and swung on trunnions made of two square-head bolts, each ¼ in. in diameter, and 1 in. long. These bolts are firmly held to the frame with brass strips, ½ in. wide and 3 in. long. The strips are drilled in their centers to admit the bolts, and then drilled at each end for the screw that fastens them to the frame. This construction is clearly shown in *Fig. 1*.

A hole is cut in the center of the frame backing and a small hole, not over ⅛ in. in diameter, is scratched through the silvering on the glass. If the trunnions are centered properly, the small hole should be exactly in line with them and in the center.

A U-shaped support is made of wood strips, ⅜ in. thick and 1 in. wide, the length of the uprights being 3½ in. and the crosspiece connecting

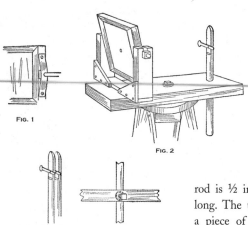

FIG. 1

FIG. 2

FIG. 3   FIG. 4

DETAIL OF THE PARTS FOR MAKING
THE MIRROR AND SIGHT ROD THAT
ARE PLACED ON A BASE
SET ON A TRIPOD TOP,
THE WHOLE BEING ADJUSTED
TO REFLECT THE SUN'S RAYS IN
ANY DIRECTION DESIRED.

their lower ends a trifle longer than the width of the frame. These are put together, as shown in *Fig. 2*, with small brackets at the corners. A slot, ½ in. deep and ¼ in. wide, is cut into the upper end of each upright to receive the trunnions on the mirror frame. Nuts are tightly turned on the bolt ends to clamp the standard tops against the brass strips on the mirror frame. The cross strip at the bottom is clamped to the base with a bolt, 1½ in. long. The hole

for this bolt should be exactly below the peep-hole in the mirror and run through one end of the baseboard, which is ¾ in. thick, 2 in. wide, and 10 in. long.

At the opposite end of the base, place a sighting rod, which is made as follows: The rod is ½ in. in diameter and 8 in. long. The upper end is fitted with a piece of thick, white cardboard, cut ¼ in. in diameter and having a projecting shank 1 in. long, as shown in *Fig. 3*. The rod is placed in a ½-in. hole bored in the end of the baseboard, as shown in *Fig. 2*. To keep the rod from slipping through the hole, a setscrew is made of a small bolt with the nut set in the edge of the baseboard as shown in *Fig. 4*.

The tripod head is formed of a wood disk, 5 in. in diameter, with a hole in the center, and three small blocks of wood, 1 in. square and 2 in. long, nailed to the underside, as shown in *Fig. 5*. The tripod legs are made of light strips of wood, ⅜ in. thick, 1 in. wide, and 5 ft. long. Two of these strips, nailed securely together to within 20 in. of the top, constitute one leg. The upper unnailed ends are spread to slip over the blocks on the tripod top. These ends are bored to loosely fit over the headless nails driven partway into the block ends. One tripod leg is shown in *Fig. 6*.

The screen, or shutter, is mounted on a separate tripod and is shown in *Fig. 7*. Cut out two slats from hardwood, ⅜ in. thick, 2½ in. wide, and 6 in. long, and taper both edges of these slats down to 3/16 in. Small nails are driven into the ends of the slats and the heads are filed off so that the projecting ends will form trunnions on which the slats will turn. Make a frame of wood pieces, ¾ in. thick and 2½ in. wide, the opening in the frame being 6 in. square. Before nailing the frame together bore holes in the side uprights for the trunnions of the slats to turn in. These holes are 1¾ in. apart. The frame is then nailed

together and also nailed to the tripod top. The shutter is operated with a key very similar to a telegraph key. The construction of this key is shown in *Fig. 7*. A part of a spool is fastened to a stick that is pivoted on the opposite side of the frame. The key is connected to the slats in the frame with a bar and rod, to which a coil spring is attached, as shown in *Fig. 8*. *Fig. 9* shows the positions of the tripods when the instrument is set to flash the sunlight through the shutter. The regular telegraph code is used in flashing the light.

To set the instrument, first turn the cardboard disk down to uncover the point of the sight rod, then sight through the hole in the mirror and adjust the sight rod so that the tip end comes squarely in line with the receiving station. When the instrument is

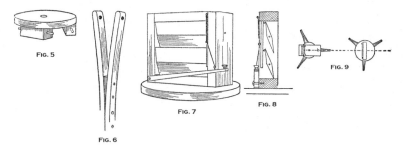

FIG. 5

FIG. 6

FIG. 7

FIG. 8

FIG. 9

THE PARTS IN DETAIL FOR MAKING THE TRIPODS AND THE SHUTTER FOR FLASHING THE LIGHT, AND DIAGRAM SHOWING THE LOCATING OF THE TRIPODS TO DIRECT THE LIGHT THROUGH THE SHUTTER.

properly sighted, the shutter is set up directly in front of it and the cardboard disk is turned up to cover the end of the sight rod. The mirror is then turned so that it reflects a beam of light with a small shadow spot showing the center made by the peephole in the mirror, which is directed to fall on the center of the cardboard sighting disk. It will be quite easy to direct this shadow spot to the disk by holding a sheet of paper 6 or 8 in. in front of the mirror and following the spot on the paper until it reaches the disk. The flashes are made by manipulating the key operating the shutter in the same manner as a telegraph key.

— AN EASILY CONSTRUCTED BALL-BEARING ANEMOMETER —

An anemometer is an instrument that measures the velocity of the wind. The anemometers used by the weather bureau consist of four hemispherical cups mounted on the ends of two horizontal rods that cross at right angles and are supported on a freely turning vertical axle. Because the concave sides of the cups offer more resistance to the wind than do the convex sides, the device is caused to revolve at a speed that is proportional, approximately, to that of the wind. The axle, to which the rotary motion is transmitted from the cups, is connected to a dial mounted at the foot of the supporting column. This dial automatically records the rotations. The reproduction of such a registering mechanism would be rather complicated. Hence, in the arrangement to be described, none will be used. Therefore, one of these improvised anemometers mounted on a high building will indicate by the changing rapidity of its revolutions only the comparative, not the real, velocity of the wind.

In constructing the instrument, straight, dished vanes will be used instead of hollow cups. The vanes operate almost as effectively and may be combined more readily into a sturdy rotating unit. A bicycle front hub is utilized to make a wear- and noise-proof bearing having minimum friction. Each of the four wings is formed from a piece of galvanized iron, measuring 4½ by 10 in., with one end cut to a curve as shown. Use tinners' rivets to fasten a 4-in. length of ¾- by

1/16-in. strap iron to each wing. Form each of the strips into a trough-shaped vane, measuring 2¼ in. from edge to edge—this being the distance between the spoke flanges of a bicycle hub. Some cylindrical object of suitable diameter will serve as a form for bending. Place the ends of the support strips between the spoke flanges and rivet them securely. The rivets pass through the spoke holes. Some trial-and-error may be required to ensure a symmetrical arrangement of the parts. Solder the curved end of each wing to the inner surface of the adjacent wing. Place a tin cap—a salve-box lid will do—under the upper locknut on the hub to exclude rain from the bearing.

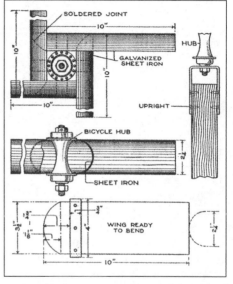

THIS ANEMOMETER IS MADE FROM GALVANIZED SHEET IRON, A BICYCLE HUB, AND A FEW IRON STRAPS. PRACTICE IN OBSERVING ITS MOTION WILL ENABLE ONE TO ESTIMATE FAIRLY CLOSELY THE WIND'S VELOCITY.

The supporting upright may be a heavy wooden rod or a piece of iron pipe. A yoke of 1 by ⅛-in. strap iron, held to the top of the upright with screws, is provided for the attachment of the hub. The locknut on the hub clamps it to the yoke. Apply a coat of metal paint to the iron parts that are exposed. Mount the device sufficiently high to give the wind free access to it from all directions. The curve at one end of each wing is an irregular one. Hence, its accurate construction involves a knowledge of sheet-metal pattern drawing. However, if it is made of a form similar to that shown it will fit sufficiently well to permit a good soldered joint.

— A SIMPLE MOTION-PICTURE MACHINE —

The drum A is a piece of wood, 1¾ in. long and 1¹¹⁄₁₆ in. in diameter, supported on the end of a round stick, B. The stick can be made in one piece with the drum if a wood lathe is at hand, but a piece cut from a curtain pole and a lead pencil inserted in a hole bored in the end will answer the purpose. Be sure to make the diameter of the drum 1³⁄₁₆ inches.

Provide a base piece, C, ½ in. thick and 2 in. square, and fasten a piece of cardboard having a slit E, as shown. The cardboard should be 2 in. wide and 2½ in. high, the slit being cut ½ in. in width, ¼ in. from the top and ¾ in. from the bottom. A hole is bored in the center of the block to admit the standard B easily.

The next step is to provide the picture and attach it to the drum. A picture of a boy pounding cobble-

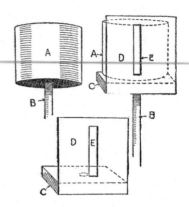

THE PARTS FOR MAKING
THE REVOLVING DRUM FOR
HOLDING THE STRIP OF PICTURES.

stones is shown in the sketch, in F, which should be made on a strip of paper 4⅜ in. long. This is glued or attached with rubber bands to the drum. The drawing can be enlarged in pen and ink. Or it can be reproduced as it is if a hand camera is at hand, and a print used on the drum.

THE DIFFERENT POSITIONS OF THE PICTURE
WILL APPEAR IN ACTION WHEN TURNING WITH THE DRUM.

It is only necessary to put the parts together, grasp the base in one hand and turn the support *B* with the other. Then, looking through the slot *E,* the viewer will see the boy pounding the stones. Various pictures can be made and the strips changed.

— AN INTERESTING WATER TELESCOPE —

A water telescope is easy to make and will offer much pleasure in exploring plant or animal life in comparatively shallow water. The device is made by fitting a heavy glass disk into the end of a round metal tube, about 2 in. in diameter. The glass is fitted between two rings of metal, prefer- ably with a small flange set against the glass. Waterproof cement is used to fix the glass between the rings. To use the "telescope," rest it on the other side of a boat or other convenient place at the water, and set the lower end containing the glass under the water. Remarkably clear views may be had in this way.

— HOW TO MAKE A WONDERGRAPH —

An exceedingly interesting machine is the so-called wondergraph. It is easy and cheap to make and will furnish both entertainment and instruction for young and old. It is a drawing machine, and the variety of designs it will produce—all symmetrical and ornamental and some wonderfully complicated—is almost without limit.

Fig. 1 is a diagram of the machine shown in the sketch. This is the easiest to make and gives as great a variety of results as any other.

Fasten three grooved circular disks with screws to a piece of wide board or a discarded box bottom, so as to revolve freely about their centers. They may be sawed from pieces of thin board or, better still, three

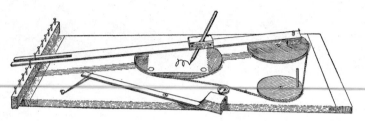

AN EASILY MADE WONDERGRAPH

of the plaques so generally used in burnt-wood work may be bought for a small amount of money. Use the largest one for the revolving table *T*. *G* is the guide wheel and *D* the driver with attached handle. Secure a piece of a 36-in. rule, which can be obtained from any furniture dealer. Nail a small block, about 1 in. thick, to one end and drill a hole through both the ruler and the block. Pivot them by means of a wooden peg to the face of the guide wheel. A fountain pen or a pencil is placed at *P* and held securely by rubber bands in a grooved block attached to the ruler. A strip of wood, *MN*, is fastened to one end of the board. This strip is made just high enough to keep the ruler parallel with the face of the table, and a row of small nails are driven partway into its upper edge. Any one of these nails may be used to hold the other end of the ruler in position, as shown in the

sketch. If the wheels are not true, a belt tightener, *B*, may be attached and held against the belt by a spring or rubber band.

After the apparatus is adjusted so that it will run smoothly, fasten a piece of drawing paper to the table with a couple of thumbtacks, adjust the pen so that it rests lightly on the paper, and turn the drive wheel. The results will be surprising and delightful. The accompanying designs were made with a very crude combination of pulleys and belts, such as described.

The machine should move at a speed that will cause the pen to move over the paper at the same rate as in ordinary writing. The ink should flow freely from the pen as it passes over the paper. A very fine pen may be necessary to prevent the lines from running together.

The dimensions of the wondergraph may vary. The larger designs in the illustration were made on a table, 8 in. in diameter, which was driven by a guide wheel, 6 in. in diameter. The size of the driver has no effect on the form or dimensions of the design, but a change in almost any other part of the machine has a marked effect on the results obtained. If the penholder is made so that it may be fastened at various positions along the ruler, and the guide wheel has holes drilled through it at different distances from the center to hold the peg attaching the ruler, these two adjustments, together with the one for changing the other end of the ruler by the rows of nails, will make a very great number of combinations possible. Even a slight change will greatly modify a figure or give an entirely new one. Designs may be changed by simply twisting the belt, thus reversing the direction of the table.

If an arm containing three or four grooves to hold the pen is fastened

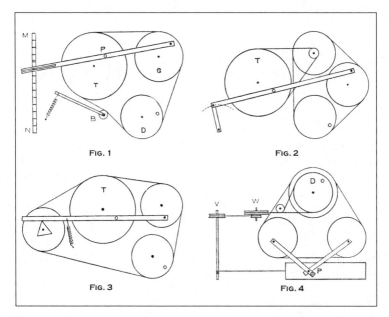

FIG. 1 FIG. 2

FIG. 3 FIG. 4

DIAGRAMS SHOWING THE CONSTRUCTION OF WONDERGRAPHS

SPECIMEN SCROLLS MADE ON THE WONDERGRAPH

to the ruler at right angles to it, still different figures will be obtained. A novel effect is made by fastening two pens to this arm at the same time, one filled with red ink and the other with black ink. The designs will be quite dissimilar and may be one traced over the other or one within the other according to the relative position of the pens.

Again change the size of the guide wheel and note the effect. If the diameter of the table is a multiple of the guide wheel, a complete figure of few lobes will result as shown by the one design in the lower right corner of the illustration. With a very flexible belt tightener an elliptical guide wheel may be used. The axis may be taken at one of the foci or at the intersection of the axis of the ellipse.

The most complicated adjustment is to mount the table on the face of another disc, table and disc revolving in opposite directions. It will go through a long series of changes without completing any figure and then will repeat itself. The diameters may be made to vary from the fraction of an inch to as large in diameter as the size of the table permits. The designs given here were originally traced on drawing paper 6 in. square.

Remarkable and complex as the curves produced in this manner are, they are but the results obtained by combining simultaneously two simple motions as may be shown in the following manner: Hold the table stationary and the pen will trace an oval. But if the guide wheel is secured in a fixed position and the table is revolved a circle will be the result.

So much for the machine shown in *Fig. 1*. The number of the modifications of this simple contrivance is limited only by the ingenuity of the maker. *Fig. 2* speaks for itself. One end of the ruler is fastened in such a way as to have a to-and-fro motion over the arc of a circle and the speed of the table is geared down by the addition of another wheel with a small pulley attached. This will give many new designs. In *Fig. 3* the end of the ruler is held by a rubber band against the edge of a thin triangular piece of wood that is attached to the face of the fourth wheel. By substituting other plain figures for the triangle, or outlining them with small finishing nails, many curious modifications such as are shown by the two smallest designs in the illustrations may be obtained. It is necessary, if symmetrical designs are to be made, that the fourth wheel and the guide wheel have the same diameter.

In *Fig. 4*, *V* and *W* are vertical wheels that may be successfully connected with the double horizontal drive wheel if the pulley between the two has a wide flange and is set at the proper angle. A long strip of paper is given a uniform rectilinear motion as the string attached to it is wound around the axle *V*. The pen *P* has a motion made of two simultaneous movements at right angles to each other produced by the two guide wheels. Designs such as shown as a border at the top and bottom of the illustration are obtained in this way. If the vertical wheels are disconnected and the paper fastened in place the well-known Lissajou's curves are obtained. These curves may be traced by various methods, but this arrangement is about the simplest of them all. The design in this case will change as the ratio of the diameters of the two guide wheels are changed.

These are only a few of the many adjustments that are possible. Frequently some new device will create a figure that is apparently like one obtained in some other way. Yet, if you watch the way in which the two are commenced and developed into the complete design you will find they are formed quite differently.

The average boy will take delight in making a wondergraph and in inventing the many improvements that are sure to suggest themselves. In any event it will not be time thrown away, for, simple as the contrivance is, it will arouse latent energies which may develop along more useful lines in later years.

— A Perpetual Calendar —

It is necessary only to set this calendar the first of each month, by sliding the insertions up or down, to get the proper month or week. The calendar, as it is shown, is set for January 1916. Saturday is the first day and the Friday the seventh, and so on. It is not confusing and can be read either by the day or date. If the day is known it will show the date, and if the date is known it will show the day. The illustration clearly shows the parts, which can be cut from heavy paper or cardboard.

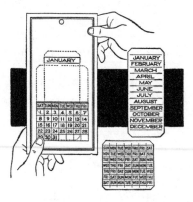

IT IS NECESSARY ONLY TO CHANGE THE SLIDING PIECES TO SET THE CALENDAR FOR EACH MONTH.

— Improvised Postcard Projector and Enlarging Camera —

An outfit that may be used for either projecting picture postcards or enlarging photographic negatives was assembled as delineated in the illustration. An ordinary camera is required to provide the lens and bellows in combination with a dark box that can be built in the home workshop. The method of construction is this:

Make a box about 8 in. square out of ½-in. planed softwood stock. Nail the sides, but omit for the present the top and the bottom. The two openings thus left will be called the front and the back. Mount an 8-by-8-by-½-in. board, *D,* on the back with hinges, for a door.

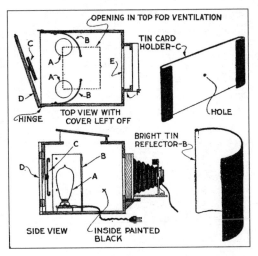

AN ORDINARY SMALL CAMERA, FITTED WITH THIS ATTACHMENT, BECOMES AN ENLARGING AND POSTCARD-PROJECTING CAMERA.

Provide a hook to hold it shut. Cut a square hole, of the same size as that of the opening in the back of the camera that is to be used, in another 8-by-8-in. piece, *E.* This will constitute the front board. This front board is cut so that it fits in between the sides of the box instead of on the ends, as does the back. In the top, cut a square hole for ventilation. A hood is provided over this hole to prevent light being thrown forward.

When using the arrangement as a projector or magic lantern, two 40-watt tungsten lamps, *A,* are required. Each lamp is mounted in a porcelain receptacle attached to the floor of the box with screws. A lamp cord, one end connecting the two lamps in multiple and the other fitted with an attachment plug, passes through a hole in the floor of the box. Form the two reflectors, *B,* of 8-by-7-in. bright tinned sheet-iron pieces, each having holes along one of its edges to allow for attachment. The reflectors are bent to a semicircular contour before mounting. The card holder is detailed in *C.* It is a piece of tinned sheet iron bent to the form shown so that it will hold a postcard. A hole is drilled in its center for a screw pivot. It can then be fastened to the center of the back door and can be turned into position for either horizontal or vertical pictures. A washer is inserted on the screw between the holder and the door. The thickness of the camera body having been determined, a slide is fastened to the front board, as in the diagram, to support this body.

Before it can be used as a projector it must be adjusted to operate with the camera of the type and size available. The adjustment must be made in a darkened room with one of its walls a white screen on which the image will be projected. This is done as follows: Remove the back from the camera and place the camera in the slide without extending the bellows. Open the shutter. Insert a card in the hold C. Light the tungsten lamps. Now move the front board, with the camera carried on it, back and forth within the box until the components are in focus. That is, until the most distinct image obtainable is reproduced on the screen. Then, illuminate the previously darkened room and nail the front board in the position thus determined. These

adjustments having been made, paint the box flat black inside and out. Everything should be painted black except the reflecting surfaces of the tin reflectors and the incandescent-lamp bulbs. The front board having been fastened, subsequent focusing can be affected by shifting the lens board of the camera longitudinally. The image of any sort of a picture that will fit in the holder can be reproduced. Colored postcards will project in their natural tints.

To make enlargements with the same box, a few minor changes are necessary. When used for enlargements the tungsten lamps, which are required for projection, are not used. They may, however, remain in the box and can be disconnected from the circuit by unscrewing them a few turns. The negative or film that is to be enlarged is held in the opening E. Where a film is to be reproduced, it is held between two pieces of glass that are fastened to the inside of the front board with small clips. If a glass negative is used, the two additional glass plates are unnecessary. If the negative does not fill the opening in the camera, a mask cut from heavy black paper will be required to cut off the light.

The light for the enlargement is

furnished by another tungsten lamp mounted in a porcelain receptacle that is screwed to a board that constitutes a base. This light source is moved about in the house until it is directly in back of the opening E in the front of the box and until the light is distributed equally over the entire negative. To focus, move the camera backward or forward. While focusing, use a yellow glass, or ray screen, to cover the lens. When focusing has been completed, the shutter is closed and the ray screen removed. Then stop down the lens to bring out detail, and expose.

— A Homemade Magic Lantern —

The essential parts of a magic lantern are a condensing lens to make the beam of light converge upon the slide to illuminate it evenly, a projecting lens with which to throw an enlarged picture of the illuminated slide upon a screen, and some appliances for preserving the proper relation of these parts to each other.

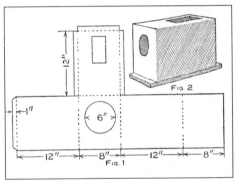

LANTERN HOUSE

The best of materials should be used and the parts put together with care to produce a clear picture on the screen.

The first part to make is the lamp house, or box, to hold the light. The illustration shows the construction for an electric light, but the same box may be used for a gas or oil lamp, provided the material is of metal.

A tin box with dimensions close to those given in the diagram may be secured from your local grocer. But if such a box is not found, one can be made from a piece of tin cut as shown in *Fig. 1*. When this metal is bent at right angles on the dotted lines it will form a box as shown in *Fig. 2*, which is placed on a baseboard, ½ to ¾ in. thick, 8 in. wide,

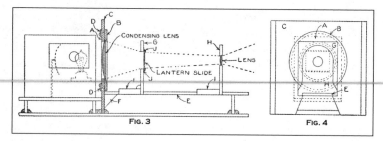

MAGIC-LANTERN DETAILS.

and 14 in. long. This box should be provided with a reflector located just in back of the lamp.

Procure a plano-convex or biconvex 6-in. lens with a focal length of from 15 to 20 in. and a projecting lens 2 in. in diameter with such a focal length that will give a picture of the required size. Or you can use a lens of 12-in. focus enlarging a 3-in. slide to about 6 ft. at a distance of 24 ft.

The woodwork of the lantern should be ½-in., well-seasoned pine, white wood, or walnut, and the parts should be fastened together with wood screws, wire brads, or glue, as desired. The board on which the condensing lens is mounted should be 16 in. wide and 15 in. high, battened on both ends to keep the wood from warping. The board is centered both ways. At a point 1 in. above the center, describe a 9-in. circle with a compass and saw the wood out with a

scroll or keyhole saw. If a small saw is used and the work carefully done, the circular piece removed will serve to make the smaller portion of the ring that holds the condensing lens. This ring is actually made up from two rings, *A* and *B*, *Fig. 3*. The inside and outside diameters of the ring *B* are ⅜ in. greater than the corresponding diameters of ring *A*, so when fastened together concentrically an inner rabbet is formed for the reception of the lens and an outer rabbet to fit against the board *C*. This is the board in and against which it rotates, being held in place by buttons, *DD*.

A table, *E*, about 2 ft. long, is fastened to the board *C* with brackets, *F*, and supported at the outer end with a standard. The slide support *G* and the lens slide *H* are constructed to slip easily on the table *E*, the strips *II* serving as guides. Small strips of tin, *JJ*, are bent as shown and fastened at the top and bottom of the rectangular opening cut in the support *G* for holding the lantern slides.

All the parts should be joined together snugly and the movable parts made to slide freely. When all is complete and well sandpapered, apply two coats of shellac varnish, place the lamp house on the bottom board behind the condensing lens, and the lantern is ready for use.

The proper light and focus may be obtained by slipping the movable parts on the board *E.* When the right position is found for each, all lantern slides will produce a clear picture on the screen, if the position of the lantern and screen is not changed.

Spy Lab

— A Simple Cipher Code —

Have you ever needed a secret code in which to couch the contents of a message intended for the eyes of one person alone? If you have, you will remember the difficulties that were experienced in making up the code and enciphering your letter. Here is a cipher code that may be mastered in a few minutes; one that is most difficult to decipher by any person other than those having the key words, and that is very simple when once understood.

It is commonly known as the "Play Fair" code and is in use in some of the foreign military services. It is a substitutive cipher that operates with one or more key words, two letters in the code being substituted for each two letters in the text of the message. In preparing the cipher code by this method the key words are selected by the correspondents and their location in the cipher square mutually agreed upon. A large square divided into 25 smaller squares is drawn, as shown in *Fig. 1,* and the letters of the key words entered into their proper spaces, the remaining spaces being filled by other letters of the alphabet. The key words must not contain duplicate letters. The letters *I* and *J* are considered as one and entered in the same space, the letter *I* being invariably used in enciphering.

Suppose that the two words "grant" and "field" have been selected for the key, the same to be entered respectively in the spaces on the

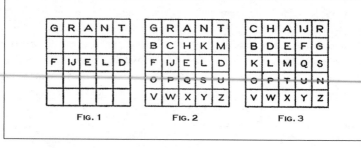

G	R	A	N	T
F	IJ	E	L	D

Fig. 1

G	R	A	N	T
B	C	H	K	M
F	IJ	E	L	D
O	P	Q	S	U
V	W	X	Y	Z

Fig. 2

C	H	A	IJ	R
B	D	E	F	G
K	L	M	Q	S
O	P	T	U	N
V	W	X	Y	Z

Fig. 3

THE CIPHER CODE ILLUSTRATED IN THESE DIAGRAMS MAY BE ADAPTED FOR WIDE USES BY THE SUBSTITUTION OF APPROPRIATE KEY WORDS FOR THOSE SHOWN.

first and third horizontal lines of the square. Then the basis of the construction would be as indicated in *Fig. 1*. Now fill in the remaining fifteen spaces of the square with other letters of the alphabet, beginning at the blank space at the left of the second line, entering the letters in rotation and not using any letter of the key words. The completed cipher would then appear as shown in *Fig. 2*.

The text of the message to be sent is then divided into groups of two letters each and the equivalent substituted for each pair. Where two like letters fall in the same pair the letter *X* is inserted between them and when the message is deciphered this additional letter is disregarded. If one letter is left over after the last pair, simply add an *X* to it and make a pair.

Suppose it is desired to send this message in the cipher: "Will you meet me as agreed?" Having three pairs of the same letter, it will be necessary to break them up by placing the letter *X* between them. The message will then be paired off as follows:

WI LX LY OU ME XE TM EA SA
GR EX ED

The message may now be enciphered, after considering three simple rules for guidance: Every pair of letters in the square must be either in the same vertical line, the same horizontal line, or at the diagonally opposite corners of a rectangle formed by the smaller squares within the large square.

In the first case, *R* and *P* are in the same vertical line (the second). The next letter below in each case is substituted for *R* and *P*, which are *C* and *W*. If the pair consists of *K* and *Y* (fourth vertical), substitute *L* for *K* and go to the first horizontal line (the second), and thus substitute the next letters to the right, which are *C* and *K*. If the pair consists of *P* and *U* (fourth horizontal), substitute *Q* for *P* and then go back to the first vertical line (fourth horizontal) and substitute *O* for *U*. In the third case, *R* and *S* are at the opposite corners of a rectangle. Each letter of the pair is substituted by the letter in the other corner of the rectangle on the same horizontal line with it. Then *R* would be represented by *N,* and *S* would be represented by *P.* To illustrate further, *NE* would be represented by *AL; BZ* would be represented *MV; TP* by *RU.*

The message may now be enciphered, applying the rules:

WI LX LY OU ME XE TM EA SA
GR EX ED
RP EY SN PO HD AQ MD QH QN
RA QA LF

In sending this message, to make it more difficult for the inquisitive cipher expert, divide the substituted letters into words of five each and give him the added task of deter-

mining whether the cipher used is the transposition or the substitution method. The message ready to hand to the telegrapher would read:

RPEYS NPOHD AQMDQ
HQNRA QALFX

In deciphering a message the method is reversed. Take the message as received, divide the letters into pairs, and disregard the final *X,* which was put in to make a five-letter word. Then apply the key reversed. Practice it on the message at left to get the system with respect to letters occurring at the end of the lines. Where the letters of a pair are in the same vertical line, substitute for each the letter above; where they are in the same horizontal line, substitute the letter to left; where they are in the corners of a rectangle, substitute the letters at the opposite corners on the same horizontal line. To test the understanding of the system, the message given in *Fig. 3,* with the key words "chair" in the first horizontal line and "optun" in the fourth line, may be deciphered. The message to be deciphered is as follows:

FQVUO IRTEF HRWDG APARQ
TMMZM RBFVU PICXM TRMXM
AGEPA DONFC BAXAX.

— DRAWER LOCKED BY SECRET DOWEL PIN —

The secret lock shown in the drawing was fitted to a drawer whose lock was rendered useless by the loss of the key. Simply drill a hole through the under rail and into the panel of the drawer. Insert a loosely fitting hardwood dowel pin, or a steel nail into this hole. A thin metal button keeps the pin in position. To remove the pin and unlock the drawer, the clip is turned to one side that causes the pin to drop out. Not being easily discovered, such a lock may be applied, for additional

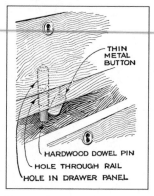

safety, to drawers whose locks are easily "jimmied."

— AN EFFECTIVE COMBINATION LOCK EASILY MADE —

The combination lock described has been used for years on lockers and letter boxes in a large public building. The details are for a lock with three disks and, in *Fig. 4,* the use of two disks is suggested. The lock is made as follows: From a piece of 3/16- or ¼-in. hardwood, saw out three disks, *A, Fig. 1,* from 1 to 4 in. in diameter, according to the size of lock desired. For one with 2-in. disks, as shown, cut slots, *B,* ½ in. wide and deep, in the edge

of the disks. For axles use ⅜- by 2-in. hardwood dowels, *C,* with a sixpenny headless wire nail in one end, leaving about ¼ in. of it exposed.

The case of the lock is shown in *Fig. 1.* It is made large enough to mount the disks, as shown. Fasten strips a trifle thicker than the disks around the edges of the inside surface of the lid. Place the disks in the positions shown, drilling small holes in the baseboard for the nail axles. The bolts *D* and the piece *E* are made of hardwood, fastened with a lap joint. On each side of the bar D fasten cleats F to hold it in position. The hand H moves in a slot in the lid, and is fixed to the bar, E.

The door, or lid, on which the lock is to be used is provided with openings, J, as shown in *Fig. 3*. The axles, C, project through openings, as bearings. When the windows J, through which the combinations are read, are made, place the ends of the bolts in the slots of the disks and screw the lock in position. Mark on each disk the point exactly in the center of the window, enabling one to work the combination temporarily. To lock the device, push the handle to the left and turn the axles. To unlock it, turn the axles until the pencil marks appear in the middle of the windows, and throw the bolts.

Next make paper dials, K, of a diameter shown in *Fig. 2*. Divide the circumference into from 50 to 100 equal parts, according to the size of the dial, and draw radii, as shown.

Number at least every fifth point. Fasten one of the dials to the face of each disk, A, with small thumbtacks, placing the combination numbers selected exactly over the pencil marks made in setting the temporary combination. Verify the combination before locking it. Unless the slots in the disks are a little wider than the ends of the bolts, the combination must be very closely adjusted. A line on the glass or a point of a black paper will be an aid in setting the combination,

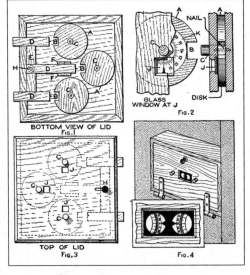

THIS WOOD COMBINATION LOCK
GIVES GOOD SERVICE AND
IS EASILY MADE.

as shown in *Fig. 2*. The combination may be changed by setting the dials in new positions. The large number of combinations possible makes it very difficult for someone to decipher the actual combination. For most purposes, two disks are sufficient in a lock of this kind.

— HOW TO TRANSFER DRAWINGS —

The young draftsman can avoid soiling drawings transferred with carbon paper by substituting a piece of unfinished paper, the surface of which has been covered with a thin coating of lead rubbed from the pencil. If an error is made in the tracing, or under pressure is applied with the hand, the resulting impressions may be removed readily with an eraser.

If a copy of a drawing is desired, and it is not necessary that the same relative left and right position be maintained, the original pencil drawing may be placed face downward on a sheet of paper and the back of it rubbed with a bone paper knife, or other smooth, rounded object. By going over the impression and making a reverse of it in the same way, a copy of the original in the same relations may be obtained.

— A COMBINATION ELECTRICALLY OPERATED DOOR LOCK —

The illustration shows a very useful application of an ordinary electric door lock in the construction of a combination lock and alarm to be operated from the outside the building.

The three numerals, 1, 2, and 4, or any other combination of numbers constituting the house number on a door, are made of some kind of insulating material and fastened in place on a base of insulating fiber, or wood, about ¼ in. thick. Fasten the numbers by means of ordinary brass-headed tacks, as indicated by the black dots. The tacks will extend through the base a short distance so that the electrical connections may be made by soldering wires to them, as shown in the diagram, alternate tacks being connected together with the exception of three; for instance, *A*, *B*, and *C*.

The terminals of the leads that

are connected to alternate tacks are in turn connected to the terminals of a circuit composed of an ordinary vibrating bell, *D,* and battery, *E.* If any two adjacent tack heads are connected together (except tacks *A, B,* and *C*) the bell circuit will be completed and the bell will ring, which will serve as an indication that someone is tampering with the circuit. The person knowing the combination connects the tack heads *A* and *B,*

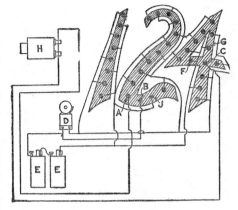

THE BRASS TACK HEADS
HOLDING THE NUMERALS IN PLACE
CONSTITUTE THE COMBINATION POINTS.

and at the same time connects the tack head *C* with *F* or *G,* or any other tack head that is connected to the plus side of the battery, whereby a circuit will be completed through the lock *H* and the door opened. A metallic substance, such as a knife, key, or finger ring, may be used in making the above indicated connection, and there will be no need to carry a key for this particular door so long as the combination is known.

The base upon which the numbers are mounted and through which the points of the tacks protrude should be mounted on a second base that has a recess cut in its surface to accommodate the wires and points of the tacks.

The combination may be made more or less complicated, as desired, by connecting the tacks in different ways and by using a separate battery for the bell and lock. The circuit leading to the door lock, if there is one already installed, may be used and then no extra circuit is needed.

Such a device has been used on a private-desk drawer with entire satisfaction. The battery was placed in the back end of the drawer, and if it happened to fail, a new one could be connected to the points *B* and *J* so that the drawer could be opened and a new battery put in.

— SIMPLE MACHINE FOR TRANSMITTING WRITING —

An interesting and novel construction for amateur or boy mechanics is a telautograph or writing telegraph machine. The instruments, as shown, are duplicates with the exception of the placing of the rubber bands. They can be made in different sizes, and satisfactory results were obtained by making

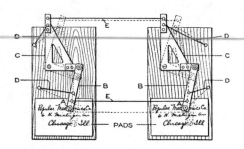

A MESSAGE WRITTEN ON THE PAD WITH A PENCIL IS TRANSMITTED TO THE OTHER PAD AT A CONSIDERABLE DISTANCE AWAY.

the base 7 by 12 in., the arm *B*, 5 in. long and ¾ in. wide, and the triangle *C*, 6 in. by 3½ in. A hole is bored in the arm *B*, slightly smaller than the pencil to be used, and a slot sawed from the edge to hole so that when the pencil is forced into the hole it will be tightly gripped, as in *A*. The arm *B* is fastened to triangle *C* to move freely. The triangle is fastened to the base and can also move freely. The rubber bands *D* are stretched tightly to hold the moving parts in position. The strings *E* should be strong and stretched taut.

The larger diagram shows the instruments placed in parallel position. The smaller diagram shows how they can be placed one above

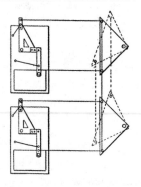

the other. An unruled pad is fastened to the base of each instrument with thumbtacks. The operation may be traced by noting the successive action of the parts when the pencil on the pad at the left is moved in writing a message. The pivoted triangle communicates the action to the string

E, which actuates the other triangle and its lever system. The rubber bands serve to steady the action. The instruments may be arranged a short distance apart for play or experimental purposes or set in rooms on different floors by making suitable pulley connections for the cords.

— USEFUL PERISCOPE THAT A BOY CAN MAKE —

Mention of periscopes is quite common in the reports from European trenches; such a device in a simple form can be made easily by boys who have fair skill with tools. The illustration shows a periscope that may be used for play and has other practical uses as well. In a store or other place where a person on duty cannot watch all parts of the establishment, such a device is convenient in that it will reflect persons entering the door. As a toy or for experimental purposes the periscope shown has many possibilities, and will appeal to youngsters.

It consists of a square box, 18 in. long, and open at the ends. It is 3½ in. wide and made of wood, ⅜ in.

THIS SIMPLE PERISCOPE IS USEFUL BOTH FOR PLAY AND PRACTICAL PURPOSES.

thick. A mirror is fitted at an angle of 45 degrees near one end of the box or tube, as shown in the sketch.

The front of the mirror is opposite a three-cornered opening in the box that extends across one side. The opposite end of the tube is also fitted with a mirror in the same manner, except that the front of the mirror faces to the opposite side of the box at which there is also an opening. In using this device, the user sights from the point indicated by the eye.

The image is reflected in the mirror at the top and thrown onto the lower mirror, where it may be seen without exposing the head above the level of the lower opening. It is this application of reflection by mirrors that makes it possible for soldiers to see distant objects without exposing themselves to fire, by the use of the periscope.

— A Flashlight Telegraph on a Kite Line —

An ordinary pocket flash lamp is prepared in the following manner: A brass spring, as shown in the sketch, is bound tightly to the flash lamp with a cord. Two wires, one at each end, are twisted around the lamp's body, forming two loops at the top. The kite string is run through the loops and over the spring. The lamp is then placed near the kite. The ordinary pull on the kite string does not close the spring, but a sharp jerk will pull the string in contact with the push button and its slight pressure causes an instant flash of the light. By this method words may be spelled out in the telegraph code.

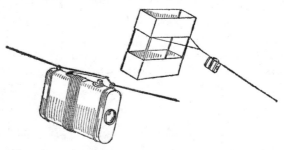

THE FLASH OF THE LIGHT ON THE STRING
MAY BE READ AS FAR AS IT CAN BE SEEN.

— A Handy Portable Lock —

Travelers who feel insecure behind the flimsy or disabled locks that may be found in many out-of-the-way hostelries—and in some city hotels—can use a detachable lock of the type shown in the drawing, and sleep with the assurance that anyone trying to force the door to which it is attached will arouse the occupant of the room. A ⅛-in. steel plate is cut to the form and dimensions given, and the two points are bent over and sharpened. Several slots are cut through the plate, and a metal wedge, or key, is provided to fit them. In use, the sharpened points of the lock are forced into the wooden door jamb against the stop strip; then the door is closed, and the wedge pushed home tightly in the proper slot.

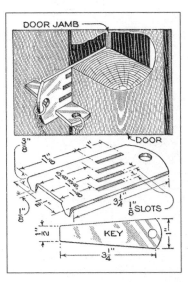

— ❖ ❖ ❖ —

{ CHAPTER 8 }

THE REALLY
GREAT OUTDOORS

—

A CANOE ADVENTURE

— PONTOONS FOR STABILITY
IN THE CANOE —

To sleep in a canoe has always been considered the equivalent of making an appointment with the coroner, because the craft is likely to capsize with a sudden shifting of weight. However, one may sleep aboard a canoe in safety and also stand upright to "play" a gamey fish, or make a difficult landing, by equipping the craft with pontoons.

Two false thwarts are first provided; these should make a snug fit between the inside of the gunwales, one at the position of the center thwart and the other at the rear off the forward seat. The length of these thwarts will depend upon the beam of the boat at those points and, as shown in *Figs. 1* and *2,* should come flush with the top of the gunwales. Angle-iron braces underneath hold the thwarts in place and make them readily removable; the guides are attached with screws down the exact center of each, the heads of the screws being countersunk. Eight iron straps are provided, made as shown in *Fig. 3*. Four are attached to each thwart, as in *Figs. 1* and *2*, the outer ones coming directly over the gunwales. A hole is drilled through each side of the center straps to accommodate pins.

The slides, or outriggers, are made of good straight-grained oak, about 6 in. longer than the outside width of the canoe at the point used. Four of these pieces will be required, and they should be smoothed down to slide easily under the straps without binding. Holes to coincide with those in the center straps are drilled in each piece at intervals of 2 or 3 in., for holding the slides in either the extended or housed position. One end of each slide is mitered for fitting to the pontoon arms. The pontoon arms are cut

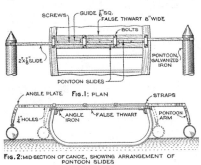

FIG. 1: PLAN

FIG. 2: MID-SECTION OF CANOE, SHOWING ARRANGEMENT OF PONTOON SLIDES

FIG. 3: END SECTION OF THWART, SHOWING STRAPS, POSITION OF SLIDES AND GUIDE

FIG. 4: DETAIL OF PONTOONS

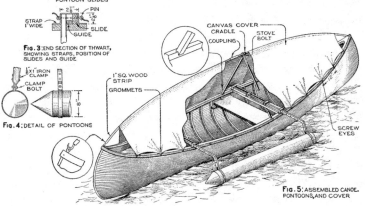

FIG. 5: ASSEMBLED CANOE, PONTOONS, AND COVER

BY EQUIPPING AN ORDINARY CANOE WITH PONTOONS AND A CANVAS COVER, THE CANOEIST IS ABLE TO STAND UP WHEN "PLAYING" A GAMEY FISH OR MAKING A DIFFICULT LANDING; HE MAY ALSO SLEEP ABOARD IN SAFETY AND COMFORT.

out and smoothed down to suit, and one end is mitered to fit the mitered ends of the slides, to which they are attached with iron angle plates, sunk flush with the wood, and fastened with countersunk screws. These plates must be flush so that they will not interfere with the operation of the slide in the straps. When the slides and pontoon arms are assembled, each will resemble a hockey stick in appearance, the pontoon arms being parallel with the sides of the canoe, as in *Fig. 2.* The pontoons are merely airtight cylinders made from fairly heavy galvanized iron, and provided with conical ends. The pontoons are held to the ends of the pontoon arms by means of iron clamps, as shown in *Fig. 4.* A hole is drilled in each clamp between the pontoon and the end of the arm to take a suitable clamping bolt, the tightening of which serves to hold the pontoons.

As a final touch for use when cruising, a canvas cover may be added as shown in *Fig. 5;* this drawing also shows the appearance of the canoe with the pontoons extended. A light, flexible wood strip is provided, a trifle longer than the distance between the bow and stern of the canoe, and a screw hook is turned into each end; a screw eye is inserted at each end of the boat to take the hooks on the end of the strip, as shown in the detail. For convenience in stowing, this strip is cut in two at the center, and the ends are rounded off for 2 or 3 in.; a coupling made from a short length of tubing is provided to slip over the rounded ends of the strip. A folding cradle, as shown in the drawing, supports the center of the strip and notches in the ends of the legs fit over the gunwales of the canoe, as in the detail. Light canvas is used for the cover, which fits over the whole canoe and buttons along the outside. This is accomplished by inserting grommets and small brass screw eyes at intervals in the edge of the canvas and the outside of the boat.

When under way and paddling along, the slides are pulled in and pinned in place so that the pontoons fit closely under the counter of the canoe. As they clear the water they will not impede progress. When it is desired to use them for any purpose, simply slide out a pair at a time to the distance required, and secure them in place with the pins. Only a slight tipping motion of the canoe will then bring one or the other of them into contact with the water, making the craft entirely stable and safe.

— ANCHOR FOR A CANOE OR SMALL BOAT —

Small craft, particularly those used for fishing or on streams where a current is encountered, should be provided with an anchor. The illustration gives details for making one that is simple in construction and inexpensive. It weighs about five pounds and is heavy enough for light craft up to 18 ft. long.

The main section was made of a piece of 1½-in. angle iron, 10 in. long. The flukes, or end pieces, were made of sheet iron, 2 in. wide and 8 in. long, bent at a right angle and riveted in place. The straps that hold the link, permitting it to swing freely, were made of band iron. The link was made of an old bicycle crank into which a ring was forged. It may be made of iron rod, forged into the desired shape and fitted with a ring. A convenient method of handling the anchor on a boat is to run the line through a pulley at the bow

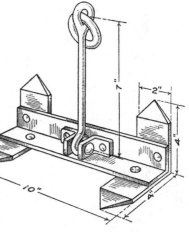

THIS HOMEMADE ANCHOR IS A PRACTICAL ADDITION TO THE EQUIPMENT OF A CANOE OR SMALL BOAT, AND WEIGHS FIVE POUNDS.

and fasten the end of it to a cleat, near the seat of the person handling the craft. Care must be taken, in a canoe or small boat, that sufficient line is provided to reach the bottom of the anchorage, as otherwise the craft may be overturned.

— A SIMPLE CANOE AWNING —

Canoeists are familiar with the disadvantages of their craft in the lack of protection from the burning effects of the sun. However, a very neat and effective protection is afforded by an awning of the type shown in the drawing.

The awning consists of five pieces,

the canvas awning and four removable uprights. Naturally, no dimensions can be given, the awning being made according to the length and width of the canoe. The uprights are made of 1-in. square material, rounded at both ends to fit into ½-in. holes in the thwarts, or gunwales, and into the stretcher across the top. If it the owner prefers not to drill holes in the canoe to hold the awning supports, there are various types of sockets that can be bought or easily made. The canvas awning strip has a stretcher inserted through a hem at each end, and a light rope is tied to the awning as indicated. After the uprights are in position, the awning is stretched across them, and the ends of the ropes are made fast through conveniently located screw eyes. An awning of this or any other type positively should not be used in waters where danger of a sudden wind exists.

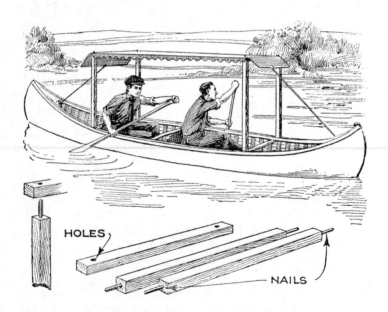

HOLES

NAILS

A NEAT AWNING FOR THE CANOE ADDS GREATLY TO THE PLEASURES OF SUCH A BOAT. THIS AWNING CAN BE STOWED AWAY COMPACTLY AND SET UP IN A FEW MINUTES.

— How to Make a Motorized Canoe —

A staunchly built canoe of sufficient length and beam may be converted into a light, serviceable, and convenient powerboat by the installation of a lightweight motor of about 2 horsepower. While the craft thus becomes less available for shallow waters and cannot be used on trips where portages are necessary, a power canoe has advantages in that longer trips may be undertaken with less regard for weather conditions. Greater speed and the fact that physical power need not be expended also increase the value and range of operations of such a craft.

Unless a motor of extremely light weight is procured, a canoe of frail construction and less than 16 ft. long is not likely to stand the jar of the driving mechanism. The canoe illustrated in the page plate is 18 ft. long, with a 36-in. beam, and strongly planked, decked, and braced. A canoe of even broader beam would tend to give more stability in rough water, and if heavy camping packs or other material must be transported, this factor should be observed particularly. Likewise, the depth and draft must be considered, because the carrying capacity and seaworthiness of a canoe depend in part on these factors. The fitting of the various parts of the mechanism and accessories must be done with the aim of balancing the load evenly. If properly disposed, the weight of these parts should tend to lower the center or gravity of the canoe, thus rendering it more stable.

The actual work of installing the motor and fittings should be preceded by careful planning and the making of a full-size diagram of the stern portion of the canoe as rebuilt. Too much care cannot be taken in this work because, if it is neglected, the craft may be rendered unsafe, or the motor and fittings may not operate correctly. The motor should be set in the stern, as shown in the illustration, because this will permit the use of a minimum of shafting and other fittings that must be accommodated. The exact location of the motor may vary with canoes and engines of different types. This should be tested by placing the motor in the canoe and noting the effect on its balance in the water. For a canoe of the dimensions indicated, and a lightweight motor, 5 ft. from the stern is a satisfactory position.

The motor should be placed as low in the canoe as possible, allowing the flywheel and crank case sufficient clearance below.

A convenient method of operation is as follows: Place the canoe on boxes or sawhorses, taking care that it its properly supported about 2 ft. from the ground, or floor. Take measurements directly from the canoe, or part to be fitted, whenever convenient. Procure two sheets of paper, 30 in. wide and 7 ft. long; mark one "diagram" and the other "templates," and use the former for the full-size detail and the other for the making of templates for curved or irregular parts.

Begin the diagram by drawing the base line *AB, Fig. 3*. This is the lower line of the engine bed and the upper surface of the ribs. Draw the line *CD* perpendicular to the baseline, and 18 in. from the left end of the sheet. The point *C* is the center of the stern end of the driving shaft. The dimensions of parts are not given, except in special instances, because they must be obtained from the particular canoe and other parts entering into the construction. Indicate the layer of ribs *E,* the planking *F,* and the keel *G.* Using the template sheet, cut a template or pattern for the curved stern. This may be readily and accurately done by fusing a straightedge to the keel and permitting it to extend to *A*. Rest the long edge of the sheet on the straightedge when fitting the template to the curve. Use the template as a guide in marking the curve on the diagram, as in *HJ.* The curve *K,* of the stern decking, may be indicated similarly.

Determine the distance the motor is to be set from the stern and indicate it by the perpendicular line *L.* Measuring from the baseline, indicate the height of the center of the

A LIGHTWEIGHT, TWO-HORSEPOWER MOTOR INSTALLED IN A STAUNCH 18-FOOT CANOE WILL INCREASE THE RANGE AND UTILITY OF SUCH A CRAFT; THE CONSTRUCTION SHOWN IS SIMPLE AND WITHIN THE CAPABILITIES OF A CAREFUL NOVICE OF FAIR MECHANICAL SKILL. A VIEW OF THE STERN FROM ABOVE IS SHOWN IN FIG. 1. THE ENGINE IS SHOWN MOUNTED ON THE ENGINE BED, AND THE SHAFT BLOCK IS SHOWN NEAR THE STERN. A PARTIAL SECTIONAL VIEW IS SHOWN IN FIG. 2. THE RELATION OF THE ENGINE AND BED, SHAFT AND FITTINGS, SHAFT BLOCK, SHAFT LOG, AND RUDDER ARE SHOWN. THE CONSTRUCTION DIAGRAM, FIG. 3, IS DESCRIBED IN DETAIL IN THE TEXT. A LARGER-SCALE VIEW AND A SECTION OF THE SHAFT BLOCK ARE INDICATED IN FIG. 4, AND FIG. 5 ILLUSTRATES THE ENGINE BED WITH DIMENSIONS AND FASTENING HOLES.

351

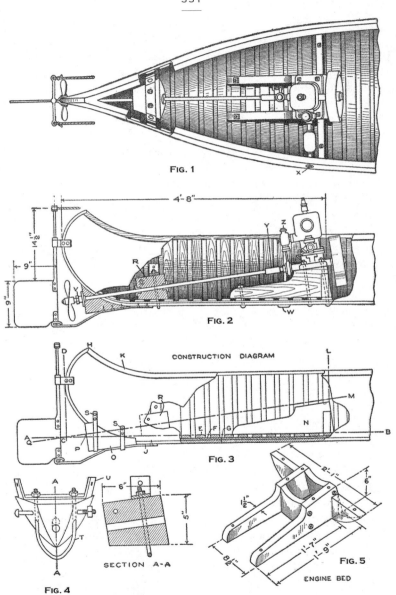

FIG. 1

FIG. 2

CONSTRUCTION DIAGRAM

FIG. 3

FIG. 4

SECTION A-A

FIG. 5

ENGINE BED

motor shaft from the floor, as in *M*. This should be made as low as possible, permitting sufficient clearance for the flywheel and the crank case. Draw a straight line from *C* to *M*, which will thus indicate the center line of the driving shaft. This line is fundamental in determining the dimensions and placing of certain parts and fittings and should be established with extreme care. The size and exact position of the engine bed *N* may now be indicated. Its dimensions, given in detail in the perspective sketch, *Fig. 5*, are suggestive only. They may be varied in order to provide proper bearing on the floor, and so that the bolts holding the bed may pass through ribs. The cross brace at the forward end is important and should be fitted carefully over a rib. The upper line of the engine bed must not be confounded with the centerline of the shaft, for in many engines they are on a horizontal line when viewed from the forward end, yet not necessarily so. The slant of the engine bed must be made accurately, as any deflection from the angle of the centerline of the shaft will disarrange the installation.

The shaft log *O* may next be indicated and a template made for use in guiding the bit when boring the hole for the shaft through it. The template used for the curve *HJ* may be altered by drawing the shaft log on it at the proper place. The point *P*, from which the bit is to be started when the shaft log is fixed into place, should be indicated and the centerline of the shaft, extended to *Q*, may then be used as a guide for the bit. If the homemade type of bearing *R* is used, it should be indicated on the diagram. A metal bearing may be made, or a suitable one obtained from dealers in marine hardware. In the latter case it will probably be necessary to block up the bottom of the canoe in order to provide a flat, horizontal bearing surface for the bearing flange.

The rudder and other parts, which are not directly connected with the motive-power unit, may be indicated in detail on the diagram or be made from sketches of a smaller scale.

Paper patterns, made full size, offer a convenient method of outlining the parts of the engine, the rudder, and other irregular pieces. When the diagram is complete, measurements may be transferred directly from it without reducing them to figures. And, wherever possible, parts should be fitted to it.

The shaft log, shaft bearing, and engine bed may be made of oak or other strong hardwood. It's desirable to have the engine bed complete before an attempt is made to fit the shaft and its connections. It is made of 1½-in. stock, bolted together with lag screws and fixed firmly into the canoe with bolts. The heads of the bolts should be provided with cotton and red-lead packing, and care should be taken that the bolts pass through the ribs.

The shaft log should be fixed into place before it is bored. Bolts may be passed through it and fastened on the inside if there is room for drawing up the nuts in the stern. Large screws may be used to aid in the fastening and smaller screws may be used from the inside. The lower rudder support will also aid in holding the log in place, and the iron straps S, Fig. 3, will ensure its rigidity. This is an important point in the construction, because if the log is not fixed positively, the thrashing of the propeller will soon loosen it.

A detail of the shaft bearing R is shown in Fig. 4. The hole to receive the shaft must be bored accurately and the use of the template, as with the boring of the shaft log, is advisable. Flanged metal bearings are provided to take up the wear in the bearing block. The method of fastening the block, as shown in the detail view, ensures a rigid bearing with a minimum of holes through the bottom of the canoe. A U-bolt, T, binds the double angle brace U and the block firmly to the keel. The angles of the brace are fixed into the sides of the canoe with bolts, and a bolt at the stern end of the block supports it further. Place the block so that it will bear on the three ribs and fits to the curve of the canoe.

The rudder is made of sheet metal supported on a rod or pipe. Its general dimensions are shown in *Fig. 2*. The fan of the rudder is riveted to its supports and rests in a bearing strip of ¼- by 1-in. strap iron, which is shaped as a guard for the propeller. The upper bearing of the rudder post is formed from a strip of iron, bolted to the stern, and the upper guide bar, to which the ropes are attached, is cut from an iron strip.

The propeller is 8 in. in diameter, but may be installed of a size suitable to the power, speed, and type of the motor used. The stuffing box *V, Fig. 2*, the bearings for the bearing block R, the intake strainer W, the exhaust outlet *X, Fig. 1*, and the shaft coupling *Y* are all of manufactured types that may be purchased from marine-supply houses.

The intake strainer *W* is placed in the bottom directly below the pump *Z*. The exhaust outlet *X* is placed above the waterline, and a muffler should be installed to avoid noise from the exhaust explosions. The exhaust may be conducted under water or to a point near the stern. No indication is given for the placing of the gasoline tank, the supply pipes, electrical-energy source, and wiring. The tank may be placed in the stern of the canoe high enough to provide a good flow. A magneto may be used to give current for the sparking circuit, or batteries may be provided. They may be placed at any point convenient and should be encased in a waterproof container.

In assembling the parts care must be taken not to wrench the shaft or other pieces out of line. In general, it is wise to fix nonadjustable parts solidly when they are fitted into place. This applies particularly to the engine bed and the shaft log. The bearing block may be adjusted vertically by adding packing or by reducing the lower surface. The rudder and its fittings may be made in regular course but should not be fitted until the power unit and driving mechanism are finally in place. The propeller may be protected from possible injury by laying it aside until needed. All the openings in the hull through which bolts or other fastenings are placed should be packed with red lead or other waterproof packing. The working parts and finished metal surfaces should be oiled or greased thoroughly as the parts are assembled, and the unfinished metal parts painted with red lead. [Editor's note: Today we use alkyd or acrylic metal primer.] This will protect them from moisture and aid in the smooth operation of the mechanism.

PROJECT CAMP

— HOW TO MAKE A TWINE HAMMOCK —

Cord hammocks may be made in two or more different ways, the knots being formed by the simple overhand tie, *Fig. 1*, the flat reef knot, *Fig. 2*, the Solomon's knot, *Fig. 3*, or by the triple throw-over, *Fig. 4*. Or they can be knotted by the process known as netting, *Fig. 5*, in which a special needle, or shuttle, is used.

In using any one of the first three methods of making the knots it is necessary to have cords arranged in pairs and long enough to reach from one end of the hammock to the other, allowing only sufficient length for the take-up in tying the knots and the spread of the meshes. The overhand knot is large and the Solomon's knot a little unwieldy, but is considered more beautiful when tied. The flat reef knot is small, is easily tied, and will not slip. The netting process has a good knot and has the advantage of a short single cord, because the meshes are made independently and the cord is carried on the netting needle.

It is a great advantage, when making a hammock with the simple overhand, the flat reef, or the Solomon's knot, to loop all the pairs of cords at the center about a rod, *Fig. 6*—which may handle—knotting from the center toward each end, one side being tied and then the

other. When the first pairs are being tied the opposite ends should be looped up together out of the way. Even half the length of a hammock makes a long cord to be drawn through each time a knot is tied. Each string can be wound about the fingers into a little bundle and secured with a half hitch, using the same cord, and left hanging, as shown in *Fig. 7*. Allow sufficient cord free to throw large loops in the

WHEN MAKING A HAMMOCK WITH THE SIMPLE OVERHAND, FLAT REEF, OR SOLOMON'S KNOT, LOOP ALL THE PAIRS OF CORDS AT THE CENTER ABOUT A ROD.

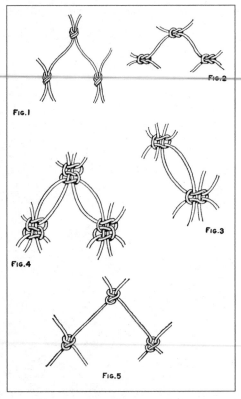

FIG.2

FIG.1

FIG.3

FIG.4

FIG.5

THE SIMPLE OVERHAND, FLAT REEF,
SOLOMON'S KNOT, TRIPLE THROW-OVER,
AND NETTING TIES.

by the first two methods of tying the knots. Seine twine of medium-hard twist and 24-ply can be obtained from a store carrying sporting goods and is about the best material to use for this purpose. These pairs of cords are looped on the center rod, and the rod is anchored to a wall as shown in *Fig. 8.* Then begin by placing the mesh stick, or rather the mesh post, *Fig. 9,* between the first pair of cords, *A* and *B,* at the left end of the center rod, as in *Fig. 8* and *Fig. 6.* The simple device illustrated in *Fig. 9* is very useful for tying any one of the first three knots. The device needs no explanation other than the illustration. It will be seen that there are two sizes on the top of the post; the smaller is for the first time across only. The mesh post should be of convenient height for a person when sitting on an ordinary chair. One foot rests on the base as the tying proceeds, but

tying and to make about 10 additional meshes. About 3 ft. would be a good length to be left free.

It will be necessary to have 24 pairs of cords—48 cords in all, each 18 ft. long—to make a hammock

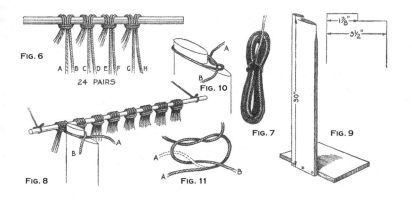

THE MESH POST HAS TWO SIZES ON ITS UPPER END,
THE SMALLER FOR KNOTTING THE FIRST ROW OF MESHES AND
THE OTHER FOR THE REMAINING ROWS. THIS ILLUSTRATION
ALSO SHOWS THE MANNER OF TYING THE KNOTS.

there is no pulling over, as the tie draws both ways on the post. This also does away with the pull on the center rod.

The cord to the right, *B,* is taken in the right hand and thrown over the left cord *A, Fig. 8,* and is held by the left hand. The left cord *A* is then tucked down behind the right, as shown in *Fig. 10.* If the right cord goes over in making the first loop, the same cord *B* must also go over in the second throw, as in *Fig. 11,* in order to have a proper square knot that will not slip. The end of *A* is then tucked under *B,* as shown by the dotted lines. This makes a very serviceable knot for the ham-

mock but can be also used for other purposes. The knot is shown in *Fig. 2.* Draw it up tightly, very hard, for knotting is not worth much if it is not tied well.

In case the simple overhand knot is preferred, the mesh post is placed between the first pair as before, and cords *A* and *B* are brought to the front as in *Fig. 12.* But with this knot they are carried parallel into a large loop that is thrown over as illustrated, then tucked up through as indicated by the dotted lines. The thumb and first finger of the left hand now slide up to the point *P,* while the right hand pulls up the loop as it nears the finish. The thumb and first finger crowd the loop down hard against the mesh post. The small part is used for the first row across. The knot formed is shown in *Fig. 1.*

After tying the first pair of cords using the knot preferred, slip the first mesh so made off the tying post and place the post between *C* and *D,* which is the next, or second, pair. Tie the second pair and pass on to the third pair, which is *E* and *F.* Continue moving and tying until all the 24 pairs of cords have been simi-larly knotted in their first mesh. The last knotting will be the twenty-fourth pair, which is represented by the cords marked *Y* and *Z.* Instead of tying cords of the same pairs on the return trip across, one cord *Y* of the twenty-fourth pair is tied with one cord *X* of the twenty-third pair. The other cord *W* of the twenty-third pair is tied with the cord *V* of the twenty-second pair, and so on across the series.

On the second row of tying, the post is first placed between cords *Y* and *X* and they are knotted together. But instead of tying about the small part of the post, the larger size is used. After cords *Y* and *X* have been tied, cords *W* and *V* are combined. It will be seen that this is tying the pairs together instead of com-bining the two cords of the same pair. The third time across the combina-tions are the same as in the first row. The large mesh is used on all but the first row. The alterna-tions of rows is continued until the cords are tied to within 2½ ft. of the end.

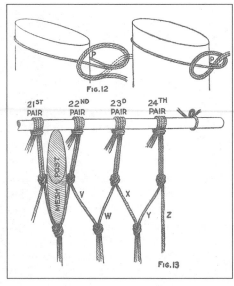

TYING THE OVERHAND KNOT AND HOW TO RUN
THE FIRST AND SECOND ROWS ACROSS.

Pull out the center rod, insert it in the second row of meshes, loosen the ends that were looped up, and begin the knotting of the opposite ends of the cords. When both sides are completed to within 2½ ft. of the ends, the center rod is

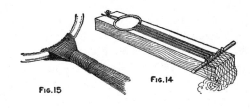

FIG.15

FIG.14

ATTACHING THE RINGS TO THE ENDS OF THE CORDS AND THE BINDING NEAR THE RINGS: ALL THE PAIRS OF CORDS ARE LOOPED ABOUT A ROD IN THE CENTER, AND THE KNOTS ARE MADE TOWARD THE ENDS.

removed and inserted in the last row of meshes. Another simple device will be found efficient, which consists of a 30-in. long board, three or more inches wide and 1 in. thick. Three nails are driven into the board at a slant, as shown in *Fig. 14,* to prevent the ring and rod from slipping off as the tying proceeds. One 1½-in. galvanized ring will be required for each end. The ring is attached to the single nail at the end with a string. This is better than just slipping the ring over the nail, because it is necessary to have a little more play in putting the cords through for the tying. The distance from the rod to the ring should be 2 ft. The tie is made in pairs as before, one cord going under and the other over the side of the ring, using the flat reef knot. There will be a few inches of ends remaining after the tie is made and

these are brought back to the main body of the cord and wound with an extra cord used for that purpose. The winding is started by looping the end of the extra cord or string about the whole bundle of cord together with the ends, pulling tightly and tying securely with flat reef knot. This is illustrated in *Fig. 15.* The winding should be about 1½ in. long where the turned-back ends are cut off. Each time the cord is wound about the bundle it should be looped through its own winding and drawn tightly. This is practically the buttonhole loop. Finish the winding the cord should be given a double looping through its own winding; then with an awl or other pointed tool, work a way through the under side of the other windings so that the end may be brought out farther back and pulled tightly to prevent unwinding when the pull comes on the hammock. Attach the ring to the opposite end in the same manner and the hammock is complete.

~~The edge can be bound the same~~ as a tennis net, or a rope can be run through the outside meshes lengthwise, as desired. A very pretty effect can be obtained by knotting, in a similar manner to the body of the ~~hammock, an apron fringe for the~~ sides.

— HOW TO MAKE A NETTED HAMMOCK —

A good hammock should be about 12 ft. long, which includes 8 ft. of network and 2 ft. at each end of long cords that are attached to rings. Seine twine, of 24-ply, is the best material and it will take 1½ lb. to make a hammock. The twine comes in ½-lb. skeins and should be wound into balls to keep it from knotting before the right time. Two galvanized rings, about 2½ in. in diameter, are required.

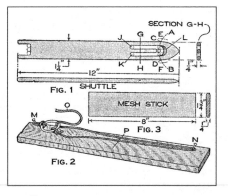

THE TOOLS NECESSARY CONSIST OF A NEEDLE, OR SHUTTLE, A GAUGE BOARD, AND A MESH STICK.

The equipment for netting a hammock consists of a wood needle, or shuttle, a gauge board for the long meshes at the ends, and a mesh stick for the regular netting of the main body of the hammock, all of which will be described in detail.

The shuttle is made of wood and is 12 in. long, 1¼ in. wide, and ¼ in. thick. The best material to use is maple or other hardwood, but very satisfactory ones can be cut from good grained pine. The sketch, *Fig. 1*, shows the general shape of the shuttle, one end being pointed and the other forked. Lay out the pointed end before beginning to cut down to size. Place a compass at the center of the end, and with a radius of 1½ in. describe the arc *AB*. With the intersections of this arc and the side lines of the needle, *C* and *D,* as centers, and the same radius, 1½ in., cut the arc *AB* at *E* and *F*. With *E* and *F* as centers draw the curves of the end of the shuttle. The reason for placing the centers outside the shuttle lines is to obtain a longer curve to the end. The curves can be drawn freehand, but will then not be so good.

The space across the needle at *GH* is divided into five ½-in. divisions. The centers of the holes J and *K* at the base of the tongue are 3½ in. from the pointed end. The opening is 2¾ in. long. Bore a ¼-in. hole at the right end of the opening, and three holes just to the left, as shown by the dotted lines. Cut out along the lines with a coping saw and finish with a knife, file, and sandpaper. Round off the edges as shown by the sectional detail. It is smart to bevel the curve at *L* so that the shuttle will wind easily. The fork is ¾ in. deep, each prong being ¼ in. wide. Slant the point of the shuttle and round off all edges throughout and sandpaper smooth.

The gauge board, *Fig. 2,* is used for making the long meshes at both ends of the hammock. It is a board

about 3 ft. long, 4 in. wide, and 1 in. thick. An eightpenny nail is driven into the board 1 in. from the right edge and 2 in. from the end, as shown by *M,* allowing it to project about 1 in. and slanting a little toward the end; the other nail *N* will be located later.

The mesh stick, *Fig. 3,* should be made of maple, 8 in. long, 1¾ in. wide, and ¼ in. thick. Round off the edges and sandpaper them very smooth.

The making of the net by a specially devised shuttle is called "natting," or netting, when done with a fine thread and a suitably fine shuttle. Much may be done in unique lacework designs, and when coarser material and larger shuttles are used, such articles as fish nets, tennis nets, and hammocks may be made. The old knot used in natting was difficult to learn and there was a knack to it that was easily forgotten, but there is a slight modification of this knot that is quite easy to learn and to make. The modified knot will be the one described.

The shuttle is first wound by looping the cord over the tongue, as shown in *Fig. 4,* then bringing it down to the forked end and up to the opening on the opposite side.

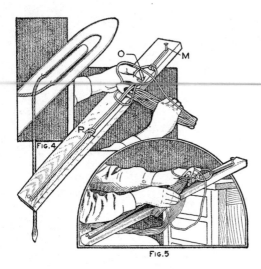

FIG. 5

THE SHUTTLE IS FIRST WOUND AND THE
LONG LOOPS AT ONE END FORMED
OVER THE GAUGE STICK.

the shuttle to the ring, bring the shuttle down and around the nail *N*. Then bring it back and pass it through the ring from the underside. The cord will then appear as shown. A part of the ring projects over the edge of the board to make it easier to pass the shuttle through. Draw the cord up tightly and put the thumb on top of the cord *O*, *Fig. 5*, to prevent it from slipping back, then throw a loop of the cord to the left over the thumb and up over a portion of the ring and pass the shuttle under the two taut cords and bring it up between the thumb and the two cords, as shown. Draw the looped knot tight under the thumb. Slip the long loop off the nail *N* and tie a simple knot at the mark *P*. This last knot is tied in the long loop to prevent looseness. Proceed with the next loop as with the first and repeat until there are 30 long meshes.

After completing these meshes, anchor the ring by its short cord to a hook or other stationary object. The

Then the cord is again looped over the tongue and returned to the fork or place of starting. Continue winding back and forth until the shuttle is full. The shuttle will accommodate from 20 to 35 complete rounds. If the shuttle is too full it crowds in passing through the meshes and delays the work.

Attach one of the galvanized rings by means of a short cord to the nail in the gauge board, as shown in *Fig. 2*. At a point 2 ft. from the lower edge of the ring, drive an eightpenny finishing nail, *N*. Tie the cord end of anchorage should be a little above the level for tying the knots of the net. Tie the cord of the shuttle to the left outside loop and always work from the left to the right. The first time across see that the long meshes do not cross over each other but are kept in the order in which they are attached to the ring.

After tying the cord to the mesh 1, *Fig. 6*, bring the mesh stick into use. Pass the cord down over the mesh stick, drawing the lower end of the loop down until it comes against the upper side of the mesh stick and put the thumb down upon it in this position to prevent slipping. Pass the shuttle up through the loop 2 and draw that down to the mesh stick. Shift the thumb from the first position to the second. Throw the cord to the left over the thumb and about the loop 2, as shown in *Fig. 7*. Bring the shuttle under both of the cords of mesh 2 and up between the large backward loop and the cords of the mesh 2.

Without removing the thumb, draw the knot up very tight. This makes the first netting knot. Continue the cord around the mesh stick, pass it up through mesh 3, throw the backward loop, put the shuttle under and up to the left of the mesh 3 and draw very tight. Do not allow a mesh to be drawn down below the upper side of the mesh stick. Some of these cautions are too often repeated, but if a mesh is allowed to get irregular, it will cause trouble in future operations.

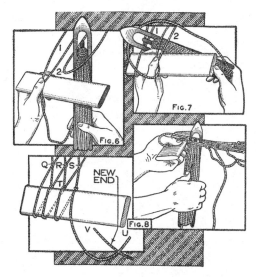

AFTER THE COMPLETION OF THE LONG MESHES, THE RING IS ANCHORED AND THE MESH STICK BROUGHT INTO USE.

Continue across the series until all of the long loops have been used; this will bring the work to the right side. Flip the whole thing over, and the cord will be at the left, ready to begin again. Slip all the meshes off the mesh stick. It makes no difference when the meshes are taken off the stick, but they must all come off before a new row is begun. Having the ring attached to the anchorage by a cord makes it easy to flip the work over. Be sure to flip to the right and then to the left alternately to prevent the twisting, which would result if turned one way all the time.

The first mesh each time across is just a little different problem from all the others, which may be better understood by reference to *Fig. 8.* The knots *Q, R,* and *S* are of the next previous series. The cord is brought down over the mesh stick and up through mesh 1, and when the loop is brought down it may not draw to the mesh stick at its center; it is apt to do otherwise and a sideways pull is necessary, which is pulled so that the knots *Q* and *R* are side by side, then the

knot at *T* may be tied. When the mesh 2 is drawn down it should pull to place without shifting, as should all the others of that row.

Continue the use of the mesh stick until a net 8 ft. long is made. When the cord gives out rewind the shuttle and tie with a small knot that will not slip. The weavers knot is good if known, or the simple square knot shown in *Fig. 9* is very good. It is too easy to make to need direction, but unless it is thrown over just right it will slip. Let *U, Fig. 8,* represent the short cord and *V* the new piece to be added. Place the cord *V* back of *U* and give *U* a complete turn around *V, Fig. 9,* and bring them together at a point above *U,* then to the front. Repeat the complete turn of *U* about *V,* shown by the dotted line, and pull tightly. If analyzed, it consists of two loops that are just

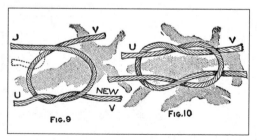

A SQUARE KNOT IS USED TO JOIN THE ENDS OF THE CORD WHEN REWINDING THE SHUTTLE.

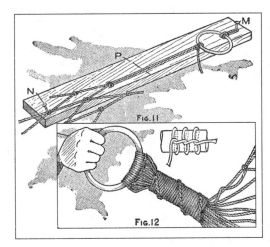

FIG. 11

FIG. 12

THE GAUGE BOARD IS AGAIN USED FOR THE
LONG LOOPS AT THE FINISHING END, AND
THEN THE CORDS ARE WOUND.

alike and linked together as shown in *Fig. 10*.

When the 8 ft. of netting has been completed, proceed to make the long loops as at the beginning. The same gauge board can be used, but the tying occurs at both ends. And because the pairs cannot be knotted in the center, two or three twists can be given by the second about the first of each pair. The long loops and the net are attached together as shown in *Fig. 11*. Slip on the meshes of the last run over the nail *N*, and when the cord comes down from the ring, the shuttle passes through the same mesh. When drawn up, the farthest point of the mesh comes against the nail. After this long loop has been secured at the ring, the first mesh is slipped off and the next put on. All of the long loops at this end will be about three inches shorter than at the other end, unless the finishing nail *N* is moved down. This will not be necessary.

With a piece of cord about 6 ft. long, start quite close to the ring and wind all the cords of the long loops together. The winding should be made very tight, and it is best to loop under with each coil. This is shown in *Fig. 12*.

The hammock is now ready for use. Some like a soft, small rope run through the outside edges lengthwise. Others prefer a fringe, and either can be added. The fringe can be attached about six meshes down from the upper edge of the sides. The hammock should have a stretcher at each end of the netted portion, but not as long as those required for web hammocks.

— DIVING TOWER
FOR THE SUMMER CAMP —

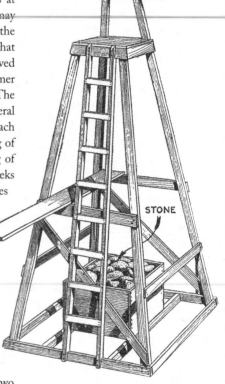

Aquatic pleasures and sports at a summer camp or lake may be considerably enlivened by the building of a diving tower like that shown in the sketch. It has proved very successful at a boys' summer camp at Crystal Lake, Illinois. The boys have made a practice for several years of building a tower early each swimming season on the opening of their camp in July and disposing of it at the close of camp some weeks later. Several resorts and cottages now boast towers made by the campers.

The tower is built largely of 2- by 4-in. stock. The longer pieces at the corners are 12 ft. in length, slanted so that the lower end of the tower is 7 ft. square and the platform at the top 3 ft. square. The handrail at the top is fixed to extensions of the rear uprights. A springboard is fastened on two horizontal braces near the middle of the tower and is reached by the ladder. The structure is built on the shore and towed out to its position. It is sunk and weighted by the box of stones supported on cross braces.

STONE

BOYS AT A SUMMER CAMP CONSTRUCT A DIVING TOWER EACH SUMMER AND DISPOSE OF IT FOR THE COST OF LUMBER WHEN THEY BREAK CAMP. THE TOWER IS BUILT LARGELY OF 2-BY-4-INCH STOCK AND IS WEIGHTED WITH A BOX OF STONES.

— Whistle Warns of Fish Catch —

A toy railroad wheel, a piece of hollow can, and pieces of wire are the materials necessary for making the whistle shown in the illustration. The whistle warns a fisherman that a fish is attempting to make away with his bait. The wheel fitted into the end of the cane and wedged into place to form a tight joint. The wires are formed into loops at the ends of the cane and fixed to it. The whistle is attached to the fish line, as shown, with the open end down and slightly below the surface of the water. The fishing pole may be fixed so that the whistle will remain in this position while the fisherman is at ease in the shade nearby. When the fish attempts to make away with the bait, as shown in the sketch, the water forces the air in the upper part of the cane out through the center hole of the wheel, and a whistling sound is the result.

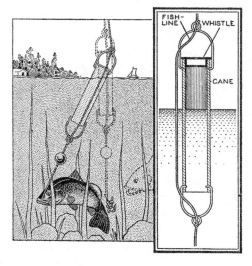

When the fish strikes the bait the water is forced up into the whistle suddenly, and the escaping air warns the fisherman.

— A Fish Scaler —

All kinds of devices, both simple and complex, have been made and patented for use in scaling fish. But for a novelty a fisherman found the following, which necessity compelled him to improvise on an outing trip, to be as efficient as any of them. As usual, the fisherman forgot the curry comb to clean the fish when packing up his gear. But, at the same time, he remembered to take a plentiful supply of bottled goods. Long before it became necessary to scale any fish, enough bottles had been opened to provide the basis of a tool for the purpose, which he constructed by using the small tin bottle caps, a few being nailed on a block of wood, about 3 in. wide by 4 in. long. This made a splendid fish scaler, as good and efficient at home as in the camp. It is both inexpensive

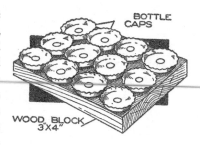

BOTTLE CAPS NAILED TO A WOOD BLOCK FOR REMOVING SCALES FROM A FISH.

and easily made. The sketch shows the general appearance.

— RAIN ALARM WITH DROP-OF-WATER CONTACT —

An annunciating device, which awakens a person sleeping in a room with the window open and warns him that it is raining so that he may close the window, is an interesting bit of electrical construction. On the outside of the house, as detailed, a funnel is fixed to the wall. Two separate wires have their terminals at the funnel's small end. The wires enter the room at the frame of the window and connect to an electric bell and a dry cell. A drop of water entering the funnel flows down to the small end, falling on the terminals of the wires. The water

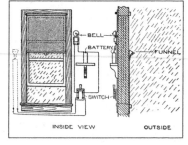

A DROP OF RAIN WATER COMPLETES THE BELL CIRCUIT, THUS GIVING WARNING OF THE RAIN.

acts as a conductor, completing the circuit and ringing the bell. A switch inside cuts out the circuit, stopping the bell's ringing.

— CORN POPPER MADE FROM COFFEE CAN AND BROOM HANDLE —

With an old coffee can or similar tin receptacle and a piece of a broom handle 2½ or 3 ft. long, it is easy to make a corn popper that is preferable in many ways to a wire one. Take a strip of wood a little shorter than the height of the can to be used and, after boring two holes in it to prevent its splitting, nail it to the end of the handle. The latter is then fastened to the side of the can

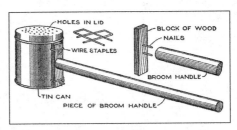

CORN POPPER MADE FROM A COFFEE CAN OR SIMILAR TIN RECEPTACLE AND A PIECE OF A BROOM HANDLE

with two wire staples, as shown. Holes are made in the can top to admit air to the corn while it is popping.

— PRESERVING LEAVES IN A SPECIMEN BOOK —

The common method of preserving leaves by pressing them with an iron rubbed on beeswax may be improved by substituting the following process. Paint the underside of each leaf with linseed oil, ironing it immediately. Then paint and iron the upper side in the same way. This treatment gives the leaves sufficient gloss, while they remain quite pliable. It is not necessary to press and dry the leaves beforehand, but this may be done if desired. The tints may even be well preserved by painting only the upper side of the leaves with the oil and then placing them, without ironing, between newspapers and under weights to dry.

— HOMEMADE KITE REEL —

This kite reel is constructed from two old pulleys and few pipe fittings. The large pulley is about 14 in. in diameter, on the face of which are riveted flat strips of iron with extending arms. These arms are reinforced by riveting smaller pieces from one to the other, which connects all arms together on both sides of the wheel. Mounted on the shaft with the pulleys is a guide for the kite wire or string. This guide permits of being moved entirely over the top of the reel. The smaller pulley is attached to the shaft and used as a brake. The brake is used only when running out the wire or string, first removing the crank

SNOW DAY

— MAKING SNOWSHOES —

Shapes of Snowshoe

We owe the snowshoe to the inventive mind of the North American Indian, and its conception was doubtless brought about through that prolific source of invention— necessity. The first models were crude web-footed affairs, but improvements in model and manner of filling the frames were gradually added until the perfected and graceful shoe of the present day was finally reached. The first snowshoes were made by Native Americans, and tribes of Maine and Canada continue to fashion the finest handmade models today.

The snowshoe is a necessity for the sportsman and trapper whose pleasure or business leads him out in the open during the winter season, when roads and trails are heavily blanketed by a deep fall of powdery snow. But the use of the web shoe is by no means confined to the dweller in the wilderness. The charm of wintry wood and plain beckons many lovers of the outdoors to participate in this invigorating sport, and snowshoe tramps are fast growing in popularity in and about our cities and towns.

All the modern snowshoes are constructed upon practically the same general lines, although the types of frames differ considerably in size as well as in shape, and the filling of hide is often woven in many varied and intricate patterns. The frame or bow—usually made of ash in order to get strength with light weight—is bent in many shapes. But the one shown in the diagram is a typical general-purpose shoe and may be called standard. The frame is held in shape by means of two wooden cross braces, neatly mortised into the frame. These braces are spaced some 15 or 16 in. apart, and so divide the shoe into three sections, known as the toe, center, and heel. The filling is woven into a lanyard, which is a light strip of hide firmly laced to the frame through a double row of holes drilled in the wood. The center filling is woven of heavy strands of rawhide, in a fairly coarse mesh, because this part of the shoe must bear the weight of the body and the brunt of wear. The end fillers for toe and heel are woven of lighter strands of hide, and the mesh is, of course, smaller.

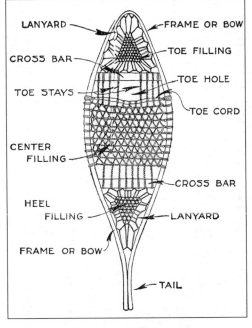

THE FRAME OF A SNOWSHOE IN ITS USUAL CONSTRUCTION, SHOWING THE CROSSPIECES WITH THEIR LACED FILLINGS OF HIDE AND DIFFERENT PARTS NAMED FOR READY REFERENCE.

As may be noted by referring to the drawing, a center opening or "toe hole" is provided. And, because the greater strain on the filling lies directly under the ball of the foot, the shoe is reinforced at this point by the "toe cord" running across, and the "toe-cord stays" that are tied in on each side of the toe hole. One end of the stays is fastened to the toe cord and the other lashed over the wooden cross bar of the frame. These reinforcing cords are formed of several strands of hide, the stays being again wound with finer strands.

The way the foot is attached to the shoe is important to prevent slipping and to secure a good foothold while walking. This is done with a toe strap, which will allow the toe to push down through the toe opening as the heel of the foot is lifted in the act of walking. A second strap, or thong, leading from the top around the foot and above the curve of the heel, is needed to lend additional support in lifting the snowshoe. This creates the easy shambling stride characteristic of the snowshoer.

There are, of course, a great number of models or styles. One style will be popular in one locality, while an altogether different style is preferred in another part of the country. The most representative types are well shown in the illustrations, and brief descriptions will point out their practical advantages. Each model possesses certain merits—one model being designed for fast traveling in the open, another better adapted for brush travel, while others are more convenient for use in hilly country where much climbing is done, and so on.

Style A is regarded by snowshoe experts as an extreme style, because it is long and narrow. It is designed for fast traveling over smooth and level country and over loose, powdery snow. This style is much used by the Cree Indian tribe, and is usually made 12 in. wide by 60 in. long, with a steeply upcurved toe. It is a good shoe for

SNOWSHOE EXPERTS CONSIDER THIS AN EXTREME STYLE BECAUSE IT IS LONG AND NARROW.

A

cross-country work, but is somewhat difficult to manage on broken trails, when the snow is packed, and also affords rather slippery footing when crossing ice. Owing to the stout construction of the frame and reinforcement needed to retain the high, curved toe, *Style A* is more difficult to manage than the more conservative models. Its frame is stiffer, making it more fatiguing to wear, while its use is a decided handicap in mountainous districts, because a curved toe always makes hill climbing more difficult.

THIS SNOWSHOE IS CONSIDERED THE ORDINARY EASTERN MODEL AND ONE BEST ADAPTED FOR ALL-AROUND USE.

Style B may be considered the ordinary eastern model, and a common style best adapted for all-around use. It is a neat and gracefully designed frame, about 12 in. wide and 42 in. long, and is usually made with a slightly upcurving toe, about 2 in. turn at the toe being correct. When made by the Native Americans of Maine, this model is fashioned with a rather heavy heel. This heel is an advantage for fast walking, but it increases the difficulty in quick turning.

Style C is a favorite model among the hunters and woodsmen of New England. This is a splendid style for general purposes in this section of the country, because the full, round toe keeps the toe up near the surface, and lets the heel cut down more than the narrow-toe models. *Style C* is an easy shoe to wear, and though it is not so fast as the long, narrow frame, its full shape is more convenient for use in the woods. It is usually made with about a 1- to 1½-in. turn at the toe.

Style D is the familiar "bear's paw," a model originating with the northeastern trapper. This model is well adapted for short tramps in the brush. Having a flat toe, it is likewise a good shoe for mountain climbing. For tramping about in thick brush, a short, full shoe enables one to take a shorter stride and turn more quickly, but it is a slow shoe for straight-ahead traveling.

When purchasing a pair of snow-shoes, some few important considerations should be kept in mind. The size and model will depend upon the man to some extent, since a large heavy man will require a larger snowshoe than would suffice for a

C

THE STYLE ILLUSTRATED HERE IS SPLENDID FOR GENERAL PURPOSES AND IS A FAVORITE AMONG HUNTERS AND WOODSMEN.

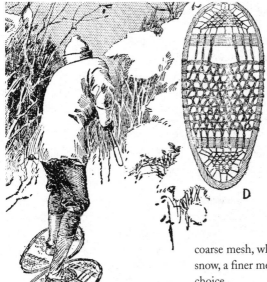

localities where the snow packs solidly and there is considerable ice, and in mountainous districts or for rough-country traveling, the smaller sizes will give more satisfaction and prove more durable also. For a wet-snow locality, the center filling should be strung in rather coarse mesh, while for soft, powdery snow, a finer mesh will be the logical choice.

THIS IS THE FAMILIAR "BEAR'S PAW" MODEL, ORIGINATED BY THE NORTHEASTERN TRAPPER FOR USE ON SHORT TRAMPS AND IN BRUSH.

There are snowshoes and snowshoes, and while there are fine models regularly stocked by a few of the better sporting-goods firms, there are likewise many poorly made snowshoes on the market. It is wise to pay a fair price and secure a dependable handmade article. Cheaper snowshoes—often filled with seine twine and the cheapest hide (commonly known in the trade as "gut")—will warp and twist in the frame, and the shoddy filling will soon become loosened up and "bag" after a little use. The best snowshoes are made by Native Americans, and

person of lighter weight. Height also enters into the choice, and while a small person can travel faster and with less fatigue when equipped with a proportionately small shoe, a tall man will naturally pick out a larger-sized snowshoe for his use. For a country where deep snows prevail, larger sizes are best. But in the filling is ordinarily made of neat's hide; cowhide for the center filling, and calfskin for the toe and heel. A first-class pair of snowshoes is a pleasure, and when possible to do so, it is best to have them made to order. This is necessary in case one wishes to incorporate any little wrinkles of his own into their making, or desires a flatter toe, lighter heel, or a different mesh from the usual stock models.

Where but one pair of snowshoes is purchased, *Style B* will probably prove the best selection. It should be ordered with the flat toe, or a turn not greater than 1 in. The frame may be in either one or two pieces, depending upon the size of the shoe and the ideas of the maker, but it is smart to specify white ash for the frames in the order. No quality maker would be guilty of using screws or other metal fastenings, but many of the cheap and poorly fashioned snowshoes are fastened at the heel with screws, thus making this a decidedly weak point. The wood is quite certain to split after a little rough service. In contrast to the poor workmanship of these low-priced snowshoes, the Native American-made article is fashioned from sound and properly seasoned wood. The

cross bars are snugly fitted by mortising to the frame and the filling is tightly woven. The heel will be properly fastened by lacing with a rawhide thong. However, Native American craftsmen are likely to make the toe small and leave the wood to form a rather heavy heel. Some few woodsmen and sportsmen may prefer this model, but the majority of users favor a fuller toe and a lighter heel for general use, because the regulation Native American model, cutting down at toe and heel equally deep, increases the difficulty of easy traveling over soft snow. It is, however, a good shoe when used over broken trails.

When buying snowshoes at the store, make sure the frames are stoutly and well made. For all-around use, it is a good idea to select a filling of good heavy weight and with a firmly woven and open mesh, say, about ¾ in. The toe and heel sections will, of course, be of finer-cut hide and smaller mesh. And it is wise to avoid those shoes employing seine twine for the end filling. Some factory-made snowshoes are given a coat or two of varnish, but this, while serving to make them partly waterproof, makes them rather slippery when crossing logs and ice. Most woodsmen prefer to leave both frame and filling in their natural condition.

The Native American-made snowshoe is always provided with a generously large toe hole, so that ample foot covering may be used. This point is generally overlooked in the machine-made products, and the toe cords are also frequently roughly formed, thus chafing the feet and making them sore. These details may or may not prove a handicap for short tramps near town, but for long trips through the woods, they are important considerations.

The Native American manner of tying the snowshoe to the foot by means of a single twisted and knotted thong is a good method of attachment. If the thong is properly adjusted to the requisite snugness in the first place, the shoes may be quickly removed by a simple twist of the ankle. A better fastening is secured by using a fairly wide (¾ in.) toe strap and a long thong. The toe strap is placed over the toes, immediately over the ball of the foot, and secured against slipping by weaving the ends in and out between the meshes of the filling until it reaches the frame on either side. This grips the toe strap firmly and does away with the necessity of tying a knot.

A narrow thong, about 4 ft. long, is now doubled, the center placed just above the heel of the foot, and the ends passed under the toe cord, just outside of the toe-cord stays on each side. The thong is then brought up and across the toes, one end passing over and the other under the toe strap. Each end of the thong is now looped around the crossed thong on either side, and then carried back over the back of the heel and knotted with a common square are reef knot. Calfskin makes a good flexible foot binding, or a suitable strip of folded cloth or canvas may be used.

The regulation snowshoe harness, consisting of a leather stirrup for the toe and an instep and heel strap, will be found more comfortable than the thong. When once adjusted snugly to the foot, the shoes may be quickly taken off and put on again by pushing the heel strap down, when the foot may be slipped out of the toe stirrup.

The use of heavy leather shoes is, of course, undesirable. The only correct footwear for snowshoeing is a pair of high-cut moccasins, cut roomy enough to allow one or more pairs of heavy woolen stockings to be worn. The heavy and long German socks, extending halfway to the knee and drawn on over the trouser legs, are by far the most comfortable for cold-weather wear. The feet, thus shod, will not only be warm in the coldest weather, but the free use of the toes will not be interfered with. Leather shoes are cold and stiff, and the heavy soles and heels, chafing against the snowshoes, will soon ruin the filling.

Making the Shoe

Snowshoe making is an art, and while few craftsmen can equal the Native American in weaving the intricate patterns they prefer to employ for filling the frames it is not difficult to fashion a good solid frame and then fill it by making use of a simple and open system of meshing. For the frames, white ash is much the best wood, but hickory and white birch are dependable substitutes, if the former cannot be obtained. Birch is perhaps the best wood to use when the sportsman wishes to cut and split up his own wood. But as suitable material for the frames may be readily purchased for a small sum, probably the majority of the readers will elect

to buy the material. Any lumber dealer will be able to supply white ash, and it is a simple matter to saw out the frames from the board. The

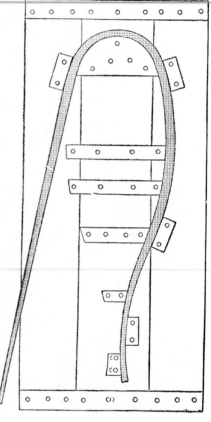

THE DESIGN OF THE SNOWSHOE IS TRACED ON A BOARD, AND BLOCKS ARE USED TO SHAPE THE FRAME OR BOW.

379

sawed-out frame is inferior to the hand-split bow. But if good, selected material can be obtained, there will be little, if any, difference for ordinary use.

When dry and well-seasoned lumber is used, the frame may be made to the proper dimensions. But when green wood is selected, the frame must be made somewhat heavier, to allow for the usual shrinkage in seasoning. For a stout snowshoe frame, the width should be about 1¹⁄₁₆ in.; thickness at the toe, ⁷⁄₁₆ in., and thickness at heel, ⁹⁄₁₆ in. The frame should be cut 2 in. longer than the finished length desired. In working the wood, remember that the toe of the finished frame will be the center of the stick; the heel, the end of the stick, and the center of the shoe will lie halfway between the heel and toe.

After the frames have been finished, the dry wood must be steamed before it can be safely bent to the required shape. Before doing this, a wooden bending form must be made. An easy way to make this form is to first draw a pattern of the model on a sheet of paper, cut out the pencil mark, and, placing this pattern on a board, carefully trace the design on the wooden form. A number of

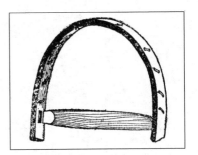

LOCATE THE CROSSBARS BY BALANCING THE FRAME, THEN FIT THE ENDS IN SHALLOW MORTISES.

cleats, or blocks, of wood will now be needed. The inside blocks will be nailed in position, but the outside stay blocks will be simply provided with nails in the holes so they may be quickly fastened in position when the steamed frame is ready for the form.

To make the frame soft for bending to shape, it must be steamed. The easiest way of doing this is to provide boiling water in a wash boiler. Place the wood over the top and soak well by mopping with the boiling water, shifting the stick about until the fibers have become soft and pliable. After 10 or 15 minutes of the hot-water treatment, wrap the stick with a cloth and bend it back and forth to render it more and more pliable. Then repeat the hot-water treatment,

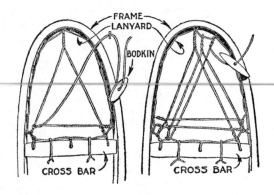

BEGIN WEAVING THE TOE FILLING AT THE CORNER OF
CROSSBAR AND FRAME, CARRYING IT AROUND
IN A TRIANGLE UNTIL COMPLETE.

a permanent set, the frame will not retain its shape. The same bending form may be used for both frames. But if you are in a hurry to finish the shoes, two forms should be made—but considerable pains must be taken to make them exactly alike in every way.

When the frames are dry, secure the tail end of the frame by boring three holes about 4 in. from the end, and fasten with rawhide. The work of fitting two crossbars may now be undertaken, and the balance of the snowshoe depends upon fitting these bars in their proper places. Before cutting the mortise, spring the two bars in the frame about 15 in. apart, and balance the shoe in the center by holding it in the hands. When the frame exactly balances, move the bars sufficiently to make the heel about 3 oz. heavier than the toe, and mark the place where the mortises are to be cut. The crossbars and mortise must be a good tight fit, and a small, sharp chisel will enable the

and repeat the process until the wood is sufficiently soft to bend easily without splintering. The toe being the greatest curve, it must be well softened before putting on the form. Otherwise the fibers are likely to splinter off at this point. When the frame is well softened, place it on the bending form while hot and slowly bend it against the wooden inside blocks to hold it to the proper curve. Begin with the toe, and after fastening the outside blocks to hold this end, finish one side, then bend the other half to shape. The bent frame should be allowed to dry on the form for at least a week. If it is removed before the wood has become thoroughly dry and has taken

AN ENDLESS THONG IS MADE WITH EYES CUT IN
THE ENDS OF THE LEATHER AND EACH PART IS
RUN THROUGH THE EYE OF THE OTHER.

builder to make a neat job. It is not necessary to cut the mortise very deep; ¼ in. is ample to afford a firm and snug mortised joint.

The lanyard to which the filling is woven is next put in by boring pairs of small holes in the toe and heel sections and lacing a narrow rawhide thong through the obliquely drilled holes. Three holes are then bored in the crossbar—one on each side about 1½ in. from the frame, and the third in the center of the bar. The lanyard is then carried through these holes in the cross bar.

Begin the toe filling first by making an eye in one end of the thong, put the end through the lanyard loop and then through the eye, thus making a slipknot. Start to weave at the corner where the bar and frame are mortised.

Carry the strand up and twist it around the lanyards in the middle of the toe, then carry it down and make a like twist around the lanyard loop in the opposite corner. The thong is now looped around the next lanyard (No. 2 from the crossbar lanyard) and fastened with the twisted loop knot illustrated. Continue the strand across the width of toe space and make a similar loop knot on No. 2 lanyard on the starting side. Twist it around the strand first made and loop it under the next crossbar lanyard loop. Then carry it up and twist it around the lanyard loop in the toe of the frame, continuing in the same manner until the last lanyard of the

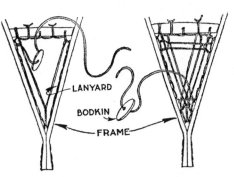

THE HEEL FILLING IS WOVEN BY MAKING THE CON-
NECTION WITH THE LANYARD IN THE SAME MANNER
AS FOR THE TOE FILLING.

toe is reached, when the space is finished by making the twisted loop knot until the space is entirely filled. It is a difficult matter to describe by text, but the illustrations will point out the correct way and show the manner of making an endless thong by eye-splicing, as well as illustrating the wooden bodkin, or

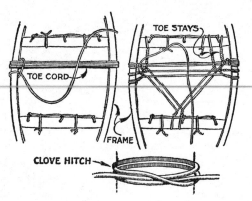

THE CENTER MUST BE WOVEN STRONG AND TIGHT, AND FOR THIS REASON A HEAVIER STRAND OF HIDE MUST BE USED.

needle, used in pulling the woven strands taut. This bodkin is easily made from a small piece of wood about ¼ in. thick and about 2 in. long. To simplify matters, the heel may be filled in the same manner as the toe.

For the center, which must be woven strong and tight, a heavier strand of hide must be used. Begin with the toe cord first. To make this amply strong, carry the strand across the frame, five or six times, finishing with a half-hitch knot, as shown. Then carry it up and twist it around the crossbar to form the first toe-cord stay.

As may be noted, the center section is filled by looping back and twisting the strands as when filling the toe. However, the filling is looped around the frame instead of a lanyard, and a clove hitch is used. A toe hole, 4 in. wide, must be provided for. When enough of the filling has been woven in to make this opening, the thong is no longer looped around the crossbar but woven through the toe cord. As the filling ends in the toe cord, it should be woven in and out at this point several times, finishing the toe hole by looping a strand around the crossbar at the side of the toe hole, then passing it down the toe-cord stay by twisting around it. Then twist it around the toe cord along the filling to the other side of the toe hole, where it is twisted around the toe-cord stay on the opposite side, looped around the frame, and ended in a clove hitch.

At the first reading, it will doubtless appear difficult. But a careful examination of the illustrations will soon show how the trick is done, and indeed it is really a very simple matter. It is one of those things that are easier to do than to describe. The method of filling has been purposely made simple, but the majority of shoes are filled in practically the same manner—which does quite as well the more intricate Native American design.

The knack of using the snowshoe is quickly mastered, providing the shoes are properly attached to allow the toe ample freedom to work down through the toe hole as each foot is lifted. The shoe is, of course, not actually lifted in the air. Instead, it is slid along the surface, half the width of one shoe covering the other when it is lifted in the act of walking. At first the novice may be inclined to think snowshoes a bit cumbersome and unwieldy, and doubt his ability to penetrate the brush. However, as the snowshoer becomes accustomed to their use, he will experience little if any difficulty in traveling where he will. When making a trail in more

or less open country, it is a good plan to blaze it thoroughly. This will enable you to return over the same trail, in case of a snowfall in the meantime, or drifting snow fills up and obliterates the trail first made. When the trail is first broken by traveling over it once by snowshoe, the snow is packed well and forms a solid foundation. Should even a heavy fall of snow cover it, the blaze marks on tree and bush will point out the trail. This will afford faster and easier traveling than breaking a new trail each time one journeys in the same direction.

A well-made pair of snowshoes will stand a couple of season's hard use, or last for a year or two longer for general wear. To keep them in good shape, they should be dried out after use, although it is never advisable to place them close to a hot fire or the hide filling will be injured. Jumping puts severe strain on the frame of the shoe. Though damage may not occur when so used in deep, soft snow, it is wise to avoid the possibility of breakage. Accidents will now and then happen, to be sure, and as a thong may snap at some unexpected moment, keep a strand or two of rawhide on hand to meet this emergency.

— A Snowball Thrower —

The snow fort with its infantry is not complete without the artillery. A set of mortars, or cannon, placed in the fort to hurl snowballs at the entrenched enemy makes the battle more real. A device to substitute for the cannon or a mortar can be easily constructed by any boy, and a few of these devices set in a snow fort will add greatly to the interest of the conflict.

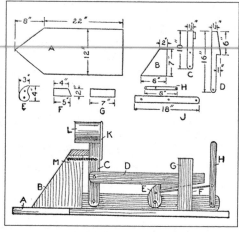

THE DIMENSIONED PARTS AND THE DETAIL OF THE COMPLETED SNOWBALL THROWER

The substitute—called a "snowball thrower"—consists of a base, A, with a standard, B, which stops the arm, C, controlled by the bar, D, when the trigger, E, is released. The tripping of the trigger is accomplished by the sloping end of D on the slanting end of the upright F, with their upper ends extending above the bar D, to prevent the latter from jumping out when it is released by the trigger.

CANNONADING A SNOW FORT WITH THE USE OF A SNOWBALL THROWER.

The trigger *E* is tripped with the handle, *H,* connected to the piece, *J,* on which all the working parts are mounted. The upper end of the arm *C* has a piece, *K,* to which is attached a tin can, *L,* for holding the snowball to be thrown. A set of door springs, *M,* furnishes the force to throw the snowball.

All the parts are given dimensions, and if cut properly, they will fit together to make the thrower as illustrated.

— BUILDING A SNOW LIGHTHOUSE —

This article describes a lighthouse made from snow that will be a big hit in the neighborhood when the candle placed inside is lit.

The lighthouse is made by rolling three large snowballs of different diameters and placing them on top of each other, the largest one at the bottom to form the base, and the smallest at the top for the light chamber. Snow is then packed tightly at the joints to make the tapered cylinder, which should be about 5 ft. high, 3 ft. in diameter at the base, and 20 in. in diameter at the top. A space is hollowed out for the light chamber, with four openings for windows, which are protected with glass. A candle is inserted in the center of the cavity. In order to make the candle burn, a hole is made in the top leading into the light chamber, and another hole from a point somewhat below the windows to conduct air to the candle. When the candle is lighted, the air supply through these openings allows it to burn perfectly.

— SIMPLY MADE COASTERS, SLEDS, AND SLEIGHS —

Make your own sled! There is no use in buying them, because your handmade sled is probably better than any purchased one and you can take so much more pride in it when you know it is of your own construction. There are so many different designs of sleds that can be made by hand that the matter can be left almost entirely to your own ingenuity. You can make one like the store-bought sleds and

FIG. 1—BARREL-STAVE SLED.

face the runners with pieces of an iron hoop that will answer every purpose. A good sled for coasting consists simply of two barrel staves and three pieces of board as shown in the picture, *Fig. 1.* No premade sled will equal it for coasting and it is also just the thing for carrying loads of snow for building snow houses. The method of its construction is so simple that no description other than the picture is needed. You can make a chair-sleigh out of this by fitting a chair on the cross

CHAIR SLEIGH

board instead of the long top board or it will be still stronger if the top board is allowed to remain, and then you will have a device that can readily again be transformed into a coasting sled. In making the chair-sleigh it is necessary to nail four L-shaped blocks on the cross boards, one for each leg of the chair, to hold the chair in place. Skating along over the ice and pushing the chair in front of him, the proud possessor of a chair-sleigh may take his mother, grown sister, or lady friend with him on his outings, and permit her to ride in the chair.

Folding-Chair Sleigh

A folding-chair sleigh is even more enjoyable and convenient than the device just described. If the ice pond is far from home this may be placed under your arm and carried where you like.

The illustrations *Figs. 2* and *3* show all the parts as they should look before being joined together. The seat may be made of a piece of canvas or carpet. The hinges are of leather. *Fig. 4* shows the folding-chair sleigh after it has been put together. Skates are used for the runners. The skates may be strapped on or taken off whenever desired. When the chair is lifted, the supports slip from the notches on the sidebars and the

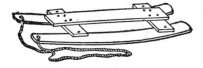

FIG. 2—
FOLDING-CHAIR SLEIGH BOTTOM

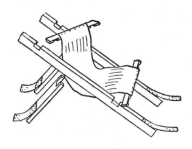

FIG. 3—
FOLDING-CHAIR SLEIGH WITH
TOP PARTS DISCONNECTED

FIG. 4—
FOLDING-CHAIR SLEIGH OPEN

chair is lifted, the supports slip from the notches on the sidebars and fall on the runner bars. The chair is then folded up so that it can be carried by a small boy. With regular metal hinges and light timbers a very handsome chair can be constructed that will also afford an ornamental lawn chair for summer.

The Toboggan Sled

When the snow is very deep a toboggan sled is the thing for real sport. The runners of the ordinary sled break through the crust of the deep snow, blocking the progress and spoiling the fun. The toboggan sled, with its broad, smooth bottom, glides along over the soft surface with perfect ease.

To make the toboggan sled, secure two boards each 10 ft. long and 1 ft. wide and so thin that they can be easily bent. Place the boards beside each and join them together with cross sticks. Screw the boards to the cross stick from the bottom and be sure that the heads of the screws

FIG. 5—
FOLDING-CHAIR SLEIGH CLOSED

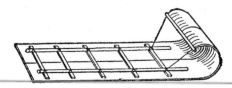

FIG. 6—THE TOBOGGAN

are buried deep enough in the wood so as not to protrude. The bottom must present an absolutely smooth surface to the snow. Fasten two side bars to the top of the cross sticks and screw them firmly. In some instances the timbers are fastened together by strings, a groove being cut in the bottom of the boards so as to keep the strings from protruding and being ground to pieces. After the side bars are securely fastened, bend the ends of the boards over and tie them to the ends of the front crossbar to hold them in position. See *Fig. 6.* The strings for keeping the boards bent must be very strong. Pieces of stout wire, or a slender steel rod, are even better. The toboggan slide is the favored device of sport among the boys in Canada, where nearly every boy knows how to make them.

Norwegian Skis

You have often read of the ski, the snowshoe used by the Norwegians and other people living in the far north. With them the men and women glide down the snow-covered mountain sides, leap across ditches, run races, and have all kinds of sport. They are just as amusing to American kids who have ever learned to manipulate them, and it is wonderful how much skill can be attained in their use. Any kid with a little mechanical ingenuity can make a pair of skis. They can be made from two barrel staves. Select staves of straight-grained wood. Sharpen the ends of each and score each end by cutting grooves in the wood, as shown in *Fig. 7.* A pocketknife or small gouge will suffice for this work. Then smear the end of the staves with oil and hold them close to a hot fire until they can be bent so as to tip the toes upward, as shown in the picture, *Fig. 7.* Then with a cord bind the staves as they are bent and permit them to remain thus tied until they retain the curved form of their own accord. Now screw on top of each ski a little block, just broad and high enough to fit in front of the heels of your shoe. Fasten a strap in front of each block through which to slip your toes, and the skis are made. The inside of the shoe heel should press firmly against the block

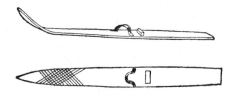

Fig. 7—Homemade skis

which to steer, and hunt for a snowbank. At first you will afford more amusement to onlookers than to yourself, for the skis have a way of trying to run in opposite directions, crosswise, and various ways. But with practice you will soon become expert in their manipulation.

and the toe be held tightly under the strap. This will keep the skis on your feet. Now procure a stick with

— MAKING SNOW BUILDING BLOCKS —

Forts, Eskimo igloos, and other buildings can be made quite elaborate architectural accomplishments if constructed of snow building blocks. The snow is compressed in a simple rectangular wooden mold, which produces a block about the same size as the standard concrete block, or 8 by 8 by 16 in., although any other size or shape may be produced by altering the mold. The mold is placed on a flat surface filled with snow that is tamped down hard,

FORTS ERECTED WITH BUILDING BLOCKS MADE OF SNOW: THE BLOCKS ARE MOLDED IN A WOODEN FORM AND THEN LAID IN A MORTAR OF WET SNOW, WHICH, WHEN FROZEN, UNITES THE BUILDING INTO ONE SOLID MASS.

and the snow struck off level with the mold top. After the snow has been sufficiently compacted, the mold is removed, and the block is set aside until a sufficient number have been made to complete a fort or other structure. In building, the blocks are held together with a "mortar" of wet snow or slush, which, when frozen, unites the building into one solid mass. The trowel used for spreading the mortar can be made from a shingle or piece of board.

— Four-Passenger Coasting Bobsled —

Coaster bobsleds usually have about the same form of construction, and only slight changes from the ordinary are made to satisfy the builder. The one shown has some distinctive features that make it a sled of luxury, and the builder will pride himself in the making. A list of the materials required is supplied. Any wood may be used for the sled, except for the runners, which should be made of ash.

Shape the runners all alike by cutting one out and using it as a pattern to make the others. After cutting them to the proper shape, a groove is formed on the under edge to admit the curve of a ⅝-in. round iron rod about ¼ in. deep. The iron rods are then shaped to fit over the runner in the groove and extend up the back part of the runner and over the top at the front end. The extensions should be flattened so that two holes can be drilled in them for two wood screws at each end. If the builder does not have the necessary equipment for flattening these ends, a local blacksmith can do it at a nominal price. After the irons are fitted, they are fastened in place.

The top edges of the runners are notched for the crosspieces so that the top surfaces of these pieces will come flush with the upper edges of the runners. The location of these pieces is not essential, but should be near the ends of the runners, and the notches of each pair of runners should coincide. When the notches are cut, fit the pieces in snugly, and fasten them with long, slim wood screws. Small metal braces are then fastened to the runners and crosspiece on the inside, to stiffen the joint.

As the rear sled must oscillate some, means must be provided for this tilting motion while at the same time preventing sidewise turning. The construction used for this purpose is a hinged joint. The heavy 2-by-5-in. crosspiece is cut sloping on the width so that it remains 2 in.

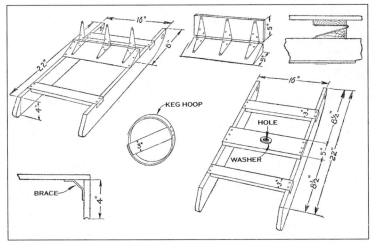

DETAILS SHOWING THE METHOD OF REAR-SLED OSCILLATION,
THE BRACING AND THE STEERING WHEEL.

thick at one edge and tapers down to a feather edge at the opposite side. This makes a wedge-shaped piece, to which surface the three large hinges are attached. The piece is then solidly fastened to the upper edges of the runners that are to be used for the rear sled, and so located that the center of the piece will be 8 in. from the front end of the runners.

The supporting crosspiece on the font sled is fastened on top of the runners, at a place where its center will be 11 in. from the front end of the runners.

The top board is prepared by making both ends round and planing the surfaces smooth. The two crosspieces are placed on the underside. Bore two ½-in. holes through the width of each crosspiece, near the ends, to receive the eyebolts. They are placed, one with its center 12 in. from the end to be used for the rear, and other with its center 8 in. from the front end, and securely fastened with screws. The shore is placed in the center of the board, and wires are run over it connecting the eyebolts. The eyebolts are then drawn up tightly to make the wire taut over the shore. This will prevent the long board from sagging.

On the upper side of the board and beginning at the rear end, the backs are fastened at intervals of 18 in. They are first prepared by rounding the corners on the ends used for the tops, and the opposite ends are cut slightly on an angle to give the back a slant. They are then fastened with the small hinges to the top board. On the edges of the top board, 1-in. holes are bored about 1 in. deep, and pins driven for footrests. These are located 18 in. apart, beginning about 5 in. from the front end. The dowel

is used for the pins, which are made 4 in. long.

The steering device consists of a broom handle, cut 18 in. long, with one end fastened in a hole bored centrally in the 5-in. crosspiece of the front sled. A hole is bored in the top board through the center of the crosspiece fastened to the underside for the steering post. The broomstick is run through this hole after first placing two metal washers on it. After running the stick through, a hardwood collar is fastened to it just

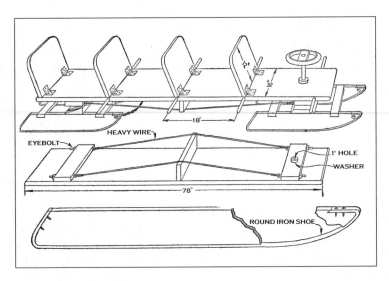

THE TOP BOARD IS WELL BRACED ON THE UNDERSIDE AND FITTED WITH FOUR BACKS ON TOP TO MAKE IT A LUXURIOUS RIDING SLED, AND THE RUNNERS ARE PROVIDED WITH METAL SHOES FOR SPEED.

above the top board, so that the top cannot be raised away from the sled. A steering wheel, made from a nail-keg hoop, is attached at the upper end of the broomstick. A piece of wood is fastened across its diameter, and the hoop is covered with a piece of garden hose and wrapped with twine. In the center of the cross-piece, a hole is bored to snugly fit on the broom handle, which is then fastened with screws.

The rear sled is fastened to the top board with screws through the extending wings of the hinges and into the crosspiece. Holes are bored in the front ends of all runners, and a chain or rope is attached in them. The loop end of the rear one is attached to the underside of the top board, and the one in the front used for drawing the sled.

Materials

1 top, 6½ ft. long, 16 in. wide, and 1¼ in. thick

4 runners, 22 in. long, 4 in. wide, and 1 in. thick

4 crosspieces, 16 in. long, 3 in. wide, and 1 in. thick

3 pieces, 16 in. long, 3 in. wide, and 1 in. thick

1 piece, 16 in. long, 5 in. wide, and 2 in. thick

1 shore, 16 in. long, 3 in. wide, and 1 in. thick

4 seat backs, 12 in. long, 16 in. wide, and 1 in. thick

1 dowel, 3 ft. long, and 1 in. in diameter

4 rods, ⅝ in. in diameter, and 30 in. long

4 eyebolts, ½ in. by 6 in. long

3 hinges, 5-in. strap

8 hinges, 3-in. strap

— How to Build a Toboggan Sled —

The first object of the builder of a sled should be to have a "winner," both in speed and appearance. The accompanying instructions for building a sled are designed to produce these results.

The sled completed should be 15 ft. 2 in. long by 22 in. wide, with the cushion about 15 in. above the ground. For the baseboard select a pine board 15 ft. long, 11 in. wide, and 2 in. thick, and plane it on all edges. Fit the baseboard with ten oak footrests, 22 in. long, 3 in. wide, and ¾ in. thick. Fasten them on the underside of the baseboard at right angles to its length and 16 in. apart, beginning at the rear. At the front

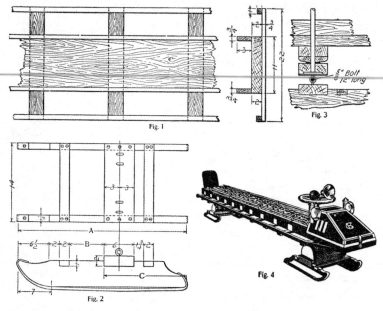

Fig. 1

Fig. 3

Fig. 2

CONSTRUCTING A "WINNER" TOBOGGAN SLED.

24 or 26 in. will be left without crossbars for fitting on the auto front. On the upper side of the crossbars at their ends on each side, screw a piece of oak 1 in. square by 14 ft. long. On the edges of the upper side of the baseboard screw an oak strip 3 in. wide by ¾ in. thick and the length of the sled from the back to the auto front. These are to keep the cushion from falling out. See *Fig. 1*. For the back of the sled use the upper part of a child's high chair, taking out the

spindles and resetting them in the rear end of the baseboard. Cover the outside of the spindles with a piece of galvanized iron.

The construction of the runners is shown in *Figs. 2* and *3*. The stock required is oak, two pieces 30 in. by 5 in. by 1¼ in., two pieces 34 in. by 5 in. by 1¼ in., two pieces 14 in. by 6 in. by 2 in., and four pieces 14 in. by 2 in. by 1 in. They should be put together with large screws about 3 in. long. Do not use nails, because they are not substantial enough. In proportioning them, the points *A*, *B*, and *C*, *Fig. 2*, are important. For the front runners these measurements are: *A*, 30 in.; *B*, 4 in.; *C*, 15½ in. For the rear runners: *A*, 34 in.; *B*, 7 in.; *C*, 16½ in. The screw eyes indicated must be placed in a straight line and the holes for them carefully centered. A variation of 1/16 in. one way or another would cause a great deal of trouble. For the steel runners use ⅜-in. cold-rolled steel flattened at the ends for screw holes. Use no screws on the running surface, however, as they "snatch" the ice.

The mechanism of the front steering gear is shown at *Fig. 3*. A ¾-in. steel rod makes a good steering rod. Flatten the steering rod at one end and sink it into the wood. Hold it in place by means of an iron plate drilled to receive the rod and screwed to block *X*. An iron washer, *Z*, is used to reduce friction; bevel block *K* to give a rocker motion. Equip block *X* with screw eyes, making them clear those in the front runner, and bolt through. For the rear runner put a block with screw eyes on the baseboard and run a bolt through.

Construct the auto front (*Fig. 4*) of ¾-in. oak boards. The illustration shows how to shape it. Bevel it toward all sides and keep the edges sharp, as sharp edges are best suited for the brass trimmings that are to be added. When the auto front is in place, enamel the sled either a dark maroon or a creamy white. First sandpaper all the wood, and then apply a coat of thin enamel. Let stand for three days and apply another coat. Three coats of enamel and one of thin varnish will make a fine-looking sled. For the brass trimmings use No. 24 B. and S. sheet brass 1 in. wide on all the front edges and pieces 3 in. square on the crossbars to rest the feet against. On the door of the auto front put the monogram of the owner or owners of the sled, cutting it out of sheet brass.

For the steering wheel procure an old freight-car "brake" wheel, brass-plated. Fasten a horn, such as used on automobiles, to the wheel.

Make the cushion of leather and stuff it with hair. The best way is to get some strong, cheap material, such as burlap, sew up one end and make the form of an oblong bag. Stuff this as tightly as possible with hair. Then get some upholstery buttons, fasten a cord through the loop, bring the cord through to the underside of the cushion, and fasten the button by slipping a nail through the knot. Then put a leather covering over the burlap, sewing it to the burlap on the underside. Make the cushion for the back in the same way. On top of the cushion supports run a brass tube to serve the double purpose of holding the cushion down and affording something to hold on to.

If desired, bicycle lamps may be fastened to the front end, to improve the appearance. It is wise to have a light of some kind at the back to avoid the danger of rear-end collisions.

The door of the auto front should be hinged and provided with a lock so that skates, parcels, overshoes, lunch, etc., may be stowed within. A silk pennant with a monogram adds to the appearance.

If desired, a brake may be added to the sled. This can be a wrought-iron lever 1½ in. by ½ in. by 30 in. long, so pivoted that moving the handle will cause the end to scrape the ice. This sled can be made without lamps and horn at a reduced cost. If the expense is greater than one can afford, a number of boys may share in the ownership.

— RUDDER FOR A TOBOGGAN —

Learning to steer a toboggan by means of the foot dragged behind it is an interesting feature of the sport, but this method is dangerous at times and results in much wear on shoes and clothes. The device shown in the illustration makes this method of steering unnecessary and gives the rider accurate control over the sled. It consists of a strip of ¼ by 1-in. iron curved to form a rudder at one end and twisted at the middle to provide a

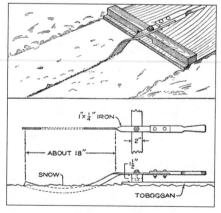

THIS RUDDER FOR A TOBOGGAN ENSURES POSITIVE CONTROL AND PREVENTS WEAR ON THE SHOES AND CLOTHES OF THE RIDER.

flat piece for pivoting it on the rear cleat of the sled, as shown in the working drawing. A handle is fastened to the front end of the strip with bolts. The rudder should not be curved too deeply or it will cut through the snow and be damaged, or ruin the track.

— HOW TO MAKE A MONORAIL SLED —

AN EXHILARATING GLIDE ACCOMPANIED BY A BUOYANT SENSE OF FREEDOM OBTAINED ONLY ON THE MONORAIL TYPE.

to the runners as follows: Blocks are nailed or bolted on either side of the upper edge of the rear runner, and the top is fastened to them with screws. The runner is also braced with strap iron, as shown. The same method applies to the front runner, except that only one pair of blocks is used at the center and a thin piece of wood fastened to their tops to serve as the fifth wheel.

A monorail sled, having a simple tandem arrangement of the runners, is very easily constructed as follows: The runners are cut from 1-in. plank of the size and shape given in the sketch, and are shod with strap iron, 1 in. wide and ¼ in. thick. Round iron or half-round iron should not be used, as these are liable to skid. The square, sharp edges of the strap iron prevent this and grip the surface just as a skate.

The top is a board 6 ft. long and 1 in. thick, securely fastened

The hole for the steering post should be 6 in. from the front end and a little larger in diameter than the steering post. The latter should be rounded where it passes through the hole, but square on the upper end to receive the steering bar, which must be tightly fitted in place.

In coasting, the rider lies full length on the board with his hands on the steering bar. This makes the center of gravity so low that there is no necessity for lateral steadying runners. In addition to the exhilarating glide of the ordinary sled,

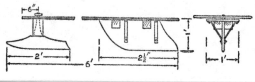

THE CONSTRUCTION IS MUCH MORE SIMPLE THAN MAKING A DOUBLE-RUNNER BOBSLED.

the rider experiences a buoyant sense off freedom and a zest peculiar to the monorail type. Then, too, the steering is affected much more easily. Instead of dragging the feet, a slight turn of the front runner with a cor-responding movement of the body is sufficient to change the direction or to restore the balance. This latter is, of course, maintained quite mechanically, as everyone who rides a bicycle well knows.

— THE RUNNING SLEIGH —

Another winter sport very popular in Sweden, and one that has already reached America, is the "running sleigh," shown in the illustration. A light sleigh is equipped with long double runners and is propelled by foot power. The person using the sleigh stands with one foot upon a rest attached to one of the braces connecting the runners and propels the sleigh by pushing backward with the other foot. An upright support is attached to the runners to steady the body. The contrivance can be used upon hard frozen ground, thin ice, and snow-

RUNNING SLEIGH

covered surfaces. Under favorable conditions it moves with remarkable speed. The running sleigh has a decided advantage over skis, because the two foot supports are braced so that they cannot come apart.

— A Ski Sled —

The sled is built low and wide so that it will not tip easily. The skis, or runners, are cut 10 ft. long and 6 in. wide, from 1-in. ash boards that are straight-grained. At the points where the curve is to be formed, plane off about ¼ in. on the upper side, but do not plane off any at the very tip end. This will allow the skis to be more easily bent. If it is not handy to steam the skis, put them in boiling water, and be sure that at least 1½ ft. of the points are covered. Provide a cover for the vessel, so that only very little steam may escape. Let them boil for at least one hour. A good method of bending the points is shown. When the skis are taken from the water, put them as quickly as possible in the bending blocks, side by side, and bend them with a slow, even pressure. Weight the extending ends and leave the skis in the blocks 8 or 10 hours to dry. Sharpen the points after they are bent.

The sled will run easier if the skis have slight rocker curve. To make this curve, have the center block 6 in. while the two end blocks are 5½ in. high. A ¼-in. flathead bolt is run through the ski, the block, and the cross strip. The holes are counter-sunk in the surface for the heads of the bolts. The top is made of three 6-in. boards, fastened to the cross-pieces. It is a good plan to brace the tips of the skis with a 2-in. strip.

THE RUNNERS ARE SHAPED LIKE A SKI AND ARE JOINED
TOGETHER WITH KNEES FOR THE TOP BOARD.

— A Motorcycle Bobsled —

Most motorcycle owners put their machines away when the snow begins to fly, and forego their use during the winter months. However, the photograph shows how one enthusiast constructed a bobsled that uses the motorcycle power plant to drive it along the frozen surface.

INSTEAD OF STORING THE MOTORCYCLE DURING THE COLD WINTER MONTHS, IT IS USED, IN THIS CASE, TO DRIVE A BOBSLED. THE FRONT WHEEL AND HANDLEBARS ARE REMOVED, AND THE MACHINE IS HELD UPRIGHT IN A WOODEN FRAMEWORK.

The front wheel and handlebars are removed from the machine, which is held vertically in a framework built as a part of the sled body. The front fork is firmly fastened and the rear wheel is placed between two guideboards, so arranged as to prevent the walls of the tire from rubbing against the sides. An old tire was used on the single wheel, and additional traction obtained by the use of a tire chain. The sled is steered by means of a steering wheel operating the front set of runners, which swivels on a pin at the center.

— Motor-Driven Sleds —

For those who wish to build a motor-driven sled but do not want to go to the trouble and expense of making or buying an aerial propeller and adapting the engine to this form of drive, the wheel-driven sleds described in this article will be of great value.

The first machine has a light steel frame supported on oak runners, shod with round steel. The sled is driven by a four-cylinder motorcycle engine, geared to the driving wheel in the same manner as in the motorcycle. The driving wheel, which is a standard motorcycle wheel, is mounted in a U-shaped angle-iron yoke. The ends of the yoke are attached to a crosspiece on the steel frame by means of stout hinges. A stiff spring is provided on each side of the yoke for holding the wheel to the surface, while at the same time permitting free vertical movement. Thus there is no loss of traction and the sled can travel over uneven ground. The wheel is covered by a sheet-metal hood, forward of which and a little above the top of the engine, the gasoline tank is mounted on a frame made of flat iron. The sled is steered by means of the front runners, which are controlled through sash-cord steering ropes running to the steering wheel. The steering wheel is located immediately behind the wheel hood, on the right-hand side of the sled. Footrests are provided on each side of the machine, and the brake lever is within easy reach of the driver's hand on the right-hand side. The brake is simply a pointed steel lever that digs into the ice when the hand lever is pulled back; the clutch-control lever is at the left of the driver's seat. The small tank seen on top of the engine, at the front, is a two-quart oilcan.

A somewhat similar sled, though less ambitious in design, is driven by a twin-cylinder motorcycle engine. This one is designed along the lines of a light automobile or cycle car.

The builder has used it on both snow and ice, and found it to be an excellent hill climber. The machine is 9½ ft. long over all, and the frame is made of light angle iron, with front and rear runners of wood. The chain-driven drive wheel, which is mounted as described in the first type, has short sections of 2-in. angle iron riveted around its circumference. The sled is guided by the front runners, through a regulation automobile steering post and drag line connected to a steering knuckle fastened to the runners. The spark and throttle control are regulated from the levers on the steering wheel.

The simplest type of these kind of sleds consists merely of an ordinary "coaster," to which is attached a motor wheel. The small drawing shows the framework to which the motor wheel is fastened. To create this frame two pieces of pine, 2 by 3

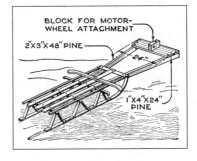

BLOCK FOR MOTOR-WHEEL ATTACHMENT

2"X3"X48" PINE

1"X4"X24" PINE

by 48 in., and a crosspiece, 1 by 4 by 24 in., are required. Combined with a block attached to the crosspiece, the pieces of pine are drilled for attaching the motor wheel, which is mounted so as to permit steering. This sled has attained a speed of 20 miles an hour on a level surface.

These brief descriptions may stimulate interest in the fascinating winter sport of motor sleighing, and will also serve to crystallize the ideas of those who wish to build such a sled, and are wondering which type to select. All of these designs have been tried out and found to be successful, and it is merely a matter of the builder's choice which one to select.

Water Sports

— How to Make a Water Bicycle —

Water bicycles afford fine sport and, like many other devices boys make, can be made of material often cast off by their people as rubbish. The principal elements necessary for the construction of a water bicycle are oil barrels. Flour barrels will not do—they are not strong enough, nor can they be made perfectly airtight. The grocer can furnish you with oil barrels at a very small cost, and may even let you have them for making a few deliveries for him. Three barrels are required for the water bicycle,

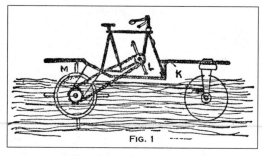

FIG. 1

WATER BICYCLE COMPLETE

although it can be made with but two. *Fig. 1* shows the method of arranging the barrels after the manner of bicycle wheels.

Procure an old bicycle frame and make for it a board platform about 3 ft. wide at the rear end and tapering to about 2 ft. at the front. Use cleats to hold the board frame, as shown in the shaded portion *K*. The construction of the barrel part is shown in *Fig. 2*. Bore holes in the center of the heads of the two rear barrels and also in the heads of the first barrel and put a shaft of wood through the rear barrels and one through the front barrel, adjusting the side pieces to the shafts, as indicated.

Next place the platform of the bicycle frame and connections thereon. Going back to *Fig. 1* we see that the driving chain passes from the sprocket driver, *L,* of the bicycle frame to the place downward between the slits in the platform to the driven sprocket on the shaft between the two barrels. Thus a center drive is made. The rear barrels are

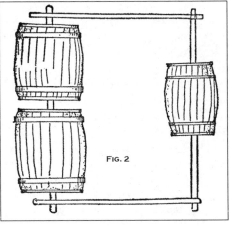

FIG. 2

BARREL FLOAT FOR BICYCLE

fitted with paddles as in *M*, consisting of four pieces of board nailed and cleated about the circumference of the barrels, as shown in *Fig. 1*.

The new craft is now ready for a first voyage. To propel it, seat yourself on the bicycle seat, feet on the pedals, just as you would were you on a bicycle out in the street. The steering is affected by simply bending the body to the left or right, which causes the craft to dip to the inclined side and the whole affair turns in the dipped direction. The speed is slow at first, but

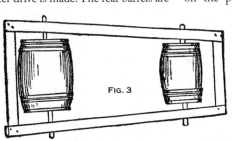

FIG. 3

ANOTHER TYPE OF FLOAT

increases as the force is generated and as one becomes familiar with the working of the bike. There is no danger, because the airtight barrels cannot possibly sink.

Another mode of putting together the set of barrels, using one large one in the rear and a small one in the front, is presented in *Fig. 3*. These two barrels are empty oil barrels like the others. The head holes are bored and the proper wood shafts are inserted and the entrance to the bores closed tight by calking with hemp and putty

or clay. The ends of the shafts turn in the wooden frame where the required bores are made to receive the same. If the journals thus made are well oiled, there will not be much friction. Such a frame can be fitted with a platform and a raft to suit one's individual fancy built upon it, which can be paddled about with ease and safety on any pond. A sail can be rigged up by using a mast and some sheeting. Or even a little houseboat, which will give any amount of pleasure, can be built.

— WATER-COASTING TOBOGGAN AND SLIDE —

Coasting down an incline and being projected through the air to plunge into the warm water of a summer lake, or other outdoor bathing spot, offers thrills and excitement to the person seeking a new aquatic diversion. The illustration shows a slide and the toboggan sled for use on it, which were built by a group of young men at a summer resort. Though the slide shown is perhaps more extensive than most boys would care to undertake, the principle involved may be adapted easily to a model one-fourth as long, less than 20 ft. The slide shown was

strongly built of 2- by 4-in. material for the framework, 2- by 6-in. planks for the slide guides, and 2- by 12-in. planks for the roller bearing. Lighter material may be used for the guides and the roller bearing on a smaller slide, but the framework should be of 2- by 2-in. stock.

The high end of the slide illustrated is about 7 ft. from the ground, but a proportionately greater incline is provided because the beach slopes gradually to the water's edge. It is reached by a ladder fixed to a tree, which acts as an end brace for the slide. If no such natural support is available, the end of the slide must be strongly braced on three sides, to ensure safety. It is inadvisable to build the slide unduly high to provide the necessary incline, because this may result in accidents. A location where the ground is suitable should be selected rather than assume danger or risk.

The end of the slide nearest the water may be given a slight upward turn, so that when the toboggan leaves it the rider is carried upward before striking the water. The hold on the toboggan should be retained when entering the water, because injury may result by failure to clear it in the plunge. With experience a dive may be made as the toboggan leaves the slide.

The construction of the slide is shown in detail in the lower sketch. The framework of 2- by 4-in. material should be only slightly wider than the guides, and the supports should be spread toward the ground to give rigidity. The supports, *A*, should be nailed firmly, or bolted, to the horizontal members, *B*. If lighter stock is used, the pieces at *B* should be nailed in pairs, one on each side of the uprights. The guides *C* and *D* should be of smooth lumber, and the edges of these pieces, as well as

of the bearing plank *E*, should be rounded off to remove splinters. The joints in the sections of the guides should be made carefully and placed over the framework supports. They should be reinforced from the lower side by plates of wood.

The bearing plank, *E*, is of 2-in. stock and 12 in. wide. It may be made of lighter material in a smaller slide. The joints in it should likewise be made carefully, to ensure smooth riding over them. They should be set directly over the framework supports, but not on those over which joints have been made in the guides. The plank forming the bearing for the roller should not extend to the end of the slide at the lower end, but should be set back about 18 in. This permits the toboggan to slide off smoothly rather than to spring directly into the air from the bearing on the rollers. The bearing plank may be nailed into place, but care must be taken to set all nails below the surface. A better construction is to use screws or bolts. Bore holes for them through the plank, countersinking their heads.

The toboggan, as shown in the detail sketches, is built strongly. It is to be fitted over the 12-in. bearing plank, allowing ¼-in. play on each side. The sides are of 1¼-in. stock

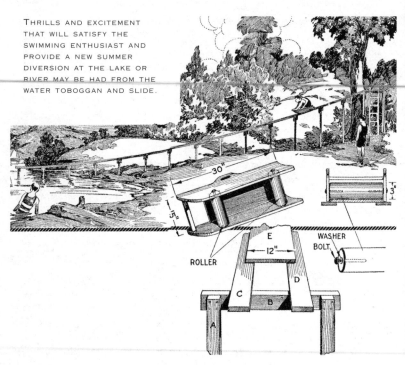

and high enough to accommodate the rollers, which should be about 3 in. in diameter. The dimensions of 15 in. in width and 30 in. in length, on the top surface, are suggestive only, and will vary with the materials used. The toboggan will not stand the necessarily hard wear unless good-quality oak or other hardwood is used. The top and foot brace should be fixed strongly with screws, their heads countersunk.

The rollers are fixed in the sides by means of screws, or a bolt may be set through the length of the roller. In either case the bearing should be in holes bored through the sidepieces. Washers should be fitted at the sides of the bearings, and the latter must be kept greased. All the edges and corners of the toboggan should be rounded off so that there is a little possibility of injury from slivers or contact with the edges.

— Making a Catamaran Raft —

A simple raft that will meet the requirements for an inexpensive and simple boat can be made from two or three logs in the manner indicated in the drawing.

Two logs, about 12 ft. long, are used for the sides. These are connected with crosspieces, spikes or wooden pegs being used to secure the parts together. A piece of split log answers for a seat, and two forked branches inserted into the sidepieces make satisfactory oarlocks. In the absence

A USEFUL BOAT, BUILT OF LOGS AS A CATAMARAN RAFT, TAKES THE PLACE OF A REGULATION ROWBOAT WHEN THE LATTER IS NOT EASILY OBTAINED.

of regulation oars, pieces of board can be cut to approximately the proper shape.

— How to Make a Sailomobile —

Having read of the beach automobiles used on the Florida coast an enthusiast noted that they were like an ice boat with a sail, except they had wheels instead of runners. So he set to work to make something to take him over the country roads.

He found and used seven fence pickets for the framework, and other things, as they were needed. He spliced two rake handles together for the mast, winding the ends where they came together with wire. (A single piece is superior if you can get one long enough.) The gaff, which is the stick to which the upper end of the sail is fastened, is a broomstick. The boom, the stick at the bottom of the sail, was made of a rake handle with a broomstick spliced to make it long enough. The innovative mechanic borrowed a sheet, which he put down on the floor and cut in the shape of a mainsail. The wind was the cheapest power to be found, thus it was utilized; the three wheels were cast-off bicycle wheels.

The rider steers with the front wheel, which is the front wheel of an old bicycle with the fork left on. The axle between the rear wheels is an iron bar, and the pulley that raises and lowers the sail.

A saw, hammer, brace, and bit were the tools used. Slats made a seat and a cushion from the house made it comfortable, and in a week everything was ready for sailing.

ON *the* ICE

— BUILDING AN ICE YACHT —

Hull Construction

Although the northern part of this country is blessed with innumerable lakes and streams where that king of winter sports, ice yachting, should be enjoyed, comparatively little definite is known of the construction of fast, easily handled craft, except around such ice-yachting centers as the Hudson and Shrewsbury rivers, Orange Lake, and some Midwestern lakes.

From the number of crude makeshift affairs so often seen, it is obvious that many real yachts would be built to the lasting delight of the owners and their friends, if their design and construction were only better understood. It is for the purpose of providing this information that this article is written. The yacht herein described, while not too large to be used on a good sized pond or small lake, is of sufficient size and speed for the most exciting races. At the same time it is perfectly safe and easily handled, provided the given measurements are strictly adhered to.

The material used in the construction depends to a great extent on available supply. In purchasing the lumber, one should always buy the driest obtainable, and the better the quality the better looking the completed boat will be. There is no reason why one who can use carpenters' tools with ordinary skill should not be able to turn out a first-class

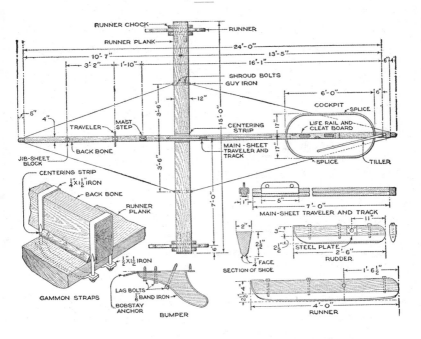

DETAILS OF THE BACKBONE, RUNNER PLANK, AND RUNNERS.
NOTE THE CURVE ON THE EDGE OF THE RUNNER, AND
THE POSITION OF THE SPLICES ON THE COCKPIT.

job with a moderate outlay—if the instructions are closely followed.

For the backbone, butternut, white pine, and basswood are the most suitable woods, although cypress may also be used. The tendency of spruce to "wind" eliminates that wood from all consideration. Because it is hardly possible to obtain one stick long enough for this part, allowance must be made for a splice of not less than 8 ft., and longer than this if possible. This splice should be made with one long, straight cut, without notches of any sort, as the notches weaken the timber. Only the best grade of pot glue should be used, and the joint thoroughly fastened with ½-in. lag bolts, put in from the bottom, with large washers under the heads. When spliced, the stick should measure 4 in. by 8 in. by 25¼ ft. It is left straight on the underside throughout its entire length and of full width. But the top of the bowsprit is tapered in a curve, beginning at the mast, down to the shoulder where the eyebolt for the forestay goes through. Here it is made 4 in. thick, and from a point 2 ft. aft of the runner plank another curved taper should run to the stern shoulder, where it is 6 in. thick. All four corners on the bowsprit are rounded, and after the cockpit is in position, the afterpart of the backbone should be slightly rounded all the way to the stern. The tip of the bowsprit is rounded for a distance of 5 in., to receive the guys and bobstay, and the stern for a distance of 4 in., as shown in the deck plan. To ensure an accurate rudderpost hole, it is bored halfway through from the top and finished from the bottom. The whole backbone should then be planed smooth, and finished with cabinet scraper, sandpaper, and generous quantities of elbow grease. It should then be soused with boiled oil. This applies to every part made of wood, because the oil prevents it from turning black should the varnish be marred.

The cockpit is the only really difficult part of the whole boat to make. The rims are made of cherry and oak, and require steaming and bending over a form, with two splices where shown. The oak rim is 4 in. wide by 1 in. thick, is finished smooth and, after forming and splicing, is placed in position and accurately centered on the backbone. Marks are made on the under edge of the rim to correspond with the edges of the backbone, and notches ½ in. deep and as wide as the backbone are cut in the rim. These notches fit over the backbone, to which the cockpit is securely fastened by two large screws at each end. A heavy iron strap, bent in the shape of an "L," is screwed to both the backbone and the inside of the cockpit rim at each end.

The bottom can be made of either ½-in. whitewood, in one piece, or of oak strips 1 in. wide, with ¼-in. space left between them. Strips are better, because the spaces permit snow and water to pass through so that no ice can form. The bottom is screwed to the underside of the oak rim shaped to the form shown, and reinforced by three strips of flat iron. The cherry covering board extends just below the joint of the bottom and rim, and is spliced on the side opposite to the splice in the oak and thoroughly screwed to the rim. All screw heads are sunk in deeply and wood-plugged. The handrail is of oak, on apple or maple spindles. The life rail and cleat board are of 1-in. oak, the same width as the backbone, with the forward end screwed to the cockpit rim and the after end raised level on an oak block.

Butternut, white pine, basswood, and ash are the most suitable woods from which to make the runner plank, although cypress is also excellent. If ash is used, the finished plank should be ½ in. thinner than the softer woods. The rough plank should measure 16 ft. long by a full 4-by-12-in. section. As in the backbone, the underside is planed perfectly straight. The center is then marked with pencil, and from this all measurements are taken. A thickness of 2½ in. measured from the under edge is marked at each end. A long, thin batten is sprung from these marks to the top edge at the center, and a line drawn to mark the curve to which the plank is finished. The four runner chocks and four brackets are made in pairs from 2-in. oak, or maple, of best quality. Lay off and mark the position of the inner starboard (right-hand, looking forward) chock, referring to the deck plan. Square the chock very accurately and bolt with four ½-in.

carriage bolts, after sinking the chock into the runner plank ¼ in. This prevents the runners from becoming twisted out of true, and applies to all four chocks, because no other part of the boat is subject to such a terrific strain. All bolts should have washers under the heads as well as under the nuts. One pair of brackets is fastened to the chock using very large screws, then fastened to the plank. Assuming that the runners are finished, mark one with an "S," indicating that it is always to be used on the starboard side. Place it in position with built-up cardboard, 1 in. thick, between it and the chock. Put the outer chock in position, and then put the runner bolt through all three, tightening the nut with your fingers. This will give the position in which the outer chock is to be bolted, with sufficient allowance of space to ensure free play for the runner. Cut an "A" with a chisel on the rear edge of the plank at the center, corresponding with the heel of the runner, indicating that this is the after edge. Mark the position of the inner chock on the port (left-hand) side, and bolt with one bolt only, without sinking the chock into the plank. Place the runner, cardboard, and the outer chock in place, as on the starboard side. Cut a 2-in. notch in the edge of a board equal in length to the runner plank, place it over the heel of the starboard runner, and make a slight mark where it rests on the heel of the port runner. Shift the plank to the forward end of the runners to find if the running edges are parallel. Repeat this, shifting the port runner and chock until the running edges prove absolutely parallel. Upon their accuracy—more than on any other one thing—depend the sailing qualities of the boat. Sink in and secure the remaining chocks and brackets permanently, and remove the cardboard strips. Saw off and round the ends of the plank, as shown. From a point opposite the inner ends of the chock brackets, spring another curve parallel with the top of the plank. Chamfer off the under edge, giving the plank a curved appearance. Strips of quarter-round hardwood are then screwed across the center in such a position that the backbone will always rest across the center of the plank.

Cast iron of the best grade is the only material that may be used for the runner shoes of an ice yacht. Therefore a wooden pattern of the exact size and shape of the finished shoe must be made, from which to have the shoes cast, and one for the rudder also. Although the drawings show the runners in detail, a description of the shoe is necessary. The running edge is a true right angle, and must be kept so in order to get the utmost speed out of the boat. The faces of the right angle are ¼ in. wide. The upper face must be trued in a planing machine and then drilled and tapped for cap screws. As a majority of foundries have a machine shop in connection with them, this should not be an expensive piece of work. The oak or maple top must be perfectly fitted and bedded to the shoe, and the joint made with a marine gasket. The cap screws are ⅜ in., with washers under the heads, and are drawn up very tight. The bolt just aft of the runner bolt hole is countersunk to clear the runner plank. The runners must be filed with the greatest possible accuracy by the following method: Place one in the vise and, using

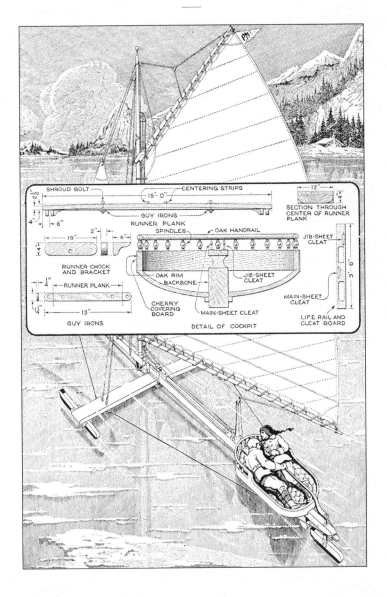

SHROUD BOLT · CENTERING STRIPS
15'-0"
GUY IRONS
RUNNER PLANK
4" 6"

SECTION THROUGH
CENTER OF RUNNER
PLANK
12"

18" 2" 6"
RUNNER CHOCK
AND BRACKET

RUNNER PLANK
1"
15"
GUY IRONS

SPINDLES · OAK HANDRAIL
JIB-SHEET
CLEAT

OAK RIM
BACKBONE
JIB-SHEET
CLEAT

CHERRY
COVERING
BOARD
MAIN-SHEET CLEAT

MAIN-SHEET
CLEAT

3'-6"

LIFE RAIL AND
CLEAT BOARD

DETAIL OF COCKPIT

a wooden straightedge as a guide, file the running edge to the perfect curve. The point beneath the bolt hole should be left untouched and the toe and heel filed down 3/16 in. The straightedge should rock back and forth smoothly. File the faces back to a sharp right angle and finish with a carborundum stone. The runner bolt holes are bushed with brass pipe of sufficient diameter to take a ½-in. bolt freely. These bolts have square heads, sunk into the chock ¼ in. to prevent turning, and are 8 in. long, with cotter pins outside the washers and nuts. A box, or crate, should be made to hold and protect the runners when not in use. Any slight damage to the running edge may mean a long job of filing. In use, the runners should always remain on the ice overnight, to prevent rusting, and the edges kept in perfect and sharp condition for racing.

A hardwood bumper, made from 2-in. stuff and bound with flat iron, screwed on, is placed just forward of the rudder. It will be necessary to take measurements for this part with the rudder in position. The bobstay anchor is of ¼- by 1¼-in. flat iron, with holes drilled for lagscrews and for attaching a turnbuckle.

The track for the main sheet traveler is made of any close-grained hardwood, in two pieces. It is screwed to the backbone, as shown. The forward part should be removable, to allow the gammon straps too be placed in position. It should be well oiled, and only the top varnished. If it is varnished all over, the traveler will stick. The traveler must be made of brass or bronze.

As soon as the oil is thoroughly dried, go over the whole lightly with fine sandpaper and apply two or three coats of the best spar varnish obtainable, rubbing lightly between coats. All metal work not of brass should be painted with aluminum paint. This completes the hull woodwork.

Spars, Rigging, and Assembling

Only the best grade of spruce is suitable for spars. Unquestionably hollow ones are lighter and stronger, but they cost a lot more. If expense is no object, buy hollow spars. Otherwise proceed as follows: For the mast

DETAILS OF SAILS, RIGGING, AND HULL FITTINGS. IN THE UPPER RIGHT-HAND CORNER IS A DETAIL DRAWING OF THE METHOD OF RIGGING THE MAINSHEET; BELOW THIS IS SHOWN THE METHOD OF FASTENING THE JIB, PEAK, AND THROAT HALYARDS TO THE PURCHASE BLOCKS.

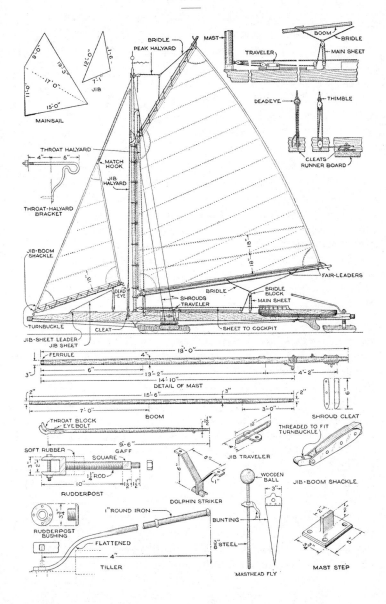

BRIDLE
PEAK HALYARD
MAST
BOOM
BRIDLE
TRAVELER
MAIN SHEET

9'-0"
12'-0"
19'-3"
1'-6"
17'-0"
7'-1"
11'-0"
15'-0"
JIB

MAINSAIL

DEADEYE
THIMBLE

CLEATS
RUNNER BOARD

THROAT HALYARD
4"
5"
MATCH HOOK
JIB HALYARD

THROAT-HALYARD
BRACKET

JIB-BOOM
SHACKLE

FAIR-LEADERS

DEAD EYE
BRIDLE
SHROUDS
TRAVELER
BRIDLE BLOCK
MAIN SHEET

TURNBUCKLE
CLEAT
SHEET TO COCKPIT

JIB-SHEET LEADER
JIB SHEET

18'-0"
FERRULE
4"
3"
6"
13'-2"
14'-10"
4'-2"

DETAIL OF MAST

2"
15'-6"
3"
2"
7'-0"
3'-0"
BOOM

SHROUD CLEAT

THROAT BLOCK
EYEBOLT
1½"
12"
9'-6"
GAFF

THREADED TO FIT
TURNBUCKLE

SOFT RUBBER
SQUARE
1¼" ROD
3"
10"
1½" 1½"
RUDDERPOST

JIB TRAVELER

JIB-BOOM SHACKLE

1"ROUND IRON
DOLPHIN STRIKER

WOODEN BALL
3"

RUDDERPOST
BUSHING
3¼"
BUNTING

FLATTENED
8" STEEL

4"
TILLER
MASTHEAD FLY

MAST STEP

select the clearest 4-by-4-in. stick to be found. For the boom and gaff use a 3-by-3-in. stick, and for the jib boom a 2-by-2-in. piece. Plane the stick for the mast fairly smooth on all four sides, then layoff a taper from a point 6 ft. from the foot, reducing the diameter to 3 in. at the heel. Plane all four sides, still keeping the stick square. From a point 5 ft. from the masthead, taper to 2½ in. Plane off all four corners, making an octagonal stick. Then, with a small plane, round the spar, and finish with enough sandpaper and elbow grease—especially the elbow grease—to remove all plane marks. If any attempt is made to round the spar before tapering, it will be found impossible to keep it straight. A brass or iron ferrule, 2 in. wide, is fitted to the foot to prevent splitting, and a mortise cut to receive the mast step. Shroud cleats of apple wood or maple, of the form shown, are screwed at the points indicated, and the throat-halyard bracket and eyebolts put in place. The boom and gaff are identical in construction to the mast. The boom tapers to 2 in. at either end, with a large hole through the after end for the sail haul-out. The gaff tapers to 1½ in. at each end, with a haul-out hole at the peak. Oak

jaws, fitted with a throat block, are riveted at the throat. It is best to buy the jaws from a ship chandler. The jib boom is not tapered, but is rounded, and the jaws of the jib-boom shackle are riveted in place. The bridle cleats for the boom and gaff are similar to the shroud cleats, but smaller.

Wherever possible, brass or bronze should be used for the fittings, although iron will do. The detail drawings show the masthead fly, throat-halyard bracket, and the two guy irons so plainly that no description is needed. The jib traveler is of ⅜-in. rod, riveted and brazed to a ¼ in. plate. Tenpenny nails make excellent cross pins for the traveler. The object of these is to prevent the sheet block from slipping around to the underside of the traveler. The two members of the mast step are also riveted and brazed. The dolphin striker is of ¼-by-1-in. stock, with a half section of pipe brazed in the lower end of the "V." The jib-boom shackle is all brass, with the end hole threaded to fit the forestay turnbuckle. The gammon-strap set cannot be made until the backbone and runner-plank parts are in place. It will probably be found advisable to cut strong paper patterns of the gammon straps for the blacksmith or machinist to work from. The bolts on the straps are riveted and brazed to the flat iron. Unless cast of bronze and turned, the rudderpost must be forged by a first-class blacksmith, it being a somewhat difficult piece of work. It is fitted with a soft-rubber bumper, which greatly relieves the shock of sailing over rough ice. Of course, the tiller must be fitted to the post so that there is no lost motion. The handle is wound with cotton cord, filled with shellac, and varnished. Plates may be used in place of the rudderpost bushings. But they will soon wear, and will, in turn, wear a groove in the post. That's why bronze or cast-iron bushings, of the form shown, are well worth the extra expense. They will last forever.

Because there are a number of first-class sailmakers who specialize in ice-yacht sails, one should be selected, and the sail plan sent to him when placing the order. Yacht twill will make strong, durable sails at a low price, but the better grades of sailcloth are more satisfactory. In giving the order, the fact that the sails are for an ice yacht should be mentioned, together with the following specifications: jib to have snap hooks for forestay, and be made to lace to the boom, or the

foot will be cut as for a sailing yacht. Mainsail to have thimbles in pairs on hoist for mast-hoop lacing, and single thimbles on foot. Otherwise leave it to the sailmaker. He knows.

The cockpit cushions are made of good-quality ticking, covered with corduroy or plush on the edges and one side only. They are filled with upholsterer's moss or the contents of a discarded hair mattress, and are 2½ in. thick. In length, the covering should be 6 in. longer than the cockpit, because proper filling shortens the cushion considerably. If made long, the finished cushions will fit tightly enough to stay in place. The buttons for tacking should be covered with the same material as the cushion.

The shrouds, forestay, and guys are made of ¼-in. iron wire, and the bobstay of ⅜-in. wire. In making up each piece, the measurements must be taken from the boat itself to avoid mistakes. Loops to fit the masthead, and the ends of the backbone are first spliced. Then the opposite ends are spliced into ⅜-in. galvanized shackle-and-shackle pipe turnbuckles of the slot and cotter-pin pattern. (Never use hook turnbuckles.) All turnbuckles should be fitted with wire-rope thimbles, and all loops and splices tightly served with hard cable-laid cotton cord about ⅛ in. in diameter, filled with shellac, and varnished. The bobstay has an eye splice formed to fit the backbone nose; from there it runs down under the dolphin striker and aft to the anchor iron screwed to the bumper. The bridles for the boom and gaff are ¼-in. wire, with loops finished as above. The halyards should be crucible cast steel, ³/₁₆ in. in diameter, finished as follows: The jib halyard is spliced in a pair of match hooks with wire-rope thimble for attaching to the jib, and the lower end spliced around a lignum-vitae deadeye. The upper end of the peak halyard is spliced into a self-locking brass bridle fitted with a thimble, and the lower end around a thimble to receive the purchase block. The throat halyard has a thimble in each end, one for attaching to the eyebolt at the jaws of the gaff, and one for a purchase block at the lower end. The splices are finished in the same manner as for the shrouds and stays. All Manila rope is ⅜-in., spliced in, with free ends moused with sail thread. The mainsheet proper is spliced into the becket of the bridle block at one end, and around a thimble at the other, for attaching to the mainsheet traveler by a screw shackle. This traveler is hauled along the track by a purchase attached to the foot of the mast, giving ample power to trim sail easily during a race, without luffing and losing speed. The remaining ropes are so plainly shown in the illustration as to require no further description.

The halyard blocks are of the type designed for wire rope only, all others being any first-class make of bronze yacht block, with fitting suited to the work for which each block is used. Galvanized blocks will not do, nor should any have hook fittings.

Together with the rigging described above, eyebolts, mast hoops, gooseneck, cleats, lacing, and screw fair-leaders must be purchased from the ship chandler. The jib and mainsail lacing is ³/₁₆-in. braided cotton, and the same material is used for the sail haul-outs. Fair-leaders are screwed into the top of the main boom, alternating with the thimbles on the foot of the sail, and through all is run a Manila stop, drawn very tight. Two fair-leaders are also used in the runner plank on each side of the backbone, for lashing the halyard-purchase ropes.

The whole boat, including the sails, but not the runners, should be set up complete outside the shop to prove that every part fits properly before putting it on the ice.

Always, when setting up, the gammon straps are first bolted tight. Then the runner plank and backbone are squared by measuring from the center of the rudderpost hole to a certain point on corresponding chocks at opposite ends of the plank, tightening the guys accordingly.

A combined sail and cockpit cover, preferably of waterproof duck and extending the full length of the boat, is necessary for protection from the elements. It should be made in one piece, with an opening to go around the mast, and have grommets along each edge for ties to bind it down tightly to the guys and bobstay. A horse set under the boom will hold the cover up, tent-fashion. Colors for a craft of this size should be 18 by 12 in. During snow, the runners should be removed, dried, greased, and carefully put away in their box.

In many things one finds that the pleasure of anticipation and preparation far exceeds the actuality. This, however, does not apply at all to ice-yachting. For though the construction of such a craft will give the builder many happy hours' employment, the sailing of it will prove the greatest imaginable joy after the tricks of the trade are mastered. And the only way properly to master them is racing with some old hand at the game. When that incurable disease, "ice-yachting fever," attacks one's blood, the only relief is ice-yachting.

— An Ice Glider —

The enthusiastic pushmobilist need not push aside his hobby during the winter. An amusement device for use on ice—one that will surpass the very best pushmobile—can be easily made as shown in the illustration.

Similar to an ice yacht only a great deal smaller, the ice glider will require three ordinary skates. Two of these are fastened to the

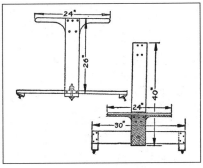

DETAIL OF THE PARTS FOR THE CONSTRUCTION OF THE ICE GLIDER.

ends of the front crosspiece so that their blades will stand at an angle of about 30 degrees with their edges outward. To get this angle, tapering blocks are fastened to the crosspiece ends, as shown. The skates are then fastened to these blocks.

The crosspiece is 30 in. long and about 8 in. wide. An upright is constructed, 26 in. high, in the center of this piece. The edges of the front crosspiece are cut on a slant so that a piece nailed to its front and back edges will stand sloping toward the rear. A handle, 24 in. long, is fastened between the two uprights at the upper end. The rear part is made of a board, 8 in. wide by 40 in. long. The remaining skate is fastened in a perfectly straight position on the rear rend. The skates may be attached with screws run through

THE GLIDER IS PUSHED OVER THE ICE SIMILARLY TO A PUSHMOBILE, AND THE SPEED THAT BE ATTAINED IS MUCH GREATER.

holes drilled in the top plates, or with straps. The front end of the rear board has a hole for a bolt to attach it to the center of the front crosspiece, so that the latter will turn to guide the glider.

A pusher is prepared from a block of wood, into which nails are driven with their ends projecting on the underside. The block is strapped to one shoe, as shown.

The glider is used in the same manner as a pushmobile.

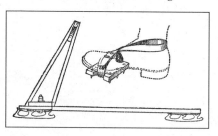

THE BLOCK OF WOOD WITH PROJECTING NAILS TO FASTEN ON THE SHOE THAT DOES THE PUSHING.

The pusher can be made in another way by using sole leather instead of the block. Small slots are cut in the sides for the straps. Nails are driven through the leather so that the points project. Either kind of pusher is especially adapted for the pushmobile to prevent wear on the shoe.

— SKATES MADE OF WOOD —

Skates that will take the place of the usual steel-runner kind and that will prevent spraining of the ankles can be made of a few pieces of ½-in. hardwood boards.

Four runners are cut out, 2 in. wide at the back and 1½ in. wide at the front. The length should be 2 in. longer than the shoe. The top edges of a pair of runners are then nailed to the underside of a board 4 in. wide, at its edges.

A piece of board, or block, 2 in. wide is fastened between the runners at the rear, and one 1 in. wide in front. Two bolts are run through holes bored in the runners, one just back of the front board, or block, and the other in front of the rear one.

Four triangular pieces are fastened,

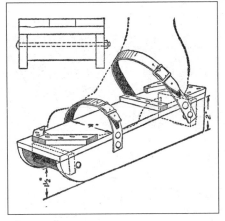

SKATES MADE OF WOOD TO TAKE THE PLACE
OF THE STEEL-RUNNER KIND AND
PREVENT SPRAINED ANKLES.

one on each corner, so that the heel and toe of the shoe will fit between them. If desired, a crosspiece can be nailed in front of the heel. Straps are attached to the sides for attaching the skate to the shoe. Both skates are made alike.

— ❖ ❖ ❖ —

CHAPTER 9

FUN *for* LITTLE ONES

—

ANIMALS *at* PLAY

— A TOY HORSE THAT WALKS —

This toy, amusing for the youngsters and their elders as well, will repay in joy the effort taken in making it. Use a cigar box for the carriage, making it about 10 in. high, and shape it in the design shown. Nail a piece of wood, ⅛ by 2 by 4 in. wide, on each side of the carriage. Drill ⅛-in. holes in these pieces for the axle. For the

THE TOY IS PUSHED
BY MEANS OF THE HANDLE,
CAUSING THE HORSE TO WALK.

horse, take a piece of wood, ½ by 4 by 6 in. long, and draw an outline of the head, neck, and body. Cut this out and drill ⅛-in. holes where the legs are attached.

Cut the legs as shown, about 3½ in. long. Attach them with small bolts, or rivets, allowing space enough for the parts to move freely. The wheels are made of pine, ½ in. thick and 3 in. in diameter. The axle is made of ³/₁₆-in. wire bent to the shape indicated, ½ in. at each offset. Fit the wheels on the axle tightly, so as not to turn on it, the axle turning in the pieces nailed to the sides of the carriage. The horse is attached to the top of the carriage by a strip of wood. A 3-ft. wooden handle is attached to the back of carriage to guide it. Wires are attached to the legs, connecting with the offsets in the axle.

— THE FIGHTING ROOSTERS —

The younger child will get a great deal of pleasure and may occupy long periods of time in playing with the toy shown in the photograph. The toy is simple to make and not apt to get out of order easily.

Two roosters are cut out of thin wood or heavy composition board and are painted in the manner illustrated. The feet of the roosters are fastened to a piece of thin spring steel by driving a tack or brad through a hole in the steel into the wood. The spring is then set into a base somewhat like the one shown, the ends being held so that the steel

TWO WOODEN ROOSTERS MOUNTED ON A PIECE OF SPRING STEEL AFFORD A COMICAL AND PERFECTLY SAFE TOY FOR THE AMUSEMENT OF A CHILD.

bends slightly upward in the middle. Finally, a wooden pin is fastened to the middle of the spring by the same method as described above. By pressing on the top of this wooden pin, the roosters are made to swing back and forth, thus giving a pretty good imitation of the belligerent barnyard fowls.

424

— Mechanical Toy Alligator of Wood —

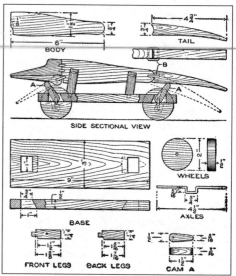

THE ALLIGATOR IS DRAWN ALONG WITH
A STRING, AND THE JAWS AND
TAIL FLIP UP AND DOWN.

A boy, using only a jackknife, can make a toy alligator that opens its mouth and wags its tail as it is pulled along. The various parts, as shown, are cut from soft wood, ½ in. thick. The method of fastening the parts is shown in the side sectional view. When the wheels turn, the cams, A, set on the crank portions of the wheel axles, raise and lower the jaw and tail. The upper jaw is 1 in. wide at the widest part, and 3 in. long. The lower jaw is smaller, and the same length. The body is 6 in. long, and tapering in width from 1½ to ¾ in. The tail is 4¾ in. long, and ¾ in. wide. Holes are drilled in each piece near the edge, at joining points, through which wires are drawn and clamped, as in B. The legs are shown in detail. They are attached to the body by drilling a 1/16-in. hole in each, and a hole though the body, through which the fastenings are passed. The lower ends of the legs are fastened to the base, which is 3 by 9 in. long. Square holes, 1 in. wide, near each end, are provided for the cams A. The axles and wheels are made as shown. The axles fit tightly in the wheels so that the latter can move the axles around with each turn. The axles are made from ⅛-in. wire, bent as shown. They should be long enough, after passing through the bottom, to extend through the wheels on each side.

— TOY DONKEY NODS
AND WAGS ITS TAIL —

The most popular toys are those that move in imitation of some well-known object. The donkey shown in the drawing is a good example of this. The outline is drawn on a ¾-in. block and sawed out with a scroll, band, or coping saw. The head is sawed off, as indicated. A slot is then sawed up through the legs and partway into the body. A similar, but narrower, slot is cut in the back of the head, and a strip of tin is used to connect the head to the body, as shown. A piece of tin, cut to the shape of a tail, is similarly attached in the slot behind. Both the tail and the tin strip that connects the head to the body are pivoted to the latter with small brads. Motion is imparted to the head and tail by wires that connect the parts to a screw eye underneath the wheeled base on which the figure is mounted. Flat strips of wood with rounded edges, attached to the revolving axles, strike the wires as the toy is pulled across a table and cause both head and tail to move up and down. The animal may be decorated as desired.

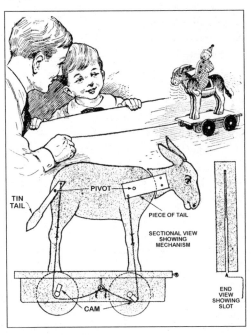

TIN TAIL

PIVOT

PIECE OF TAIL

SECTIONAL VIEW
SHOWING
MECHANISM

CAM

END
VIEW
SHOWING
SLOT

A TOY DONKEY THAT WAGS ITS TAIL AND NODS
ITS HEAD WHEN DRAWN ACROSS A TABLE
HAS A SIMPLE MECHANISM THAT MAKES
IT EASY TO CONSTRUCT.

— A Jumping-Frog Toy —

An entertaining little toy can be made from the wishbone of a fowl after it has been well cleaned and freed from flesh.

Take a piece of strong thin string and double it, tying it securely to opposite sides of the wishbone about 1 in. from the ends, as in the drawing. Cut a strip of wood a little shorter than the bone, and make a circular notch about ½ in. from one end. Push the stick through the doubled string for about half its length, twist the string tightly by means of the stick, then pull the stick through until the notch is reached. From a piece of

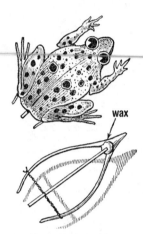

wax

paper or thin cardboard cut out the outline of a frog. Paint it to resemble the animal as nearly as possible, and paste this to one side of the wishbone. The only material now required is a piece of shoemaker's wax, which is placed on the underside of the bone, just where the free end of the stick will rest. When a child wants to make the frog jump, he only needs to push the stick down and press the end into the wax. Place the frog on the table, and after a short while the toy will, all of a sudden, make a very lifelike leap as the end of the stick pulls away from wax.

Incredible Flying Machines

— How to Build Model Airplanes —

The model airplanes illustrated, while they do not exemplify the very best performance or design, nevertheless have proved to be very satisfactory in flight. They also include structural features that make them easy to build. Because of this simplicity of design, they will appeal to the person who likes to build, whether he has the experience in this line or not. He will be able to complete the style of his choice, provided he has the necessary patience and consideration for detail.

Because the "race," *Fig. 1,* the "fly-about," *Fig. 2,* and the "rise-off-ground," *Fig. 9,* are nearly alike, they will be described first. The wings of all three are built up in the same manner, using materials of the same kind, but differing in their dimensions. To build the wings for any of these, two strips of white pine, basswood, or spruce are selected. They should be a trifle over the required length, and planed down to measure exactly ⅛ by ¼ in., and then cut to length. Mark the middle of the strips and drill a ¹⁄₁₆-in. hole through each. In the center of each end of the strips drill a ¹⁄₁₆-in. hole ½ in. deep. Next, cut several strips of tough paper 1 in. wide, coat them with glue, and bind each end and the middle of the spars, wrapping two or three thicknesses of paper around them. This is to prevent splitting. From a piece of soft wire, ¹⁄₁₆ in. in diameter, cut a piece 1 in. longer than the distance between the centers of the spars and bend right angles ½ in. from each end. Flatten the ends of the wires on an anvil or vise, lay the spars flat on a smooth surface, and insert the

short ends of the wires into the holes in the ends of the strips. Force them in as far as they will go, as indicated in *Fig. 5.* When these wires are bent to control the direction of flight they will stay so, because they are soft and because the flattened ends prevent them from moving up and down. This method bends the rear spar a little, but it has proved satisfactory on many models. After the wing frame has been assembled, lay it on a piece of tough paper, mark the outline, and then cut it out. Leaving a ½-in. margin on all sides. Now coat the underside of the frame with glue, place it on the paper, with the margin even all around. Work out the wrinkles, being careful not to bow in the spars. Cut the ends of the paper to fit between the spars, coat them with glue, fold over the wires, and stick to the top side of the paper. After the glue has dried thoroughly, lay the wing on a smooth board and trim off the surplus paper. Punch a hole through the paper binding over the holes in the spars, and give the whole a coat of waterproof varnish to make an exceedingly tough and durable unit.

For the motor bar, cut a piece of pine or spruce, ¼ by ⅜ by 24½ in. Lay it flat, drill a ¹⁄₁₆-in. hole about

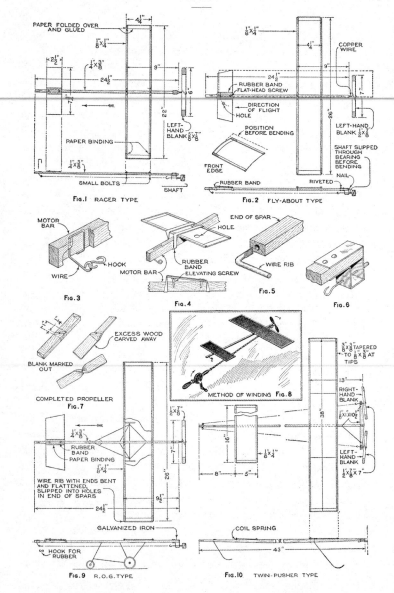

PAPER FOLDED OVER AND GLUED

$\frac{1}{8}'' \times \frac{1}{4}''$

$\frac{1}{4}'' \times \frac{3}{8}''$

$2\frac{1}{2}''$

$24\frac{1}{2}''$

$9''$

$22''$

$6''$

LEFT-HAND BLANK $\frac{5}{8}'' \times 7''$

PAPER BINDING

$\frac{1}{4}'' \times \frac{3}{8}''$

SMALL BOLTS

SHAFT

FIG. 1 RACER TYPE

$\frac{1}{8}'' \times \frac{1}{4}''$

$4\frac{1}{4}''$

COPPER WIRE

$24\frac{1}{2}''$

$9''$

$7''$

$26''$

RUBBER BAND
FLAT-HEAD SCREW

DIRECTION OF FLIGHT
HOLE

POSITION BEFORE BENDING

FRONT EDGE

RUBBER BAND

LEFT-HAND BLANK $\frac{1}{2}'' \times \frac{5}{8}''$

SHAFT SLIPPED THROUGH BEARING BEFORE BENDING

NAIL

RIVETED

FIG. 2 FLY-ABOUT TYPE

MOTOR BAR

HOOK

WIRE

FIG. 3

HOLE

RUBBER BAND

MOTOR BAR

ELEVATING SCREW

FIG. 4

END OF SPAR

WIRE RIB

FIG. 5

FIG. 6

$\frac{1}{2}'' \times \frac{3}{4}''$

EXCESS WOOD CARVED AWAY

BLANK MARKED OUT

COMPLETED PROPELLER
FIG. 7

METHOD OF WINDING FIG. 8

$\frac{1}{4}'' \times \frac{3}{8}''$

RUBBER BAND
PAPER BINDING

$\frac{1}{8}'' \times \frac{1}{4}''$

$\frac{1}{2}'' \times \frac{7}{8}''$

$7''$

$26''$

$24\frac{1}{2}''$

$9\frac{1}{2}''$

WIRE RIB WITH ENDS BENT AND FLATTENED, SLIPPED INTO HOLES IN END OF SPARS

GALVANIZED IRON

HOOK FOR RUBBER

FIG. 9 R.O.G. TYPE

$16''$

$8''$ $5''$

$\frac{1}{8}'' \times \frac{1}{4}''$

$38''$

$\frac{3}{8}'' \times \frac{3}{8}''$ TAPERED TO $\frac{1}{8}'' \times \frac{3}{8}''$ AT TIPS

$13''$

RIGHT-HAND BLANK

$\frac{1}{8}'' \times 1 \times 10\frac{1}{2}''$

LEFT-HAND BLANK

$\frac{1}{2}'' \times \frac{7}{8}'' \times 7''$

COIL SPRING

$43''$

FIG. 10 TWIN-PUSHER TYPE

¾ in. from one end, and another ½ in. from the first. Bend a piece of soft wire as in *Fig. 3,* slip it through the holes, and bend the ends as shown. The propeller bearing on the racer is made from a piece of sheet metal, drilled for the ¹⁄₁₆-in. diameter shaft, and fastened to the bar as shown in *Fig. 6.* It can be bound to the shaft with glued paper, which will, perhaps, be the better way for the beginner. *Fig. 7* shows how to make the propeller. The shaft should be made of wire, bent as shown in *Fig. 1,* and slipped through the hole drilled in the center of the propeller. By indenting the hub a little with the short end of the shaft, the exact position for the extra hole can be found. When this is drilled, slip the shaft through the hub again, pressing the short end into the extra hole. This prevents any chance of the propeller turning on its shaft. Another way is to flatten the end of the shaft and force the widened part into the wood, parallel with the grain.

The elevator, *Fig. 4,* is made of pine or basswood. It is bound in the middle with glued paper, as described for the wing spars and indicated by the shaded section in *Fig. 1.* Plane down the wood to ¹⁄₁₆ in. in thickness, and cut a piece of the proper size; for the racer, it should measure 2½ by 8 in., for the flyabout 2½ by 8½ in., and for the rise-off-ground model 3 by 9 in. Bind the edges with a strip of paper and varnish. The elevator of the racer is not movable but is attached with two roundhead screws to the motor bar. This makes it impossible to alter the angle of the elevator on this model without removing it from the bar. Two or three small washers underneath the forward edge serve to place it at the correct angle. On the flyabout and rise-off-ground models, however, the elevator is adjustable, and is fastened with but one screw near the rear edge. This serves as a pivot. Use a rubber band to hold the elevator down against a flat-headed screw located under the front edge, and keep it straight. To increase or decrease the angle of the elevator, merely turn it to one side, so that the

THE FOUR STYLES OF MODEL AIRPLANES ILLUSTRATED HAVE PROVED SATISFACTORY IN FLIGHT, AND POSSESS FEATURES THAT MAKE THEM EASY TO BUILD. THE LINE OF FLIGHT AND ALTITUDE OF THE MODELS ARE REGULATED BY ADJUSTING THE WINGS AND ELEVATORS. THE DRIVING POWER IS FURNISHED BY RUBBER BANDS.

hole shown in the drawing will come over the screw head. Then, with a small screwdriver, turn the screw in or out as needed, and allow the elevator to return to its normal position. The rubber band also prevents the elevator from breaking by absorbing some of the landing shock.

The rise-off-ground model, *Fig. 9,* is just like the fly-about, except that it has a little more surface than the latter, and the wing is set at an angle large enough to give it a good lift. This is done with small washers or coiled wire of sufficient thickness to raise the front wing spar about ⅛ in. The drawing shows how the landing gear, which consists of three wheels mounted on hard wire, is attached. Make the wheels of cigar-box wood, drill the centers, and use the same size of wire for the axles as for the wire supports. The ends should be looped around the axles. The small front wheel must be a little lower than the others so that the forward end of the motor bar will be higher than the rear when the model is resting on the ground. The diameter of the front wheel is 1½ in., and the larger ones are 2 in. in diameter.

The "twin pusher," *Fig. 10,* is more elaborate than the other three but is not beyond the amateur's abil-ity. Its elevator does not swing, but it is made in exactly the same manner as the other models. This is also true of the wing, except that in this case the spars are ⅜ in. square in the middle, tapered down to ⅛ by ⅜ in. at their tips. Two extra wire ribs are placed 6 in. from the center between the spars. The holes are drilled and the ribs inserted before the paper wing covering is applied. The motor bar is of pine or spruce, ½ by 1 by 43 in., shaped as shown in the drawing. Make the front hook from a 4-in. length of wire, insert it in a small hole drilled near the front of the bar, and bend the loops. The crossbar that takes the bearings should be of ash or other hardwood, and be braced with 1/16-in. hard wire. The bearings are strips of sheet metal, bent to U-shape and riveted to the crossbar. Hard wire is used for the landing skids. The front edge of the wing should be raised about 1/16 in. The elevator is adjustable and is attached to the motor bar by two screws. The front one runs through a small coil spring between the spar and motor bar, and furnishes a means of changing the angle of the elevator.

The power on all these models is furnished by rubber bands, about 3/64 in. thick, 3/16 in. wide, and 4 in.

ABOVE, LEFT: THE "FLY-ABOUT" MODEL SHOWN WITH TWO EXTRA WING RIBS.
CENTER: THE "TWIN-PUSHER" TYPE WITH A CRUISING RADIUS OF FROM 600
    TO 800 FEET.
BELOW, LEFT: THIS VIEW OF THE FLY-ABOUT MODEL SHOWS HOW THE MOTOR
    IS ASSEMBLED.
CENTER: A TINY MODEL COMPARED WITH THE 12-INCH RULE; IT IS DRIVEN
    BY A TWO-INCH PROPELLER.
RIGHT: ONE OF THE MODEL PLANES IN FLIGHT.

long. They should be linked together chain fashion, so that three of the bands will only make a length of 6 in. instead of 12 in. This method allows broken bands to be replaced with new ones quickly and easily.

A wire hook, inserted in the chuck of a hand drill, as shown in *Fig. 8,* will serve as a winder. After linking the bands together on the mold, release the front end of the "motor," and hook it to the drill. Stretch the rubber to about twice its length and turn until about half wound. Then keep turning, but gradually release

the tension so that the rubber will be straight when fully wound, and hook on again. The number of turns needed will be found through experience; the twin model will stand more than 1,000 turns to each propeller, which means that with a gear ratio of 4 to 1 on the drill, the handle will have to be turned 250 times. The two propellers on this model must revolve in opposite directions.

To launch, hold the motor bar with the right hand, just ahead of the wing, and the propeller with the left. Then, with a quick upward push, send the airplane into the air. If it has a tendency to climb too steeply, the elevator should be lowered a little; if it loses altitude, the elevator should be raised enough to correct this fault. With both wingtips flat, the planes will have a tendency to turn to the right. Curving the right wingtip down a little will give a straightaway flight; a left turn can be made by curving the right tip down still more. Several trial flights will probably be necessary before the proper adjustment is obtained.

— A TOY WATER PLANE —

The toy water plane shown in the drawing is something of a novelty in the way of model water craft, as the hull only rests upon the water when the propeller is not revolving. In traveling at full speed, the hull leaves the water quickly and rides with the fins on the surface of the water, as illustrated.

The sides and bottom of the hull are built up from strips of pine, about ⅛ in. thick. Blocks are used to space the sides the proper distance apart and for the attachment of the wooden supports for the propelling mechanism and fins. The sheet-aluminum planes, or fins, are mounted as shown, so that each is tilted at the same angle. The plane is driven by a model-airplane propeller. For a 24-in. water plane, the propeller should be about 7 in. long. The power is derived from a motor made of a number of rubber bands linked together.

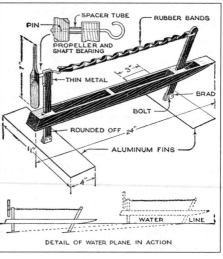

DETAIL OF WATER PLANE IN ACTION

A TOY WATER PLANE THAT RIDES ON THE
SURFACE OF THE WATER WHEN ITS
PROPELLER IS REVOLVING.

— A Simple Aerial Toy —

An interesting little toy that involves no more than a small piece of tin and an empty thread spool can be made in a few minutes. Two small wire brads are driven into one end of the spool, at diametrically opposite points. The heads are clipped off, leaving studs, ¾ in. long. A "whirler" is made from a piece of tin in the form of an airplane propeller, the blades being bent in opposite directions, as indicated. Holes to permit the propeller to make an easy fit on the studs are provided at the proper points. In use, the spool is placed on a shouldered stick, slightly smaller than the hole of the spool.

Then about 4 ft. of strong twine is wrapped around the spool and the propeller is placed on the studs. Holding the spool by its shaft in one hand, the string is given a sharp pull with the other hand, and the propeller flies off into space.

— A Feather Airplane Dart —

Four feathers, a nail, and some string are all the materials needed for making a glider that will fly gracefully through the air for considerable distances.

The feathers are cut and fitted together as shown in the drawing, the nail being placed horizontally in front of the wings, to keep the glider "trimmed."

The feather dart is shot in the same manner as a paper dart, and because

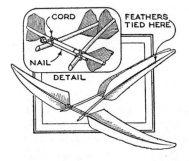

the feathers are stronger, it will last much longer then a paper version.

— How to Make a Model Old-Four Monoplane —

The old-four mono-plane model, made famous by its wonderful flights, is one of the most graceful that has been built. Its large size and slow, even glide make it a much more desirable flier than the ordinary dart-like model. It gives one a true insight into the phe-nomena of heavier-than-air flight. This machine, when complete, should weigh 9 oz. and fly 1,200 ft., rising from the ground under its own power and landing lightly. Its con-

THE MECHANICAL BIRD WILL RUN
ABOUT FIVE FEET ON THE GROUND
AND THEN RISE AND FLY.

struction is simple, and with careful reference to the sketches, an exact reproduction may be made.

For the motor bases, *A, Fig. 1,* secure two spruce sticks, each 48 in. long, ⅜ in. wide, and ¼ in. thick. Fasten a wire hook on one end of each stick with thread wound around after giving it a coat of glue. These hooks are to hold one end of the rubber bands that act as the motive power, and are designated by the letter *B*. At the opposite ends of the

sticks, at *C*, bearings are provided. These consist of blocks of wood, each 1 in long, 1 in. wide, and ⅜ in. thick. These are also bound in place with thread after gluing them. Holes are drilled through the blocks length-wise and then lined with bushings made of brass tubing, ¹⁄₁₆ in. inside diameter. The two motor bases *A* are connected with four cross sticks, *D*, each 9 in. long and ³⁄₁₆ in. square. These are bound and glued on the underside, one near each end and the others equidistant each from the other and from the nearest end stick. The front bumper, *E*, is made of round rattan, ⅛ in. in diameter.

The alighting gear is next in order of construction. This is made, as shown, entirely of bamboo 3/16 in. square. The pieces marked *F* are 11 in. long; *G*, 9½ in. long, and the crossbar *H*, 11 in. long. At the rear, the pieces *J* are 13 in. long; *K*, 4½ in. long, and the crosspiece *L*, 11 in. long. The distance between the points *M* and *N*, *Fig. 2*, is 6 in., and between *O* and *P*, 9 in. The bamboo is easily curved by wetting and holding it for an instant in the flame of a candle. It will hold its shape just as soon as it becomes cold.

The wheels are made of tin, 1½ in. in diameter, borrowed from a toy automobile. The axles are made from wire, 1/16 in. in diameter.

The wing spars *Q* are made of spruce, 3/16 in. wide and ¼ in. thick. Those for the front are 30 in. long, and for the rear, 36 in. long. The ribs *R* are made of bamboo pieces, 1/16 in. square, 5 in. long for the front plane, and 6 in. for the rear. These are bound and glued on top of the spars, 3 in. apart. They are given a slight upward curve. The round ends are made of 1/16-in. rattan.

It is rather difficult to make good propellers, but with a little time and patience they can be shaped and formed into good proportions.

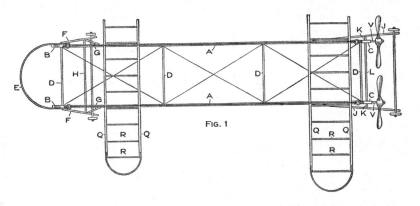

FIG. 1

THE MOTOR BASE IS MADE OF TWO SPRUCE STICKS JOINED TOGETHER WITH FOUR CROSS STICKS, BOUND AND GLUED TO THE UNDERSIDE.

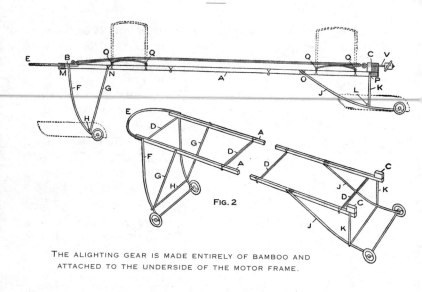

FIG. 2

THE ALIGHTING GEAR IS MADE ENTIRELY OF BAMBOO AND
ATTACHED TO THE UNDERSIDE OF THE MOTOR FRAME.

Procure two clear, straight-grained blocks of white pine, 8 in. long, 1½ in. wide, and ¾ in. thick. Draw a diagonal line on one block from opposite corners as shown in *S, Fig. 3*, then on the other block *T*, draw the line in an opposite direction. Turn the blocks over and draw opposite diagonals, as shown by the dotted lines. Draw a circle on each side exactly on the center, ½ in. in diameter. Drill 1/16-in. holes through the centers of the circles for the propeller shafts. The wood is then cut down to the lines drawn, leaving only enough materials that they will not break easily. The face of the blades should be flat and the back rounded. Leave plenty of stock near the hub. After the faces have been finished, the blades are shaped as shown at *U*. The propellers should be finished with sandpaper to make them perfectly smooth, as much of the success of the model will depend upon them. It is wise to shellac them and also the frame and the alighting gear. Aluminum paint costs but little, and it makes a fine finish for a model aeroplane.

The propeller shafts, *V, Fig. 1, 2, and 4*, are cut from bicycle spokes. An eye for the rubber band is bent in the spoke, about 2 in. from the threaded end. The end having the threads is run through the bearing block, *C, Fig. 4,* and the propeller fastened on with a small washer on each side of it by means of two nuts, *W,* cut from a bicycle nipple. These nuts may be turned up tightly with pliers.

The planes are covered with tissue paper put on tightly over the tops of the ribs, using a flour paste. The planes are movably fixed on the motor bases *A* by tying at the four points of contact with rubber bands. This makes it possible to adjust the fore-and-aft balance of the machine by changing the position of the planes.

The motive power, which is the most important part of the entire machine, consists of rubber bands. There are three ways of obtaining these bands. It is best, if possible, to purchase them from an aeroplane supply house. In this case, procure about 100 ft. of 1/16-in. square rubber, 50 ft. for each side. These are wound closely between the hooks *X*. This rubber can be taken from a golf ball. It will require about

40 strands of this rubber on each propeller. The rubber is removed by cutting into the ball. Another way of obtaining the bands is to purchase No. 19 rubber bands and loop them together, chain-fashion, to make them long enough to reach between the hooks without stretching. About 30 strands on each propeller will be sufficient. The hooks *X* are made in the shape of the letter "S," to provide a way for taking out the rubber bands quickly. To prevent the hooks from cutting the rubber, slip some 1/16-in. rubber tubing over them. The rubber bands, or motor, when not in use, should be kept in a cool, dark place and powdered with

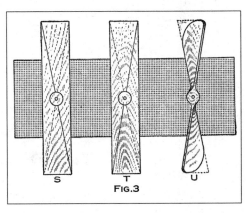

S   T   U
FIG.3

THE MOST DIFFICULT PART OF MAKING
THE PROPELLERS CAN BE OVERCOME
WITH A LITTLE PATIENCE.

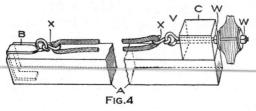

FIG.4

THE MOTIVE POWER, WHICH IS THE MOST
IMPORTANT PART OF THE MACHINE,
CONSISTS OF RUBBER BANDS.

French chalk to prevent the parts from sticking together.

With the model complete, flying is the next thing in order. With a machine as large as this one, quite a field will be necessary to give it a good flight. Test the plane by gliding it, that is, holding it up by the propellers and bearing blocks on a level with your head and throwing it forward on an even keel. Shift the planes forward or back until it balances and comes to the ground lightly.

Winding up the propellers is accomplished by means of an eye inserted in the chuck of an ordinary hand drill. While an assistant grasps the propellers and motor bearings, the rubber is unhooked from the front of the machine and hooked into the eye in the drill. Stretch the rubber out for about 10 ft., and as it is wound up, let it draw back gradually. Wind up the propellers in opposite directions, turning them from 4,000 to 800 revolutions. Be sure to wind both propellers the same number of turns, as this will assure a straight flight.

Set the machine on the ground and release both propellers at once, and at the same time push it forward. If everything is properly constructed and well balanced, the mechanical bird will run about 5 ft. on the ground and then rise to 15 or

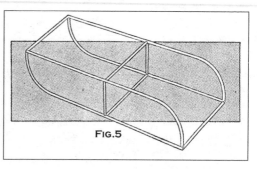

FIG.5

FRAMEWORK FOR CONSTRUCTING PONTOONS
BY COVERING THEM WITH WRITING PAPER
SOAKED IN PARAFFIN.

20 ft. and fly from 800 to 1,200 ft., descending in a long glide and alighting gracefully.

If the machine fails to rise, move the forward plane toward the front. If it climbs up suddenly and hangs in the air and falls back on its tail, move it toward the back.

After the novelty of overland flights has worn off, try flights over the water. To do this the wheels must be removed and four pontoons put in their place as shown by the dotted lines in *Fig. 2.*

Patience is the one thing necessary in model building. Sometimes a machine carefully made will not fly, and no one can make it do so until some seemingly unimportant alteration is made.

TRACTOR PULL

— A TOY FARM TRACTOR —

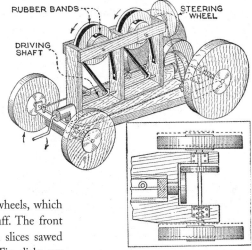

Driven by rubber bands—but in a manner entirely different from that in which model airplanes are operated—the toy tractor illustrated will furnish interesting work for the amateur maker. Most of the wooden parts are of ½-in. whitewood, with the exception of the rear wheels, which are made of ½-in. stuff. The front wheels are made from slices sawed from a curtain pole. Tin disks are fastened on both sides at the center of all wheels, for bearings. The axles are lengths of soft-iron wire, the ends

DRIVEN BY RUBBER BANDS, THIS MODEL TRACTOR WILL FURNISH AN INTERESTING OBJECT FOR THE AMATEUR TOYMAKER'S SKILL.

of which are flattened; the rear axle is also flattened near one end for a part of its length, to prevent the drive disk from turning. Heavy tin is used for the axle bearings. The power from the rubber-band motor is transmitted to the rear wheels by means of friction disks. A small compression-coil spring is placed between the wheel and axle bearing on the side opposite the drive disk, to keep the friction disks in contact. This arrangement also serves as a clutch, allowing the drive disk to run free while the motor is being wound. This is done by pushing the rear axle to the position indicated by the dotted lines in the lower detail. A steering wheel is mounted at the rear of the engine frame, and turns the front wheels by means of cord fastened to the ends of the pivoted

front-axle bearing. In building up the motor, two small disks are fastened to larger ones with small nails, and a short rubber band attached to each small disk and to the frame upright, as shown. A longer rubber band has one end fastened to each of the larger disks, and the other end is fastened to eyes formed on the drive shaft. The disks are then mounted in the motor frame, as shown. After bending the eye in the driving shaft, it is important that the wire on either side be straightened accurately. The winding band should be nearly $1/16$ in. thick, $1/8$ in. wide, and long enough to reach once around the large pulley, and should be used single. The short band should be twice as strong as the former, or it may be of the same size and doubled.

— TOY TRACTOR PROPELLED BY CLOCKWORK —

A powerful toy tractor can be made by mounting the works of an old alarm clock on a small truck. Remove the balance wheel, which leaves four gears besides the mainspring gear. Cut a spool in half and secure it tightly to the shaft from which the hands were

removed, to form the driving pulley. The front-axle support is a block of wood, tightly fitted between the spacing rods that hold the side plates together. The front axle is made from a round stick, and the front wheels are two checkers. The axle is held to the support by a small tin scrap. The rear-axle support is a wood block, cut to fit between the side plates and held by small brads through openings in the plate. The block rests against the bottom of one of the spacing rods and no other fastening is required. Tin straps are used for securing the rear axle, which is ⅜ in. in diameter, to the block. An old spool, cut in half, forms the rear wheels, which are tightly fitted to the axle. To secure traction, small brads are driven into the rim of the wheels and cut off about ⅛ in. from it. The rear wheel on the same side as the drive pulley is grooved to take a string belt, which transmits the energy of the clock mechanism to the wheels.

— A Toy Tractor Built with Dry Cell and Motor —

An ordinary two-volt dry cell, a small motor, and the necessary wooden parts, as shown in the illustration, are all that is needed to make a toy tractor that will give its builder a great deal of fun. A good feature is that the parts can be taken down quickly and use for other purposes when desired. A base, ½ by 3 by 9 in. long, is made of wood, and two axles of the same thickness are set

A BOY CAN MAKE THIS SIMPLE ELECTRIC TRACTOR IN A SHORT TIME, AND WILL GET MUCH FUN OUT OF IT.

under it as shown. The wheels are disks cut from spools, or cut out of thin wood for the rear wheels and heavier wood for the front ones. They are fastened with screws and washers, or with nails. The dry cell is mounted on small strips and held by wires. The motor is fastened with screws and wired to the dry cell in the usual manner. One of the front wheels serves as the driver, and is grooved to receive the cord belt.

MAKING WAVES

— MAKING A TOY WATER "SCOOTER" —

The drawing shows a water "scooter" that can easily be made by the average boy from a few bits of light board, some stiff wire, and a handful of rubber bands. The pontoons are tapered at the stem of the craft and are held the right distance apart by cross strips. The propulsive mechanism of the scooter is mounted overhead. The propeller is the most difficult part to make, and possibly some

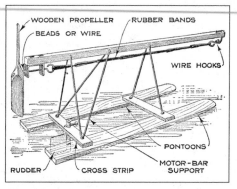

A WATER "SCOOTER" DRIVEN BY A RUBBER-BAND MOTOR, AND THAT CAN BE EASILY MADE FROM LIGHT STRIPS OF WOOD. IT IS CAPABLE OF GOOD SPEED FOR VOYAGES THAT AVERAGE ABOUT 50 FEET.

experimentation will be necessary to get the most effective result. However, the important thing to remember is that it must be balanced accurately and lined up well to ensure smooth running. It is mounted on a wire shaft supported by a tin bracket. But before assembling the propeller in its bearing, a few beads or a few loose turns of wire should be slipped over the shaft, as indicated, to provide clearance. The actual power is furnished by a long rubber strip, or a number of rubber bands looped together. The rubber strip thus obtained being dusted with talcum powder and fastened at one end to the propeller, and at the opposite end to the overhead wooden strip, as shown. Powerful rubber bands can be cut from an old inner tube. If desired, a rudder may be added to the boat so that it can be made to travel in a circle instead of a straight line. Such a scooter, lightly constructed and with a sufficiently powerful rubber-band motor, will travel at good speed for about 50 ft.

— BUILDING MODEL BOAT HULLS —

The amateur naval constructor speedily learns that a boat hull is no simple thing to make, easy though it may look. However, by carving the bow and stern from blocks of wood and using tin or other sheet metal for extending the hull, a very satisfactory piece of work is obtained. After the bow and stern have been completed, they are joined together at the desired distance apart with wooden strips, one at the bottom and one at each side, as shown in the drawing. These strips fit flush into mortises that have been cut in the blocks to receive them. The open space between the stem and stern is closed by tacking a

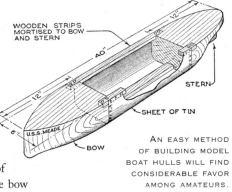

AN EASY METHOD OF BUILDING MODEL BOAT HULLS WILL FIND CONSIDERABLE FAVOR AMONG AMATEURS.

sheet of tin to the strips and wooden ends, with strips of rubber between to make watertight joints. A wooden deck may be provided and, if desired, masts, funnels, gun turrets, and other gear may be added, depending on whether one is building a battleship or a merchantman.

— LIVE BALLAST FOR THE MODEL YACHT —

When the skipper of a racing sailboat goes out for a speed trial he usually carries "live ballast." That is, two or three of his crew shift their weight to the windward side of the boat as may be necessary. This permits him to carry a greater

spread of canvas than would otherwise be possible.

The same effect can be obtained with a model yacht by using the attachment shown. A 1¼-in. length of brass tubing, large enough to slip over the mast, is obtained. A

strip of sheet brass is
bent around the tube
and soldered, the end of
the boom being lashed
between the ends of
the strip. A similar
brass arm, about half
the length of the beam,
or width, of the boat,
is soldered to the tub-
ing exactly opposite the
boom. A ball of lead is
soldered to the outer
end of the second arm.

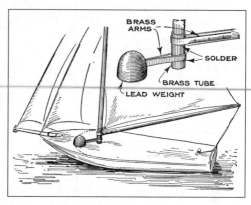

A SIMPLE COUNTERBALANCE APPLIED TO THE
MAINSAIL BOOM OF A MODEL YACHT TAKES
THE PLACE OF "LIVE BALLAST."

When completed,
the tube is slipped over the mast and
several turns of wire are made around
the mast just above it to keep the
boom from working up. The proper
weight for the lead ballast must be
found by testing the boat in water.

The action of the device is simple; when the boom is forced out by
the wind, the ball of lead is swung
out over the windward side, tending
to balance the pressure of the wind
on the sail.

— MODEL PADDLE-WHEEL BOATS —

Only a few boys
have ponds of
their own, in a pasture,
perhaps. But there are
miniature lakes in our
city parks, pools at our
summer camps, and
old water holes in the

woods. If all of these fail, a boy can
still sail his ships on the bathtub

sea. A simple side-wheeler, built
of wood, is shown in the sketch. It

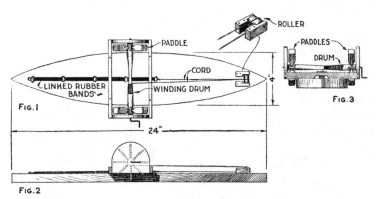

winds up with a crank and runs 15 to 20 ft. A float is made by pointing the ends of a thick board, the dimensions of which are given in *Fig. 1,* the side view, *Fig. 2,* and the end view, *Fig. 3.* It is made of thin wood. A broom-handle section, just long enough to slip into this frame, is whittled to form

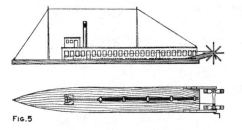

THE STERN-WHEELER IS SIMILAR IN CONSTRUCTION TO THE SIDE-WHEELER AS TO DRIVING MECHANISM.

a winding drum and fitted with paddles, wire axles, and a crank. A second, shorter section of the broom handle, set between blocks nailed to the stern, serves as a roller for the rubber bands. These, linked together and tied to a length of heavy cord, as shown in *Fig. 1,* are fixed to the bow

and run over the roller to the drum. The addition of a top, or lid, of cardboard, wood, or tin, and painted to resemble cabins and pilot house, and fitted with masts and a smokestack, completes the model. *Fig. 5* shows a similarly built stern-wheeler with the stern-wheel shaft set on brackets.

— A Spring-Driven Toy Boat —

A boat that is propelled by springs, and that will furnish much amusement to children, may easily be made from no more elaborate materials than a piece of board, a pair of corset steels or hacksaw blades, and some pieces of tin.

The board is cut to approximately the outline of a boat, and a piece is cut from the stern to accommodate the paddle wheel, the latter being made by inserting pieces of tin into slots cut into a round wooden axle. Staples are used to secure the ends of the axle to the board. The two springs are mounted opposite each other, as shown, and a piece of stout string is attached to the free ends and to each side of the paddle-wheel axle. When the paddle wheel is wound up, the string will draw the springs up in

A SPRING-DRIVEN TOY BOAT THAT USES CORSET STEELS OR HACKSAW BLADES AS THE SOURCE OF POWER CAN BE DRIVEN IN A FORWARD OR BACKWARD DIRECTION, DEPENDING ON HOW IT IS WOUND UP.

arcs as illustrated, and as soon as the wheel is released, the tendency of the springs to resume their horizontal position will revolve the paddle wheel and cause the boat to move forward or backward, depending on which direction the wheel is turned when winding.

— How to Make a "Water Skate" —

A novel little water craft, using a rubber band to furnish power, has a rudder at the stern that is swung from side to side to produce an effect similar to that obtained when a rowboat is culled forward with a single oar at the stern.

A short piece of light board is curved at the front end to form the hull of the boat, and a vertical keel is fastened to the underside. The rudder or, more properly in this case, the propeller is mounted in a bearing fastened to

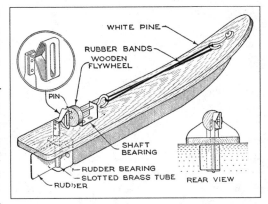

WHITE PINE

RUBBER BANDS
WOODEN
FLYWHEEL

PIN

SHAFT
BEARING

RUDDER BEARING
SLOTTED BRASS TUBE
RUDDER

REAR VIEW

A WATER SKATE IS A TOY BOAT MADE FROM A PIECE OF LIGHT BOARD AND SCULLED FORWARD EXACTLY AS A ROWBOAT IS PROPELLED FROM THE STERN.

the rear end of the keel. The upper end of the rudder is provided with a slotted tiller that is engaged by the crankpin on the wooden flywheel. The method of supporting the flywheel and the shaft to which it is attached as well as the manner in which the rubber-band motor is hooked up are so clearly shown in the drawing that a detailed description is unnecessary. The boat is made ready for operation by turning the flywheel so that the rubber band will be twisted tightly, producing sufficient tension to drive the little craft forward when it is placed in the water.

— SPRING-PROPELLED TOY BOAT —

A length of shade-roller spring forms the motive power for a model side-wheel boat, the hull of which is built along the usual lines for such craft.

The paddle wheels are mounted on a stiff wire shaft on which a cork pulley, about ½ in. in diameter, is forced. The wheel assembly is mounted amidships. The pulley-and-shaft assembly, mounted at the stern, consists of a grooved pulley tacked to the end of a spool, the whole revolving smoothly on a shaft made from a wire nail.

The spring is cut to such a length that, when one end is secured at the stem, the other will reach halfway to the pulley axle at the stern. One end of a stout string is tied to the free end of the spring, the other end being fastened to the spool with a small brad. Power is transmitted to the paddle wheels by means of a string belt.

The craft is "wound up" by turning the paddles backward until the spring has been stretched to double its length. By using two or more pulleys to increase the ratio of revolutions of the paddles to the drive pulley such a boat can be made to develop considerable speed and make quite extended voyages.

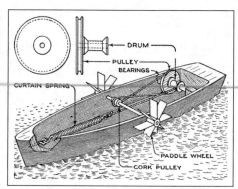

A SPRING-PROPELLED TOY BOAT THAT CAN BE EASILY MADE FOR THE ENTERTAINMENT OF THE CHILDREN. THERE ARE FEW PARTS TO BREAK OR GET OUT OF ORDER.

KEEP IT MOVING

— HOW TO MAKE A CHILD'S ROLLING TOY —

Secure a tin can or a pasteboard box about 2 in. in diameter and 2 in. or more in height. Punch two holes, *A, Fig. 1,* in the cover and the bottom, ¼ in. from the center and opposite each other. Then cut a curved line from one hole to the other, as shown

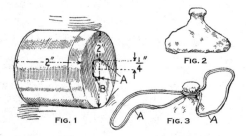

in *B*. A piece of wood, which can be procured from a woodworker, is cut

FIG. 4

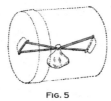

FIG. 5

ROLLING CAN TOY

holes A are turned up, as in *Fig. 4,* and the ends of the bands looped over them. The flaps are then turned down on the band and the can parts put together as in *Fig. 5.* The can may be decorated with brilliant colored stripes, made of paper strips pasted on the tin. When the can is rolled away from you, it winds up the rubber band, thus storing the propelling power that makes it return.

in the shape shown in *Fig. 2,* the size being 1 by 1⅛ by 1¼ in. An ordinary rubber band is secured around the neck of the piece of wood, as shown in *Fig. 3,* allowing the two ends to be free. The pieces of tin between the

— SEMAPHORE SIGNALS FOR TOY RAILWAY —

With only a few simple and easily obtainable materials, a full set of electric semaphore signals can be built for the toy railroad. The semaphore mast is made of wood, while the arm may be of thin wood, cardboard, or metal. The mast is mounted on a small block, as shown. The signal is operated by a solenoid attached to the bottom of the mast with tape or a small metal clamp. The solenoid consists of several yards of bell wire, wound in a coil around a small brass tube. A light cord or thread is attached to the semaphore arm, and a small piece of iron or steel is attached to the opposite end and is

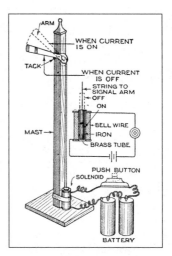

dropped into the hollow core of the solenoid. The string should be just long enough so that when the arm is raised the metal on the string will be drawn entirely inside the coil. By connecting the ends of the coil to a dry battery and pushbutton, the metal weight will be pulled to the bottom and the semaphore arm will fly up in the "clear" position shown by the dotted lines. As soon as the current ceases to flow, the arm will drop into the horizontal, or "danger," position. An automatic block-signal system can be arranged by insulating sections of the track from others and connecting the semaphores to the track circuit so that as soon as the train enters that "block," or section, the signals will operate.

— CHILDREN'S ADJUSTABLE PUSHCYCLE —

Boys between the ages of five and ten years old hate to do "girlish" things, such as riding three-wheeled velocipedes. Their chief ambition is to own a bicycle, which few boys are allowed to do, owing to the dangers of the streets and to the fact that they soon outgrow a bicycle suitable to their age. The pushcycle shown in the drawing will fill the gap and can be readily made from a pair of wheels from an old baby carriage and strips of wood. As shown in the drawing, this cycle has all the features of the regular article with the exception of pedals, chain, and sprockets, the device being pushed

A PUSHCYCLE WILL FURNISH SPORT FOR THE SMALL BOY AND TEACH HIM TO BALANCE, IN ANTICIPATION OF THE DAY WHEN HE WILL OWN A REAL BICYCLE.

along by the feet of the rider. As the owner grows older and larger, the height of the seat is readjusted by removing the bolt at the center and putting it in another hole. For smaller children, the seat is brought nearer the ground in the same manner.

— A Child's Playhouse —

The child's playhouse is an expensive luxury if it is purchased ready to set up. But by following the instructions given herewith a large and inexpensive one may be constructed.

Procure about 100 ft. of 1¾ by 1½-in. boards, and saw out pieces, as shown. It will be much easier to construct using iron corner brackets rather than using mortises, nails, and glue. The frame will also be much stronger.

When the frame is completed, burlap is tacked on to make the covering. The burlap can be purchased cheaply, and the best color to use is green, red, or brown. This material should be fastened on the different sections before they are hinged together. To prevent the burlap from unraveling, turn the edges under before tacking them down.

A piece of wire screen is used for

THE COVERED FRAMEWORK CAN BE USED IN- OR OUTDOORS, AS DESIRED, AND WHEN SET UP AND THE WINGS SWUNG BACK, IT PRESENTS THE APPEARANCE OF A HOUSE.

the door. An old piece will do, if it is well coated with black or dark-green paint. It is then tacked on the inside of the door. Fasten the different parts together with the hinges. The hinges are fastened on the inside of

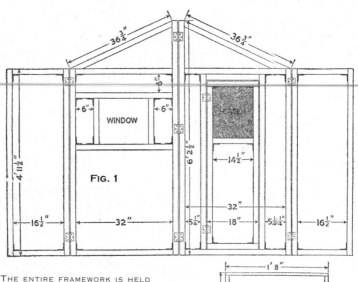

WINDOW

FIG. 1

THE ENTIRE FRAMEWORK IS HELD
TOGETHER WITH BRACKETS AND IS
HINGED AT THE JOINTS SO IT CAN
BE FOLDED UP AND PUT INTO A
SMALL SPACE. THE SECTIONS ARE
COVERED WITH COLORED BURLAP
TO MAKE THEM APPEAR SOLID. ON
THE RIGHT IS SHOWN THE AWNING-
FRAME CONSTRUCTION.

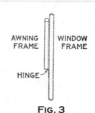

the side wings and on the outside of
the two front pieces. With the hinges
placed in this manner, the house can
be folded into a small space.

For the one built for this article,
green burlap was used. By trimming
the door and window frames along
the edges with white paint, a very
pretty effect was produced.

A small awning was made over
the window, which improved the
appearance very much. Roller shades
on the door and window, and an
electric doorbell, completed a very
neat and practical playhouse.

— HOMEMADE TOY BANK —

The little bank illustrated is not exactly burglar-proof, but once put together it cannot be opened except by the destruction of one of the units of which it is composed. It requires but little skill to

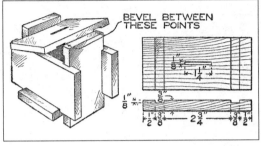

SIX PIECES OF WOOD AS THEY ARE PUT TOGETHER TO FORM A TOY BANK.

make, and would be a good problem for manual training, as it offers an excellent opportunity for teaching certain rudiments of woodworking by the application method.

Its construction requires six pieces of hardwood of the dimensions shown in the sketch. White wood will do if there is no hardwood at hand. The coin slot is ⅛ in. wide by 1¼ in. long, and is cut in only one piece.

The first five pieces should be easy to put together, but the sixth, or top, piece shown in the sketch, will not go in, because the bottom edge of the raised side will strike the inside of the piece to the right. By beveling this edge with a chisel from top to bottom between the dadoes, or grooves, it can be forced down quite a distance. It can be sprung in place by placing a block of wood on the high side and striking it a sharp blow with a heavy hammer.

— HOW TO MAKE A MINIATURE WINDMILL —

The following description outlines how a miniature windmill is made. This will produce considerable power for its size, even in a light breeze. Its smaller parts, such as blades and pulleys, were constructed of 1-in. sugar pine on account of its softness.

The eight blades were made from pieces 1 by 1½ by 12 in. Two opposite edges were cut away until the blade was about ⅛ in. thick. Two

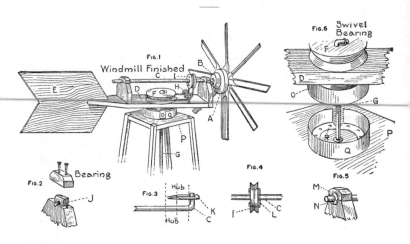

FIG.1
Windmill Finished

DETAILS OF MINIATURE WINDMILL CONSTRUCTION

inches were left uncut at the hub end. They were then nailed to the circular face plate, *A, Fig. 1*, which is 6 in. in diameter and 1 in. thick. The center of the hub was lengthened by the wooden disk, *B, Fig. 1*, which was nailed to the face plate. The shaft, *C, Fig. 1*, was ¼-in. iron rod, 2 ft. long, and turned in the bearings detailed in *Fig. 2. J* was a nut from a wagon bolt and was placed in the bearing to ensure easy running. The bearing blocks were 3 in. wide, 1 in. thick and 3 in. high without the upper half. Both bearings were made in this manner.

The shaft *C* was keyed to the hub of the wheel by the method shown in *Fig. 3*. A staple, *K*, held the shaft from revolving in the hub. This method was also applied in keying the 5-in. pulley, *F*, to the shaft, *G, Fig. 1*, which extended to the ground. The 2½-in. pulley, *I, Fig. 1*, was keyed to shaft *C*, as shown in *Fig. 4*. The wire, *L*, was put through the hole in the axle and the two ends curved so as to pass through the two holes in the pulley. They were then given a final bend to keep the pulley in place. The method by which the shaft *C* was kept from working forward is shown in *Fig. 5*. The washer, *M*, intervened between the bearing block and the wire *N*, which was passed through the axle and then bent to prevent its falling out. Two washers were placed on shaft *C*, between the forward bearing and the hub of the wheel to lessen the friction.

The bed plate, *D, Fig. 1*, was 2 ft. long, 3 in. wide, and 1 in. thick and was tapered from the rear bearing to the slot in which the fan, *E*, was nailed. This fan was made of ¼-in. pine 18 by 12 in., and was cut to the shape shown.

The two small iron pulleys with screw bases, *H, Fig. 1*, were obtained for a small sum from a hardware dealer. Their diameters were 1¼ in. The belt that transferred the power from shaft *C* to shaft *G* was top string, with a section of rubber in it to take up slack. A rubber band was placed in the grooves of each of the two wooden pulleys to prevent it from slipping.

The point for the swivel bearing was determined by balancing the bed plate, with all parts in place, across the thin edge of a board. There, a ¼-in. hole was bored in which shaft *G* turned. To lessen the friction, washers were placed under pulley *F*. The swivel bearing was made from two lids of baking-powder cans. A section was cut out of one to permit its being enlarged enough to admit the other. The smaller one, *O, Fig. 6*, was nailed top down, with the sharp edge to the underside of the bed plate, so that the ¼-in. hole for the shaft *G* was in the center. The other lid, *G*, was tacked, top down also, in the center of the board *P*. The lid was attached with brass-headed furniture tacks, *R, Fig. 6*, which acted as a smooth surface for the other tin to revolve upon. Holes for shaft *G* were cut through both lids. Shaft *G* was only ¼ in. in diameter, but to keep it from rubbing against the board *P*, a ½-in. hole was bored for it, through the latter.

The tower was made of four 1-by-1-in. strips, 25 ft. long. They converged from points on the ground forming an 8-ft. square to the board, *P*, at the top of the tower. This board was 12 in. square and the corners were notched to admit the strips as shown, *Fig. 1*. Laths were nailed diagonally between the strips to strengthen the tower laterally. Each strip was screwed to a stake in the ground so that by disconnecting two of them the other two could be used as hinges and the tower could be tipped over and lowered to the ground. This is necessary in certain instances as, for instance, when the windmill needs oiling. Bearings for the shaft *G* were placed 5 ft. apart in the tower. The power was put to various uses.

— DECORATIVE TOYS AND BOXES MADE AT HOME —

Homemade toys and gifts, as well as the "treasure boxes" in which they are contained, have an added interest both to the one making and the one receiving them. The holiday season makes this work especially attractive, which affords opportunity for individuality in construction and design limited only by the skill of the worker. The decorated toys and the box described in detail in this article are suggestive only, and may be adapted to a large variety of forms and designs. The gorgeously colored parrot and the gaily caparisoned rider and horse suggest a host of bird and animal forms, those having possibilities for attractive coloring being most desirable. The decorated box shown in *Fig. 7* may be adapted as a gift box, to be used where its decoration may be seen, as in a nursery. It can be made in forms as varied as cardboard boxes are. Plant, animal, or geometrical forms may be used to work out designs, and appropriate color schemes applied to them. A

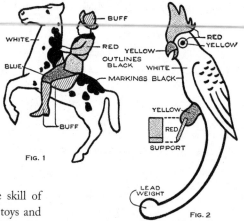

THE OUTLINES FOR THE HORSE AND RIDER AND THE PARROT MAY BE MADE BY ENLARGING THESE SKETCHES. THE COLOR SCHEME INDICATED IS SUGGESTIVE ONLY AND MAY BE VARIED TO SUIT INDIVIDUAL TASTE.

good plan in determining a color scheme is to use the colors of the flower or other motif. If the design is not associated with objects having varied colors—a geometrical design, for instance—harmonious colors should be chosen. These may be bright and contrasting, such as red and green, and violet and orange, or they can be more subdued in tone.

A brightly colored design for a horse and rider is shown in *Fig. 1.* The form is cut out of thin wood and the color applied. The painted figure is mounted on the curved wire, weighted at one end, as shown in *Fig. 6.* The toy adds a touch of novelty to a room when suspended from the corner of a mantel, a shelf, or other suitable place. Balanced in a striking attitude, forefeet upraised, even grown-ups can hardly resist tipping the rider to see his mount rear still higher. The parrot shown in *Fig. 2* is made similarly and is weighted at the end of its tail. The point of balance is at the feet, which

may be fastened to a trapeze, or can be arranged to perch on a convenient place, like that suited to the horse and rider.

The tools and equipment necessary for the making of such toys are simple and are generally available in most boys' workshops or tool chests. A coping saw, like that shown in *A, Fig. 3,* is suitable for cutting the wood. A fretsaw, operated by hand, foot, or power, may be used. Such a tool makes this work proceed rapidly. To use the coping saw to the best advantage, particularly if the work is to be done on a table that must not be marred, a sawing board should

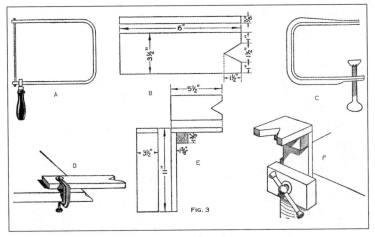

THE TOOLS REQUIRED ARE FOUND IN MOST BOYS' WORKSHOPS, AND A SATISFACTORY SAW TABLE MAY BE MADE EASILY, AS SHOWN IN DETAIL.

be made. In its simplest form, this consists of a board as shown in *B*, about ⅞ in thick, 3½ in. wide, and 6 in. long, with one end notched. This is clamped to the end of the table, as in *D*, with a clamp. An iron clamp of the type shown in *C* is best. Another form of sawing table, especially useful when the woodworker wants to stand up at the work, is shown in *E* in detail, and clamped in the vise in *F*. It consists of a notched board, 3½ in. wide, fixed at right angles to a board of similar width, 11 in. long, and braced at the joint with a block about 1⅜ in. square. In using the coping saw with either of these saw tables, the wood is held down on the support, as shown in *Fig. 5*. The saw is drawn downward for each cutting stroke, thus tending to hold the board more firmly against the saw table. It is, of course, important that the saw be inserted in the coping-saw frame with the teeth pointing toward the handle so that the method of cutting described may be followed. The wood must be sawed slowly, especially at the beginning of a cut. The operator soon learns the kinks in handling the saw and wood to the best advantage and can then make rapid progress.

An outline drawing of the form to be cut out of the wood must first be made to the exact size the object is to be. It can be very satisfying to work out the form of the animal or other figure, especially for the boy or girl who has the time necessary to do good work. If desired, the figure may be traced from a picture taken from a

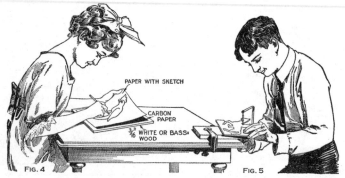

THE DESIGN IS TRACED CAREFULLY ONTO THE WOOD
AND THEN CUT OUT WITH THE COPING SAW, ON THE SAW TABLE.

book, magazine, or other source. Cut a piece of wood to the size required for the design and place a sheet of carbon paper over it. Or if none is available, rub a sheet of paper with a soft pencil, and use this as a carbon paper, the side covered with the lead being placed on the surface of the wood. The carbon paper and the sheet bearing the design should then be held in place on the wood with thumbtacks or pins, and the transfer made with a pencil, as shown in *Fig. 4.* The design should be placed on the wood so that the weaker parts, such as the legs of the horse, will extend with the length instead of across the grain of the wood.

In some instances, where a complicated form is cut out, it is necessary to use wood of several plies. Where this type of wood is available it is worthwhile to use it for all of this work. For smaller objects, wood 3/16 in. thick is suitable, and stock up to ½ in. in thickness may be used. Whitewood, basswood, poplar, and other soft, smooth-grained woods are suitable.

When the design has been satisfactorily outlined, place the piece of wood on the saw table with the design on the upper side. Holding the wood down firmly, as shown in *Fig. 5,* and sawing in the notch of the saw table, cut into the edge slowly. Apply light pressure on the downstroke only, as the upstroke is not intended to cut. Turn the piece to keep the saw on the line and in the notch. It is important that the saw be held vertically so that the edge of the cutout portion will be square. With proper care and a little practice, the edges may be cut so smoothly that only a light sandpapering will be required to produce a smooth edge. When the figure has been cut out, smooth the edges by trimming them carefully with a sharp knife, if necessary. Sandpaper them lightly to remove sharp corners. A fine sandpaper, about No. 1/2, is suitable for this purpose. The figure is then ready for painting. The white is put on first and, when dry, the other colors applied over it.

Oil paints may be used, and a varnish or shellac applied over them to give a high-grade appearance. But this process requires much care, considerable skill, and long drying time between coats to prevent "runs" in the colors.

Watercolor paint, which can be purchased in powder form at paint stores and mixed with water to the consistency of cream, is a satisfactory coloring material and is easy to apply. A small amount of each of the colors used—yellow, red, blue, black, and white—will be sufficient for several toys. Mix each color in a separate saucer and use a small watercolor brush to apply the paint. In painting the horse and rider, the horse is first painted entirely white, and then the black spots are applied after the color is dry. The rider's coat is painted red; the trousers blue; the hat and leggings buff, as indicated in *Fig. 1*. For buff, mix a brushful of yellow with a brushful of red and add about three brushfuls of white. A half brushful of black may be added to dull the color, if desired. The flesh tone for the rider's face is made by mixing a little red with white. When the colors are dry, all edges are outlined with a heavy line of black, not less than ⅛ in. in width. This outline may be evenly applied with the point of the brush.

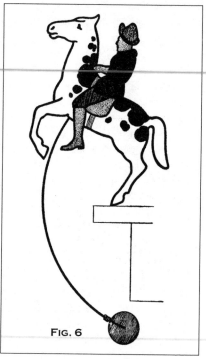

FIG. 6

The method of making the parrot is similar to that described for the horse and rider, and the color scheme is suggested in *Fig. 2*.

It should be obvious that no attempt is made to secure a lifelike, or realistic effect in painting these toy shapes. All colors are flat, that is, without light and shade. The toys are really decorative designs, and the maker is at liberty to use any colors desired, whether natural or not.

The horse and rider construction is balanced on the hind foot, as shown in *Fig. 6*, by attaching a lead weight to a 1/16-in. wire as a counterweight. The wire should be set into the body of the horse, behind the foreleg, to a depth of ¾ in. The weight of the metal and the curve of the wire should be adjusted to obtain the proper balance. The parrot is balanced in the same way, except that the weight is fixed to the end of the tail, which is curved like the wire.

These and other homemade toys or gifts may be sent or contained appropriately in boxes decorated to match them. They may be made complete, or commercial boxes of suitable sizes may be covered and decorated. If good materials are used, such a box makes a pretty and useful gift in itself. The complete process of making a typical box is described for those who prefer to make one of special size. The dimensions given are thus only suggestive and may be adapted to suit particular needs.

The materials necessary are: cardboard, cover paper, lining paper, bond paper, paste, and watercolors. The latter should be of the opaque variety, since white or other light shades may then be used on darker-colored paper. A sharp knife, a scissors, a metal-edge ruler, and bookbinder's paste are also needed. Suitable substitutes for the various kinds of paper may usually be obtained in the home, if they are not readily available at local stationery stores or printing establishments.

The box is made as follows: Decide on the proper size and select cardboard and colored paper to use as cover material to carry out the design. Cut out a square of the cardboard, with sides 12½ in. long, as shown in G. Then mark it as indicated and cut on the full line to remove the square corners. Crease it on the dotted lines and fold to form a box. To hold the cardboard in box shape, strips of bond paper—ordinary writing paper—are cut, 3¾ in. long and 1 in. wide, then creased along their centers and pasted to the corners. The paste should be applied to the paper strip first, then on the corners of the box. Apply the piece of paper over the corner of the box on the outside, pressing it to make a snug fit. Repeat this operation on the other corners.

Lay off the dimensions given on the selected color of cover paper—which will be the background color for your design—and score the lines indicated. Spread paste smoothly over the surface of the colored paper, between the lines drawn ⅜ in. from the long edges, and then spread a thin layer of paste over the outer surface of one of the sides of the box. Apply the paper to the pasted surface and press it down, rubbing

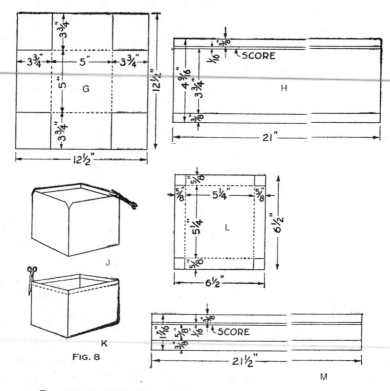

THE VARIOUS STEPS IN THE PROCESS OF MAKING AND COVERING A
RECTANGULAR CARDBOARD BOX ARE SHOWN IN DETAIL. THE METHOD
OF MAKING A PATTERN FOR THE DESIGN IS SHOWN ABOVE.

gently out from the center to remove air bubbles. Fold the ⅜-in. laps at the top and bottom over the upper edge of the box and around the lower corner. Repeat this process, covering the four sides. To form a smooth fold at the corners, it is best to miter the paper as shown at *J* and *K*, before pasting it down. Then paste a square of the same paper 4⅞ in. wide on the bottom of the box, taking care to match the edges evenly all around.

Line the box with a strip of lining paper, 20 in. long and 4 in. wide. Try the lining by folding it into the box so that its upper edge is about ⅛ in. from the edge of the box, and crease it carefully into the corners. Remove it, apply paste, and press it well into the corners when pasting it down. Paste a square of the same paper, 4⅞ in. wide, in the bottom of the box.

The cover is made by the same process as the main portion of the box. The dimensions of the cardboard are shown in *L,* and the covering in *M.* Notice that the cover is slightly wider than the box, so that it will fit easily.

When the box is thoroughly dry, it is ready to receive decorations on the top and sides. The design may be created in different colored papers and adapted from a leaf, flower, or similar form, as well as from geometric or animal forms.

— MINIATURE METAL-BOUND CHESTS —

Boys in shop class became very enthusiastic over the making of small chestlike boxes, bound with ornamental metal, and adapted them to a great variety of uses. The boxes were designed to suit the taste of the maker and for use as glove, handkerchief, jewelry, treasure, and other boxes. The boxes were lined with silk and finished in wax and varnish, in various stains. Oak was used for most of these, and the metals employed were largely copper and brass, although silver is suitable for small boxes. They are simple in construction, as shown in the working drawings, and can be made in the home workshop. The photograph reproduced shows a group of boxes, for various purposes, and in several styles of metal binding. The long box at the top is for gloves or ties; the larger ones are for boys' personal use, caring for collars, handkerchiefs, etc.; the smaller boxes are for the dresser, providing a place for jewelry and similar small articles. The boxes proved great favorites as gifts, and the monogram of the recipient may be etched into the metal.

Well-seasoned oak is the most suitable material for the making of the boxes, as it harmonizes well with the plain metal trimmings. The quarter-sawn variety is preferable, being more ornamental and less

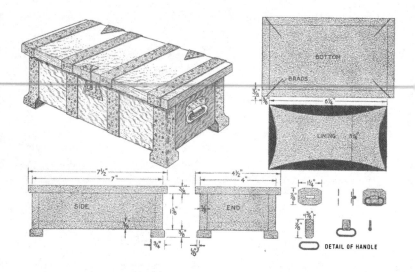

THE CONSTRUCTION OF THE JEWELRY BOX IS TYPICAL OF THE OTHERS.
THE HANDLE IS SHOWN IN DETAIL. THE NAILING OF THE BOTTOM
AND THE FITTING OF THE LINING ARE SHOWN AT THE RIGHT.

likely to warp or twist. For most of the boxes, stock ⅜ in. thick is suitable, although this may be cut down to 5/16 in. for the smaller boxes, if convenient. The method of joining the pieces is similar in all the varieties of boxes, and the jewel box illustrated in the working drawings will be taken as a specimen. The sides of box are butted against the ends, lapping over them, flush, and nailed with small brads. The bottom is fitted between the sides and ends, and nailed so that the nails are concealed by the metal bands at the four corners and at other points, if bands are placed near the middle. The stock for the box is cut and finished on all sides to the following dimensions: all pieces to be ⅜ in. thick, top, 4½ by 7½ in.; two sides, 1⅞ by 7 in.; two ends, 1⅞ by 4 in.; bottom, 3¼ by 6¼ in.

All the pieces should be scraped carefully to a smooth finish. Nails should be started with an awl or a slightly flattened nail of the same size, fitted into a hand drill. Extreme care must taken in nailing to ensure that the surface of the wood is not marred. Damage is likely to occur if the nails are driven into the wood too rapidly or without guide holes. The feet are cut from a strip, ⅜ in. thick and ¾ in. wide, the cut edges being sandpapered smooth without destroying the squareness of the sharp corners. They are nailed to the bottom of the box with brads, care being taken to have the end grain of each block at the end of the box—particularly if the metal trimmings do not cover the blocks.

The cover is fixed in place with small plain butts. The butts are countersunk into the wood, one leaf into the top and the other into the back of the box. A simpler method is to set both leaves of the hinge into the edge of the back. Care must be taken in fitting the hinges so that they are set in line with the back of the box. Holes should be made for the screws before driving them into place. Excessive care should be taken with the fitting of the hinges, because the proper fitting of the lid—both as to resting level and being in line with the edges of the box—depends on the fitting of the hinges.

After the construction work and nailing are completed, the box may be sandpapered carefully. Sand in the direction of the grain and be careful not to round off the edges. Excessive sanding of the woodwork marks the work of the careless novice. The box should be handled as little as possible while the metal trimmings are being fitted and, before the finish is applied, should be sanded lightly to remove dirt. When the metal pieces are fitted and ready to be fastened in place, the finish may be applied to the box. Warm browns or other dark oak finishes are best suited to the simple style of chest and the metal fittings. A coat of stain should be applied and followed, when dry, with a coat of filler, rubbed well into the pores of the wood. The filler should be permitted to dry hard, and the surface then sanded very lightly with a fine grade of paper—No. 00 is best. Do not rub through the filler or stain, particularly at the corners. Wax is the most commonly applied outer finish. Several coats may be used to give a substantial finish. For a high-gloss finish, apply a coat of shellac followed by coats of rubbing varnish. Allow each coat to dry well and sand between coats with No. 00 sandpaper. This is a more involved process and requires that the varnish be rubbed down with pumice stone and water and finished with an oil polish.

No. 20 gauge or lighter copper or brass is suitable for the trimmings. The details of the handles are shown in the sketch. Cut a back plate, ⅞ in. by 1¼ in., and fit the handle of wire to it by means of a strap bent from a strip of metal, ⅜ in. by ⅞ in. The other bands are merely strips, ½ to ¾ in. in width and fitted to the size of the box, where applied. Strap hinges of the same metal may be made, but the most convenient method for the amateur is to fit the metal strips into place at the hinges merely as ornamental features. Various types of locks may be fitted to the box. For the worker who has the skill, a hasp can be a very interesting feature, as indicated in the sketch.

The designing and making of the metal trimmings affords unlimited opportunity for originality. It's wise to test-fit the desired strips cut from paper before making them of metal. Also keep in mind that the simple bands and forms are better suited to the plain box than ornate trimmings. Having decided upon suitable patterns for the metal strips, cut them from the sheet with snips or tinner's shears, being careful to produce a smooth edge. A file may be used to smooth and round the edges of the metal slightly. The metal is fastened with escutcheon pins, which add to the ornamental effect if properly spaced. Holes for them must be drilled or punched through the metal.

The metal may be left smooth and polished or hammered with the round end of a ball-peen hammer to produce the dented effect shown on several of the boxes in the group. This, as well as other finishing of the metal, must be done before it is fixed in place. Beautiful colors may be given to the metal by heating it and observing the colors as they "run." A trial will enable one to judge the proper heat for the various colors, which "run" from a light straw to a deep purple, with various reddish intermediate tones. A brown oxidized finish, or a verd-antique—greenish—finish may also be obtained. The metal should be polished with wax to preserve the finish if other than the latter type is used.

The boxes are lined with silk or other suitable material. The method is as follows: Cut cardboard pieces to fit against the inner sides of the bottom, sides, and ends. Pad one side of them with cotton batting, and cover with silk, gluing the edges of it on the back of the cardboard, as shown in the sketch. By bending the pieces slightly, they may be inserted and glued in place. Be careful in handling the glue that the silk is not soiled. Pads of felt, or chamois skin, may be glued to the bottom of the feet of the box to ensure that the box does not mar the surface upon which it rests.

The most popular boxes, which are especially suitable for gift purposes, are the jewelry, glove, and handkerchief boxes. Their dimensions are: jewelry box, 2¾ by 4 by 7½ in.; glove box, 3¼ by 5 by 13 in.; handkerchief box, 4 by 6 by 10 in. Other sizes suited to special purposes may, of course, be readily designed. They can be made in walnut, mahogany, or other cabinet woods.

JUST *for* FUN

— A WHIRLIGIG CLAPPER —

A good noisemaker for Halloween—or any other occasion—can be made by carefully following the directions given here. The box is the first thing to make. It is constructed of wood pieces, ½ in. thick, and consists of two ends and two sides. The ends are each 1½ in. square and the sides 1½ in. wide and 6 in.

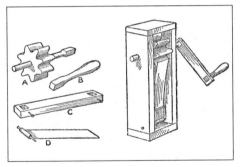

DETAIL OF THE PARTS AND HOW THEY ARE ASSEMBLED TO MAKE THIS CLAPPER.

long. These parts are nailed together with the ends lapping the sides.

The ratchet wheel *A* is a disk of hardwood, 1½ in. in diameter. Its rim is divided into eight equal parts and notched with a knife as shown.

It is placed in the forward end of the box on a wood axle of ⅜-in. diameter to which it is glued. One end of this axle is squared and projects 1 in. beyond the side of the box. The squared end passes through a square hole in the end of the crank *C*, which is a piece of wood ¾ in. thick, 1 in. wide and 4 in. long, and is fastened with brads and glue. At the other end of the crank, a similar hole connects with a handle whittled to the shape shown in *B*.

A flat piece of steel spring, ½ in. wide and long enough to reach from the rear end of the box to the teeth of the ratchet wheel, is shaped as shown in *D*. The spring may be made from a stiff piece of corset steel or bicycle trousers guard. The spring is fastened with a nail through the end and box sides and a second nail passes through the sides over the spring, about 2 in. forward of the first nail. This is to give the spring tension on the teeth.

To operate the clapper, allow it to hang straight down. The right hand grasps the handle and whirls the box in a circle around to the left.

— Making and Using the "Bandilore" —

An East Indian toy, known as a "bandilore," is made from a piece of spool, about ½ or ¾ in. thick, and two tin disks, about 4 in. in diameter.

The section of spool is tacked between the two disks, exactly in the center. Tie one end of a 3- or 4-ft. length of stout cord to the spool. The bandilore is operated by winding the cord around the spool and holding the free end of the string in the hand. The toy is dropped and descends with great speed; just before the end of the cord is reached, the whole thing is given a quick upward jerk. This increases the speed and momentum of the disks so that the

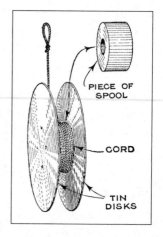

PIECE OF SPOOL

CORD

TIN DISKS

cord is wound in the opposite direction, and the bandilore climbs upward, the process being repeated as often as desired.

— A Perpetual Whirligig —

Camphor is the motive power that drives the device shown in the illustration. It will cause the whirligig to revolve for several days, or until the camphor is consumed.

The whirligig is made of a piece of cork, ½ in square, with a needle stuck into each of its four sides. Smaller pieces of cork, to which pieces of camphor have been attached with sealing wax, are stuck on the ends of the needles. Take care to keep the needles and cork free from oil or grease, because this will retard their movement. As soon as the device is placed in a dish of water it will start whirling and continue to do so as long as motive power is supplied. A small flag or other ornament may be attached to the center cork.

— ❖ ❖ ❖ —

FUN *for* OLDER KIDS

—

CLEVER AMUSEMENTS

— JUMPING TOYS FROM MAGAZINE PICTURES —

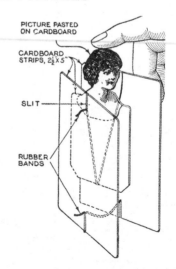

PICTURE PASTED ON CARDBOARD

CARDBOARD STRIPS, 2½"X 5"

SLIT

RUBBER BANDS

Jumping jacks without boxes will provide endless entertainment for the juvenile members of the household. These can be made from no more elaborate materials than a few strips of pasteboard and some rubber bands. Three strips of stiff cardboard, of uniform size, are required to make one of the toys. Two of the strips are placed together and slits, about ½ in. deep, are cut in both ends, as shown in the drawing. Two long rubber bands are required. These are cut open at one end and the ends are inserted in the slits of the opposite cards, as shown. Only one rubber band is used at a time, the other one being provided in case the first breaks. This will allow the toy to be turned upside down and used without interruption. The third card has a suitable picture pasted at one end, and the cardboard is cut away around the edges of the picture. Hold the toy in the hand and insert the strip containing the picture at the top. Press down against the rubber band in the manner indicated. When the pressure of the hand is relieved, the tension of the rubber band causes it to jump out above the upper edge of the strips.

— A Toothpick "Popper" —

This particular "popper" is made from six toothpicks and is entirely harmless. The toothpicks are arranged as shown in the drawing. The center slivers put the others under considerable tension, and at the same time hold them together. To "touch off" this popper, it is held in the hand, and one corner lit with a match. As the corner ends are weakened by the flame, the toothpicks will fly apart with considerable force. The experiment should be per-

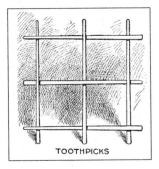

TOOTHPICKS

formed only in a place where there is no danger of fire, and the "popper" artist should be careful of his eyes.

— How to Make Paper Balloons —

This project involves using flammable materials to create a miniature hot-air balloon, and because of the danger of fire, the balloon should be ignited and flown only under the supervision of adults and with the appropriate safety precautions including a fire extinguisher. The balloon should be flown only over water.

This type of balloon, made spherical or designed like the regular aeronaut's hot-air balloon, are the best kind to make. Those having an odd or unusual shape will not make good ascensions, and in most cases, the paper will catch fire from the torch and burn before they have flown very far. The following description is for making a tissue-paper balloon about 6 ft. high.

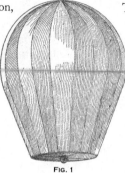

FIG. 1

PAPER BALLOON.

The bottom of the gore is one-third the width of the widest point. The dimensions and shape of each gore are shown in *Fig. 2.*

The balloon is made up of 13 gores pasted together, using about ½-in. lap on the edges. Any good paste will do—one that is made up of a well-cooked mixture of flour and water will serve the

The paper may be selected in several colors. The gores cut from these and pasted in alternately will produce a pretty array of colors when the balloon is in flight. The shape of a good balloon is shown in *Fig. 1.* The gores for a 6-ft. balloon should be about 8 ft. long or about one-third longer than the height of the balloon. The widest part of each gore is 16 in. The widest place should be 53½ in. from the bottom end, or a little over halfway from the bottom to the top.

purpose. If the gores have been put together correctly, the pointed ends

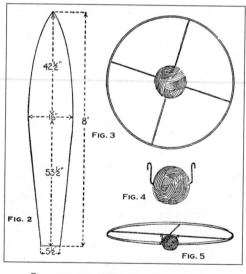

PATTERN AND PARTS TO MAKE BALLOON.

will close up the top entirely and the wider bottom ends will leave an opening about 20 in. in diameter. A light wood hoop having the same diameter as the opening is pasted to the bottom end of the gores. Two cross wires are fastened to the hoop, as shown in *Fig. 3*. These are to hold the wick ball, *Fig. 4*, so that it will hang as shown in *Fig. 5*. The wick ball is made by winding wicking around a wire, with the wire ends bent into hooks as shown.

The balloon is filled with hot air in a manner similar to that used with the ordinary cloth balloon. A small trench or fireplace is made of brick with a chimney over which the mouth of the paper balloon is placed. Use fuel that will make heat with very little smoke. Hold the balloon so it will not catch fire from the flames coming out of the chimney. Have some alcohol ready to pour on the wick ball, saturating it thoroughly. When the balloon is filled with hot air, carry it away from the fireplace, attach the wick ball to the cross wires, and light it under the supervision of an adult.

In starting the balloon on its flight, take care that it leaves the ground as nearly upright as possible.

— HOW TO MAKE A FLUTTER RING —

The flutter ring is for enclosing in an envelope and to surprise the person opening it by the revolving of the ring. The main part is made of a piece of

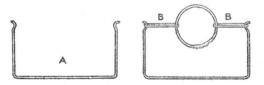

THE SHAPE OF THE WIRE AND MANNER OF ATTACHING THE RUBBER BANDS TO THE RING.

wire, *A,* bent so that the depth will be about 2 in. and the length 4 in. Procure or make a ring 2 in. in diameter. The ring should be open like key ring. Use two rubber bands, *BB,* in connecting the ring to the wire.

To use it, turn the ring over repeatedly until the rubber bands are twisted tightly, and then lay it flat in a paper folded like a letter. Hand it to someone in this shape or after first putting it into an envelope. When the paper is opened up, the ring will do the rest.

— PAPER CUBES THAT "PUFF UP" —

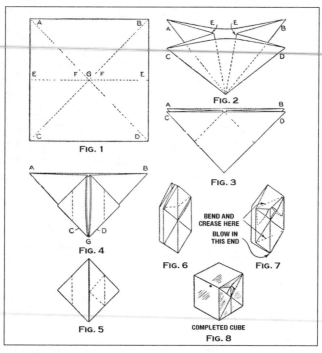

FIG. 1

FIG. 2

FIG. 3

FIG. 4

BEND AND CREASE HERE
BLOW IN THIS END

FIG. 6

FIG. 7

FIG. 5

COMPLETED CUBE
FIG. 8

PAPER CUBES, OR BOXES, THAT EXPAND ARE EASILY MADE
FROM SQUARE PIECES OF PAPER. THE ILLUSTRATION
SHOWS THE VARIOUS STEPS IN CONSTRUCTION.

Paper cubes, or boxes, that will provide considerable amusement for the children are easily made. A square piece of paper is folded, as shown by the dotted lines in *Fig. 1*, from points *A* to *D* and from *B* to *C*. The paper is spread out and folded on the opposite side from points *E* to *F*. The square of paper is again spread out and folded into the form shown in *Figs. 2* and *3*. The corners *A*, *B*, *C*, and *D* are folded on the dotted lines shown in *Fig. 3*, to the center *G* in *Fig. 4*. When all four corners have been folded, the paper will appear as shown in *Fig. 5.* The four corners are folded toward the center, as indicated by the dotted lines in *Fig. 5.* When this is done the paper will appear as in *Fig. 6.* The corners *A, B, C,* and *D* are bent on the dotted lines in *Fig. 6* and folded inside the flap, as in *Fig. 7.* When the paper has been folded into the form shown in *Fig. 7,* a hole will be left at one end and the cube, or box, is expanded by blowing into it. The inflated cube is shown in *Fig. 8.*

— AN ARMY IN A SMALL BOX —

A play device that will afford much amusement and is interesting for boys to make is shown in the sketch. To make the peephole cabinet, obtain a box of suitable size. Fasten a piece of looking glass inside, at each end. Make a peephole at one end of the box and rub the silvering from the back of the looking glass at the hole. Place a few metal soldiers, horses, etc., along the sides of the box 1 or 2 in. apart, one being set to hide the reflection of the hole.

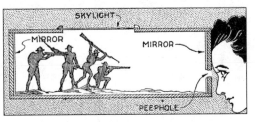

WITH THE HELP OF THE MIRRORS, A FEW SOLDIERS ARE MADE TO APPEAR AS AN ARMY.

When a boy looks through the hole, he'll see an endless army. Light is provided through the skylight at the top, which is fitted with ground glass or tissue paper. This device perplexes most people who are not familiar with its construction.

— A RECORDING ANNUNCIATOR TARGET —

In rifle practice it is often desirable to provide a target that will indicate to the marksman when the bull's-eye is struck. The device shown in the sketch, arranged behind an ordinary card target, has given satisfactory results on a private range and can easily be adapted to other uses.

Referring to *Fig. 1, A* indicates a wooden base, 4-by-8-by-½ in., on which is mounted a strap hinge, *B,* 6½ in. long, by means of a block, 1⅜ in. high. An opening, *C,* 1½ in. in diameter, is provided in the base. A plate, *D,* 1¾ in. square, is riveted to the strap hinge opposite to the opening.

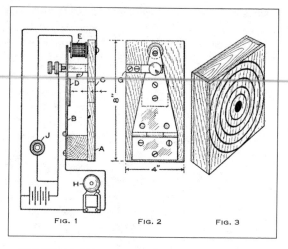

FIG. 1   FIG. 2   FIG. 3

THE BULLET FORCES THE HINGE AGAINST THE THUMB-SCREW, CAUSING THE BELL TO RING.

An electromagnet, *E,* obtained from an electric bell, is mounted upon the base under the small end of the hinge. A standard, *F,* provided with a cross arm, *G,* is secured upon the base between the opening and the magnet. A thumbscrew with a locknut extends through the cross arm, engaging the rear side of the strap hinge, and permits an adjustment of distance between the core of the magnet and the surface of the hinge. A bell or buzzer, *H,* is connected as indicated, through the battery circuit. The electromagnet is connected through the battery and push button *J.*

The strap hinge normally rests against the electromagnet. The force of any projectile passing through the opening against the plate closes the bell circuit and indicates to the marksman that the bull's-eye has been hit. By the closing the magnetic circuit, the strap hinge is drawn again into normal position and the bell circuit is broken. *Fig. 2* shows a front view of the circuit-closing device. The device may be mounted in any suitable box, as suggested in *Fig. 3.* The front of the box is covered with sheet metal, ¹⁄₁₆ in. thick, and the standard target card is mounted thereon.

— The Somersaulting "Bunny" Target —

The somersaulting "bunny" target shown in the drawing is intended for target practice with the bow and arrow. But, by substituting sheet-iron parts for the wooden ones described, it may be used as well for small-caliber rifle practice.

The rabbit is outlined on a 10-by-24-in. board with the rings and bull's-eye of the target a trifle off center to the right; the bull's-eye is formed by drilling a 1½-in. hole through the board.

A 2-by-6-in. post is used for supporting the target, which is mounted on a shaft so as to revolve freely. A piece of gas pipe, about 12 in. long, will answer for the shaft. This is inserted through a hole drilled in the post and is attached to the back of the target with a floor flange. A washer on each side of the post, together with cotter pins driven through holes in the shaft, serve to maintain the proper space between the post and target for operation of the trigger.

The trigger is made by fastening two blocks of wood

to the opposite ends and sides of a piece of spring steel. One of the blocks is nailed to the post in such a position as to bring the other block directly behind the bull's-eye block and, by bearing against a nail in the back of the target, to hold the rabbit vertically until the trigger is released by a properly placed shot.

The somersaulting effect is produced by the weight arrangement

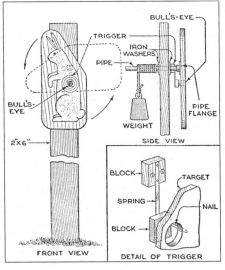

WHENEVER THE MARKSMAN MAKES A BULL'S-EYE ON THIS TARGET THE "BUNNY" MAKES A COMPLETE SOMERSAULT, AND TURNS AGAIN TO AN UPRIGHT POSITION READY FOR ANOTHER SHOT.

shown in the drawing. A piece of stout twine is wound around the projecting end of the shaft, behind the post, and a weight is attached to the free end. The target remains stationary until a lucky shot springs the trigger. The weight then unwinds the rope, and the rabbit makes a complete revolution, the nail striking the block again and stopping the target when it is in an upright position.

From 10 to 20 bull's-eyes may be recorded by the somersaulting bunny before it has to be rewound, depending on the number of turns of rope around the shaft.

— SHOOTING GALLERY FOR TOY PISTOLS —

Skill in shooting toy pistols, blowguns, and similar harmless weapons that use peas, marbles, or wooden darts for ammunition can be easily honed by practicing on a target of the type shown in the drawing. Clothespins, spools, and some wire are about the only materials required. The clothespins are placed on a stiff wire or small rod with a spool between each pair. The wire is then fitted in a box, as shown. In back of the clothespins and a little above their lower ends is a second wire that holds them upright. This

A PISTOL FOR INDOOR USE, BY MEANS OF WHICH THE YOUNG MARKSMAN CAN IMPROVE HIS "SHOT" WITH HARMLESS AMMO SUCH AS MARBLES, PEAS, AND DARTS.

wire should be placed so that the pins will lean forward a little. When these targets are knocked over by an expert—or lucky—shot, they are caught by the pin-setting rod at the back. This rod is bent from a piece of stiff wire and is held horizontally by a rubber band. When all the targets have been knocked over, or after each marksman's turn is over, the pins are reset by a pull on the cord tied to the pin-setting rod. If desired, the clothespins can be painted and designated by numbers.

— AN ILLUMINATED INDICATING TARGET BOX —

The joys of target practice are often hampered by the delays in the settlement of hits. It takes time and is annoying to be constantly advancing to the target to examine it. To do away with this, an illuminated target

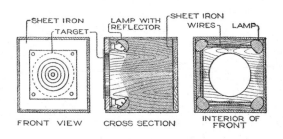

FRONT VIEW CROSS SECTION INTERIOR OF FRONT

THE LOCATION OF HITS IS RECORDED BY A BEAM OF LIGHT STREAMING THROUGH THE HOLE SHOT IN THE PAPER TARGET.

was constructed that enables the shooter to locate every hit without leaving his post. To make the device, a square wooden box of convenient size is obtained. In one side of this, cut a round hole as large as the largest ring on the targets used. The side opposite this is fitted with a piece of sheet iron to stop the bullets. Paint this iron and the interior white. Inside the box, arrange four electric lights so their rays will be thrown on the hole, as shown. Candles may be used, if necessary. The lamps must be out of range of the bullets that hit the target, and protected by an iron plate. The targets are painted on thin paper and fastened over the front of the hole. The lights are turned on while shooting. Each shot punctures the paper, and the light streaming through the hole will show the location of the hit.

— GOLD FISH TRAVEL FROM BOWL TO BOWL —

An interesting and entertaining arrangement—permitting goldfish in one bowl to travel to another—is created as shown in the drawing. An extra fish bowl is provided and filled with water to the same height as the one containing the fish. Then a piece of glass tube, of large diameter, is made into an elongated U by heating where the bends are to be and slowly bending. After it has cooled, this U-shaped tube is filled with water and one end is placed in each bowl. The water will remain in the glass tube, even though above the level of the two bowls, so long as the water in both is kept above the ends of the tube.

AN ARRANGEMENT THAT PERMITS GOLDFISH IN ONE BOWL TO SWIM TO ANOTHER THROUGH A GLASS TUBE.

NOISEMAKERS

— A HOMEMADE HAWAIIAN UKULELE —

The one-string banjo, the cigar-box guitar, and similar vaudeville favorites are giving way to the tantalizing ukulele. The home mechanic, to be up to date in his musical craftsmanship, must fall in line. The size of this instrument makes it especially suited to the cigar-box type of body construction, as detailed in the several sketches. This neat ukulele was made inexpensively by careful selection of materials from the shop scrap stock.

A cigar box of good-quality Spanish cedar, about 2½ by 6 by 9 in., as shown in *Fig. 1,* is used for the body. Remove the paper carefully so as not to mar the surface, soaking

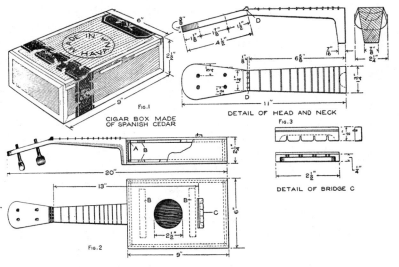

FIG. 1

CIGAR BOX MADE
OF SPANISH CEDAR

DETAIL OF HEAD AND NECK

FIG. 3

FIG. 2

DETAIL OF BRIDGE C

TO KEEP IN FASHION HIS MUSICAL CRAFTSMANSHIP, THE HOME
MECHANIC MAY MAKE A CIGAR-BOX UKULELE AS DETAILED.

it if necessary. Take it apart; if the nail holes are too numerous or broken out, trim off the edges. Fit the parts of the body together, as shown in *Fig. 2*. The top and bottom pieces should rest against the side and end pieces, and the latter between the sides. Cut the 2½-in. hole in the top piece, as shown, 3¾ in. from the neck end. To reinforce the body make strips, *A*, ¼ in. square, and fit them to be glued into the corners at the top and bottom. Make strips, *B*, ¼ by ⅝ by 4½ in., and glue them under the top and on the bottom as indicated

in *Fig. 2*. The final assembling and gluing of these parts, using animal glue, should be done after the bridge *C* is in place, and the other parts are made. The bridge is of hardwood hollowed underneath the notched edge, as detailed, and is fitted with a metal string contact.

Spanish cedar or mahogany is suitable for the neck, as detailed in *Fig. 3*. A single piece is best, but the extension for the pegs and the wide end at the body may be joined and glued to the main portion of the neck. Dowels should then be used to reinforce the joints. The outline of the parts of the neck are shown in detail in *Fig. 3*. In the sectional view, the shape of the neck at the thinnest and thickest parts is shown by the two upper curved, dotted lines. The nut, *D*, is made of mahogany, walnut, or other hardwood, the grain extending lengthwise, and the notches for the strings spaced as shown.

The making and spacing of the frets must be done very carefully. They are aluminum, although brass and other metals are suitable. Make the frets 1/16 by 3/16 in. and cut grooves 1/8 in. deep for them. The spacing of the frets is determined as follows, a standard practice: The distance from the metal string contact on the bridge to the nut should be measured carefully. The first fret, near the head, is 1/18 of this distance from the nut, the total length being in this instance,

13 in. The second fret is set 1/18 the distance from the first fret to the bridge; the third 1/18 from the second fret to the bridge, etc. The frets must fit tightly in the grooves, requiring no special fastening. The tuning pegs may be bought or made.

In assembling the parts, fasten the end of the body to the neck with glue and reinforce with screws. Set its upper edge parallel with the fingerboard and so that the latter is flush with the top of the body when fitted to it. Assemble the body, without the top, gluing it to the end fixed to the neck. When this portion is thoroughly dried, fit the top into place finally and glue it. The whole construction is then cleaned, sandpapered, stained, and shellacked or varnished. The stringing of the instrument is simple, and the strings may be purchased in sets.

— A Guitar That Is Easy to Make —

A guitar having straight lines, giving it an old-fashioned appearance, can be made by the home mechanic. If care is taken in selecting the material and having it thoroughly seasoned, the finished instrument will have a fine tone. The sides, ends, and bottom are made of hardwood, preferably hard

maple, and the top should be made of a thoroughly seasoned piece of soft pine. The materials required are listed in the materials list.

Cut the fingerboard tapering and fasten pieces cut from hatpins with small wire staples for frets. All dimensions for cutting and setting are shown in the sketch. The neck is

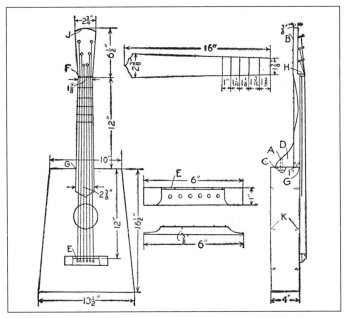

DETAILS OF GUITAR

cut tapering from *G* to *F* and *J* to *F*, with the back side rounding. A drawknife is the proper tool for shaping the neck. Cut a piece of hardwood, ¼ in. square and 1⅞ in. long, and glue it to the neck at *F*. Glue the fingerboard to the neck and hold it secure with clamps while the glue sets.

The brace at *D* is 1 in. thick, cut to any shape desired. The sides are glued together and then the front is glued on them. Place some heavy weights on top and give the glue time to dry. Fasten pieces of soft wood in the corners for braces. Glue the neck to the box, making it secure by the addition of a carriage bolt at *A*. A small block *C* is glued to the end to reinforce it for the bolt. Glue strips of soft wood, as shown by *K*, across the front and back to strengthen them. The back is then glued on and the outside smoothed with sandpaper.

Make the bottom bridge by using an old hatpin or wire of the same size used for *E* secured with pin staples.

Glue the bridge on the top at a place that will make the distance from the bridge *F* to the bottom bridge *E* just 24 in. This dimension and those for the frets should be made accurately. Six holes, 3/16 in. in diameter, are drilled in the bottom bridge for pins. The tuning plugs *B* and strings can be purchased at any music store.

List of Materials
1 top, 3/16 by 14 by 17 in.
1 bottom, 3/16 by 14 by 17 in.
2 sides, 3/16 by 3⅝ by 16¾ in.
1 end, 3/16 by 3⅝ by 13⅛ in.
1 end, 3/16 by 3⅝ by 9⅝ in.
1 neck, 1 by 2 5/16 by 18½ in.
1 fingerboard, 3/16 by 2⅝ by 16 in.

— A MUSICAL WINDMILL —

Make two wheels out of tin. They may be of any size, but wheel A must be larger than wheel B. On wheel *A* fasten two pieces of wood, *C,* to cross in the center, and place a bell on the four ends, as shown. The smaller wheel, *B,* must be separated from the other with a round piece of wood or an old spool. Tie four buttons with split rings to the smaller wheel, *B*. The blades on the wheels should be bent opposite on one wheel from the others so as to

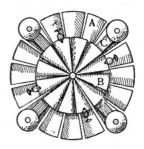

make the wheels turn in different directions. When turning, the buttons will strike the bells and make them ring constantly.

GAME DAY

— A SNAKE GAME —

Ask any Canadian Native American what a snow snake is, and he will tell you that it is a piece of twisted wood, such as wild grape vine, about 5 or 6 ft. long, and 1 in. or more in thickness, stripped of its bark and polished. It is grasped with one hand in the center and

THROWING THE SNOW SNAKE IN TRACKS MADE THROUGH THE SNOW WITH A LOG. EACH PLAYER TRIES TO GET HIS SNAKE FIRST OUT AT THE END OF THE TRACK MORE TIMES THAN HIS OPPONENTS.

given a strong forward throw at the tail end by the other hand, while at the same time the hold in the center is loosened. With a hard bottom and about 1 in. or more of light snow on top—ideal conditions for playing the game—the snake will travel for long distances when thrown by an expert. To a novice seeing the snake traveling along at a rapid speed, raising and lowering its head as the wood vibrates from side to side, its resemblance to the real reptile is perfect.

When the Native Americans have tests of skill with the snake they make tracks through the snow by drawing a log in it. Sometimes as many as dozen tracks are made side by side, and a dozen snakes are sent along at once. The one who makes his snake emerge from the end of the track first the most times out of a certain number of throws takes the prize. The trick of throwing the snake is not at all hard to acquire, and it makes for an exciting game.

— A MARBLE-UNDER-BRIDGE GAME OF SKILL —

The object of this game is to pass a marble from one end to the other of the "roadway," under the "bridges," and over the "inclines," without dropping it. A stop must be made at each hole. The device is made as follows: Cut two pieces of wood, ¼ by 1¾ by 12 in., and join them to form a right angle.

Cut pieces of cardboard, 4 each, 1¾ by 2½ in. wide, with a ¾-in. hole in the center, for inclines B, and 1¾ by 3 in., for bridges A. Also cut two pieces 1¾ in. square for stops C. Fasten them with tacks as shown. The marble should be large enough so that it will rest in the holes at B.

— MAGNETIZED CHECKERMEN —

Anyone who has played checkers knows how easy it is to have the pieces become disarranged, usually at the most interesting point of the game. Two methods of preventing this are illustrated in the accompanying drawing. One of these ideas requires small magnets made from clock springs, which are attached to the bottom of the checker men. A

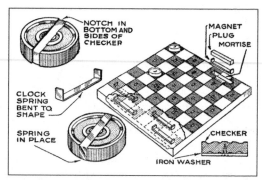

MAGNETISM IS CALLED UPON TO PREVENT CHESS AND CHECKER MEN FROM BECOMING DISARRANGED ON THE BOARD.

metal board is required. Three or four of the checkers are clamped in a vise, and grooves are filed on opposite edges and one side, as shown. Some pieces of clock spring of good thickness—but not more than ¼ in. wide—are cut into pieces of the proper length and bent to fit neatly and snugly into the filed grooves, and flush with the face of the checker. These pieces are magnetized by bringing them into contact with an ordinary horseshoe magnet. The checkerboard used with these checkers may be an ordinary board with a covering of galvanized iron, or tin plate, on which the squares are painted. Chessmen are fitted with magnets in the same manner as checkers.

The second idea is to embed the magnets in the checkerboard, and is preferred because heavier magnets may be used. This means they will be stronger and longer-lived. As shown in the drawing, mortises are cut into the board so that the ends come at the centers of two black squares. The magnets are formed and magnetized in the manner described, and put in place, after which the opening is plugged up with wood to match the rest of the board. After all the magnets have been put in place, the surface of the board is finished smooth so that the ends of the magnets will just come flush with the top. The checkers are held to the magnets by means of soft-iron washers that are attached to one side with small screws, as indicated.

— AN INDOOR BASEBALL GAME —

An indoor game of baseball may be played on a board 5 ft. long and 4 ft. wide. A diamond is laid off at one end of the board and pins representing the hits are attached to the board so they will project above the surface. The locations of the players are designated by holes bored partway in the wood with an expansive bit.

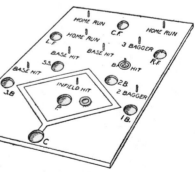

BASEBALL DIAMOND ON A BOARD.

These holes should be large enough to receive the rings easily. The rings may be gaskets or they may be made of rope, and should have an inside diameter of about 3 in.

Only two people can play this game. The distance from the board to the thrower may be from 10 to 100 ft., according to the size of the room. This distance should be marked and each thrower stands at the same place.

If the ring is thrown over one of the "base-hit" or "two-bagger" pegs, it shows the number of bases secured. Throwing a ring over one of the "home run" pegs means a score, of course. The "infield hit" secures a base. If the ring slips into a hole, that counts as one out. A player must throw until he has three outs. The score is kept for the runs made.

— A BUCKET-BALL GAME —

This is a new indoor game that follows out in principle a regular game of baseball. It is an exciting and interesting pastime. And while a certain amount of skill is required to score runs, a person who cannot play the regular game can score as many runs, and as often as the best players in the professional leagues.

THE PLAYER MUST THROW THE BALL SO THAT IT WILL ENTER AND STAY IN ONE OF THE BUCKETS, WHICH DESIGNATES THE BASE HITS BY THE NUMBER IN ITS BOTTOM.

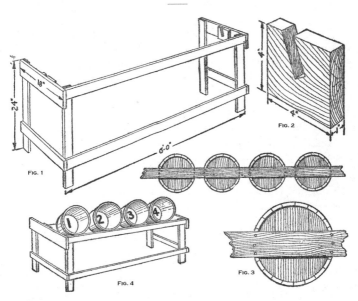

THE FRAME IS MADE UP WITHOUT A BACK, TO HOLD THE BUCKETS
AT AN ANGLE THAT MAKES IT DIFFICULT TO TOSS THE BALL
SO THAT IT WILL STAY IN ANY ONE OF THEM.

Anyone that is just a little handy with tools can make the necessary parts for this game. The tools required are a hammer and a saw. The materials consist of some finishing nails; three strips of wood, 6 ft. long, 2 in. wide, and 1 in. thick; two strips, 18 in. long, 4 in. wide, and 1 in. thick; four strips, 24 in. long, 2 in. wide, and 1 in. thick; two strips, 18 in. long, 2 in. wide, and 1 in. thick; two blocks, 4 in. square, and 1 in. thick; and four wood buckets.

A frame is built up as shown, 6 ft. long, 18 in. wide, and 24 in. high, without a back. One of the long pieces is fastened to the bottoms of the buckets as shown, spacing the latter equally on the length of the piece. This piece is then set in notches cut in the blocks of wood at an angle of 45 degrees. These blocks are fastened to the upper crosspieces at the ends of the frame. The upper part of the buckets rest on the upper front piece of the frame.

The rules for playing the game are as follows: Three baseballs are used.

The players stand about 10 ft. away and in front of the buckets. Each player, or side, is permitted to throw only three balls an inning, irrespective of the number of runs scored. Any kind of delivery is permitted, but an underhand throw will be found most successful. The buckets are numbered from 1 to 4, and represent, respectively, one-, two-, and three-base hits, and home runs. The one in which the ball stays designates the run.

Plays are figured as in a regular ballgame. For instance, if a ball should stay in bucket *No. 2* and the next in bucket *No. 3*, the first man would be forced home, counting one run, and leaving one man on third base. If the next ball stays in bucket *No. 4*, the man on third base is forced home, as well as the one who scored the home run, making three runs for that inning. The runs should be scored as made.

— PIN SETTER FOR THE HOME TENPINS —

Bowling with a set of small tenpins, which can be purchased at a department store, is a very interesting game. The chief drawback, however, is the setting of the pins. With a little rack like the one shown in the illustration, the interest in the game may be increased considerably. It not only helps in setting the pins rapidly but also ensures a good setting with the proper spacing between the pins. It is very simple to make, because it consists of a triangular piece of wood with ten holes bored into it at the proper places, the dimensions of which will be governed by the size

ALL THE TENPINS ARE QUICKLY SET, AND EACH IN ITS PROPER PLACE.

of the pins, and three supports. The pins are dropped in the holes and the rack lifted from them.

— ELECTRIC SCOREBOARD FOR INDOOR GAMES —

A very good electric scoreboard, for use in scoring basketball and other games played indoors, is shown in the illustration. It is constructed entirely of wood but should be lined with backing board or sheathing. The dimensions are a matter of choice, but one 4 ft. long, 2 ft. wide, and 18 in. deep is a good size. The back of the box is provided with two cleats, each 2½ ft. long, fastened at each end. This allows a projection of 3 in. at the top and bottom, for fastening the scoreboard to the wall. The manner of construction is shown in *Fig. 1*, and a cross section of the box, in *Fig. 2*.

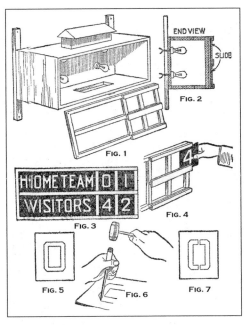

ELECTRIC INDOOR SCOREBOARD, SHOWING ITS CONSTRUCTION AND MANNER OF CUTTING OUT THE LETTERS AND NUMBERS.

The front of the box should be fastened with screws to make its removal easy in case of repairs. This part of the box carries the frame for inserting the numbers and the words "Home Team" and "Visitors," as shown in *Fig. 3*. Because the words are a permanent fixture, the cards carrying them are fastened to the front. At the end of these words a frame is constructed as shown in *Fig. 4*, in which the cards having the numbers are inserted in slides.

Numerals and letters can be cut

out of heavy cardboard or tin. The design of a letter having sharp angles and straight edges, as shown in *Fig. 5,* is very easily cut out with a chisel. The method of cutting is shown in *Fig. 6.*

Because portions of the letters and numerals, such as the center in an O, would fall out if cut entirely around, some way must be provided to hold the parts in place. The way to prepare stencils is to leave a portion uncut, which is known as a tie, and the letter will appear as shown in *Fig. 7.*

The best method of making these letters and figures is to cut out the letter entirely, then to paste thin paper over the back and replace the parts removed by the cutting in their original position.

— MARBLE-AND-CHECKERS "BASEBALL" GAME —

A light 8-by-16-in. board is elevated at one end by means of a square stick and drilled with five holes, about 1 in. in diameter, in the positions shown in the drawing. The two upper holes are called "singles," the hole just below this is a "double," the next a "triple," and the last one is a "home run." Small wire brads are driven into the board around these holes. The brads are placed irregularly but with sufficient space between them to allow a marble to pass. The outline of a ball diamond is drawn

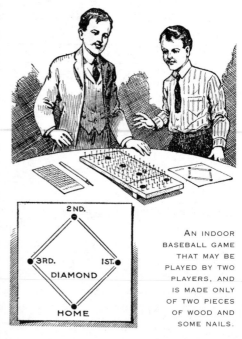

AN INDOOR BASEBALL GAME THAT MAY BE PLAYED BY TWO PLAYERS, AND IS MADE ONLY OF TWO PIECES OF WOOD AND SOME NAILS.

upon a card, and the three bases and home plate are indicated on it. Each of the two players is provided with nine checkers that correspond to the players on his team.

When the game is on, one of the players places a checker on the home plate as a batter. Then, the marble is placed between the two nails at the top center of the inclined board and allowed to roll. If it falls into the "single" hole, the "batter" is advanced to first base, and another checker is put up. The game is played just as the regular game, and when three men are out, the second player's team of checkers comes to bat, and the other team takes the field. If the marble lodges in the tacks below the horizontal line on the board, it is a "base on balls" and if the marble stops above the line, it counts as a "strikeout." Should the marble roll entirely off the board without entering any of the holes, it counts as an "out." Scorecards can be prepared and the game made almost as exciting as a real game.

— A PARLOR CUE ALLEY —

Parlor cue alley is really a game of bowling except that it is played on a small raised board. Instead of throwing the balls by hand, an ordinary billiard cue is used, the balls being about 1¼ in. in diameter. The automatic feature of this new game saves the time usually required to set up the pins, and assures that they will be set absolutely true each time.

To build this alley, first procure three planed boards. Use hardwood

A CUE IS USED TO SHOOT THE BALL ON THIS ALLEY.

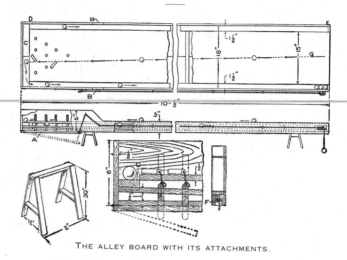

THE ALLEY BOARD WITH ITS ATTACHMENTS.

even though it is more difficult to work. Two of the boards should be 10 ft. long, 9 in. wide, and ½ in. thick, and the other 10 ft. long, 15 in. wide, and ½ in. thick. Place the first two boards side by side and fasten them with cleats, the first cleat being placed 18 in. from the end to be used for the pins. The cleats should be of ¾- or ⅞-in. material and cut as long as the upper board is wide, or 15 in. These are placed on top of the lower boards, or between the two. By placing the first one 18 in. from the end, clearance is obtained for the trap *A*. The other board is placed on the cleats and fastened, after it has been centrally located, with screws from the underside. The screws must not

come through or the surface of the upper board marred in any way that might prevent the balls from rolling freely. The difference in width of the lower board and the upper one provides a 1½-in. clearance on each side as grooves for the return of the balls.

Enclose the alley with boards, 3 in. wide and ½ in. thick, to the point *B*, and from there around the pin end with boards, 6 in. wide. The upper board should be cut to such a length that a space of 2 in. at the end *C* will be provided. Into this space is fitted a block of wood, about ⅞ in. thick, with its upper surface slightly pitched toward the sides of the alley to start the balls back to the front of the board. From the ends of this block two 1½ in. wide strips are fitted into the side grooves, from *D* to *E*. They should be set on an incline, to return the ball after each shot.

The location of each pin is marked on the end of the upper board. Small holes are drilled just large enough to allow pieces of stout cord, like a fish line, to pass through freely. The pins are made of hardwood and are carefully balanced; one end should not be heavier than the other. The lower end of each pin is drilled to make a recess, *F*, in which the cord is fastened with a screw or nail. Holes are bored through the bottom board, ⅜ in. in diameter, to correspond to the 10 small holes made through the upper one. Lead weights of about 2 oz. are fitted in the holes and attached to the strings from the pins. The ends of the weights should extend about ½ in. from the underside of the alley.

Attach a board, 18 in. square, with hinges to the end of the alley so that it will hang under the weights. A stout cord is run along the underside of the alley to the front end through screw eyes, and attached to the swinging board. By letting the board swing down the weights are released and they draw the pins into a standing position, accurately set for the next break. When set, the line is drawn, and the swinging board pushes the weights up and releases the pins.

The balls used are made of hardwood. If it is not possible to make them, they can be purchased from a toy store. They are 1¼ in. in diameter. Each player has three shots. The ball is placed on the spot *G* and shot with a billiard cue, the object being to knock down as many pins as possible. The score is kept as in bowling.

Horses can be made of metal and wood, as shown, for holding the alley at the proper height. The alley can be used on a large table, but horses are more convenient.

GOOD SPORTS

— A CIRCULAR SWING —

Many a farm or country house features a circular swing like the one constructed, which proves very attractive to boys and their friends. The circular swing will be far more popular than the regular version, becoming a favorite with all the younger people, boys and girls alike.

To make the one in the illustration, a 10-ft. length of chain was looped around a branch of a large elm and 18 or 20 ft. from the tree trunk. To the hanging end of this chain a 1-in. rope nearly 10 ft. longer than was needed to reach the ground was made fast.

Directly beneath the point where the chain went around the limb, as determined by a plumb bob, was set a 6-in. piece of cedar post 3½ ft. above the ground. Into the top of this post was set a ½-in. rod, to serve as a pivot for the swing. It was set

THE CIRCULAR SWING WILL BE FOUND VERY SAFE AND PLEASURABLE. BUT, AS IN THE CASE OF AN ORDINARY SWING, ANYONE CARELESS ENOUGH TO GET IN THE WAY OF IT WILL GET BADLY BUMPED.

in firmly about 6 in. and projected about 3 in. from the top of the post.

A straight-grained piece of pine board, 15 ft. long, 8 in. wide, and 1 in. thick, was procured and a hole bored in one end large enough to make it turn freely on the pin in the upper end of the post. Two holes were bored in the other end of the board large enough to admit the rope. The first hole was 6 in. from the end, and the second hole, 3 ft. The hanging end of the rope was passed down through one of these holes and back up through the other and then made fast to itself about 3 ft. above the board after the board had been adjusted so that it would swing throughout its length at the height of the post, or 1½ ft. from the ground. The swing was then complete except for a swivel, which was put in the rope within easy reach of one standing on the board, so that it could be oiled.

One good push would send the board with a boy on the end three or four times about the 90-ft. circle. The little fellows would like to get hold of the board in near the post and shove it around. Once started, it could be kept going with very little effort.

In putting up such a swing, make sure to set the post solidly in the ground, because it has a tendency to work loose. Tie all the knots tightly. Do not look upon the swivel as unnecessary. The first swing put up was without one, and the rope twisted off in a few days.

It is not necessary to climb a tree; just throw a stout cord over the limb by means of a stone or nut tied to the end. Then haul the rope and chain up over the limb with the cord. Before the chain leaves the ground, loop the end of it and pass the cord through the loop. The higher the limb from the ground, the better the swing will work, but 25 ft. will be about right.

— An Adjustable Punching-Bag Platform —

A punching-bag platform, suitable for the tall athlete as well as the small boy, is shown in the accompanying sketch. The platform is securely fastened to two strong wooden arms or braces, which in turn are nailed to a 2-by-12-in. plank as long as the diameter of the platform. This plank, as shown in the small drawing at the upper left-hand corner of the sketch, is placed in grooves or slots fastened against the side of a wall. The plank with the platform attached may be raised or lowered to the desired height and held there by a pin or bolt put through the bolt-hole of the plank and into a hole in the wall.

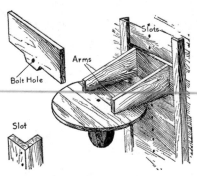

ADJUSTABLE PLATFORM

— TO PRACTICE BATTING FOR BASEBALL PLAYING —

A boy with a very great desire to make a good ballplayer found that he could not hit a ball tossed to him. Try as he might, the bat never hit the ball. Someone suggested that a ball hung by a cord would help to a great extent, and it was tried out with excellent results. An inexpensive ball was suspended from the limb of a tree so that it would be at the proper height for the batter. In striking at the ball it was not necessary to hit home runs, as this is liable to break the cord, or get it tangled to its support. If the strikes are made properly, the ball will swing out and come back in a perfect curve, or can be made to come back bounding and in no straight line. This will teach the

eye to locate the ball and make hits where it cannot be taught by having someone toss the ball to the striker.

THRILLS *in* MOTION

— HOMEMADE OVERHEAD TROLLEY COASTER —

The accompanying sketch shows a playground trolley line that furnished a great deal of amusement to many children at a minimum cost. The wire, which is 3/16 in. in diameter, was stretched between a tree and a barn across vacant quarter block. The strength of the wire was first tested by a heavy man. When not in use the wire is unhooked from the tree and hauled into the barn and coiled loosely in the hay loft. The wire was made taut for use by a rope that was fastened to the beams in the barn. The trolley was made, as shown in *Figs. 1* and *2*, of strips of wood bolted with stove bolts on two grooved pulleys. The middle wide board was made of hardwood. The wheels were taken from light pulley blocks and stove bolts were purchased from a local hardware store to accurately fit the hubs. Because it was necessary to keep the bearings greased, we used Vaseline. This coaster made great sport for the youngsters and at no time were they in danger of a serious fall because the line was hung low and the slant of the wire was moderate.

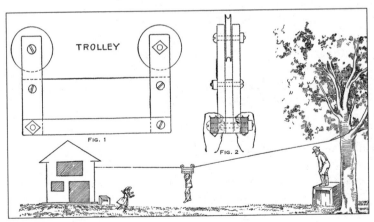

DETAILS OF THE TROLLEY AND HOW IT IS USED.

— EASILY RENEWED COASTER BRAKE —

The brake that forms a part of most models of children's toy wagons and coasters of various kinds is usually unsatisfactory because of its short life. The wooden lever wears down rapidly, and an iron brake wears the tires, and there is usually no way to renew either.

The drawing and photograph illustrate an iron brake handle that has provision made at its lower end for holding a wooden-block brake shoe. As soon as there is any amount of wear, a new block can be inserted, and the brake will be as good as new. The brake lever is forged from a piece of round iron, with one end flattened to accommodate the brake-shoe holder, to which it is riveted. The brake lever is fastened to the wagon by means of a stud attached to the underside of the wagon box.

— A BOY'S MOTOR CAR —

Even though the home-built "bearcat" roadster or other favorite model does not compare in every detail with the luxurious manufactured cars, it has an individuality that puts it in a class by itself. The amateur mechanic, or the ambitious boy who is fairly skilled with tools, can build at least the main parts for his own small car of the simple, practical design shown in the sketch and detailed in the working drawings. If necessary, he can call more skilled mechanics to his aid. A motorcycle engine or other small gasoline motor is used for the power plant. The control mechanism of the engine and the electrical connections are similar to those of a motorcycle. They are installed to be controlled handily from the driver's seat. The car is built without springs, but these may be included, if desired. Or the necessary comfort may provided—in part, at least—by a cushioned seat. Strong bicycle wheels are used, the 1½-by-28-in. size being suitable. The hood may be of wood, or of sheet metal, built over a frame of strap iron. The top of the hood can be lifted off, and the entire hood can also be removed, when repairs are to be made. The toolbox on the rear of the frame can be replaced by a larger compartment, or rack, for transporting loads, or an extra seat for a passenger.

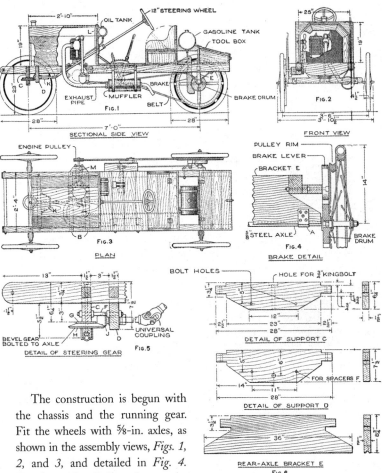

FIG.1 — SECTIONAL SIDE VIEW

12" STEERING WHEEL
OIL TANK
GASOLINE TANK
TOOL BOX
BRAKE
BRAKE DRUM
EXHAUST PIPE
MUFFLER
BELT
2'-10"
19"
23"
28"
7'-0"
28"

FIG.2 — FRONT VIEW

25"
19"
4½"
3'-6"
3'-10½"

FIG.3 — PLAN

ENGINE PULLEY
M
B
2'-4"

FIG.4 — BRAKE DETAIL

PULLEY RIM
BRAKE LEVER
BRACKET E
14"
⅝" STEEL AXLE
A
BRAKE DRUM

FIG.5 — DETAIL OF STEERING GEAR

13"
1½" 3" 1½"
C F
G
H J D
BEVEL GEAR BOLTED TO AXLE
UNIVERSAL COUPLING

FIG.6

BOLT HOLES
HOLE FOR ¾" KINGBOLT
DETAIL OF SUPPORT C
5"
12"
23"
28"
2½"
6¼"

DETAIL OF SUPPORT D
6"
14"
11"
28"
FOR SPACERS F
7½"

REAR-AXLE BRACKET E
36"
6¼"

The construction is begun with the chassis and the running gear. Fit the wheels with ⅝-in. axles, as shown in the assembly views, *Figs. 1, 2,* and *3,* and detailed in *Fig. 4.* Fit the ends of the axles to the hubs of the wheels, providing the threaded ends with lock nuts. Make the wooden supports for the frame, as detailed in *Fig. 6.* The axles are fastened into half-round grooves cut in the bottoms of the supports and secured by iron straps, as shown in

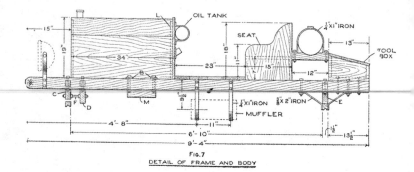

FIG. 7
DETAIL OF FRAME AND BODY

A, Fig. 4. Make the sidepieces for the main frame 2½ by 3¼ in. thick, and 9 ft. 4 in. long, as detailed in *Fig. 7*. Mortise the supports through the sidepieces, and bore the holes for the bolt fastenings and braces. Glue the mortise-and-tenon joints before the bolts are finally secured. Provide the bolts with washers, and lock the nuts with additional jam nuts where needed. Keep the woodwork clean, and apply a coat of linseed oil, so that dirt and grease cannot penetrate readily.

Finish only the supporting structure of the chassis in the preliminary woodwork. Set the front-axle and steering-rigging supports *C* and *D*, and adjust the spacers *F* between them. Bore the hole for the kingbolt, as detailed in *Fig. 6*. Fit the bevel gears and the fifth wheel *G*, of ¼-in. steel, into place, as shown in

Fig. 5. The gear *H* is bolted to the axle support. The pinion *J* is set on the end of a short ¾-in. shaft. The latter passes through the support *D*, and is fitted with washers and jam nuts, solidly, yet with sufficient play. A bracket, *K*, of ¼-by-1¾-in. strap iron, braces the shaft, as shown in *Fig. 3*. The end of this short shaft is joined to one section of the universal coupling, as shown, and, like the other half of the coupling, is pinned with a 3/16-in. riveted pin. The pinion is also pinned, and the lower end of the kingbolt provided with a washer and nut, guarded by a cotter pin. Suitable gears can be procured from old machinery. A satisfactory set was obtained from an old differential of a well-known small car.

Before fitting the steering column into place, make the dashboard, of ⅞-in. oak, as shown in the assembly view, and in detail in *Fig. 7*. It is 19½ in. high and 2 ft. 4 in. wide, and set on the frame and braced to it with 4- by 4- by 1½-in. angle irons, ¼ in. thick. Fit a ⅞-in. strip of wood around the edge of the dashboard, on the front side, as a rest for the hood, as shown in *L, Figs. 1* and *7*. A brass edging protects the dashboard, and gives a neat appearance. Lay out carefully the angle for the steering column, which is of ⅞-in. shafting, so as to be convenient for the driver. Mark the point at which it is to pass through the dashboard, and reinforce the hole with an oak block, or an angle flange of iron or brass, such as is used on railings or boat fittings. A collar at the flange

counteracts the downward pressure on the steering post. The 12-in. steering wheel is set on the column by a riveted pin.

The fitting of the engine may next be undertaken. The exact position and method of setting the engine on the frame will depend on the size and type. It should be placed as near the center as possible, to give proper balance. The drawings show a common air-cooled one-cylinder motor. It is supported, as shown in *Figs. 1* and *3* and detailed in *Fig. 8*. Two iron strips, *B*, riveted to 1½-by-1½-in. angle irons, extend across the main frame, and support the engine by means of bolts and steel clamps, designed to suit the engine. Cross

To simplify this small but serviceable motor car for construction by the young mechanic, only the essential parts are considered. Other useful and ornamental features may be added as the skill and means of the builder make possible.

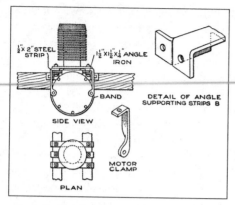

DETAIL OF THE MOTOR SUPPORT.
THE ENGINE IS MOUNTED ON REINFORCED
ANGLE IRONS, AND SECURED BY CLAMPS
AND A SUPPORTING BAND UNDER
THE CRANKCASE.

strips of iron steady the engine, and the clamps are bolted to the crank case. The center clamp is a band that passes under the crankcase.

The engine is set so that the crankshaft extends across the main frame. Other methods may be devised for special motors, and the power transmission changed correspondingly. One end of the crankshaft is extended beyond the right side of the frame, as shown in *Fig. 3*. This extension is connected to the shaft by means of an ordinary setscrew collar coupling. A block *M, Figs. 3* and *7*, is bolted to the frame, and a section of heavy brass pipe fitted as a bearing.

The ignition and oiling systems, carburetor, and other details of the engine control and allied mechanism are the same as those used on the motorcycle engine originally, fitted up as required. The oil tank is made of a strong can, mounted on the dashboard, as shown in *Figs. 1* and *2*. It is connected with the crankcase by copper tubing. A cut-out switch for the ignition system is mounted on the dashboard. The controls used for the engine of the motorcycle can be extended with light iron rods, and the control handles mounted on the dashboard or other convenient position. The throttle can be mounted on the steering column by fitting an iron pipe around the post and mounting this pipe in the angle flange at the dashboard. A foot accelerator may also be used, suitable mountings and pedal connections being installed at the floor.

In setting the gasoline tank, make only as much of the body woodwork as is necessary to support it, as shown in *Figs. 1, 3,* and *7*. The tank should be made and properly fitted in the same way and with the same materials as gasoline tanks in commercial cars. The feed is through a copper tube, as shown in *Fig. 1*. A small vent hole, to guard against a vacuum in the tank, should be made in the cap. The muffler from a motorcycle is used, fitted with a longer pipe, and suspended from the side of the frame.

The transmission of the power from the motor shaft to the right rear wheel is accomplished by means of a leather motorcycle belt. This is made by fitting leather washers close together over a bicycle chain, oiling the washers with neat's-foot oil. A grooved iron pulley is fitted on the end of the motor shaft, and a grooved pulley rim on the rear wheel as shown in *Figs. 1* and *3*, and detailed in *Fig. 4*. The motor is started by means of a crank, and the belt drawn up gradually, by the action of a clutch lever and its idler, detailed in *Fig. 9*. The clutch lever is forged, as shown, and fitted with a ratchet lever, *N*, and ratchet quadrant,

O. The idler holds the belt to the tension desired, giving considerable flexibility of speed.

The brake is shown in *Figs. 1* and *3*, and detailed in *Figs. 4* and *9*. The fittings on the rear wheel and axle are made of wood, and bolted, with a tension spring, as shown. The brake drum is supported on iron bands, riveted to the wheel, and to the pulley rim. The brake arm is connected to the brake wheel by a flexible wire. When the pedal is forced down, the wire is wound on the brake

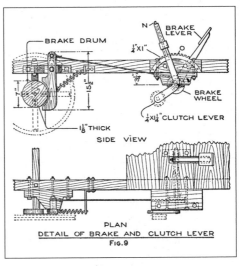

DETAIL OF BRAKE AND CLUTCH LEVER
FIG.9

THE BRAKE IS CONTROLLED BY A PEDAL, AND A CLUTCH LEVER IS MOUNTED ON THE CENTRAL SHAFT, AND SET BY MEANS OF A RATCHET DEVICE AND GRIP-RELEASE ROD.

wheel, thus permitting adjustment. The pedal is of iron and fixed on its shaft with a setscrew. An iron pipe is used as a casing for the central shaft. The shaft carrying the clutch lever, and the pipe carrying the brake pedal and the brake wheels. The quadrant *O* is mounted on a block, fastened to the main frame. The central shaft is carried in wooden blocks, with iron caps. A catch of strap iron can be fitted on the floor, to engage the pedal, and lock the brake when desired.

The engine is cooled by the draft through the wire-mesh opening in the front of the hood, and through the openings under the hood. If desirable, a wooden split pulley, with grooved rim and rope belt, may be fitted on the extension of the engine shaft, and connected with a two-blade metal fan, as shown in *Fig. 2.*

The lighting arrangement may finally be installed. Use gas or electric lamps, run on batteries. Mudguards are desirable if the car is to be used on muddy roads. Strong bicycle mudguards can be installed with the guard braces bolted on the axles. A strong pipe, with a draw bolt passing through its length, is mounted across the front of the frame. The body is built of ⅞-in. stock, preferably white wood, and is 2 ft. 4 in. wide. A priming coat should be applied to the woodwork, followed by two coats of the body color, and one or two coats of varnish. The metal parts, except at the working surfaces, may be painted or enameled.

— A CYCLEMOBILE —

The cyclemobile is a three-wheeled vehicle that can easily be constructed in the home workshop with ordinary tools. The main frame is built up of two sidepieces, *AA, Fig. 1*, each 2 in. thick, 4 in.

THREE-WHEELED CYCLEMOBILE PROPELLED LIKE A BICYCLE
AND STEERED AS AN AUTOMOBILE.

wide, and 7 ft. long. These are joined together at the front end with a crosspiece, *B*, of the same material, 17 in. long. The sides are made to be slightly tapering so that the rear ends are 11 in. apart at the point where they are joined together with the blocks and rear-wheel attachments. A crosspiece, *C*, 13 in. long, is fastened in the center of the frame.

The place for the seat is cut out off each sidepiece, as shown by the notches in *D*. These notches are 2 ft. from the rear ends. Two strips of wood, *E*, ½ in. thick, 4 in. wide, and 22 in. long, are nailed to the rear ends of the sides, as shown. The rear wheel is a bicycle wheel, which can be taken from an old bicycle or may be purchased cheaply at a bicycle store. It is held in place with

two pieces of strap iron, *F*, shaped similar to the rear forks on a bicycle. Each piece is bolted to a block of wood 3 in. thick, 4 in. wide, and 6 in. long, fastened to the sidepiece with the same bolts that hold the strap iron in place. The blocks are located 20 in. from the rear ends of the sidepieces.

The pedal arrangement, *Fig. 2*, consists of an ordinary bicycle hanger with cranks and sprocket wheel set into the end of a piece of wood, 2 in. thick, 4 in. wide and 33 in. long, at a point 4 in. from one end. The pieces *GG* are nailed on across the frame at the front end of the car to hold the hanger piece in the center between sidepieces, as shown in *Fig. 1*. A small pulley, *H*, is made to run loosely on a shaft fastened between the

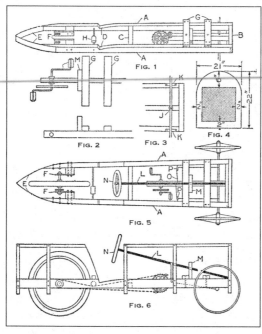

DETAIL OF THE PARTS FOR CONSTRUCTING AN
AUTOMOBILE-TYPE FOOT-POWER CAR.

riage and are about 21 in. in diameter.

A good imitation radiator can be made by cutting a board to the dimensions given in *Fig. 4.* A large-mesh screen is fastened to the rear side to imitate the water cells.

The steering gear *L, Fig. 5,* is made of a broom handle, one end of which passes through the support *M* and fits into a hole bored into the lower part of the imitation radiator board. A steering wheel, *N,* is attached to the upper end of the broom handle. The center part of a rope, *O,* is given a few turns around the broom handle, and the ends are passed through the openings in screw eyes, *PP.* They are then turned in to the inner surfaces of the sidepieces *AA,* and tied to the front axle.

The seat is constructed of ½-in. lumber and is built in the notches cut into the main frame shown in

sidepieces. This is used as an idler to keep the upper part of the chain below the seat.

The front axle is 30 in. long, pivoted as shown in *J, Fig. 3,* 6 in. from the front end of the main frame. Two small brass plates, *KK,* are screwed to the under edge of each sidepiece, as shown, to provide a bearing for the axle. The front wheels are taken from a discarded baby car-

D, *Fig. 1*. The body frame is made of lath, or other thin strips of wood, that can be bent in the shape of the radiator and nailed to the sidepieces, as shown in *Fig. 6*. These are braced at the top with longitudinal strip. The frame is then covered with canvas and painted as desired.

— HAND CAR MADE OF PIPE AND FITTINGS —

BOY'S HAND CAR.

Although it appears complicated, the construction of the car shown in the accompanying illustration is very simple. With a few exceptions all the parts are short lengths of pipe and common tees, elbows, and nipples.

The wheels were manufactured for use on a baby carriage. The sprocket wheel and chain were taken from a discarded bicycle, which was also drawn upon for the cork handle used on the steering lever. The floor is made of 1-in. white pine, 14 in. wide and 48 in. long, to which are bolted ordinary flanges to hold the framing and the propelling and steering apparatus together. The axles were made from ⅜-in. shafting. The fifth wheel consists of two small flanges working on the face surfaces. These flanges and the auxiliary steering rod are connected to the axles by means of holes stamped in the piece of sheet iron that encases the axle. The sheet iron was first properly stamped and then bent around the axle. The levers for propelling and steering the car work in fulcrums made for use in lever valves. The turned wooden handles by which these levers are operated were inserted through holes drilled in the connecting tees. The working joint for the steering and hand levers consists of a ½-by-⅜-by-⅜-in. tee, a ½-by-⅜-in. cross and a piece of rod threaded on both ends and screwed into the tee. The cross is reamed and, with the rod, forms a bearing.

The operation of this little hand car is very similar in principle to that of the ordinary tricycle. The machine can be propelled as fast as a boy can run. It responds readily to the slightest movement of the steering lever.

— A HOMEMADE ROLLER COASTER —

The popular roller coaster that furnishes untold amusement for the multitudes that patronize amusement parks during the summer can be easily duplicated in a smaller way on a vacant lot or backyard for the children of the home. Alternatively, the boys of the neighborhood could contribute to a fund and construct quite an elaborate affair, on the same lines as described, for the combined use of the owners. The one described was built with a track, 90 ft. long, 5 ft. high at one end and 3 ft. at the other, the track between being placed on the ground. In coasting from the high end to the low one, the coaster will run up on the incline, then drift back to within 24 ft. of the starting end. The car was built to seat four children or two adults. The cost of all the materials was modest.

The track is of simple construction and requires but little description. It is necessary to make it straight and nailed firmly to the cross ties on the ground and to the trestles where it is elevated. The ties and trestles are placed about 6 ft. apart. The two trestles for the starting platform should be set so that there is a slant to

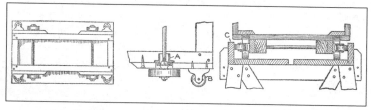

DETAIL OF THE CAR, WHEELS, AND THE TRESTLE,
WHICH IS ATTACHED TO A TIE.

the track of about 6 in. for starting the car without pushing it. The car can be carried back for starting by adults, but for children a small rope can be used over the platform to draw it back on the track, or a small windlass may be arranged for the purpose.

The main frame of the car is 3 ft. long and about 13 in. wide, firmly fastened at the corners. The axles for the wheels are machine steel, 19 in. long, turned up on the ends and

INEXPENSIVE BACKYARD ROLLER COASTER, SUITABLE FOR THE ENJOYMENT OF THE YOUNG AS WELL AS THE OLDER PERSON.

threaded in the manner of a bicycle axle to fit parts of bicycle hubs, attached to the main frame as shown in *A*. The wheels are solid, 4 in. in diameter and 1 in. thick, and are set

on the bicycle cone of the ball cup, after they are properly adjusted, and securely fastened between washers with a nut on the end of the axle. Guide wheels, *B*, are placed on the sides in the manner shown. These wheels are ordinary truck casters—not the revolving kind— 2 in. in diameter.

About ½-in. clearance should be provided between the guide wheels *B* and the guardrail *C*, on the track. When the car is made in this manner it runs close to the track and there is no place where a child can get a foot or hand injured under or at the sides of the car. The one described has been used by all the children, large and small, for a year without accident.

— HOW TO MAKE A FLYMOBILE —

The boy owning a pushmobile, or even a power-driven auto car, is often very much disappointed because motion soon stops when the power is not applied. The car illustrated is of a little different type, being equipped with a flywheel that will propel the car and carry the rider a considerable distance after pedaling is stopped. The flywheel also aids the operator, as it will steady the motion and help him over a rough place or a bump in the road.

The main frame of the flymobile is made up a few pieces of 2-by-4-in. timbers. The pieces *A* are 6 ft. 4 in. long, and the end crosspieces, *B*, 24 in. long. These are jointed, glued, and screwed together, as shown in *Fig. 1*. The frame that supports the driving parts consists of a piece, *C*, 6 ft. 2 in. long, and a piece, *D*, 2 ft. 11 in. long. These are fitted in the main frame and securely fastened to the end crosspieces *B*. Two other crosspieces, *E* and *F*, are used to strengthen the driving parts frame.

The entire hanger *G*, with its bearings, cranks and pedals, can be procured from a discarded bicycle and fastened to the piece *C*. The barrel holding the bearings is snugly fitted into a hole bored in the piece with an expansive bit. The location will depend on the builder and should be marked as follows: Place the hanger on top of the piece *C*, then put a box or board on the frame where the seat is to be and set the hanger where it will be in a comfortable position for pedaling. Mark this location and bore the hole.

The transmission, *H*, consists of a bicycle coaster-brake hub, shown in detail in *Fig. 2*. A split pulley, *J*, 6 in. in diameter, is bored out to fit over the center of the hub between the spoke flanges. The halves of the pulley are then clamped on the hub with two bolts run through the holes in opposite directions. Their heads and nuts are set into countersunk holes so that no part will extend above the surface of the pulley. The supports for the hub axle consist of two pieces of bar iron, 4 in. long, drilled to admit the axle ends, and screws for fastening them to the frame pieces *C* and *D*. This construction is clearly shown in *Fig. 2*.

The arrangement of the coaster-brake hub produces the same effect as a coaster brake on a bicycle. The one propelling the flymobile may stop the foot-power work without interfering with the travel of the machine. A little back pressure on the pedals will apply the brake in the same manner.

The flywheel, *K*, should be about 18 in. in diameter with a 2-in. rim, or face. Such a wheel can be purchased cheaply from any junk dealer. The flywheel is set on a shaft, turning between the pieces *C* and *D* and back of the coaster-brake wheel *H*. Two pulleys, *L*, about 3 in. in diameter, are fastened to turn with the flywheel on the shaft and are fitted with flanges to separate the belts. The ends of the shaft should run in good bearings, well oiled.

Another pulley, *M*, 6 in. in diameter, is made of wood and fastened to the rear axle. An idler wheel, shown in *Fig. 3*, is constructed of a small pulley or a large spool attached to an L-shaped piece of metal, which in turn is fastened on the end of a shaft controlled by the lever *N*. The function of this idler is to tighten up the belt or release it, thus changing the speed in the same manner as on a motorcycle.

THE FLYMOBILE IS A MINIATURE AUTOMOBILE IN APPEARANCE AND IS PROPELLED BY FOOT POWER.

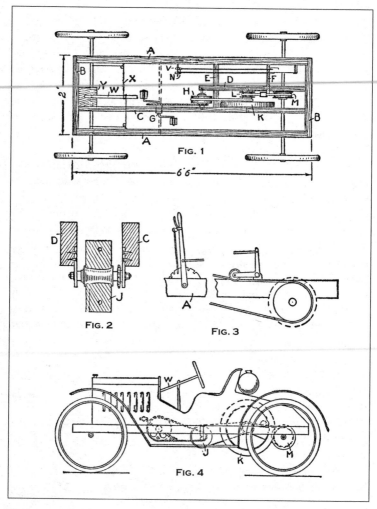

FIG. 1

FIG. 2

FIG. 3

FIG. 4

PLAN AND ELEVATION OF THE FLYMOBILE, SHOWING THE LOCATION OF THE WORKING PARTS, TO WHICH, WITH A FEW CHANGES, A MOTORCYCLE ENGINE CAN BE ATTACHED TO MAKE IT A CYCLE CAR. ALSO DETAILS OF THE BRAKES, BELT TIGHTENER, AND COASTER-BRAKE HUB.

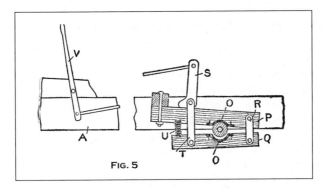

Fig. 5

The elevation of the flymobile is given in *Fig. 4*, which shows the arrangement of the belting. The size of the pulleys on the flywheel shaft causes it to turn rapidly, and, for this reason, the weight of the wheel will run the car a considerable distance when the coaster hub is released.

The rear axle revolves in bearings. Half of the axle is recessed in the under edges of the pieces *A*, while the other half is fastened to a block, screwed on over the axle. A simple brake is made as shown in *Fig. 5*. Two metal pieces (preferably brass), *O*, are shaped to fit over the shaft with extending ends for fastening them to the pieces *P* and *Q* as shown. These pieces are hinged with strap iron, *R*, at one end. The other end of the piece *P* is fastened to the crosspiece *F*, *Fig. 1*, of the main frame. The lower piece

Q is worked by the lever *S* and side bars, *T*. A small spring, *U*, keeps the ends of the pieces apart and allows the free turning of the axle until the brake lever is drawn. The lever *S* is connected by a long bar to the hand lever *V*.

The steering apparatus, *W*, *Figs. 1* and *4*, is constructed of a piece of gas pipe, 3 ft. 4 in. long. It has a wheel at one end and a cord, *X*, at the other. The center part of the cord is wound several times around the pipe and the ends are passed through screw eyes in the main-frame pieces, *A*, and attached to the front axle. The axle is pivoted in the center under the block *Y*. The lower end of the pipe turns in a hole bored slanting in the block. A turn of the steering wheel causes one end of the cord to wind and the other unwind, which turns the axle on the center pivot.

The wheels are bicycle wheels, and the ends of the front axle are turned to receive the cones and nuts, instead of using the regular hub axles. The ends of the rear axle are turned to closely fit the hubs after the ball cups have been removed. A large washer and nut clamp each wheel to the axle so that it will turn with it.

The body can be made up as desired, from sheet metal, wood, or cloth stretched over ribs of wood, and painted in the manner of an automobile. A tank and tires can be placed on the back to add to the appearance. Fenders and a running board can be attached to the main frame.

With the addition of some cross-pieces in the main frame at the front and a motorcycle engine fastened to them so that the driving sprocket will be in line with the sprocket on the coaster hub, the builder will have a real cycle car.

— ❖ ❖ ❖ —

{CHAPTER 11}

THE TOY WORKSHOP

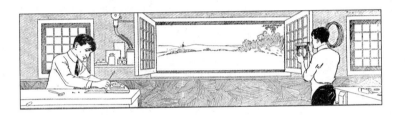

— A HOMEMADE VISE —

While making a box a woodworker had some dovetailing to do, and because there was no vise on the bench the clever mechanic rigged up a substitute. He secured a board ¾ in. thick, 3 in. wide, and 20 in. long and bored a ½-in. hole through it, 1 in. from each end. He then attached the board to the bench by driving two screws through washers and the holes in the board into the bench top. The screws

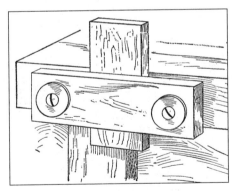

VISE ON BENCH.

should be of a length suitable to take in the piece to be worked.

— GAUGE FOR WOODWORK —

Aconvenient gauge can be quickly made by using a block of wood and an ordinary nail, or several nails for different widths can be placed in one block. Drive the nails straight into the block until the distance between the head and block is the required distance to be gauged. The rim of the nail head makes the mark as the block is drawn over the wood surface.

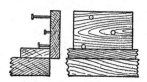

— NAIL CABINET WITH MUFFIN-PAN TRAYS —

Muffin-pan trays used by the housewife in baking make serviceable containers for nails, screws, and other small articles used in the shop. The illustration shows the pans fitted into a box and sliding in grooves cut into the sides with a saw.

The box is made with the end pieces overlapping at top and bottom, this being a better construction to carry the weight of the trays. The wood used in the sides is ⅞ in. thick, so that a saw cut may be made to the depth of ¼ in. without weakening the support. Thinner wood may be used if instead of saw cuts small

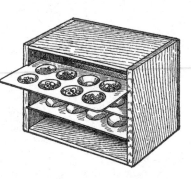

THE METAL TRAYS ARE SUBSTANTIAL AND MAY BE REMOVED READILY FOR USE ELSEWHERE.

strips of wood are nailed against the sides as tray slides.

— A Workbench
for the Amateur —

The accompanying detail drawing shows a design of a portable workbench suitable for the amateur woodworker. This bench can be made easily by anyone who has a few sharp tools and a little spare time. If the stock is purchased from the mill ready planed and cut to length, much of the hard labor will be saved. Birch or maple wood makes a very good bench, and the following pieces should be ordered:

Materials

4 legs, 3 by 3 by 36 in.
2 side rails, 3 by 3 by 62½ in.
2 end rails, 3 by 3 by 20 in.
1 back board, 1 by 9 by 80 in.
1 top board, 2 by 12 by 77 in.
1 top board, 1 by 12 by 77 in.
2 crosspieces, 1½ by 3 by 24 in.
1 piece for clamp, 1½ by 6½ by 12 in.
1 piece for clamp, 1½ by 6½ by 14 in.
4 guides, 2 by 2 by 18 in.
1 screw block, 3 by 3 by 6 in.
1 piece, 1½ by 4½ by 10½ in.

Make the lower frame first. Cut tenons on the rails and mortise the posts, then fasten them securely together with ⅜-by-5-in. lag screws as shown. Also fasten the 1½-by-3-by-24-in. pieces to the tops of the posts with screws. The heads should be countersunk or else holes bored in the top boards to fit over them. Fasten the front top board to the crosspieces by lag screws through from the underside. The screws can be put in from the top for the 1-in. thick top board.

Fasten the end pieces on with screws, countersinking the heads of the vise end. Cut the 2-in. square holes in the 1½- by 4½- by 10-in. pieces for the vise slides, and fit it in place for the side vise. Also cut square holes in the one end piece of the end vise slides as shown. Now fit up the two clamps. Fasten the slides to the front pieces with screws. Countersink the heads of the screws so they will not be in the way of the hands when the vise is used. The two clamp screws should be about 1½ in. in diameter. They can be purchased at a hardware store. A block should be fitted under the crosspiece to hold the nut for the end vise. After you have the slides fitted, put them in place and bore the holes for the clamp screws.

The back board can now be fastened to the back with screws as shown in the top view. The bench is now complete, except for a couple of coats of oil that should be applied to give it a finish and preserve the wood. The amateur workman, as well as the patternmaker, will find this a very handy and serviceable bench for his workshop.

Because the amateur workman does not always know just what tools he will need, a list is given that will serve for a general class of work. This list can be added to as the workman becomes more proficient in his line and has need for other tools. Only the better grade of tools should be purchased, as they are the cheapest in the long run. If each tool is kept in a certain place, it can be easily found when needed.

Tools

1 bench plane or jointer
1 jack plane or smoother
1 crosscut saw, 24 in.
1 ripsaw, 24 in.
1 claw hammer
1 set of gimlets
1 brace and set of bits
2 screwdrivers, 3 and 6 in.
1 countersink
1 compass saw
1 set chisels
1 wood scraper
1 monkey wrench
1 2-ft. rule
1 marking gauge
1 pair pliers
1 nail set
1 pair dividers
1 pocket level
1 6-in. try square
1 oilstone
No. 1, 2, and 00 sandpaper

— ❖ ❖ ❖ —

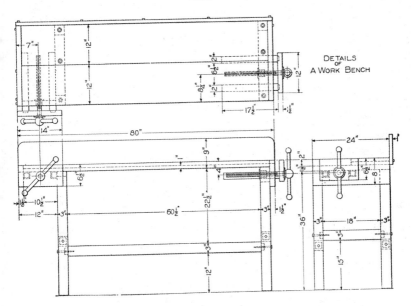

DETAILS
OF
A WORK BENCH

DETAIL OF THE BENCH

WORKBENCH COMPLETE

INDEX